Lecture Notes in Compu ⌄ ⌄ ⌄2

Commenced Publication in 1973
Founding and Former Series Editors:
Gerhard Goos, Juris Hartmanis, and Jan van Leeuwen

Kurt Bauknecht   Martin Bichler
Birgit Pröll (Eds.)

E-Commerce and Web Technologies

5th International Conference, EC-Web 2004
Zaragoza, Spain, August 31 - September 3, 2004
Proceedings

 Springer

Volume Editors

Kurt Bauknecht
University of Zurich, Department of Informatics
Winterthurer Straße 190, CH-8057 Zurich, Switzerland
E-mail: baukn@ifi.unizh.ch

Martin Bichler
Technical University of Munich, Internet-based Information Systems (IBIS)
Boltzmannstr. 3, D-85748 Garching, Germany
E-mail: bichler@in.tum.de

Birgit Pröll
Johannes Kepler University Linz, Institute for Applied Knowledge Processing (FAW)
Altnbergerstr. 69, A-4040 Linz, Austria
E-mail: bproell@faw.uni-linz.ac.at

Library of Congress Control Number: 2004110714

CR Subject Classification (1998): H.4, K.4.4, J.1, K.5, H.3, H.2, K.6.5

ISSN 0302-9743
ISBN 3-540-22917-5 Springer Berlin Heidelberg New York

Springer is a part of Springer Science+Business Media

springeronline.com

© Springer-Verlag Berlin Heidelberg 2004
Printed in Germany

Typesetting: Camera-ready by author, data conversion by Olgun Computergrafik
Printed on acid-free paper   SPIN: 11315261   06/3142   5 4 3 2 1 0

Preface

We welcome you to the proceedings of the 5t International Conference on E-Commerce and Web Technology (EC-Web 2004) held in conjunction with DEXA 2004 in Zaragoza, Spain. This conference, first held in Greenwich, United Kingdom in 2000, now is in its fifth year and very well established. As in the four previous years, it served as a forum to bring together researchers from academia and commercial developers from industry to discuss the current state of the art in e-commerce and Web technology. Inspirations and new ideas emerged from intensive discussions during formal sessions and social events.

Keynote addresses, research presentations and discussions during the conference helped to further develop the exchange of ideas among the researchers, developers and practitioners present.

The conference attracted 103 paper submissions and almost every paper was reviewed by three program committee members. The program committee selected 37 papers for presentation and publication, a task which was not easy due to the high quality of the submitted papers.

We would like to express our thanks to our colleagues who helped with putting together the technical program: the program committee members and external reviewers for their timely and rigorous reviews of the papers, and the organizing committee for their help in the administrative work and support. We owe special thanks to Gabriela Wagner, Mirella Köster, and Birgit Hauer for their helping hands concerning the administrative and organizational tasks of this conference.

Finally, we would like to thank all the authors who submitted papers, authors who presented papers, and the participants who together made this conference an intellectually stimulating event through their active contributions.

We hope that those who attended enjoyed the hospitality of Zaragoza.

August/September 2004   Martin Bichler
                                                          Birgit Pröll

Program Committee

General Chairperson

Kurt Bauknecht, University of Zurich, Switzerland

Conference Program Chairpersons

Martin Bichler, Technical University of Munich, Germany
Birgit Proell, FAW, Johannes Kepler University, Linz, Austria

Program Committee Members

Sourav S. Bhowmick, Nanyang Technological University, Singapore
Susanne Boll, University of Oldenburg, Germany
Walter Brenner, University of St. Gallen, Switzerland
Stephane Bressan, National University of Singapore, Singapore
Tanya Castleman, Deakin University, Australia
Wojciech Cellary, Poznan University of Economics, Poland
Jen-Yao Chung, IBM T.J. Watson Research Center, USA
Roger Clarke, Australian National University, Australia
Asuman Dogac, Middle East Technical University, Turkey
Eduardo Fernandez, Florida Atlantic University, USA
Elena Ferrari, University of Insubria at Como, Italy
Farshad Fotouhi, Wayne State University, USA
Yongjian Fu, Cleveland State University, USA
Chanan Glezer, Ben Gurion University of the Negev, Israel
Rüdiger Grimm, University of Technology, Ilmenau, Germany
Manfred Hauswirth, EPFL, Switzerland
Thomas Hess, LMU Munich, Germany
Yigal Hoffner, IBM Zurich Research Laboratory, Switzerland
Christian Huemer, University of Vienna, Austria
Gregory E. Kersten, University of Ottawa, Canada
Hiroyuki Kitagawa, University of Tsukuba, Japan
Wolfgang Koenig, Frankfurt University, Germany
Gabriele Kotsis, Johannes Kepler University, Linz, Austria
Winfried Lamersdorf, University of Hamburg, Germany
Alberto Laender, Federal University of Minas Gerais, Brazil
Juhnyoung Lee, IBM T.J. Watson Research Center, USA
Leszek Lilien, Purdue University, USA
Ee-Peng Lim, Nanyang Technological University, Singapore
Huan Liu, Arizona State University, USA

Heiko Ludwig, IBM T.J. Watson Research Center, USA
Sanjay Kumar Madria, University of Missouri-Rolla, USA
Bamshad Mobasher, DePaul University, USA
Natwar Modani, Oracle, India
Mukesh Mohania, IBM India Research Lab, India
Gustaf Neumann, Vienna University of Economics and Business Administration, Austria
Wee Keong Ng, Nanyang Technological University, Singapore
Rolf Oppliger, eSECURITY Technologies, Switzerland
Stefano Paraboschi, University of Bergamo, Italy
Oscar Pastor, Valencia University of Technology, Spain
Günther Pernul, University of Regensburg, Germany
Evangelia Pitoura, University of Ioannina, Greece
Gerald Quirchmayr, University of Vienna, Austria
Indrakshi Ray, Colorado State University, USA
Werner Retschitzegger, Johannes Kepler University, Linz, Austria
Tomas Sabol, Technical University of Kosice, Slovakia
Nandlal L. Sarda, Indian Institute of Technology, Bombay, India
Michael Stroebel, BMW Group, Germany
Roger M. Tagg, University of South Australia, Australia
Kian-Lee Tan, National University of Singapore, Singapore
Stephanie Teufel, University of Fribourg, Switzerland
Bruce H. Thomas, University of South Australia, Australia
A Min Tjoa, Technical University of Vienna, Austria
Aphrodite Tsalgatidou, National and Kapodistrian University of Athens, Greece
Krishnamurthy Vidyasankar, Memorial Univ., St. John's, Newfoundland, Canada
Hans Weigand, Tilburg University, The Netherlands
Christof Weinhardt, University of Karlsruhe, Germany
Hannes Werthner, University of Trento, Italy
Andrew Whinston, University of Texas, USA

External Reviewers

Bugrahan Akcay, Middle East Technical University, Turkey
George Athanasopoulos, University of Athens, Greece
Peter Bednar, Technical University of Kosice, Slovakia
Daniel Beimborn, Frankfurt University, Germany
Stefan Blumenberg, Frankfurt University, Germany
Sudip Chakraborty, Colorado State University, USA
Radoslav Delina, Technical University of Kosice, Slovakia
Rainer B. Fladung, Frankfurt University, Germany
Ozgur Gulderen, Middle East Technical University, Turkey
Yavuz Gurcan, Middle East Technical University, Turkey
Yildiray Kabak, Middle East Technical University, Turkey
George-Dimitrios Kapos, Harokopio Univ. of Athens, Greece

Table of Contents

Security and Trust in e-Commerce

Techniques for B2B e-Commerce

Negotiation Strategies and Protocols

Modeling of e-Commerce Applications

e-Commerce Intelligence

e-Retailing and Web Site Design

DRM and EC Strategies

Author Index

Using Attributes to Improve Prediction Quality in Collaborative Filtering

Taek-Hun Kim and Sung-Bong Yang

Dept. of Computer Science, Yonsei University
Seoul, 120-749, Korea
{kimthun,yang}@cs.yonsei.ac.kr

Abstract. To save customers' time and efforts in searching the goods in the Internet, a customized recommender system is required. It is very important for a recommender system to predict accurately by analyzing customer's preferences. A recommender system utilizes in general an information filtering technique called collaborative filtering, which is based on the ratings of other customers who have similar preferences. Because a recommender system using collaborative filtering predicts customer's preferences based only on the items without useful information on the attributes of each item, it may not give high quality recommendation consistently to the customers. In this paper we show that exploiting the attributes of each item improves prediction quality. We analyze the dataset and retrieve the preferences for the attributes because they have not been rated by customers explicitly. In the experiment the MovieLens dataset of the GroupLens Research Center has been used. The results on various experiments using several neighbor selection methods which are quite popular techniques for recommender systems show that the recommender systems using the attributes provide better prediction qualities than the systems without using the attribute information. Each of the systems using the attributes has improved the prediction quality more than 9%, compared with its counterpart. And the clustering-based recommender systems using the attributes can solve the very large-scale dataset problem without deteriorating prediction quality.

1   Introduction

Nowadays, customers spend so much time and efforts in finding the best suitable goods since more and more information is placed on-line. To save their time and efforts in searching the goods they want, a customized recommender system is required. A customized recommender system should predict the most suitable goods for customers by retrieving and analyzing their preferences. A recommender system utilizes in general an information filtering technique called collaborative filtering which is widely used for such recommender systems as Amazon.com and CDNow.com[1][2][3][4]. A recommender system using collaborative filtering, we call it *CF*, is based on the ratings of the customers who have similar preferences with respect to a given (test) customer.

K. Bauknecht, M. Bichler, and B. Pröll (Eds.): EC-Web 2004, LNCS 3182, pp. 1–10, 2004.

CF calculates the similarity between the test customer and each of other customers who have rated the items that are already rated by the test customer. CF uses in general the Pearson correlation coefficient for calculating the similarity, but it assumes that there must exist at least one item which has already been rated by both the test customer and one of the other customers. A weak point of the "pure" CF is that it uses all other customers including "useless" customers as the neighbors of the test customer. Since CF is based on the ratings of the neighbors who have similar preferences, it is very important to select the neighbors properly to improve prediction quality. Another weak point of CF is that it never considers customer's preferences on the attributes of each item.

There have been many investigations to select proper neighbors based on neighbor selection methods such as the k-nearest neighbor selection, the threshold-based neighbor selection, and the clustering-based neighbor selection. They are quite popular techniques for recommender systems[1][4][6][7][10]. These techniques then predict customer's preferences for the items based on the results of the neighbors' evaluation on the same items.

The recommender system with the clustering-based neighbor selection method is known to predict with worse accuracy than the systems with other neighbor selection methods, but it can solve the very large-scale problem in recommender systems. With millions of customers and items, a recommender system running existing algorithms will suffer serious scalability problem. So it is needed a new idea that can quickly produce high prediction quality, even for the very large-scale problem[8][10].

CF works quite well in general, because it is based on the ratings of other customers who have similar preferences. However, CF may not provide high quality recommendations for the test customer consistently, because it does not consider the attributes of each item and because it depends only on the ratings of other customers who rated the items that are already rated by the test customer. To improve prediction quality, CF needs reinforcements such as utilizing "useful" attributes of the items and using a more refined neighbor selection method. Item attributes mean its originality of the item it holds which differs from the others. In general, they can be obtained through the properties of the goods in real world.

In this paper we show that exploiting the attributes of each item improves prediction quality. We analyze the dataset and retrieve the preferences for the attributes, because they have not been rated by the customers explicitly. In the experiment the MovieLens dataset of the GroupLens Research Center has been used[11]. The dataset consists of 100,000 preferences for 1,682 movies rated by 943 customers explicitly.

We show the impact of utilizing the attributes information on the prediction qualities through various experiments. The experimental results show that the recommender systems using the attribute information provide better prediction qualities than other methods that do not utilize the attributes. Each of the systems using the attributes has improved the prediction quality more than 9%, compared with its counterpart. And besides the clustering-based CF using the attributes can solve the very large-scale problem without deteriorating prediction quality.

The rest of this paper is organized as follows. Section 2 describes briefly CF and several neighbor selection methods. Section 3 illustrates how to utilize the attributes of items for recommender systems in detail. In Section 4, the experimental results are presented. Finally, the conclusions are given in Section 5.

2   Collaborative Filtering and Neighbor Selection Methods

CF recommends items through building the profiles of the customers from their preferences for each item. In CF, preferences are represented generally as numeric values which are rated by the customers. Predicting the preference for a certain item that is new to the test customer is based on the ratings of other customers for the 'target' item. Therefore, it is very important to find a set of customers, called *neighbors*, with more similar preferences to the test customer for better prediction quality.

In CF, Equation (1) is used to predict the preference of a customer. Note that in the following equation $w_{a,k}$ is the Pearson correlation coefficient as in Equation (2) [2][3][4][6][8].

$$P_{a,i} = \overline{r_a} + \frac{\sum_{k} \{w_{a,k} \times (r_{k,i} - \overline{r_k})\}}{\sum_{k} | w_{a,k} |} . \tag{1}$$

$$w_{a,k} = \frac{\sum_{j} (r_{a,j} - \overline{r_a})(r_{k,j} - \overline{r_k})}{\sqrt{\sum_{j} (r_{a,j} - \overline{r_a})^2 \sum_{j} (r_{k,j} - \overline{r_k})^2}} . \tag{2}$$

In the above equations $P_{a,i}$ is the preference of customer a with respect to item i. $\overline{r_a}$ and $\overline{r_k}$ are the averages of customer a's ratings and customer k's ratings, respectively. $r_{k,i}$ and $r_{k,j}$ are customer k's ratings for items i and j, respectively, and $r_{a,j}$ is customer a's rating for item j.

If customers a and k have similar ratings for an item, $w_{a,k} > 0$. We denote $| w_{a,k} |$ to indicate how much customer a tends to agree with customer k on the items that both customers have already rated. In this case, customer a is a "positive" neighbor with respect to customer k, and vice versa. If they have opposite ratings for an item, then $w_{a,k} < 0$. Similarly, customer a is a "negative" neighbor with respect to customer k, and vice versa. In this case $| w_{a,k} |$ indicates how much they tend to disagree on the item that both again have already rated. Hence, if they don't correlate each other, then $w_{a,k} = 0$. Note that $w_{a,k}$ can be in between -1 and 1 inclusive.

Although CF can be regarded as a good choice for a recommender system, there is still much more room for improvement in prediction quality. To do so,

CF needs reinforcements such as utilizing "useful" attributes of the items as well as a more refined neighbor selection. In the rest of this section we describe several neighbor selection methods.

2.1   The k-Nearest Neighbor Selection

The k-nearest neighbor method selects the nearest k neighbors who have similar preferences to the test customer by computing the similarities based on their preferences. It only uses the k neighbors who have higher correlation with the test customer than others, while CF suffers from considering all the customers in the input dataset for calculating the preference of the test customer. Thus CF should even consider some customers who may give bad influences on prediction quality. It has been shown in several investigations that the recommender system with the k-nearest neighbor selection method has better quality of prediction than the "pure" CF[1][4][6].

2.2   The Threshold-Based Neighbor Selection

The threshold-based neighbor selection method selects the neighbors who belong to a certain range with respect to the similarities of the preferences. Contrary to the k-nearest neighbor selection method, the number of neighbors selected by this method varies, because it selects neighbors according to a certain threshold value τ.

In the recommender system with the threshold-based neighbor selection, the positive neighbors whose correlations to the test customer are greater than and equal to τ are selected as the neighbors[6]. However, it is also needed that we include the "negative" neighbors whose correlations to the test customer are less than and equal to τ, because they could contribute toward the better neighbor selection for the test customer as they provide negative "opinions" to the test customer. It is obvious that selecting only negative neighbors results in worse prediction qualities than the case in which only positive neighbors are selected, intuitively.

2.3   The Clustering-Based Neighbor Selection

The k-means clustering method creates k clusters each of which consists of the customers who have similar preferences among themselves. In this method we first select k customers arbitrarily as the initial center points of the k clusters, respectively. Then each customer is assigned to a cluster in such a way that the distance between the customer and the center of a cluster is minimized. The distance is calculated using the Euclidean distance, that is, a square root of the element-wise square of the difference between the customer and each center point. The Pearson correlation coefficient can be substituted for the Euclidean distance.

We then calculate the mean of each cluster based on the customers who currently belong to the cluster. The mean is now considered as the new center of

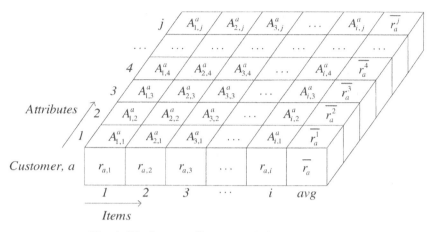

Fig. 1. The item-attributes matrix for a customer

the cluster. After finding the new center of each cluster, we compute the distance between the new center and each customer as before in order to find the cluster to which the customer should belong. Recalculating the means and computing the distances are repeated until a terminating condition is met. The condition is in general how far each new center has moved from the previous center; that is, if all the new centers moved within a certain distance, we terminate the loop.

If the clustering process is terminated, we choose the cluster with the shortest Euclidean distance from its center to the test customer. Finally, prediction for the test customer is calculated with all the customers in the chosen cluster.

3   Using Attributes to Improve Prediction Quality

In order to utilize the attributes of the items in the process of prediction, we consider a matrix of items-attributes for a customer as in Fig. 1. This figure shows the information of the items-attributes for customer a. In this figure $r_{a,i}$ denotes customer a's rating for item i. Note that $r_{a,i} \in \{-, 1, 2, 3, 4, 5\}$, where '$-$' indicates "no rating". An item may have an arbitrary combination among j attribute values as its attribute values; $Attribute(i) \subset \{1, 2, 3, \ldots, j\}$. Note that $Attribute(i) \neq \emptyset$. And $A_{i,j}^a \in \{0, 1\}$.

$$P_{a,i} = A(\overline{r_{a,i}}) + \frac{\sum_k \{w_{a,k} \times (r_{k,i} - A(\overline{r_{k,i}}))\}}{\sum_k |w_{a,k}|} . \qquad (3)$$

$$A(\overline{r_{a,i}}) = \frac{\sum_j \{A_{i,j}^a \times \overline{r_a^j}\}}{N_{a,i}} , \quad \overline{r_a^j} = \frac{\sum_i \{A_{i,j}^a \times r_{a,i}\}}{M_{a,j}} . \qquad (4)$$

$$A(\overline{r_{k,i}}) = \frac{\sum_{j}\{A_{i,j}^{k} \times \overline{r_{k}^{j}}\}}{N_{k,i}} \quad , \quad \overline{r_{k}^{j}} = \frac{\sum_{i}\{A_{i,j}^{k} \times r_{k,i}\}}{M_{k,j}} \quad . \tag{5}$$

We propose Equation (3) as a new prediction formula in order to predict customer's preferences. In this equation, $A(\overline{r_{a,i}})$ and $A(\overline{r_{k,i}})$ in Equations (4) and (5) are the averages of customer a and k's attribute values, respectively. In each equation, $N_{a,i}$ and $N_{k,i}$ is the number of "valid" attributes for item i and $M_{a,j}$ and $M_{k,j}$ is the number of "valid" items that has attribute j for a customer, respectively. The valid attribute means $A_{i,j}^{a} = 1$ and $A_{i,j}^{k} = 1$ and the valid item means $r_{a,i}$ and $r_{k,i}$ is not "-", respectively. All other terms in the above equations are the same terms defined for the previous equations.

There are a lot of items which have different attributes for the item for new prediction. Therefore, if we retrieve the attributes of the items more accurately and use them to the prediction process with Equation (3), then we can get more accurate prediction quality than the case without considering the attributes.

4   Experimental Results

4.1   Experiment Environment

In order to evaluate the prediction accuracy of the proposed recommendation system, we used the MovieLens dataset of the GroupLens Research Center [11]. The dataset consists of 100,000 preferences for 1,682 movies rated by 943 customers explicitly. The customer preferences are represented as numeric values from 1 to 5 at an interval of 1, that is, 1, 2, 3, 4, and 5. A higher value means higher preference. In the MovieLens dataset, one of the valuable attributes of an item is "the genre" of a movie. There are nineteen different genres as shown in Table 1.

Table 1. The genre attributes of a movie

Unknown	Action	Adventure	Animation	Children's
Comedy	Crime	Documentary	Drama	Fantasy
Film-Noir	Horror	Musical	Mystery	Romance
Sci-Fi	Thriller	War	Western	

For the experiment, we have chosen randomly 10% of customers out of all the customers in the dataset as the test customers. The rest of the customers are regarded as the training customers. For each test customer, we chose ten movies randomly that are actually rated by the test customer as the test movies. The final experimental results are averaged over the results of five different test sets for a statistical significance.

4.2 Experimental Metrics

One of the statistical prediction accuracy metrics for evaluating a recommender system is the mean absolute error (MAE). MAE is the mean of the errors of the actual customer ratings against the predicted ratings in an individual prediction [1][6][7][8]. MAE can be computed with Equation (6). In the equation, N is the total number of predictions and ε_i is the error between the predicted rating and the actual rating for item i. The lower MAE is, the more accurate prediction with respect to the numerical ratings of customers we get.

$$| E | = \frac{\sum_{i=0}^{N} | \varepsilon_i |}{N} .$$

(6)

4.3 Experimental Results

We compared the recommendation systems using the attribute information with those without using them. We have implemented three recommender systems each of which uses different neighbor selection method. The first system is CF with the k-nearest neighbor selection method ($KNCF$). The second system is CF with the threshold-based neighbor selection ($TNCF$). The third one is CF with the k-means clustering ($KMCF$).

For TNCF, three different systems have implemented. The first system is TNCF with positive neighbors ($TNCF\_P$). The second one is TNCF with negative neighbors ($TNCF\_N$). And the last one is TNCF with both positive and negative neighbors ($TNCF\_A$).

For KMCF, we also have two different settings. One is KMCF with the Euclidean distance as a distance ($KMCF\_E$). And the other is KMCF with the Pearson correlation coefficient as a distance ($KMCF\_C$).

The experimental results are shown in Table 2. We determined the parameters which gave us the smallest MAE through various experiments. The value of k for KNCF is the number of neighbors with k highest correlation. Among the parameters in TNCF, positive and negative values denote that the τ values for the Pearson correlation coefficients. For example, if the positive vale is 0.2 and the negative value is -0.1, then we select a neighbor whose similarity is either smaller than and equal to -0.1 or larger than and equal to 0.2. If there is a single parameter, then we select neighbors whose similarities with respect to the value only. And the last the value of k for KMCF is the number of clusters.

As shown in Table 2, each system has been tested both with and without utilizing the attributes. The results in the table show that the systems using the attributes outperform those without considering them. The prediction accuracy improvement ratio of each system using the attributes to the one without considering them is more than 9% except for the clustering systems, KMCF_E and KMCF_C.

Table 3 shows four cases of combination according to whether Equation (4) or (5) is applied to Equation (3) or not. If Equation (4) or (5) is not used,

Table 2. The experimental results

Recommender systems	MAE's	Parameters	Attributes	Improvement ratios
KNCF	0.686170	k=130	Used	9.86%
	0.761210	k=120	Not used	
TNCF_P	0.689162	τ=0.2	Used	9.41%
	0.760716	τ=0.2	Not used	
TNCF_N	0.745659	τ=-1.0	Used	11.02%
	0.838030	τ=-1.0	Not used	
TNCF_A	0.681760	τ=(0.2,-0.1)	Used	9.66%
	0.754619	τ=(0.2,-0.1)	Not used	
KMCF_E	0.744384	k=2	Used	3.88%
	0.774412	k=2	Not used	
KMCF_C	0.729218	k=2	Used	4.41%
	0.762834	k=2	Not used	

Table 3. The usage of the attributes in prediction

Cases	A	B	C	D
Used equations	(4) and (5)	(4) only	(5) only	none

then the item corresponded to Equation (1) is substituted. Table 4 shows the experimental results on these cases.

The experimental results in Table 4 show us that the prediction with case A that the attributes are applied to both the test customer and the neighbors, provides the best prediction accuracy in KNCF and TNCF. And in these methods the prediction with case B also has as good prediction quality as the prediction with case A. On the other hand KMCF provides the best prediction when we use the case B in both KMCF_E and KMCF_C. The prediction accuracy improvement ratio of KMCF with case B to the case D is more than 9%.

In the results we found the TNCF_A (case A) is the best prediction quality among others. And we can see the fact that the prediction with case A through C provides more prediction accuracy than the one with case D which never considers the attributes of an item. And the last the KMCF_C (case B) provides as good as TNCF_A in prediction quality. This fact means that the clustering-based CF can solve the very large-scale problem without deteriorating prediction quality.

5 Conclusions

It is very crucial for a recommender system to have a capability of making accurate prediction by retrieving and analyzing of customer's preferences. Collaborative filtering is widely used for recommender systems. Hence various efforts to overcome its drawbacks have been made to improve prediction quality.

It is important to select neighbors properly in order to make up the weak points in collaborative filtering and to improve prediction quality. In this paper

Table 4. The experimental results(for four cases)

Methods	MAE	Parameters	Types
KNCF	0.686170	$k=130$	A
	0.692809	$k=200$	B
	0.767625	$k=120$	C
	0.761210	$k=120$	D
TNCF_P	0.689162	$\tau=0.2$	A
	0.696775	$\tau=0.2$	B
	0.767223	$\tau=0.2$	C
	0.760716	$\tau=0.2$	D
TNCF_N	0.745659	$\tau=-1.0$	A
	0.745667	$\tau=-1.0$	B
	0.838022	$\tau=-1.0$	C
	0.838030	$\tau=-1.0$	D
TNCF_A	0.681760	$\tau=(0.2,-0.1)$	A
	0.687949	$\tau=(0.2,-0.1)$	B
	0.761572	$\tau=(0.2,-0.1)$	C
	0.754619	$\tau=(0.2,-0.1)$	D
KMCF_E	0.744384	$k=2$	A
	0.704240	$k=2$	B
	0.811596	$k=2$	C
	0.774412	$k=2$	D
KMCF_C	0.729218	$k=2$	A
	0.692414	$k=2$	B
	0.796347	$k=2$	C
	0.762834	$k=2$	D

we showed that the recommender systems that exploit the attributes of each item indeed improve prediction qualities. The experimental results show the recommender systems have improved the prediction qualities more than 9%. And besides the clustering-based CF using the attributes can solve the large-scale problem without deteriorating prediction quality.

Acknowledgements

We thank the GroupLens Research Center for permitting us to use the MovieLens dataset. This work was supported by the Korea Sanhak Foundation and the Brain Korea 21 Project in 2004.

References

1. Badrul M. Sarwar, George Karypis, Joseph A. Konstan, John T. Riedle: Application of Dimensionality Reduction in Recommender System - A Case Study. Proceedings of the ACM WebKDD 2000 Web Mining for E-Commerce Workshop. (2000)

2. Konstan, J., Miller, B., Maltz, D., Herlocker, J., Gordon, L., and Riedl, J.: GroupLens: Applying Collaborative Filtering to Usenet News. Communications of the ACM, Vol. 40. (1997) 77-87
3. Resnick, P., Iacovou, N., Suchak, M., Bergstrom, P., and Riedl, J.: GroupLens: An Open Architecture for Collaborative Filtering of Netnews. Proceedings of the ACM CSCW94 Conference on Computer Supported Cooperative Work. (1994) 175-186
4. Badrul M. Sarwar, George Karypis, Joseph A. Konstan, John T. Riedl: Analysis of Recommendation Algorithms for E-Commerce. Proceedings of the ACM E-Commerce 2000 Conference. (2000)
5. Basu, C., Hirsh, H., and Cohen, W.: Recommendation as Classification: Using Social and Content-Based Information in Recommendation. Proceedings of the AAAI. (1998) 714-720
6. Jonathan L. Herlocker, Joseph A. Konstan, Al Borchers, and John Riedl: An Algorithmic Framework for Performing Collaborative Filtering. Proceedings of the 22nd International ACM SIGIR Conference on Research and Development in Information Retrieval. (1999)
7. O'Connor M., and Herlocker J.: Clustering Items for Collaborative Filtering. Proceedings of the ACM SIGIR Workshop on Recommender Systems. (1999)
8. John S. Breese, David Heckerman, and Carl Kadie: Empirical Analysis of Predictive Algorithms for Collaborative Filtering. Proceedings of the Conference on Uncertainty in Artificial Intelligence. (1998) 43-52
9. J. Benschafer, Joseph Konstan and John Riedl: Recommender Systems in E-Commerce. Proceedings of the ACM Conference on Electronic Commerce. (1999)
10. Badrul M. Sarwar, George Karypis, Joseph A. Konstan, John T. Riedle: Recommender Systems for Large-Scale E-Commerce: Scalable Neighborhood Formation Using Clustering. Proceedings of the Fifth International Conference on Computer and Information Technology. (2002)
11. MovieLens dataset, GroupLens Research Center, url: http://www.grouplens.org/.

Using Association Analysis of Web Data in Recommender Systems

María N. Moreno, Francisco J. García, M. José Polo, and Vivian F. López

Dept. Informática y Automática, University of Salamanca, Salamanca. Spain
mmg@usal.es

Abstract. The numerous web sites existing nowadays make available more information than a user can manage. Thus, an essential requirement of current web applications is to provide users with instruments for personalized selective retrieval of web information. In this paper, a procedure for making personalized recommendations is proposed. The method is based on building a predictive model from an association model of Web data. It uses a set of association rules generated by a data mining algorithm that discovers knowledge in an incremental way. These rules provide models with relevant patterns that minimize the recommendation errors.

1 Introduction

A critical issue of modern Web applications is the incorporation of mechanisms for personalized selective retrieval of Web information. In the e-commerce environment, this is a way of increasing customer satisfaction and taking positions in the competitive market of the electronic business activities. Traditional, not electronic, companies usually improve their competitiveness by means of business intelligence strategies supported by techniques like data mining. Data mining algorithms find consumers' profiles and purchase patterns in the corporate databases that can be used for effective marketing and, in general, for business decision making. In the field of the e-commerce these procedures can also be applied but they have been extended to deal with problems of the web systems, such as information overload [3]. The incorporation of efficient personalization methods in these applications contributes to avoiding this problem and therefore, increases business benefits. The aim is to take advantage of the information obtained from customers' accesses in order to be able to make recommendations for a given customer about products that could be among his preferences.

Two types of error can appear in poor recommender systems: *false negatives*, which are products that are not recommended, though the customer would like them, and *false positives*, which are products that are recommended, though the customer does not like them [4]. False positive errors are less accepted by the clients than the false negative ones, therefore they are the most influential in the customer churn phenomenon. Data mining techniques contribute to the development of efficient personalized recommender systems by finding customers characteristics that increase the probability of making right recommendations. Data mining problems can be resolved by employing *supervised* and *unsupervised* algorithms. Unsupervised algorithms are usually used in knowledge discovery modeling, but they can be successfully used for

K. Bauknecht, M. Bichler, and B. Pröll (Eds.): EC-Web 2004, LNCS 3182, pp. 11–20, 2004.

predictive tasks in classification problems. The process of applying data mining techniques on web data is known as *web mining*. There are three categories: Web content mining, Web structure mining and Web usage mining. Web content mining is the process of discovering useful information on Web contents (text, image, audio, video, etc.). Web structure mining is based on the hyperlinks' structure of Web pages. Web usage mining aims to find interesting patterns, such as user profiles, from user logs [2].

Web mining tasks can be carried out automatically by means of software agents. The use of agents in web applications is widely extended, mainly in search engines and e-commerce environments, where they play diverse roles. The dynamic search of relevant information is one of the major roles [10] [2] [9]. Their autonomy, learning capability and the possibility of working in cooperation with other agents are suitable properties for their use in the personalization of web systems by means of data mining techniques. We have used them in an e-commerce intermediary site architecture [5], and we are now focused in its personalization aspect.

In this work, we present a web mining method for making recommendations based on the predictive use of an association rules' model that relates user and product attributes. Most of the existing association algorithms have the drawbacks that they discover too many patterns which are either obvious or irrelevant and, sometimes, contradictions between rules appear. We propose a refinement method in order to obtain stronger rules that reinforce the relation between items. An architecture of intelligent agents is suggested for systems implementing the method; one of the agents is in charge of doing data mining tasks, generating the associative models used in the recommendations. As products, customers and preferences change with time, models must be frequently modified. The cooperation between the system agents allows the automatic updating and the fitting of the recommendations to the new models. Our proposal should provide recommender systems with more relevant patterns that minimize the recommendation errors. The main contributions of this work are discussed in the section of results and also in the conclusions.

The next sections of the paper are outlined as follows. Section 2 summarizes research related to recommender systems. In section 3.1 the association analysis foundations and the proposed refinement algorithm are described. The proposed recommender system is presented in section 3.2. Section 4 includes the experimental study and results. Finally, we present the conclusions and future work.

2   Related Work

Recommender systems are used to increase sales by offering a selection of products or services a consumer is likely to be interested in. There are two main categories of recommendation methods: collaborative filtering and a content-based approach [8]. The first technique was originally based on nearest neighbor algorithms, which predict product preferences for a user, based on the opinions of other users. The opinions can be obtained explicitly from the users as a rating score or by using some implicit measures from purchase records such as timing logs [18]. In the content based approach text documents are recommended by comparing their contents and user profiles [8]. The lack of mechanisms to manage Web objects such as motion pictures, images or music constitutes the main weakness of this approach in the e-commerce application area. Besides, it is very difficult to handle the big number of attributes obtained from the product contents. Collaborative filtering also has limitations in the e-commerce environment. Rating schemes can only be applied to homogeneous domain information. Besides, sparsity and scalability are serious weaknesses which would lead to poor recommendations [4]. Sparsity is due to the number of ratings needed for prediction is greater than the number of the ratings obtained because usually collaborative filtering requires user explicit expression of personal preferences for products. The second limitation is related to performance problems in the search for neighbors.

In the last years many recommender systems based on the last approach have been developed. The GroupLens research system [7], Ringo [18] and Video Recommender [6] are three examples based on this approach. The usual technique used in these systems is based on correlation coefficients. The method requires user ratings about different recommendable objects. Correlation coefficients showing similarities between users are computed from the ratings. Then, recommendations based on these coefficients can be made. The procedure presents the sparsity problem and the first-rater problem that takes place when new products are introduced [7].

There are two approaches for collaborative filtering, *memory-based* (*user-based*) and *model-based* (*item-based*) algorithms. **Memory-based** algorithms, also known as *nearest-neighbor* methods, were the earliest used [18]. They treat all user items by means of statistical techniques in order to find users with similar preferences (*neighbors*). The prediction of preferences (recommendation) for the active user is based on the neighborhood features. A weighted average of the product ratings of the nearest neighbors is taken for this purpose. The advantage of these algorithms is the quick incorporation of the most recent information, but they have the inconvenience that the search for neighbors in large databases is slow [19].

Data mining technologies, such as Bayesian networks, clustering and association rules, have also been applied to recommender systems. **Model-based** collaborative filtering algorithms use these methods in the development of a model of user ratings. This recent approach was introduced to reduce the sparsity problem and to get better recommender systems.

The Bayesian network analysis is a technique that formulates a probabilistic model for collaborative filtering problem. The underlying structure used for classification is a decision tree representing user information. The predictive model is built off-line by a machine learning process and used after to do recommendations to the active users. The process is fast and simple and this is very suitable for systems in which consumer preferences change slowly with respect to the time needed to build the model [19].

In a recent work [3], the authors propose the use of methods from both categories in order to avoid the commented problems. The support vector machine (SVM) memory-based technique is used for content-based recommendations, and the latent class model (LCM), that is a model-based approach, is used for collaborative recommendation.

Rule-based approaches have also been applied to overcome problems that personalized systems have [8]. The data should be processed before generating the rules. In [4] a recommendation methodology that combines both data mining techniques is proposed. First a decision tree induction technique is used in the selection of target customers. Later, association rules are generated and used for discovering associations between products.

Clustering techniques identify groups of users who appear to have similar preferences. Predictions are based on the user participation degree in the clusters. These
techniques are not very accurate and they can be useful in a preliminary exploration
of the data.

A graphical technique that has yielded better results than nearest neighbors is horting [21]. Nodes in the graph represent users and edges between nodes indicate degree
of similarity between users. Prediction is produced by walking the graph to nearby
nodes and combining the opinions of the nearby users.

The algorithm of nearest neighbors has also been applied in combination with data
mining techniques. Lee et al. [8] create a user profile that is effective within a specific
domain by using a nearest neighborhood-based method. They expand the traditional
method to find profiles valid over all the domains. For each user, neighbors' transaction information is used to generate Web object association rules.

The main advantage of Web mining methods is that they allow avoiding the problems associated with traditional collaborative filtering techniques [12].

Our proposal is a different model-based approach that deals with the case of new
users in which an initial user profile is not available. We apply an association rule
algorithm in order to find initial patterns. Rating and users information is used in the
rule generation procedure. We use other users' attributes to refine the rules and obtain
specific rules that consider the particularities of each user. The algorithm drives the
refinement procedure for obtaining the most useful rules for the desired objective
(recommendation of products).

3   Making Personalized Recommendations

The recommendation procedure is based on searching the user profile in order to
personalize the recommendations for him/her. The profiles are given by a set of refined association rules that relate information about products preferences and user
attributes. The procedure for obtaining them is explained below.

3.1   Generating and Refining Association Rules

Mining association rules from data is mostly used for finding purchase patterns in
commercial environments. Algorithms for discovering rules, such as "Apriori", the
first to be introduced [1], are not complex; however, they usually generate a large
number of rules, even restricting them with high values of support and confidence. In
this work, we present a refinement algorithm that reduces the number of association
rules generated and produces the best rules considering their purpose, which is, in our
case, product recommendation. The refinement process is based on the concept of
unexpectedness. The foundations of association rules and unexpectedness [16] are
introduced below.

Consider the set of N transactions $D=\{T_1 , T_2 ,..... ..,T_N \}$ over the relation schema
$\{i_1 , i_2 ,..... ...,i_m \}$ consisting on a set of discrete attributes. Also, let an atomic condition be a proposition of the form $value_1 \leq attribute \leq value_2$ for ordered attributes and
$attribute = value$ for unordered attributes where $value$, $value_1$ and $value_2$ belong to the
set of distinct values taken by attribute in D. In [16] rules are defined as extended

association rules of the form $X \to A$, where X is the conjunction of atomic conditions (an itemset) and A is an atomic condition. The Rules' strength and applicability is given by the factors: *Confidence* or *predictability*. A rule has confidence c if $c\%$ of the transactions in D that contain X also contain A. A rule is said to hold on a dataset D if the confidence of the rule is greater than a user-specified threshold value chosen to be any value greater than 0.5. *Support* or *prevalence*. The rule has support s in D if $s\%$ of the transactions in D contain both X and A. *Expected predictability*. This is the frequency of occurrence of the item A. So the difference between expected predictability and predictability is a measure of the change in predictive power due to the presence of X [3].

In [15] the initial rules are a set of beliefs that come from domain knowledge. A rule $A \to B$ is defined to be unexpected with respect to the rule $X \to Y$ on the database D if the following conditions hold:

- B and Y logically contradict each other (B AND Y != FALSE);
- A AND X holds on a "large" subset of tuples in D;
- The rule A, X $\to$ B holds.

For example, an initial rule $X \to Y$ is that women like comedy movies (women $\to$ comedy). The rule scientist $\to$ documentary ($A \to B$) is unexpected with respect to the initial rule if the above conditions hold.

The concept of unexpectedness, is the basis of the proposed algorithm. The procedure also uses the best attributes for classification in order to find the more suitable rules for the purpose of recommendation. As a result, a small set of appropriate and highly confident rules that relate user data and product attributes is produced. It constitutes a very simple model for recommending products.

In this work, we are using a discovery-knowledge technique for solving a classification problem. We aim to build a model that relates some user attributes with product attributes in order to make recommendations of products. Thus, either the product or the category of products can be considered as the class label. The *label* attribute is the target of prediction in classification problems. Importance of columns is a technique that determines how important various attributes (columns) are in discriminating the different values of the label attribute [11]. A measure called *purity* (a number from 0 to 100) informs about how well the columns discriminate the classes (different values of the label attribute). It is based on the amount of information (entropy) that the column (attribute) provides. We use this technique for finding the best attributes used in the refinement algorithm.

The algorithm requires generating initial beliefs and unexpected patterns. In [15] the beliefs can either be obtained from the decision maker or induced from the data using machine learning methods. In our case, those beliefs were generated from the entire data-base by an association rule algorithm [11]. In an earlier work [14] we found that the use of refined rules for prediction in the projects' management area improved the results obtained with supervised techniques [13]. The recommender procedure proposed in this paper follows the approach of using good attributes for clasification in a rules' refinement algorithm wich works with Web usage data. We start with a set of beliefs which relate items. Then we search for unexpected patterns that could help us to increase the confidence or to solve ambiguities or inconsistencies between the rules representing the beliefs.

The refinement process used for software size estimation [14] has been modified in order to adapt it to Web data, which are mostly discrete. The steps to be taken are described below:

1. Obtain the best attributes for classification and create the sequence: seqA = $<A_k>$, $k = 1...t$ (t: number of attributes). The attributes in the sequence are ordered from greater to lesser purity.
2. The values of the attribute A_k are represented as $\{V_{k,l}\}$, $l = 1...m$ (m: number of different values).
3. Set $k = 1$ and establish the minimal *confidence* c_{min} and minimal *support* s_{min}.
4. Generate initial beliefs with confidence $c \geq c_{min}$ and support $s \geq s_{min}$.
5. Select beliefs with *confidence* near c_{min} or with conflicts between each other:

   Let $X_i \rightarrow Y_i$ and $X_j \rightarrow Y_j$ be two beliefs, R_i and R_j respectively. There is a conflict between R_i and R_j if $X_i = X_j$ and $Y_i \neg= Y_j$.
6. With the selected beliefs create the rule set setR = $\{R_i\}$, $i = 1...n$ (n: number of selected beliefs)
7. For all beliefs $R_i \in$ setR do:

   7.1. Use the values $\{V_{k,l}\}$ of the attribute A_k for generating unexpected pattern fulfilling conditions of unexpectedness and *confidence* $\geq c_{min}$. The form of the patterns is: $V_{k,l} \rightarrow B$.

   7.2. Refine the beliefs by searching for rules R' like:

   $X_i, V_{k,l} \rightarrow B$

   $X_i, \neg V_{k,l} \rightarrow Y_i$

   7.3. Let setR' be the set of refined rules, then the beliefs refined in step 7.2 should be added to it:

   setR' = setR' $\cup$ { R'_u}, $u = 1...f$ (f: number of refined rules obtained in the iteration i).
8. Set $k = k + 1$ and setR = setR'.
9. Repeat steps 7 and 8 until no more unexpected patterns can be found.

A positive aspect of this approach is the incremental knowledge discovery by using good attributes for classification progressively. Other methods for association rules mining take all available attributes. Thus, a great set of rules is generated, which is pruned later without considering classification criteria. Our algorithm simplifies the process of patterns selection and generates the best rules for the predictive purpose of recommending products.

3.2 Recommender System

The main objective of this proposal is to provide a simple procedure, which contribute to avoid the problems of the recommender systems, mentioned previously.

Firstly, we build the associative model that will be used for making the recommendations. In order to reduce the number of association rules generated and to obtain rules applicable to a wide range of customers, a list of the best rated products is generated. A minimum threshold value of the ratings was established for selecting the products. Afterward, the association rules are generated from the list. The recommendations are based on the patterns obtained. The initial rules are refined by means of an algorithm described in the section 3.1 in order to obtain strong patterns that contribute to avoid the false positive errors. The refined rules, which relate product attributes with user attributes and preferences, represent customer profiles. They are used for building a predictive model that finds interesting products for a given customer with a specific profile. Recommendation for new users can be made by checking their characteristics. The procedure allows the recommendation of new products whose characteristics belong to the user profile. New products with new characteristics are always recommended. This is the way to deal with the first-rater problem. The information about new products and new users provides feedback to the system. New association models are built periodically from the new information.

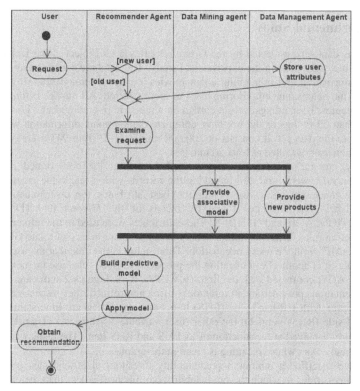

Fig. 1. UML activity diagram for the recommendation scenario

The system architecture contains three main agents that take charge of interacting with the user, managing the information and generating the recommender models. Their cooperation in the recommendation scenario is shown in figure 1. The **data mining agent** applies the proposed algorithm for generating association rules' model, which is composed by rules at different levels of refinement. This agent uses the information provided by the data management agent periodically. The **recommenda-**

tion agent transforms the associative model in a predictive model. It receives the requests from the users, takes their profiles and uses the predictive model for making the personalized recommendations. The most refined rules are used in the first instance. If the user has a profile coincident with the antecedent part of the rule, the preferential recommendation is constituted by products that satisfy the consequent part. If there are not rules that match the profile, previous level of refinement is used, and so forth. These levels are also used for secondary recommendations. The problem of finding more than one rule matching the profile is solved by taking the more confident rule for preferential recommendation. The **data management agent** collects and manages the storage of the information about new user preferences and new products. It is connected with the data mining agent to provide the data that are used periodically in the generation of new models.

4 Experimental Study

MovieLens data sets, collected by the GroupLens Research Project at the University of Minnesota, were used in the experimental study. The database contains user demographic information and user rating about movies, collected through the MovieLens Web site (movielens.umn.edu) during a seven-month period. All movies belong to 18 different genres. User ratings were recorded on a numeric five point scale. Users who had less than 20 ratings or did not have complete demographic information were removed from the data set. It consists of 100,000 ratings (1-5) from 943 users on 1682 movies (each user has rated at least 20 movies).

Initially, the rating information was used to extract the best valued movies. Association rules were produced by taking the records with a rate value greater than 2. Before generating rules, we obtain the best attributes for discriminating the GENRE label. The attributes found by means of the *Mineset* tool [11] were OCCUPATION, AGE, and GENDER. These attributes were used in the refinement of the association rules. Thus, the initial beliefs in our case are rules that relate GENRE-TIME STAMP" with the user's occupation. Time stamp is the time that the user spent in a product; it is another way of rating the products. Refined rules use the next "best attribute", AGE, combined with the first, OCCUPATION. Figures 2 and 3 are graphical representations provided by *mineset* tool of first and refined rules respectively on a grid landscape with left-hand side (LHS) items on one axis (genre-time stamp), and right-hand side (RHS) items on the other (user attributes). Attributes of a rule (LHS → RHS) are displayed at the junction of its LHS and RHS item. The display includes bars, disk and colors whose meaning is given in the graph.

We have specified a minimum predictability threshold of 30%. Rules generator does not report rules in which the predictability (confidence) is less than the expected predictability, that is, the result of dividing predictability by expected predictability (pred_div_expect) should be greater than one. Good rules are those with high values of pred_div_expect. The colors and the height of the bars in graphs (figures 2 and 3) show that these values increase in the refined rules. After the refinement process a reduced number of rules with high confidence have been obtained. Therefore, an enhancement of the recommendations based in these rules is produced.

The algorithm produces the most useful rules for the recommendation process, due to the fact that it uses the best attributes for classification, that is, the most important attributes in discriminating the different values of the class attribute, which is the

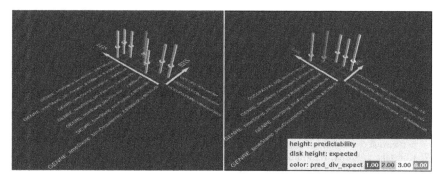

Fig. 2. Initial beliefs   **Fig. 3.** Refined beliefs

target of the recommendations. Other rule refinement methods do not consider this issue, thus they reduce the number of rules, but they do not obtain the most suitable rules for the desired objectives.

The simplicity of the models obtained with the refined rules lead to their efficient application for recommendation. On the other hand, these models are built off-line, a fact which implies an enhancing of the recommender procedure efficiency in terms of computer response time.

With respect to the advantages of using association instead of classification, the first is the lower number of attributes required and the second, the greater efficiency of the association algorithms. Clustering is another technique used habitually for finding neighbors, but it also presents computer time problems previously discussed.

5 Conclusions

In this paper, an agent based methodology for recommendation is proposed. The methodology deals with the case of making recommendations for new users and with the firs-rated problem. The recommender procedure is based on a predictive model built from an associative model that contains association rules between attributes that can be obtained from a database containing Web usage information. Recommendations provided by the predictive model are founded on strong patterns that contribute to reduce the false positive errors. Besides, there are not performance problems at recommendation time due to these models contain reduced number of highly confident rules and they are built off-line. Time spent in building the associative models is also short because association algorithms are, in general, more efficient than the classification ones. On the other hand, de refinement algorithm proposed selects the best rules for recommendation by using the best attributes for classification.

References

1. Agrawal, R., Imielinski, T., Swami, A.: Mining associations between sets of items in large databases. Proc. of ACM SIGMOD Int. Conference on Management of Data, Washington, D.C. (1993) 207-216.

2. Chau, M., Zeng, D., Chen, H., Huang, M., Hendriawan, D.: Desing and evaluation of a multi-agent collaborative Web mining system. Dec. Support Systems, 35 (2003), 167-183.
3. Cheung, K.W., Kwok, J.T., Law, M.H. and Tsui, K.C.: Mining customer product ratings for personalized marketing. Decision Support Systems, 35 (2003) 231-243.
4. Cho, H.C., Kim, J.K., Kim, S.H.: A personalized recommender system based on Web usage mining and decision tree induction. Exp. Syst. with App. 23 (2002), 329-342.
5. García, F.J., Gil, A.B., Moreno, M.N., Curto, B.: A Web Based E-Commerce Facilitator Intermediary for Small and Medium Enterprises: A B2B/B2C hybrid proposal. Proc. of EC-Web 2002, LNCS Vol. 2455, (2002) 47-56.
6. Hill, W., Stead, L., Rosenstein, M. and Furnas, G.: Recommending and evaluating choices in a virtual community of use. Proc. of Conf. Human Fac. in Comp. Sys. CHI'95, (1995).
7. Konstant, J. Miller, B., Maltz, D., Herlocker, J. Gordon, L. and Riedl, J.: GroupLens: Applying collaborative filtering to usenet news. Comm. ACM, 40 (1997), 77-87.
8. Lee, CH., Kim, Y.H., Rhee, P.K.: Web personalization expert with combining collaborative filtering and association rule mining technique. Expert Systems with Applications 21 (2001), 131-137.
9. Lee, J.H., Park, S.C.: Agent and data mining based decision support system and its adaptation to a new customer-centric electronic commerce. Expert Systems with Applications 25 (2003), 619-635.
10. Menczer, F.: Complementing search engines with online Web mining agents. Decision Support Systems, 35 (2003), 195-212.
11. Mineset user's guide, v. 007-3214-004, 5/98. Silicon Graphics (1998).
12. Mobasher, B., Cooley, R. and Srivastava, J.: Automatic personalization based on Web usage mining, Communications of the ACM, 43 (8) (2000), 142-151.
13. Moreno, M.N., Miguel, L.A., García, F.J., Polo, M.J.: Data mining approaches for early software size estimation. Proc. 3rd ACIS International Conference On Software Engineering, Artificial Intelligence, Networking and Parallel/Distributed Computing (SNPD'02), 361-368, Madrid, Spain (2002).
14. Moreno, M.N., Miguel, L.A., García, F.J., Polo, M.J.: Building knowledge discovery-driven models for decision support in project management. Dec. Support Syst., (in press).
15. Padmanabhan, B., Tuzhilin, A.: Knowledge refinement based on the discovery of unexpected patterns in data mining. Decision Support Systems 27 (1999) 303– 318.
16. Padmanabhan, B., Tuzhilin, A.: Unexpectedness as a measure of interestingness in knowledge discovery. Decision Support Systems 33 (2002) 309– 321.
17. Resnick, P., Iacovou, N., Suchack, M., Bergstrom, P. and Riedl, J.: Grouplens: An open architecture for collaborative filtering of netnews. Proc. of ACM CSW'94 Conference on Computer.Supported Cooperative Work, 175-186, (1994).
18. Sarwar, B., Karypis, G., Konstan, J., Riedl, J.: Item-based collaborative filtering recommendation algorithm. Proc. of the tenth Int. WWW Conference (2001), 285-295.
19. Schafer, J.B., Konstant, J.A. and Riedl, J.: E-commerce recommendation applications. Data Mining and Knowledge Discovery, 5 (2001), 115-153.
20. Shardanand, U. and Maes, P. "Social information filtering: algorithms for automating 'Word of Mouth'. Proc. of Conf. Human Fac. in Comp. Sys. CHI'95, 1995.
21. Wolf, J., Aggarwal, C. Wu, K.L. and Yu, P.: Horting hatches an egg. A new graph-theoretic approach to collaborative filtering. Proc. of ACM SIGKDD International Conference on Knowledge Discovery and Data Mining, San Diego, C.A., (1999).

An Intelligent System for Personalized Advertising on the Internet*

Sung Ho Ha

School of Business Administration,
Kyungpook National University,
Sangyeok-dong, Buk-gu, Daegu, Korea, 702-701
hsh@bh.knu.ac.kr

Abstract. An Internet advertising system proposed here clusters Web site users with similar preferences into numerous segments through Web usage mining. It utilizes fuzzy rules which express user segments' surfing patterns and appropriate Web ads. It selects proper Web ads by fuzzy inference, stores them in recommendation sets database, and forwards them to the target user. To verify the effectiveness of the system, changes in click-through-ratio scores per e-newspaper section are observed.

1   Introduction

Rapid development of the Internet and Web technologies enables customers to have more choices than ever before about what to buy, where to buy, and how to buy. The emerging electronic commerce has also changed many aspects of existing business and business process. At this time, successful companies provide a bundle of customized services acceptable, which satisfy the customers' needs, to gain a competitive advantage.

As the range of the Internet techniques available to online advertisers expands, Web advertising attracts public attention as a new communication channel. Among others, banner ad continues to dominate spending in online advertising and the market for that is steadily growing [1]. Online advertisement will become the most important revenue for many companies on the Web in the near future.

Conventional advertising, however, is passive, targeted to mass audiences, and has suffered poor responses from customers. To raise the effectiveness of banner ads, Web sites need to be able to put the right message to the right customer at the right time, and to provide personalized advertising messages to every desirable customer. Therefore their online marketing solutions should possess the functionality to identify a customer, predict and understand his or her preferences and interests, choose appropriate ads, and deliver them in a personalized format directly to him or her during his or her online session [11].

In this study, an adaptive and personalized system for the Internet advertising will be introduced. It provides personalized ads to users whenever they visit an e-newspaper

---

* This research was supported by Kyungpook National University Research Fund, 2003.

K. Bauknecht, M. Bichler, and B. Pröll (Eds.): EC-Web 2004, LNCS 3182, pp. 21–30, 2004.

Web site, which enables an online advertiser to practice one-to-one marketing. As a result, the system improves users' satisfaction and their responses to ads. In doing so, the Web ad system mines Web server logs containing users' Web navigation patterns with machine learning techniques, identifies their current tastes and interests, and decides on proper ads through fuzzy reasoning which will be forwarded to users.

2 Internet Advertisement

Advertising on the Web refers to advertising that delivers electronic information services to users. Until now, several literatures on online advertisement focus on using the Web for supporting commerce in terms of electronic marketing, digital publishing and dissemination. They analyze online ads' effectiveness from the marketing perspective [10]. Langheinrich et al. [7] classify online advertisement approaches into four categories: untargeted, editorial, targeted, and personalized. Personalized advertisement is regarded as a next generation advertisement approach and typically uses machine learning methods, such as neural networks, to allow personalized ad selection and recommendation based on the browsing and interaction history of a particular user as well as other demographic information.

Currently available personalization techniques comprise decision rule-based filtering, content-based filtering, collaborative filtering, and non-intrusive personalization [9]. Decision rule-based filtering asks users a series of questions to obtain user demographics or static profiles, then lets marketing experts manually specify rules based on them, and delivers the appropriate items (Web ads) to a particular user based on the rules. However, it is not particularly useful, since it is difficult to obtain valuable rules from marketing experts and to validate the effectiveness of the extracted rules.

Content-based filtering recommends items being similar to what a user has liked previously. Collaborative filtering selects items based on the opinions of other customers with similar past preferences. However, traditional recommendation techniques, including content-based or collaborative filtering, have some limitations, such as reliance on subject user ratings and static profiles, or the inability to capture richer semantic relationships among Web objects and to scale to a large number of items.

To overcome these shortcomings, non-intrusive personalization attempts to incorporate Web usage mining techniques. Web usage mining uses data mining algorithms to automatically discover and extract patterns from Web usage data and predict user behavior while users interact with the Web. Recommendation based on Web usage mining has several advantages over traditional techniques. It can dynamically develop user profiles from user patterns while reducing the need to explicitly obtain subjective user ratings or registration-based personal preferences. Therefore the recommendation system's performance does not degrade over time.

In the e-commerce environment, analyzing such information embedded in click-stream data residing in Web logs is critical to improve the effectiveness and performance of Web marketing for online service providers. Recently there have been many researches on Web server log analysis from both industry and academia. Some of these efforts have shown how Web usage mining techniques can be used to characterize and model Web site access patterns and how well they are useful to recommendation in electronic commerce scenarios [5].

3   Personalized Advertising System

The overall architecture of adaptive Web ad personalization system comprises two components: online and offline. Fig. 1 depicts the online architecture showing the system's essential functionality.

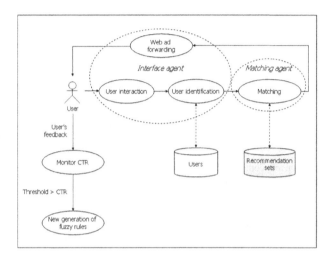

Fig. 1. Online components of the ad recommender system. It always monitors users' feedbacks to determine the timing of new fuzzy rules to generate

The online components consist of *interface agent*, *matching agent*, and *HTTP server*. The interface agent provides an interface between the HTTP server and its users for user interaction. The Web server helps identify a user and tracks the active user session as the interface agent makes HTTP requests. The matching agent looks up a recommendation sets database to extract a set of recommended ads for a target user. It then sends the ads to the client browser through the interface agent. Clickthrough ratio (CTR) score, which is the percentage of times that viewers of a Web page click on a given banner ad, measures the effectiveness of the recommended ads, and further determines the timing of new fuzzy rules to generate.

The offline is divided into four parts, as shown in Fig. 2: *customer clustering*, *fuzzy inference*, *Web ad clustering*, and *Web ad segment selection*. Customer clustering uses a self-organizing map (SOM), a neural clustering method, to divide Web site users into numerous groups with similar surfing preferences through mining Web server logs. Browsing patterns and recommendation sets for a user segment form fuzzy rules used in fuzzy inference. Fuzzy rules are mainly obtained from the previous recommendation and effect histories.

Fuzzy inference receives each user's fuzzified page views by news section from the Users database which stores each user's Web site navigation history. It draws conclusions about recommended types of ads, which are fed into Web ad segment selection.

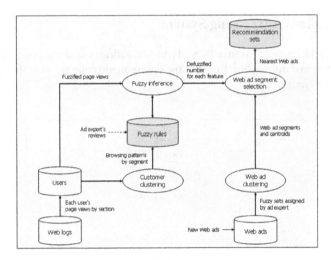

Fig. 2. Offline components comprise four functions: customer clustering, fuzzy inference, Web ad clustering, and Web ad segment selection

Web ad clustering uses another SOM to divide Web ads into groups with similar ad features. Web ad segment selection chooses appropriate Web ad segments by calculating Hamming distance measures and then Web ads by calculating Euclidean distance measures. The system stores the selected Web ads in the recommendation sets database for site users, which will be forwarded to a target user.

3.1 Segmentation of Web Site Users and Web Ads

To maximize the effectiveness of Web ads through recommending the right ads to the right users, service providers should determine Web site users' habits and interests first, which can be discovered by mining their Web page navigation patterns (Web usage mining) [4, 6].

When extracting users' access histories, on which the mining algorithms can be run, several data preprocessing issues – cleaning data, identifying unique users, sessions, and transactions – have to be addressed. Data cleaning eliminates irrelevant items including all entries with filename suffixes which indicate graphic files in server logs. It leaves log entries indicating e-news pages. Individual users and their sessions can be identified by various preprocessing methods [2, 12].

Once users and their access histories have been identified, segmenting users follows. It breaks users into peer groups with similar Web page navigation behaviors. Behaviors among the groups, however, differ significantly. Segmentation by traversal history uses a segmentation variable on the basis of how many times a user visits each section.

Fig. 3 shows a process of segmenting users and fuzzifying segments' characteristics. For analytical convenience, this study classifies electronic newspaper's sections into seven categories, such as POL (politics), ECO (economy), SOC (society), WOR (world), CUL (culture and life), SCI (science and technology), and SPO (sports). These

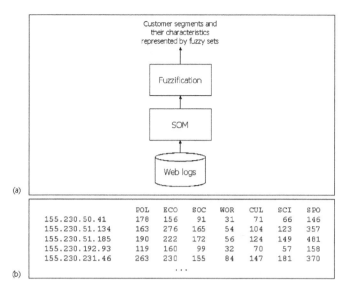

(a)

(b)

	POL	ECO	SOC	WOR	CUL	SCI	SPO
155.230.50.41	178	156	91	31	71	66	146
155.230.51.134	163	276	165	54	104	123	357
155.230.51.185	190	222	172	56	124	149	481
155.230.192.93	119	160	99	32	70	57	158
155.230.231.46	263	230	155	84	147	181	370

· · ·

Fig. 3. (a) A process for segmenting users and fuzzifying segments' characteristics. (b) Sample users' browsing counts per news section

sections are later used as antecedents of fuzzy rules. The number of times each user has visited each section during the analysis period is counted from the Web log, and is fed into the SOM which builds user behavior models. In training SOM, managerial convenience decides on nine as the number of output units.

Fig. 4(a) shows fuzzy partitions of sections SOC and SCI. Fig. 4(b) summarizes seven dominant segments derived from a three-by-three SOM, and their average access counts expressed by fuzzy numbers. Because users' characteristics are generally fuzzy and can not be specified in crisp values, fuzzy numbers are suitable for expressing users' navigation histories. Therefore four triangular fuzzy numbers such as S (small), MS (medium small), MB (medium big), and B (big), or three ones such as S, M (medium), and B are used.

To build an experimental Web ads database for the Web ad system, I chose sample ads randomly from a major e-newspaper provider in Korea; ten ads under each section. After examining these ads, I extracted six categorical features as follows: MAG (newspaper and magazine-related ads), ECO (business and financial ads), COM (computer and telecommunication-related ads), SPO (sports-related ads), ENT (culture and entertainment-related ads), and RAN (the others). Note that each ad has fuzzy characteristics which can be represented as the combination of these six features.

Membership degrees ranging from zero to one are appropriately assigned to each ad's features. SOM then clusters Web ads with six features (i.e., six input dimensions) into numerous groups with similar ad characteristics. A cluster centroid represents average membership degree for each feature. Each of the six features has triangular fuzzy number which is used as consequents in fuzzy rules executed only to the degree that antecedents are true.

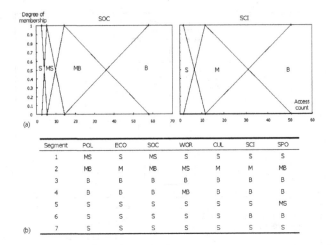

(b)

Segment	POL	ECO	SOC	WOR	CUL	SCI	SPO
1	MS	S	MS	S	S	S	S
2	MB	M	MB	MS	M	M	MB
3	B	B	B	B	B	B	B
4	B	B	B	MB	B	B	B
5	S	S	S	S	S	S	MS
6	S	S	S	S	S	B	B
7	S	S	S	S	S	S	S

Fig. 4. (a) Fuzzy partitions of the society, and science and technology sections. (b) Dominant user segments and their characteristics expressed in fuzzy numbers

3.2 Fuzzy Rules Generation and Fuzzy Inference

Fig. 5 shows how to generate fuzzy rules and describes sample rules. A fuzzy rule has a form of IF-THEN in which the left-hand side is a condition part and a conjunction of triangular fuzzy numbers for access counts by section, and the right-hand side is an action part and a conjunction of triangular fuzzy numbers for ad features.

The advertising system utilizes its previous recommendation and response histories of segmented users to make fuzzy rules for them. It is based on which ads have been recommended to each peer group and have received good responses. Ad experts may refine the fuzzy rules with domain knowledge of which ads are suitable to each user segment.

Once a fuzzy rule base has been established, a fuzzy inference engine receives fuzzified user access counts per section as an input vector value. Fuzzy inference is a mathematical process to calculate the fuzzy output probability from the probability values of the input functions. It processes the information through the fuzzy rule base and produces a fuzzy set for each ad feature, which is converted to a real number through defuzzification.

Mamdani's popular MIN-MAX reasoning strategy is used as a fuzzy inference method [3][8]. When an access count vector is given as $(x_1, x_2, x_3, x_4, x_5, x_6, x_7) =$ (POL, ECO, SOC, WOR, CUL, SCI, SPO), the probability of fuzzy output function can be calculated as follows (1):

$$W_k = \mu_{A_1}(x_1) \wedge \mu_{A_2}(x_2) \wedge \mu_{A_3}(x_3) \wedge \mu_{A_4}(x_4) \wedge \mu_{A_5}(x_5) \wedge \mu_{A_6}(x_6) \wedge \mu_{A_7}(x_7)$$
$$\mu_C(z) = \bigvee_{j=1}^{rule\#} [W_j \wedge \mu_{C_j}(z)] \tag{1}$$

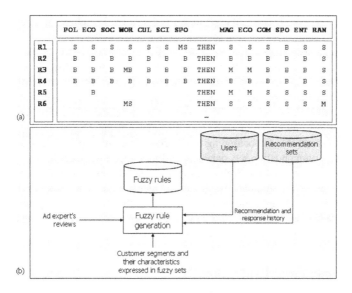

	POL	ECO	SOC	WOR	CUL	SCI	SPO		MAG	ECO	COM	SPO	ENT	RAN
R1	S	S	S	S	S	S	MS	THEN	S	S	S	B	S	S
R2	B	B	B	B	B	B	B	THEN	B	B	B	B	B	S
R3	B	B	B	MB	B	B	B	THEN	M	M	B	B	B	S
R4	B	B	B	B	B	B	B	THEN	B	B	B	B	B	S
R5		B						THEN	M	M	S	S	S	S
R6				MS				THEN	S	S	S	S	S	M

(a)

(b)

Fig. 5. Fuzzy rules generation. (a) Sample fuzzy rules. (b) A process generating fuzzy rules

where $\mu_C(z)$ is a fuzzy set for an ad's z^{th} categorical feature, $\mu_{A_i}(x_i)$ is the membership degree for the ith news section, and x_i is the ith element in an access count vector.

Because seven antecedents exist in each rule, seven membership degrees are obtained. Each fuzzy rule's fitness value is then determined by a MIN ($\wedge$) operation on these membership degrees. After applying the fitness values to the consequents of the rules, combining multiple outputs through a MAX ($\vee$) operation completes the fuzzy inference process.

3.3   Web Ads Recommendation and Continuous Monitoring

Defuzzification is to determine a crisp correspondence in a set of real numbers from the fuzzy sets derived from fuzzy inference per each ad's feature [3]. The central gravity ($Z_{defuzzified}$) is chosen as a defuzzification method and is calculated by using the following equation (2):

$$Z_{defuzzified} = \frac{\int \mu_C(z) z \, dz}{\int \mu_C(z) \, dz} \tag{2}$$

After a set of defuzzified real numbers are obtained, the ad system calculates a set of Hamming distance between a set of defuzzified numbers and centroids of ad segments. A Hamming distance is calculated by using the following equation (3):

$$d(A, B) = \sum_{\substack{i=1 \\ x_i \in X}}^{n} |\mu_A(x_i) - \mu_B(x_i)| \tag{3}$$

where X is categorical features of each ad, μ_A is defuzzified numbers made from fuzzy inference, μ_b is centroid of each ad segment, and $d(A, B)$ is the Hamming distance.

For example, assuming that a set of defuzzified numbers are (MAG, ECO, COM, SPO, ENT, RAN) = (0.64, 0.21, 0.16, 0.35, 0.2, 0.19), a Hamming distance to a cluster centroid, (MAG, ECO, COM, SPO, ENT, RAN) = (0.0, 0.0, 0.0, 1.0, 0.5, 1.0), reaches 2.77. The closer the Hamming distance, the more similar preference the ad segment has with regard to a target user. The member ads in the closest ad segment are the candidates for recommendation to the user. Euclidean distance measures between the cluster centroid and the ads belonging to the cluster are, in sequence, calculated and stored in the recommendation sets database for future recommendation.

Whenever a user visits the Web site, the ad system looks up the recommendation sets database to find the suitable ads and display them on the user's browser. However, because customers' interests and needs continuously change, the system must capture this change. When average CTR goes down a set threshold, it starts deriving new user profiles and new fuzzy rules for new recommendation.

4   Experiment and Evaluation

Generally, several metrics used to measure the effectiveness of Web ads include the CTR. In most Web ads, a 2% CTR would be considered successful. Especially as ads become familiar to users, the CTR is well below 1%.

In order to verify the effect of the proposed system on the increase in CTR scores per section of the e-newspaper, an experimental architecture for measuring the Web ad system's performance consists of multiple Web servers, which operate together and deal with actual users of the e-newspaper provider. When a user requests e-news services, a

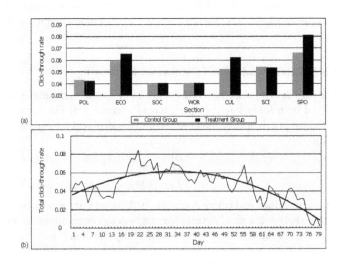

Fig. 6. (a) The CTR scores of the Web ad system. (b) Changes in total average CTR scores over time

virtual server receives the request and redirects it to any free-traffic actual Web server. Users do not know which server they connect. If every server is busy, the virtual server, then, redirects the request to the randomly selected actual server. Actual servers are divided into two groups for the experiment: the treatment group (Web servers with the ad system) and the control group (Web servers without the ad system). The treatment group and control group hold the same e-news articles, but only the treatment group shows the recommended ads to users.

Fig. 6(a) illustrates the average CTR scores per section for the treatment and control groups after a 80-day experiment. Several sections including Economy, Culture and Life, and Sports show a clear improvement in the average CTR after adoption of the Web ad system, while recommending ads to users frequently looking at Political, Social, World, or Science and Technology section seems less effective.

Fig. 6(b) illustrates changes in total average CTR scores and a trend line during the experiment (Equation for the trend line is $y = -2E - 6x^2 + 0.0001x + 0.0396$ with $R^2 = 0.6644$). The CTR scores fluctuate during the analysis period, but the general pattern for users to view Web ads shows increase in the score at first and decrease afterward. If a threshold is set to 0.02 of the CTR, the system advises segmenting new users and creating new fuzzy rules at the 76th day after starting the experiment.

5   Conclusion and Future Research

An adaptive and personalized Web ad system is proposed to raise the effectiveness of banner ads on the Internet. It consists of online and offline components: online has an interface agent, matching agent, and HTTP server; offline has customer clustering, fuzzy inference, Web ad clustering, and Web ad segment selection functionalities.

The work presented here can be extended in several ways for future research. First, clustering analysis used to segment user's access patterns can be extended to include richer information. The current clustering analysis uses an access count value (frequency value) as a base variable for user segmentation. Utilizing RFM (recency, frequency, and monetary) values altogether can be a way to improve clustering results, since they encompass the entire user's behavior.

Second, deriving and maintaining accurate fuzzy rule sets is an issue of a fuzzy system. The larger the number of sets, the more accurately a fuzzy system reflects the true relationship among variables. However, it increases complexity, decreases robustness of the system, and makes it more difficult to modify the system.

References

1. Allen, C., Kania, D., Yaeckel B.: One-To-One Web Marketing: Build a Relationship Marketing Strategy One Customer at a Time. John Wiley & Sons, Inc., New York (2001)
2. Cooley, R., Mobasher, B., Srivastava, J.: Data preparation for Mining World Wide Web Browsing Patterns. Int. J. Knowl. Inform. Syst. 1(1) (1999) 5-32
3. Cox, E.: The Fuzzy Systems Handbook: A Practitioner's Guide to Building, Using, and Maintaining Fuzzy Systems. AP Professional, Boston (1994)
4. Eirinaki, M., Vazirgiannis, M.: Web Mining for Web Personalization. ACM T. Internet Tech. 3(1) (2003) 1-27

5. Kohavi, R., Provost, F. (ed.): Applications of Data Mining To Electronic Commerce: A Special Issue of Data Mining and Knowledge Discovery. Kluwer Academic Publishers, Boston (2001)
6. Kosala, R., Blockeel, H.: Web Mining Research: A Survey. SIGKDD Explorations. 2(1) (2000) 1-15
7. Langheinrich, M., Nakamura, A., Abe, N., Kamba, T.: Unintrusive customization techniques for Web advertising. Comput. Netw. 31(11-16) (1999) 1259-1272
8. Lee, C.C.: Fuzzy Logic in Control Systems: Fuzzy Logic Controller - Part I, Part II. IEEE T. Syst. Man, Cyb. 20(2) (1990) 404-435
9. Lee, W-P., Liu, C-H., Lu, C-C.: Intelligent agent-based systems for personalized recommendations in Internet commerce. Expert Syst. Appl. 22(4) (2002) 275-284
10. Ngai, E.W.T.: Selection of web sites for online advertising using the AHP. Inform. Manage. 40(4) (2003) 233-242
11. Peppard, J.: Customer Relationship Management (CRM) in Financial Services. Eur. Manage. J. 18(3) (2000) 312-327
12. Srivastava, J., Cooley, R., Deshpande, M., Tan, P.-N.: Web usage mining: Discovery and applications of usage patterns from web data. SIGKDD Explorations. 1(2) (2000) 12-23

Supporting User Query Relaxation in a Recommender System

Nader Mirzadeh[1], Francesco Ricci[1], and Mukesh Bansal[2]

[1] Electronic Commerce and Tourism Research Laboratory
ITC-irst, Via Solteri 38, Trento, Italy
{mirzadeh,ricci}@itc.it
[2] Telethon Institute of Genetics and Medicine, Via Pietro Castellino 111, Napoli
bansal@tigem.it

Abstract. This paper presents a new technology for supporting flexible query management in recommender systems. It is aimed at guiding a user in refining her query when it fails to return any item. It allows the user to understand the culprit of the failure and to decide what is the best compromise to chose. The method uses the notion of hierarchical abstraction among a set of features, and tries to relax first the constraint on the feature with lowest abstraction, hence with the lightest revision of the original user needs. We have introduced this methodology in a travel recommender system as a query refinement tool used to pass the returned items by the query to a case-based ranking algorithm, before showing the query results to the user. We discuss the results of the empirical evaluation which shows that the method, even if incomplete, is powerful enough to assist the users most of the time.

1 Introduction

Business to consumer web sites have quickly proliferated and nowadays almost every kind of product or service can be bought on-line. In order to improve the effectiveness of user decision making support, recommender systems have been introduced in some domains. For instance, it is very popular the books recommender system included in amazon.com or the movie recommender system MovieLens [1]. In a previous paper we have introduced Trip@dvice, a travel planning recommendation methodology that integrates interactive query management and case-based reasoning (CBR) [2]. In this methodology, product research is supported by an interactive query management subsystems that cooperates with the user and provides information about the cause of query failure and its possible remedies. The goal is to help the user to autonomously decide what is the best compromise when not all his wants and needs can be satisfied. CBR supports the modelling of the human/computer interaction as a case and is exploited to extract, from previously recorded recommendation sessions, useful information that enable to intelligently sort the results of a user's query.

In this paper we focus on the Trip@dvice relaxation algorithm and its evaluation in practical usage. Interactive query management, and in particular dealing

K. Bauknecht, M. Bichler, and B. Pröll (Eds.): EC-Web 2004, LNCS 3182, pp. 31–40, 2004.
© Springer-Verlag Berlin Heidelberg 2004

with failing queries has been addressed in a number of researches in the area of cooperative database [3–5]. Chu et al. suggested to explore an abstraction hierarchy among values of a feature/attribue, and to use that knowledge for moving along the hierarchy for relaxation or tightening the result set [3]. Godfrey extensively studied the cause of failure of boolean queries, and proposed an algorithm for query relaxation [5].

Our new query relaxation algorithm extends that presented in [6], introducing the notion of abstraction-hierarchy. This is a relationship among features describing the product and not, as in [3], a partition of a feature domain (grouping of values). Moreover our approach is not limited to boolean constraints, as that discussed in [5], as we address the problem of relaxing range constraints on numeric attributes. In principle our goal is to relax the minimum number of constraints for a given query, such that a non void result is returned. But, finding such relaxed query is in general an NP-hard problem [5], hence we focussed on a simpler, incomplete but practically feasible and effective approach.

In this paper we first present the motivation for using interactive query management (IQM) in recommender systems and then we describe the architecture of the IQM module implemented in Trip@dvice. Then we present the empirical evaluation of IQM, that was conducted by exploiting log data derived from the evaluation a recommender system based on Trip@dvice [2]. The results show the method is powerful enough to find at lease one successful relaxed query most of the time.

2   Interactive Query Management

In previous researches on knowledge-based recommender systems the problem of dealing with the failure of an over-constrained query was typically addressed by exploiting similarity-based retrieval [7, 8]. In Trip@dvice [2], as well as in other proposals [9], it is argued that the system should not autonomously determine the best attainable approximate match, as in a similarity-based retrieval, but should actively support the user and let him understand what is the best relaxation/compromise. Hence in Trip@dvice when a query fails to return any item a dedicated interactive query management component (IQM in Figure 1) suggests some refinement(s) in terms of query constraints to discard or change.

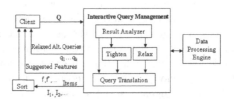

Fig. 1. Intelligent Mediator architecture.

A user will typically interacts with IQM through a Graphical User Interface, submitting a query and getting as reply a reasonable set of items. If this cannot be achieved then IQM suggests to the user some refinements to the failing query. Two types of failures are considered: the query returns either too many results or no result at all. When a query returns an empty set, IQM tries to find some relaxed alternative queries that change or remove the minimum number of constraints in the failing query and would make the subquery to produce some results. IQM reports these alternative options to the user so that he can decide what is the best relaxation (from his point of view) and opt for this with the certainty that the query will now return some result. Conversely, in case too many items would be returned, a set of candidate features are suggested as those that should be constrained in addition to those already included in the original query (this last topic is not discussed here, see [6]).

The query language supported in Trip@dvice is simple but expressive enough to cope with standard web forms. Let $X = \prod_{i=1}^{n} X_i$ be an item space (e.g., a set of hotels). We shall refer to a feature of X, as f_i with its associated domain X_i for all i, $1 \leq i \leq n$. A query, say q is obtained by the conjunction of atomic constraints; $q = c_1 \wedge \cdots \wedge c_m$ (or simply $q = \{c_1, \cdots, c_m\}$), where $m \leq n$ and each c_k ($1 \leq k \leq m$) constrains the feature f_{i_k}. Each constraint is defined as follows

$$c_k = \begin{cases} f_{i_k} = \mathsf{true} & \text{if } f_{i_k} \text{ is boolean} \\ f_{i_k} = v & \text{if } f_{i_k} \text{ is nominal} \\ f_{i_k} \in [l, u] & \text{if } f_{i_k} \text{ is numeric} \end{cases} \tag{1}$$

where $v, l, u \in X_{i_k}$.

Note that the query language we consider here does not support inquiries across catalogues, because we assume that a catalogue is a custom view that is possibly built over a set of joint tables.

We now focus on the Relax module in Figure 1. We shall refer to a relaxed version of a query by calling it simply a *subquery*, and a *successful subquery* if it returns a non-empty result set.

Example 1. Let $q : \{[2 \leq category \leq 3], [parking = \mathsf{true}], [30 \leq price \leq 50]\}$ be a query, then $q' : \{[category \geq 3], [price \leq 35]\}$ is a subquery of q, where the constraint on parking is relaxed.

The relaxation method makes use of the notion of *feature abstraction hierarchy*, i.e., a hierarchy among some features of an item space. For example, assume the *accommodation* item space contains the *category* (i.e., 1-star,2-star,...), *price* and *parking* features. Then we say that the feature *category* is more abstract than the *price* because the knowledge of the price greatly reduces the uncertainty over the category (i.e the conditional entropy of the category given the price is low [10]). The idea is to use such relationships in the relaxation process to sort a set of related constraints and start relaxation on the constrained-feature with lowest abstraction level. If this relaxation does not produce any result, then this constraint is removed and the constraint on the feature with next-lower abstraction is tried.

More formally, we denote with $FAH = \{F^1, \ldots, F^k\}$ a collection of feature abstraction hierarchies, where each $F^i = (f_1^i, \ldots, f_{n_i}^i)$ is an abstraction hierarchy, i.e., an ordered list of features in X (comparable features). We mean that f_j^i is more abstract than f_l^i iff $j < l$, and there are no common features in two different F^is, i.e. features in different F^i are not comparable.

Figure 2 depicts the algorithm used in Trip@dvice to find relaxing sub-queries of a failing query[1]. The constraints in the query $q = \{c_1, \ldots, c_m\}$ are partitioned in the set $CL = \{cl_1, \ldots, cl_{m'}\}$, where each cl_i is a ordered list of constraints of q, such that the features in cl_i belongs only to one F^j (line 1). If the constrained feature in any constraint c does not belong to any abstraction hierarchy, then a singleton list, containing only c, is built. So for instance, let $q = \{c_1, c_2, c_3\}$ be the query as in Example 1, and let the feature abstraction hierarchy be $FAH = \{(category, price)\}$, then $CL = \{(c_1, c_3), (c_2)\}$ is the partition of q according to this FAH. The proposed algorithm outputs at most two subqueries, one for each element in CL. The first subquery is obtained by relaxing a constraint in (c_1, c_3) the second by relaxing c_2. To find the first subquery, the algorithm first checks if the relaxation of c_3 (price) produces a successful subquery, otherwise it removes c_3 and relaxes also c_1.

More precisely, the loop at line 3 tries to relax the set f related constraints (i.e., $cl \in CL$) while keeping the rest of the constraints in q unchanged. The related constraints in cl are relaxed starting from the one on the feature with lowest abstraction by the *for* loop at line 6. ch is a list containing all the modified versions of the current constraint, and it is initialized with c at line 8. The variable *relax* is a flag that indicates whether a wider or shorter range should be tried for a numerical constraints. It is initially set to *true*.

$q = \{c_1, \ldots, c_m\}$: a query to be relaxed.

```
RelaxQuery(q)
1   CL ← Partition constraints in q according
        to the defined FAH;
2   QL ← ∅; % the list of subqueries
3   for each cl ∈ CL do
4       q' ← q;
5       suggest ← ∅;% a subquery suggestion
6       for j = |cl| to 1 do
7           c ← get jth constraint from cl
8           ch ← {c} % constraint history
9           relax ← true
10          do
11              q' ← q' − {c}
12              c ← ModifyRange(c, ch, relax)
13          while ( Analyse(q', c, ch, relax, suggest) )
14          if suggest ≠ ∅ then
15              QL ← QL ∪ suggest;
16              j ← 0; % no need to go to higher abstr.
17          end:if
18      end:for
19  end:for
20  return QL
```

```
ModifyRange(c, relax, ch)
1   c' ← c;
2   if c is numeric then
3       if relax then
4           c' ← IncreaseRange(c);
5       else
6           c' ← DecreaseRange(c, ch);
7       end:if
8   return c'
```

```
Analyse(q', c, ch, relax, suggest)
1   retValue ← false;
2   if ( c ≠ null and
        length(ch) < max_length ) then
3       if c is numeric then
4           retValue ← true;
5           q' ← q' ∪ {c};
6       end:if
7       n ← Count(q');
8       if (n = 0 and relax = false) then
9           retValue ← false;
10      else if (n = 0) then
11          ch ← ch ∪ {c};
12          relax ← true;
13      else if n > α then
14          relax ← false;
15      if n > 0 then
16          suggest ← {(q', n)};
17  end:if
18  return retValue
```

Fig. 2. Relaxation algorithms.

----

[1] Variables are in *italic* and literals are in sans serif

Then the *do-while* loop at lines 10-13 tries different ranges for a numerical constraint, or it iterates only once for a non-numerical constraint. The ModifyRange function modifies only the numerical constraints. It returns a modified version of the input (numeric) constraint depending on the *relax* flag. The returned constraint contains either a wider or shorter range than the one specified in c depending on the value of *relax*. It returns null if increasing (decreasing) a range would not increase (decrease) the result size of the subquery. For instance, if the current range specifies the whole range of values in the catalogue for the constrained feature, then increasing the range would not improve the result size of current subquery.

Let $c : [l \leq f_i \leq u]$ be current range constraint. The IncreaseRange function relaxes c to $[\lfloor l - \delta \rfloor \leq f_i \leq \lceil u + \delta \rceil]$, where

$$\delta = \begin{cases} 0.1(u - l) & \text{if } u > l \\ 0.1(v_{max} - v_{min}) & \text{if } u = l \end{cases} \tag{2}$$

and $v_{\min}, v_{\max}$ are the minimum and maximum values of feature f_i in the catalogue, respectively.

Example 2. (Example 1 cont.) Assume q returns an empty set. If we call Relax-Query to find all the relaxed subqueries of q, the IncreaseRange will be called in turn to find a new wider range for *price*, and it would return $[28 \leq price \leq 52]$.

The DecreaseRange will find a range between that range that caused an empty result set and the current one that makes the subquery to return too many results. Let $[l_1, u_1]$, and $[l_2, u_2]$ be two such ranges. Using this method to shorten $[l_2, u_2]$, it would return a new constraint specifying the range $[l', u']$ where $l' = (l_2 - 1_1)/2$ and $u' = (u_2 - u_1)/2$.

Example 3. (Example 2 cont.) Assume trying the wider range $[28, 52]$ for the *price* returns too many items by the corresponding subquery q' (i.e., Count$(q') > \alpha$). The next call to the ModifyRange will call the DecreaseRange in order to reduce the current range, and it will return the constraint $[29 \leq price \leq 51]$.

The Analyse procedure determines whether or not the maximum number of attempts to find a suitable constraint for a numeric feature has been reached. If not, it examines the result size (n) of the current subquery. If the result size is 0, it sets the *relax* flag to true to indicate a wider range should be tried, otherwise if the current range has made the subquery to produce a large result set, then the *relax* is set to false to indicate a shorter range has to be tried. If at any stage the subquery produces some results, then the method creates a new suggestion (i.e, *suggest*) which is a set containing a pair made of the subquery and its result size (line 16, in the Analyse).

After the *do-while* loop (lines 10-13), if there is any suggestion, then there is no need to relax the constraint on feature with higher abstraction, and hence the loop at line 6 terminates and the suggestion is added to the return set (QL).

The algorithm terminates when all the lists $cl \in CL$ of q are tried. Obviously, the running time of RelaxQuery is $O(|q|)$ where $|q|$ is the number of constraints in the query q, since each constraint is considered a constant number of times.

It is worth to note that the RelaxQuery returns at most the same number of successful subqueries as there are elements in the partition set of the query q, where each subquery represents a compromise (i.e., relaxation of a subset of constraints in the query) the user has to make in order to receive some results. Hence, it is up to the user to judge which subquery is the best one according to her preferences and constraints. For instance, if the RelaxQuery returns two subqueries, one that relaxes the constraints on price and the category, and another that relaxes the parking feature, then the user can choose either view more expensive hotels or to miss the parking.

3   Evaluation

We developed a prototype, based on Trip@dvice [2], and empirically evaluated that with real users. In fact two variants of the same system (*NutKing*[2]) were built. One supports intelligent query management (IQM) and intelligent ranking based on cases (*NutKing+*), and the other without those functions (*NutKing-*). In fact *NutKing+* used a previous version of the relaxation algorithm, that did not use the notion of feature-abstraction hierarchy [6]. The subjects had randomly been assigned to one of the two variants.

Table 1 shows some objective measures relative to the IQM. It includes the average values and standard deviations of the measures taken for each recommendation session. Values marked with * (**) means a significant difference at the 0.1 (0.05) probability level, according to an unpaired t-test. Relaxation was suggested by the system 6.3 times per session, and this means that approximately 50% of the queries had a "no result" failure. The user accepted one of the proposed subqueries 2.8 times, i.e. almost 45% of the time. We consider this a good result, taking into account the user behavior that is often erratic and not always focussed in solving the task.

Table 1. Comparison of NutKing+ and NutKing-.

Objective Measure	NutKing-	NutKing+
queries issued by the user	20.1±19.2	13.4±9.3*
number of features in a query	4.7±1.2	4.4±1.1
results size per query	42.0±61.2	9.8±14.3**
system suggested query relaxations	n.a.	6.3±3.6
# of times the user accepted query relaxations	n.a	2.8±2.1

We now provide a more detailed description of the queries issued to each of the five catalogues used in the experiment and of the performance of the RelaxQuery algorithm. In particular we shall show how often RelaxQuery can effectively assist users.

Five catalogues/collections are considered in NutKing: accommodations, cultural attractions, events, locations, and sport activities. We do not consider here the *cultural attractions* catalog since it has only three features and relaxation of 1-constraint in a failing culture-query has always produced some results.

[2] http://itr.itc.it

We mined the log file of users' interactions in the empirical evaluation, and extracted all the users' queries submitted to different catalogues in NutKing±. We grouped queries according to their type (i.e. the catalogue they queried) and the number of constraints they contained. Let Q^j denote the set of queries submitted to a catalogue where each query contains j constraints. The log also contained the result size of each query, which enabled us to determine the set of failing queries, i.e., those that had a void result set. Let $FQ^j \subseteq Q^j$ denote the set of such failing queries. Then we ran (again) the RelaxQuery algorithm on each query $q \in FQ^j$ to compare the subset of failing queries, say SQ^j that the RelaxQuery could find a successful subquery, with and without the notion of feature-abstraction-hierarchy (FAH) (Table 2). The relaxation algorithm that does not exploit FAH is described in [6]. In total using FAH the proposed algorithm was able to find a successful subquery 83% of the cases (232/279), whereas the same algorithm not using FAH was successful 61% (172/279). It is worth noting that, this is obtained by loosing a property of the previous method, i.e., the capability to find all the successful subqueries that relax 1-single constraint. In other words there are cases in which using FAH two constraints in a hierarchy are relaxed even when only one is necessary. This happen when relaxing the more abstract and still keeping the lees abstract does give some results. But, in practice, using FAH we can find a successful subquery in more cases.

Table 2. Queries submitted to the catalogues.

Catalogue	$\sum Q^j$	$\sum FQ^j$	$\sum SQ^j$	$\sum SQ^j$ FAH
Accommodation	186	112	73	94
Location	116	64	29	50
Event	92	57	39	52
Sport	102	49	31	46
Total	496	279	172	232

The figures 3(a)-(d) compare the size of the sets Q^j, FQ^j, and SQ^j for the location, accommodation, event, and sport catalogues, respectively, when FAH is used.

This shows that RelaxQuery can always find a successful subquery when the user query contains up to three constraints. This number is even higher for the queries submitted to event and lodging catalogues. In particular, considering the accommodation catalogue, we observe that more than half of queries failed to return any item, and the RelaxQuery could find a subquery 83% of the time(Table 2). We also see the method performs worse for the location-queries. One reason for this is location has more features than the others, and as the number of constraints in a query increases, the likelihood increases that a failing query cannot return any result even by *removing one* constraint. In other words, the more constraints a query has, the more likely it is to have a situation that 3 constraints are inconsistent such that no item can satisfy those constraints and we have to remove at least 2 constraints in order to receive some results. This is the case for many queries of the location catalogue with 8 constraints or more.

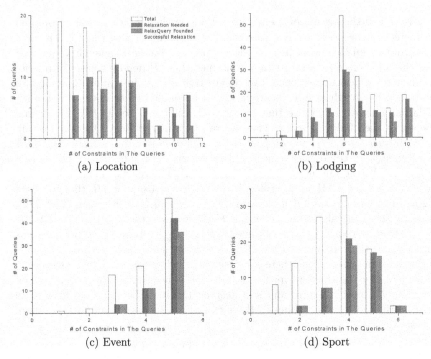

(a) Location   (b) Lodging

(c) Event   (d) Sport

Fig. 3. Behavior of the RelaxQuery algorithm for different catalogues.

Finally, we want to illustrate how difficult it would be for a user to refine autonomously her failing query. We note that we did not mined the log data coming from NutKing-, to measure if and how the user relaxed the failing queries (without system assistance). The discussion here is hypothetical, and is aimed at understanding, in the worse case, the number of query change attempts (constraint removals, that are needed to receive some results discarding the minimum number of constraints. Let $q = \{c_1, \ldots, c_m\}$ be a query, and assume the RelaxQuery method can find k successful subqueries. The *maximum* number of attempts the user needs in order to find a successful change to her failing that relaxes only one constraint is $m - k + 1$. In fact, if a user query receives zero results, then in a second attempt, the user must remove one constraint, and submit the new query. If this again fails he must put back the *removed* constraint and discard another constraint, and submit the new query. He must proceed until receives some results, which could be, in the worse case at the $(m + k - 1)^{\text{th}}$ attempt. In fact, this number will be even larger if q contains some range constraint, because different ranges should be tried. In practice this is not feasible for a user.

4   Related Work

The research on failing queries goes back to the work of Kaplan [11], where he described a system that supported a cooperative query answering to queries expressed in natural language. He argued that it is more informative to let the user understand the cause of failure, and provide answers that partially satisfy the query, than just reporting a void answer like the empty result set.

Value abstraction was introduced in the CoBase system [3], where an abstraction hierarchy among feature values is built, and the relaxation operators use it to move up and down the hierarchy. In our approach, a hierarchy is a relationship between features (e.g., country≻county≻city), derived from domain knowledge, and is exploited to find successful sub-queries of a failing query. While building a values abstraction hierarchy is quite complex and costly in CoBase, in our approach the feature hierarchy can be achieved with minimal effort.

Gaasterland et al. described in [4] a logic-based approach to develop a cooperative answering system that accepts natural language queries, and can explain the cause of any failing query. Godfrey has extensively investigated the problem of identifying the cause of a failing boolean-query [5]. He has derived an algorithm (called ISHMAEL) to find successful maximal subquery (called XSS), i.e., not contained in any other successful subquery. He shows that finding only one XSS can be done in linear time proportional to the number of constraints in q, but finding all XSS is intractable. The major difference between RelaxQuery and ISHMAEL relates to the search mode. While the latter does a depth-first-search to find an XSS subquery, the former takes a breath-first-search to find a subquery that relaxes minimum number of constraints, hence must be incomplete to avoid the combinatorial explosion of search states.

McSherry [9] has approached the relaxation problem differently by looking at the products that do not satisfy the query. For each product in the catalogue the set of attributes (called compromise set) that do not satisfy the query is computed, and a case representative (i.e., with highest similarity to the query) is put in a set called *retrieval set*. The problem with this approach is the retrieval set may contain up to $2^{|q|}$ elements.

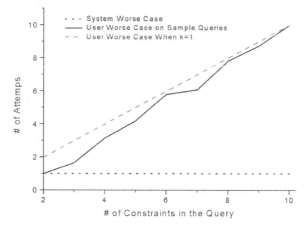

Fig. 4. Steps needed to find a relaxation.

5   Conclusions and Future Work

In this paper we presented a linear time incomplete algorithm for query relaxation. If it finds a solution this is maximal with respect to the number of constraints kept in the successful subquery found. Thus, since a query represents
user's preferences, the algorithm relaxes as few as possible user's preferences.
This algorithm is simple enough to be easily integrated into any eCommerce application. An empirical evaluation of the algorithm was presented, and showed
the algorithm is powerful enough to recover from a failure situation most of the
time.

In the future we plan to introduce *user modelling* principles that would enable
to assign weights to user's preferences such that the preferences with lowest
weight will be relaxed first. Moreover, we are extending RelaxQuery to cope
with the general case, i.e., when more than one constraint must be relaxed to
find a successful subquery.

References

1. Schafer, J.B., Konstan, J.A., Riedl, J.: E-commerce recommendation applications.
   Data Mining and Knowledge Discovery **5** (2001) 115–153
2. Ricci, F., Venturini, A., Cavada, D., Mirzadeh, N., Blaas, D., Nones, M.: Prod-
   uct recommendation with interactive query management and twofold similarity.
   In Aamodt, A., Bridge, D., Ashley, K., eds.: ICCBR 2003, the 5th International
   Conference on Case-Based Reasoning, Trondheim, Norway (2003) 479–493
3. Chu, W.W., Yang, H., Chiang, K., Minock, M., Chow, G., Larson, C.: Cobase:
   A scalable and extensible cooperative information system. Journal of Intelligence
   Information Systems **6** (1996)
4. Gaasterland, T., Godfrey, P., Minker, J.: Relaxation as a platform for cooperative
   answering. Journal of Intelligent Information Systems **1** (1992) 293–321
5. Godfrey, P.: Minimization in cooperative response to failing database queries.
   International Journal of Cooperative Information Systems **6** (1997) 95–159
6. Ricci, F., Mirzadeh, N., Venturini, A.: Intelligent query managment in a mediator
   architecture. In: 2002 First International IEEE Symposium "Intelligent Systems',
   Varna, Bulgaria (2002) 221–226
7. Burke, R.: Knowledge-based recommender systems. In Daily, J.E., Kent, A.,
   Lancour, H., eds.: Encyclopedia of Library and Information Science. Volume 69.
   Marcel Dekker (2000)
8. Kohlmaier, A., Schmitt, S., Bergmann, R.: A similarity-based approach to attribute
   selection in user-adaptive sales dialogs. In: Proceedings of the 4th International
   Conference on Case-Based Reasoning. Volume 2080 of LNAI., Vancouver, Canada,
   Springer (2001) 306–320
9. McSherry, D.: Similarity and compromise. In Aamodt, A., Bridge, D., Ashley,
   K., eds.: ICCBR 2003, the 5th International Conference on Case-Based Reasoning,
   Trondheim, Norway (2003) 291–305
10. MacKay, D.J.C.: Information Theory, Inference and Learning Algorithms. First
    edn. Cambridge University Pres (2003)
11. Kaplan, S.J.: Indirect responses to loaded questions. In: Proceedings of the theo-
    retical issues in natural language processing-2. (1978) 202–209

Accelerating Database Processing at e-Commerce Sites

Seunglak Choi, Jinwon Lee, Su Myeon Kim, Junehwa Song, and Yoon-Joon Lee

Korea Advanced Institute of Science and Technology
373-1 Kusong-dong Yusong-gu Daejeon 305-701, Korea

Abstract. Most e-commerce Web sites dynamically generate their contents through a three-tier server architecture composed of a Web server, an application server, and a database server. In such an architecture, the database server easily becomes a bottleneck to the overall performance. In this paper, we propose WDBAccel, a high-performance database server accelerator that significantly improves the throughput of the database processing, and thus that of the overall Web site. WDBAccel eliminates costly, complex query processing needed to obtain query results by reusing previous query results for subsequent queries. This differentiates WDBAccel from other database cache systems, which replicate a database into multiple conventional DBMS's and distribute queries among them. We evaluate the performance of WDBAccel by using the queries of the TPC-W benchmark. The measurement results show that WDBAccel outperforms DBMS-based cache systems by up to an order of magnitude.

1 Introduction

With the explosive growth of the Internet, numerous value-generating services are provided through WWW. In most e-commerce Web sites, those services are usually deployed on a three-tier server architecture, which consists of Web servers, application servers, and database servers. Web contents are dynamically generated upon a request through such system components. Due to its low scalability and complexity of query processing, a database server is a major bottleneck to the overall site performance.

We propose a high-performance database server accelerator, called WDBAccel, which significantly improves the throughput of database processing in multi-tier Web sites (see Figure 1). The main approach of WDBAccel is to cache results of frequently-issued queries and reuse these results for incoming queries. Upon a query hit, the query result is immediately served from the cache. WDBAccel keeps cached results consistent to an origin database by invalidating staled results. In addition, WDBAccel is designed to use main memory as the primary storage, minimizing disk operations. Thus, WDBAccel can improve the performance of database processing more than an order of magnitude.

WDBAccel differs from other existing DB cache system [6, 11, 9, 1] in that the primary purpose of WDBAccel is to accelerate the database processing. On

K. Bauknecht, M. Bichler, and B. Pröll (Eds.): EC-Web 2004, LNCS 3182, pp. 41–50, 2004.

Fig. 1. WDBAccel deployment in an e-commerce Web site

the contrary, the primary purpose of other cache systems is to distribute the load of database processing into multiple cache nodes. Those systems replicate a database into multiple nodes and distribute queries among them. In serving queries, they rely on the underlying DBMS, which executes costly query processing to obtain a query result. Thus, the performance of DBMS-based cache systems is limited by their underlying DBMS.

Our WDBAccel design incorporates three policies that effectively utilize the limited space of main memory. First, WDBAccel employs the *derived matching*. Even when the cache does not store the identical query result, the result for a query can be derived from one or more previously stored queries. In many Web-based applications, selection regions of queries tend to overlap each other. Thus, WDBAccel performs the derived matching by containment checking among selection regions of stored query results. Second, WDBAccel removes the storage redundancy of the tuples belonging to two or more query results. In many cases, query results contain identical tuples. Therefore, WDBAccel eliminates such a storage redundancy by storing query results in the unit of tuples. Third, a cache replacement policy in WDBAccel evaluates storage cost in a different way from other Web caching systems. In many systems, the policy considers the size of cached data items. However, it is not appropriate in WDBAccel due to the tuples shared among multiple query results. WDBAccel considers both the size of query results and shared tuples.

WDBAccel provides several advantages to database-driven Web sites. The most competitive advantage is that it drastically improves the throughput of the Web sites. Second, WDBAccel reduces the total cost of ownership. WDBAccel is a light-weight system optimized in caching and serving query results. Thus, it can be deployed even on lower-end H/W system while achieving a high level of performance. Third, WDBAccel can be easily deployed as a middle-tier solution between the Web application server and the database server. By supporting the standard interfaces like JDBC or ODBC, WDBAccel does not require Web applications to be modified. Forth, the high-performance nature of WDBAccel reduces the total number of cache nodes managed by an administrator, reducing administration cost.

This paper is organized as follows. In section 2, we describe the architecture of WDBAccel. In section 3, we explain technical details including query matching, cache storage, and cache replacement. In section 4, we evaluate and analyze the performance of WDBAccel. In section 5, we describe related works and compare them to our system. Finally in section 6, we present conclusions.

2   System Architecture

WDBAccel is a Web database server accelerator which processes queries delivered from the front-side Web application servers (WAS's) on behalf of database servers. It is designed as a middle-tier system which can be deployed between WAS's and database servers without extensive modification to either system as other middle-tier cache systems [6, 11, 9]. To deploy WDBAccel on an existing e-commerce service system, it is only required to change an existing database driver to WDBAccel's driver at the WAS.

WDBAccel is a query result caching system. As mentioned, it stores the results of previous queries and then serves incoming queries delivered from WAS. The query result caching is extremely useful when a workload is read-dominant. The workload of most e-commerce applications is read-dominant. In e-commerce sites, visitors spend the most time finding and reading some information, *e.g.*, product catalogs, news, articles, etc. Update interactions such as ordering products are relatively very infrequent. For example, the TPC-W benchmark [12][1] specifies that the portion of read queries, in an average case, is 80% of the entire workload. Thus, we can expect that the query result caching will show a high level of performance in many e-commerce sites.

Figure 2 shows the overall architecture of WDBAccel and the processing flow. The WAS sends a query to the Query Redirector (QR) (1), then QR checks whether the given query is *read* or *write*. If the query is a *write*, it sends the query to the Consistency Maintainer (CM) (A). CM forwards the query to the origin database server (B) and performs the process to maintain cache consistency. If the query is a *read*, then it forwards the query to the Fragment Processor (FP) (2). FP references the Cache Dictionary (CD) to decide whether the result for the incoming query can be constructed based on cached fragments (3). A fragment is a query result stored in a cache. If fragments for the incoming query are found, FP retrieves the fragments (4). Otherwise, FP sends the query to the database server (a) and receives the result for the query (b). Then, it forwards both the query and the query result to the Cache Controller (CC) (c). CC inserts the query into CD and the query result into the Cache Pool (CP) (d). (When the cache does not have enough space to store new query results, CC executes a cache replacement algorithm.) FP constructs and sends the query result to QR (5). Finally, QR sends the query result to the WAS (6).

CD is a collection of meta information about fragments stored in the Cache Pool (see Figure 3). Each entry stores meta information on a fragment (*e.g.*, selection region, fragment size, and pointer to data). Entries are classified into different *query groups* according to the structure of queries. Then, each group is indexed by selection regions of the queries. The index is used to reduce the search time for fragments matching a query.

The caching inherently incurs the inconsistency between cached results and an origin database. If a data element in an origin database is updated, the fragments derived from the updated data will be stale. WDBAccel includes CM which ensures the consistency. The primary goal of CM is to minimize the consistency overhead. It matches an update against the common parts of many

---

[1] The TPC-W benchmark is an industrial standard benchmark to evaluate the performance of database-driven Web sites. It models an e-commerce site (specifically, an online bookstore).

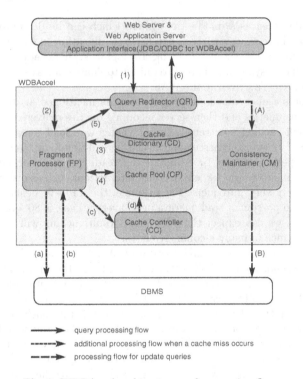

Fig. 2. WDBAccel architecture and processing flows

queries, not individual queries. Thus, it avoids repeated matching of each query. In addition, CM ensures strong cache consistency by invalidating affected query results before the completion, *i.e.*, the transaction commit, of a database update. For some pages, strong consistency is critical to service them always in an up-to-date version (*e.g.* the cost of products in Web shopping sites). [5] describes our consistency mechanism in detail.

3   Technical Details

3.1   Derived Matching

WDBAccel employs the derived matching to maximize the main-memory hit ratio, *i.e.*, the rate of reusing query results cached in main memory. When WD-BAccel fails to find an exactly matching fragment, it tries to find one or more fragments from which a query result can be derived. We give an example of the derived matching. In this example, a query Q can be derived from the union of fragments F_1 and F_2 although Q does not exactly match either F_1 or F_2.

Fig. 3. Cache Dictionary

Example 1. Given fragments and a query as follows,

F_1 : SELECT * FROM ITEM
    WHERE I_PUB_DATE >= '01/01/2003' AND I_PUB_DATE <= '01/20/2003'
F_2 : SELECT * FROM ITEM
    WHERE I_PUB_DATE >= '01/10/2003' AND I_PUB_DATE <= '01/30/2003'
Q : SELECT * FROM ITEM
    WHERE I_PUB_DATE >= '01/05/2003' AND I_PUB_DATE <= '01/25/2003'

Q can be derived from the union of F_1 and F_2 since the selection region of the union contains the selection region of Q.

WDBAccel utilizes the *selection region dependency* in order to maximize finding the derived matching. A selection region dependency is a computational dependency in selection regions. In example 1, a query Q has the selection region dependency on a union of a fragment F_1 and a fragment F_2 in that the selection region of the union contains the selection region of Q. By investigating the dependencies among selection regions, WDBAccel is highly likely to find a derived matching. This is due to the characteristic of the queries used in many Web-based applications: selection regions from different queries with the same template tend to overlap each other and may form a hot range. In example 1, selection regions on I_PUB_DATE will frequently fall together near to the present time. This is because customers in an online bookstore prefer to select new books.

When a query is matched by a derived matching, the process of the *query result deriving* follows the matching process. For the query result deriving, two operations, *union* and *trim*, are applied to matching fragments. The union operation is used to merge the matching fragments and to eliminate tuple duplication. In the Example 1, by the union, the tuples of the matching fragments F_1 and F_2 are merged and the duplication of the tuples ('01/10/2003' ≤ I_PUB_DATE ≤ '01/20/2003') is removed. We used the selection attributes of tuples to identify duplicate tuples. They are located in overlapping selection regions among the matching fragments.

The trim operation is used to cut off the tuples that do not constitute a query result when matching fragments contain a query. In the Example 1, the tuples ('01/01/2003' ≤ I_PUB_DATE < '01/05/2003') of the matching fragment F_1 and the tuples ('01/25/2003' < I_PUB_DATE ≤ '01/30/2003') of the matching fragment F_2 is cut off by the trim operation. In order to determine whether a tuple is a part of a query result, the attribute values of the tuple is compared to the selection predicates of the query.

3.2   Cache Storage

To increase the utilization of a limited cache storage, it is crucial to avoid redundant storage of identical data. Query results can include identical tuples. In
example 1, the tuples located in the overlapping selection region (I_PUB_DATE,
'01/10/2003', '01/20/2003') can be included in both fragments F_1 and F_2. As
mentioned in section 3.1, overlaps among query results as above are common in
many Web applications.

To remove the redundant storage, WDBAccel identifies overlaps in selection
regions of fragments and eliminates redundant storage of tuples. The storage
policy of WDBAccel stores query results in the unit of tuples. Before storing
each tuple in a new query result, it determines if the tuple already exists in the
cache. This is done by comparing the values of the selection attributes of each
tuple with those of the cached tuples. To speed up the comparison, the policy
scans only the tuples of the fragments overlapping the new query result. Note
that these fragments have already been retrieved in the query matching process.
We refer to the Cache Pool adopting this policy as the *Cache Pool in the unit
of Tuples* (CPT).

3.3   Cache Replacement

Hit ratio is improved if the cache stores the query results which are frequently
accessed and consume less storage space. Thus, we evaluate the profit of a query
result as follows:

$$profit(f) = \frac{popularity(f)}{s\_cost(f)}$$

where $s\_cost(f)$ is the storage cost of a fragment f and $popularity(f)$ represents
the popularity of a fragment f. When a cache space is full, the Cache Controller
evicts the query result with the lowest *profit* value (called a victim). Usually,
the last access time or the number of accesses are used for *popularity*. Under
CPT, we consider that some tuples are shared among multiple fragments. We
divide the storage cost of a shared tuple among sharing fragments. In this case,
s_cost is computed as follows.

$$s\_cost(f) = \sum_{t_i \in T(f)} size(t_i)/n\_frag(t_i)$$

where $T(f)$ is a set of tuples belonging to a fragment f, $size(t_i)$ is the size of a
tuple t_i, and $n\_frag(t_i)$ is the number of the fragments containing a tuple t_i.

4   Experiments

In this section, we compare the processing capability of WDBAccel with that of
DBMS-based systems by measuring their throughputs.

(a) WDBAccel   (b) DBMS-based cache system

Fig. 4. Experimental setup

Experimental Setup. Figure 4 (a) shows the setup for evaluating the WDBAccel system. The *Query Generator* emulates a group of Web application servers, generating queries. It runs on a machine with a Pentium III 1GHz, 512MB RAM. We implemented the prototype of WDBAccel which included all components and core functions described above. WDBAccel is deployed between the Query Generator and the database server. WDBAccel runs on the machine with a Pentium III 1GHz, 512M RAM. For the origin database server, we used Oracle 8i with the default buffer pool size of 16MB. The database server runs on a machine with a Pentium IV 1.5GHz, 512M RAM. We populated the TPC-W database in the database server at two scales: 10K and 100K (cardinality of the ITEM table)[2]. All three machines run Linux and are connected through a 100Mbps Ethernet.

Figure 4 (b) shows the experimental setup for evaluating the throughput of the DBMS-based cache system. The DBMS-based system conceptually consists of the cache-related components and the underlying DBMS. We used the simplified system by omitting the cache-related components. For the underlying DBMS, we used Oracle 8i. We also assume that the DBMS-based system achieves 100% cache hit ratio. Thus, the Oracle database is fully populated with the entire TPC-W database. Note that the throughput measured under this simplified setup will be higher than that taken under a real situation using the DBMS-based cache systems. Both systems run on the Linux machine with a Pentium III 1GHz, 512MB RAM and are connected through a 100Mbps Ethernet.

Workload Traces. We used for experiments the trace of the search-by-title query specified in TPC-W. This query searches for all the books whose titles include the keyword specified by users. It is the most frequently-used query in TPC-W; in an average case, its usage frequency constitutes 20% of the entire TPC-W workload. We believe that the query is frequently used in many e-commerce sites in general. The following is the query template of the query. We refer to the search-by-title query as the *keyword query*.

```
SELECT TOP 50 I_TITLE, I_ID, A_FNAME, A_LNAME FROM ITEM, AUTHOR
WHERE I_A_ID = A_ID AND I_TITLE LIKE '%@Title%' ORDER BY I_TITLE
```

Performance Comparison Between WDBAccel and the DBMS-Based Cache Systems. The experiment was performed through two steps: the *fill phase* and the *test phase*. In the fill phase, we fill the cache space with fragments

---

[2] In TPC-W, the scale of database is determined by the cardinality of ITEM table.

48   Seunglak Choi et al.

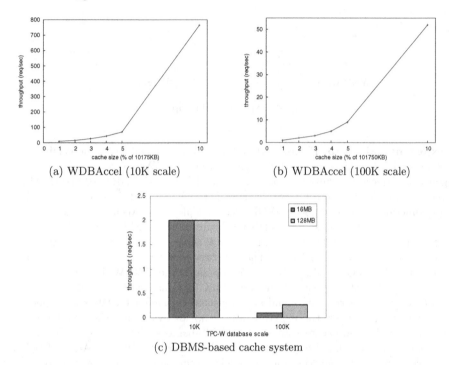

(a) WDBAccel (10K scale)

(b) WDBAccel (100K scale)

(c) DBMS-based cache system

Fig. 5. The throughputs for the keyword query

by issuing 100,000 queries. This phase warms up the cache space so that the throughput can be measured under normal condition, *i.e.,* within a normal range of cache hit ratio, during the test phase. The cache size of WDBAccel is set to range from 1% to 10% of the sum of ITEM and AUTHOR table sizes. ITEM and AUTHOR are the tables which are accessed by the keyword and the range queries. The sums of two table sizes corresponding to the 10K and 100K scales of TPC-W are around 10MB and 100MB, respectively. The buffer pool size of the DBMS-based system is set to 16MB and 128MB.

Figure 5 shows the results for the keyword query. It shows that WDBAccel outperforms the DBMS-based system by an order of magnitude. This implies that reusing query results can significantly save the query processing cost. In ordinary database servers, the keyword query needs a linear search on the ITEM table. This is because the keyword query uses the LIKE operator, which includes wild card characters and does a pattern matching. Such a LIKE operator cannot benefit from the index structure on the attribute I_TITLE. On the other hand, in WDBAccel, the query processing time increases slightly with the number of fragments no matter what a query type is. Also, WDBAccel does not require any disk accesses.

Another interesting observation is that the throughput of WDBAccel rapidly improves as the cache size increases. With the cache size up to 5%, the origin database server is the bottleneck. In that case, the cache miss ratio (and thus hit ratio) is an important factor of the throughput. For example, if the cache miss ratio decreases from 2% to 1%, the throughput will be doubled.

5   Related Work

Recently, several query result caching systems have been reported in the context of dynamic Web content services. Form-based cache [10] is the first effort for a query result caching. It extended the URL-based proxy caching for active proxy query caching with limited query processing capability. The proposed framework could effectively work for a top-n conjunctive queries generated from the HTML forms. However, it only addressed keyword queries. Weave [13] caches data in the unit of XML and HTML pages as well as query results. Weave focuses on the declarative specification for Web sites through a logical model and a customizable cache system that employs a mix of different cache policies. DBProxy [1] employs a conventional DBMS for storing and retrieving query results like the DBMS-based caching systems. Therefore, its performance could be limited by the complex query processing of the underlying DBMS. The main focus of WDBAccel is to efficiently scale the performance of database-driven Web sites. It provides a framework for a high-performance query result caching and an efficient storage structure for it.

The *HTML caching* has also been used to improve the performance of e-commerce sites. It selects cacheable data in the unit of the whole HTML page or HTML components which are parts of a HTML page. It then caches the data in front of Web servers or inside WAS's. We call the former *HTML page caching* [8, 3] and the latter *HTML component caching* [4, 7, 2]. The main advantage of the HTML caching is that the performance gain on a cache hit is better than that of others. This is because it saves much or all of the cost of HTML page generation as well as database processing. However, the HTML page caching is not effective in caching dynamic pages. HTML component caching can be effective to some extent in caching dynamic contents. A problem in the component caching is that it incurs high administration cost; cache administrators should go through a complex process of marking cacheable and non-cacheable units.

6   Conclusions

We have presented the design and implementation of a high-performance database server accelerator. WDBAccel improves throughput of the database processing, which is a major bottleneck in serving dynamically generated Web pages. To improve the performance, it reuses previous query results for subsequent queries and utilizes main memory as a primary cache storage. WDBAccel performs the derived matching to effectively find a set of query results required to construct a result of an incoming query. It employs the storage policy that reduces storage redundancy. In addition, the cache replacement policy takes into account storage costs of query results and overlaps among them. The experimental results show

that WDBAccel outperforms DBMS-based cache systems by up to an order of
magnitude.

References

1. Khalil S. Amiri, Sanghyun Park, Renu Tewari, and Sriram Padmanabhan.
   DBProxy: A self-managing edge-of-network data cache. In *19th IEEE International Conference on Data Engineering*, 2003.
2. Jesse Anton, Lawrence Jacobs, Xiang Liu, Jordan Parker, Zheng Zeng, and Tie
   Zhong. Web caching for database applications with oracle web cache. In *Proceedings of ACM SIGMOD Conference*, 2002.
3. K. Selcuk Candan, Wen-Syan Li, Qiong Luo, Wang-Pin Hsiung, and Divyakant
   Agrawal. Enabling dynamic content caching for database-driven web sites. In
   Proceedings of ACM SIGMOD Conference, Santa Barbara, USA, 2001.
4. Jim Challenger, Arun Iyengar, Karen Witting, Cameron Ferstat, and Paul Reed.
   A publishing system for efficiently creating dynamic web content. In *Proceedings of IEEE INFOCOM*, 2000.
5. Seunglak Choi, Sekyung Huh, Su Myeon Kim, JuneHwa Song, and Yoon-Joon Lee.
   An efficient update management mechanism for query result caching at database-driven web sites. *Under submission*.
6. Oracle Corporation. Oracle9ias cache.
   http://www.oracle.com/ip/deploy/ias/index.html?cache.html.
7. Anindya Datta, Kaushik Dutta, Helen Thomas, Debra VanderMeer, Suresha, and
   Krithi Ramamritham. Proxy-based acceleration of dynamically generated content
   on the world wide web: An approach and implementation. In *Proceedings of ACM SIGMOD Conference*, 2002.
8. Vegard Holmedahl, Ben Smith, and Tao Yang. Cooperative caching of dynamic
   content on a distributed web server. In *Proceedings of the 7th IEEE International Symposium on High Performance Distributed Computing*, 1998.
9. Qiong Luo, Sailesh Krishnamurthy, C. Mohan, Hamid Pirahesh, Honguk Woo,
   Bruce G. Lindsay, and Jeffrey F. Naughton. Middle-tier database caching for e-business. In *Proceedings of ACM SIGMOD Conference*, 2002.
10. Qiong Luo and Jeffrey F. Naughton. Form-based proxy caching for database-backed
    web sites. In *Proceedings of the 27th VLDB Conference*, Roma, Italy, 2001.
11. TimesTen Performance Software. Timesten library.
    http://www.timesten.com/library/index.html.
12. Transaction Processing Performance Council (TPC). TPC benchmark[TM]W (web
    commerce) specification version 1.4. February 7, 2001.
13. Khaled Yagoub, Daniela Florescu, Valerie Issarny, and Patrick Valduriez. Caching
    strategies for data-intensive web sites. In *Proceedings of the 26th VLDB Conference*, 2000.

Optimized Query Delivery
in Distributed Electronic Markets

Stefan Böttcher[1] and Dimiter Dimitriev[2]

[1] University of Paderborn
Faculty V (EIM) - Computer Science
Fürstenallee 11
D-33102 Paderborn, Germany
stb@uni-paderborn.de
[2] Citigroup Global Markets
Global Fixed Income Technology
250 West St.
New York, NY 10013
dimiter.dimitriev@citigroup.com

Abstract. Whenever product data is supplied by multiple product providers in a distributed electronic market and customer queries are submitted to all providers of this electronic market, the query workload is one of the major bottlenecks. We present a technique which reduces query workload and communication costs in distributed electronic market places involving multiple providers. The key idea is to guide customer queries through a network of brokers which aggregate the result information of previous queries, such that a query is posted only to those providers which may eventually provide products matching the query. A performance evaluation of our approach includes product data from a large number of car dealers as providers. It shows that our approach outperforms the standard query broadcasting technique by a factor of up to 50 - depending on the set of customer queries considered. Therefore, we consider our approach to be an important improvement towards the reduction of the query workload within distributed electronic markets.

1 Introduction

1.1 Problem Origin and Motivation

Whenever an electronic market integrates the distributed product data of several suppliers, and there exists a high frequency of queries submitted to this electronic market, then the query processing workload is one of the primary bottlenecks for the scalability of such a distributed market place. An important aspect of the query workload in the electronic market – and the focus of our contribution – is how many suppliers have to compute answers for each customer query. The standard approach, which we call broadcasting, is to send every query to every supplier. Whenever the number of suppliers and the number of customer queries is high, broadcasting may become infeasible within the market place. In comparison, it may be considerably advantageous to submit queries for products only to those suppliers which can contribute to the answer of the query. Our key idea is to use previous queries and statistical informa-

K. Bauknecht, M. Bichler, and B. Pröll (Eds.): EC-Web 2004, LNCS 3182, pp. 51–65, 2004.
© Springer-Verlag Berlin Heidelberg 2004

tion of their results in order to submit new queries to only those providers which can contribute to the answer of a query.

We have implemented our approach, and taken a market place for used cars as the data source for benchmark tests. Within our electronic market place for used cars, our providers are 60 car dealers which offer used cars over the market place. Our market is structured in such a way, that most of the car dealers have typical sets of offers, e.g. there are very few luxury car dealers, few dealers for vintage cars, and quite a lot of dealers offering cars produced by only a few companies. While the advantage of an electronic market is that a customer asking for a specific type of car can obtain relevant offers from all car dealers connected to the market place, the market places should avoid unnecessary query workload. Therefore, the market place should not send each customer query to each dealer, but only to those dealers which might provide an offer matching the customer's query. For example, a dealer offering luxury cars may prefer not to receive queries for the cheapest family cars every day, or a dealer offering vintage cars will not be interested in queries for a one year old BMW. Furthermore, most used car dealers located in Hamburg (northern Germany) will not be interested in a query from customers located in Munich (southern Germany) – since used car dealerships in general are local businesses – perhaps with the exception of luxury and vintage cars.

1.2 Basic Assumptions and Problem Definition

Within our market place, we assume that providers and customers agree on some kind of global relational schema of ordered domains, i.e. we assume that properties of products are represented as (attribute,value) pairs, where the attribute values are restricted by finite ordered domains. For example, an attribute like the construction year of a car is associated with an ordered range of values, e.g. the interval [1900:2004]. Whenever A1,...,AN are the N attributes of the global relational schema, which are used in common by providers and customers of the electronic market, and D1, ..., DN are the finite discrete domains of A1, ..., AN (i.e. each attribute value of AI must be an element of DI), we call D1 x ... x DN the *schema* of the electronic market, and each subset of D1 x ... x DN is called a *search space* of the electronic market.

For example, a query can restrict the interval for the construction year of a car to [2000:2004], and thereby look for product offers within a smaller search space.

Within our approach to optimized query delivery, we are especially interested in search spaces which correspond to so called conjunctive point or range queries, i.e. queries which can be defined as follows.

A *point query* is a query of the form
        Attribute = value.
A *range query* is a query of the form
        Attribute < value
or a query of the form
        Attribute > value.
A conjunctive point or range query is a query of the form

        Condition1 and … and ConditionN   (with N>0)

where each ConditionI (1<=I<=N) is either a *point query* or a *range query*. Note however that our approach still allows the customers to submit other (more general) queries. For some, but not for all of these other queries our optimization applies as well.

A search space is said to *correspond* to a conjunctive point or range query, if and only if the query condition `Condition1 and ... and ConditionN` is equivalent to `true` for every element of the search space, and it is equivalent to `false` for every element of the schema which is not an element of the search space.

Whatever the internal presentation of the data at the provider's side is, we assume that each provider transforms a query of the market place into its internal query format, and conversely converts its data into the data format (i.e. attributes and values) supported and required by the market place. This can be achieved by using mapping technologies for product classifications (as defined in [4]), by general query mapping across heterogeneous data sources ([8]), or by XML based mappings (as defined in [16]). Similarly, we assume that each customer application transforms its queries in such a way that they use the common attributes A1, ..., AN of the electronic market, and conversely transforms the answers retrieved, i.e. from the data format of the electronic market, into the data format required by the customer.

A major requirement of our market place is that query processing supports the efficient evaluation of frequently asked conjunctive point or range queries. The state of the art approach to query processing is to broadcast customer queries to all providers. The broadcast approach does not use small search spaces in order to restrict a query's application. Instead, queries are applied to the whole schema, and every query is therefore submitted to all the connected providers. In comparison, the goal of our approach is to send a query only to those providers which contribute to the answers of the query. By using our approach to optimized query delivery, query workload is significantly reduced compared to the broadcast approach. The possible degree of optimization depends on the given query, the set of supported search spaces and the distribution of product offers. The problem to be solved is how to reduce the overall query workload of the providers which are connected to a distributed market place. The query workload does not only include the amount of queries that are transferred from the customer to a provider, but also includes the queries which are needed to maintain the optimized query routing system.

1.3 Related Work

Our work is related to contributions in different fields including electronic markets, schema mapping, data warehousing and the use of aggregated data in query optimization. Within the field of electronic markets, a lot of work has been done in the area of structuring electronic market places, e.g. by product classifications (like eClass [11], ECCMA[13], ETIM [14], Edibatec [12]). These classifications are fixed, i.e. they are not dynamically adapted to queries. In contrast, our approach focuses on customer queries and performs dynamic clustering on product offers according to the most frequent customer queries.

Within related contributions to schema mapping, two approaches to data and query translation can be distinguished. While the majority of contributions (e.g. [10], [1], [22]) map the data to a unique representation, we follow [7] and [8] to deliver the queries to those domains (or providers) where the data resides. Our approach is compatible with this work and with further work on schema and query mapping for federated databases [6] and data warehouses [25], [20], and even with mapping tools like

BizTalk Mapper [21]. However in comparison to these contributions, we focus on the reduction of the query workload on the providers connected to the market place.

In common with data warehouses, we use aggregate information on attributes in order to answer queries. While the majority of data warehouse approaches query for the aggregated information itself, our main use of aggregated information is to guide query processing, i.e. to deliver customer queries to the appropriate providers.

Within our search structure, we maintain aggregated data that stores certain statistical information about the data distribution. Aggregated data has been used for query optimization by many other contributions, which can be classified into two categories [23]. While some contributions consider only the data distribution and focus on an estimation of query result size (e.g. [18], [19], [24]), we follow [9], [15], and [5] which also regard the query patterns. Furthermore, there are different methods used to represent data distribution. While parametric representations use mathematical formulas (e.g., [9]), we use enclosing hyper-rectangles to represent tuple sets, like most non-parametric representations. Various solutions exist for how these rectangles are represented, divided and updated based upon changes in underlying data. R-Trees [17] and their further developments like R*-Trees [3], use B-Tree-based structures and heuristic algorithms for dividing rectangles, which results in a set of partially overlapping shapes. In terms of rectangle division, our approach is similar to contributions using multi-dimensional histograms (e.g. [5]). More precisely, it corresponds to recursive, non-overlapping histogram partitioning over multiple attributes. Like [2], [5] and others, but unlike typical R-Trees, we use incoming queries to adapt the collection of statistical information to a query profile. Unlike these solutions – which are aimed at selectivity estimation – and which are similar to R-Trees, we maintain exact statistics at all times, allowing us to guarantee complete, deterministic results despite routing queries only to a selected number of brokers or dealers. Therefore, unlike [2] or [5], we do not use the results of queries to directly acquire data distribution statistics, as this leads to a fragmentation of data space that is expensive to keep up-to-date upon changes to the underlying data. Instead, we only use the queries themselves to identify leaves in our decision tree that need further refinement. And we generate custom queries with specially chosen ranges to acquire statistical information for each newly generated node in our decision tree. Solutions based on sampling (e.g. [24]) also, in essence, generate custom queries to acquire statistical information, but they do not account for query profiles and, more importantly, they are not aimed at ensuring compatibility between different decision trees (as described in sections 3.3. and 3.4).

In comparison to all of the other approaches, our data structure and the method for its modification combines an adaptation of brokers to different query sets (which is useful for selective routing) with a development of decision trees in such a way that allows bottom-up propagation of data updates (which is a pre-condition for the scalability of our solution to a large number of brokers).

The remainder of the paper is organized as follows. Section 2 presents the key ideas of our approach, i.e., how a hierarchy of brokers can pass a query directly to the providers which can contribute to the answer of the query. Section 3 outlines when and how such a hierarchy of brokers is developed and maintained. Section 4 outlines the results of our performance evaluation, and Section 5 outlines the summary and conclusions.

2 Key Ideas

2.1 Aggregated Information for Clusters of Product Offers

An initial idea is to aggregate data about clusters of offered products within the electronic market. A *cluster* of product offers is a set of product offers which match a certain conjunctive point or range query (or as we say, which *are found in a certain search space*). Note that a cluster is only a name for certain set of product offers, i.e. it contains no physical data referring to the product offers. *Aggregation* includes the counting of product offers found in a cluster, and the computation of minimum and maximum attribute values (e.g. for attributes like price, year, etc.) of product offers found in the cluster. This aggregated data can be used in order to estimate the number of positive answers to a query, and to support various types of queries (e.g. a query for the minimum price of a two year old BMW).

One major goal of the use of aggregated information is to reduce the further submission of unsuccessful queries to the connected providers. For example, if the minimum price for a set of stored offers is larger than the upper price limit given in a query, we are then sure that there can not be an answer which meets the query, i.e. based on the aggregated values alone, we can avoid to send the query any further.

2.2 Hierarchical Clustering and Query Passing by Brokers

A second idea is to use a hierarchical structure of so called *brokers* which control the flow and distribution of queries. Each broker is associated with its own search space, and via its search space, it is associated to its own cluster of product offers which are contained in the search space. For the purpose of query optimization, each broker stores the aggregated values for both the number of offers contained in its associated cluster, and the minimum and maximum attribute values found in each attribute of the product offers of its associated cluster. The brokers are arranged in a broker hierarchy in such a way that whenever two brokers exist in a parent-child relationship, the search space associated to the child broker is a subset of the search space associated with the parent broker, and thus the cluster of each child broker contains a subset of the product offers that are contained in the parent broker. At the bottom layer of our broker hierarchy, each provider is connected to the electronic market via a private bottom layer broker, which transforms all queries into the provider's native data format and transforms the answers back to the data format of the market place, i.e. each bottom layer broker operates as a proxy for the provider.

Our goal is to identify the bottom layer brokers which can answer a customer's query completely, but submit queries to as few associated providers (and brokers respectively) as possible. In order to minimize the submission of queries to bottom layer brokers, we introduce *intermediate brokers* which summarize the information of brokers that provide 'similar' offers to the given queries. The idea behind the introduction of intermediate brokers is to cluster similar offers of different providers depending on the queries. Clustering shall be performed in such a way, that those offers which match the same query are likely to be in the same cluster, and other offers are not in the same cluster. Each cluster of offers is managed by its own broker, such that the hierarchy of brokers supports hierarchical clustering of product offers. Having introduced hierarchical clustering, a query is always passed along the cluster hierarchy, i.e. from a parent broker to a subset of its child brokers. Within the following sections, we describe how queries are passed through the hierarchy of brokers.

In comparison to query passing, the aggregated information, which is used in order to optimize query passing from a parent broker to a child broker, is always passed in the opposite direction, i.e. from the child broker to the parent broker.

2.3 The Idea Behind Expanding the Search Space

A third basic idea is to determine typical queries and to use queries in order to expand the search space as follows. The whole search space is divided into multiple search spaces in such a way that many queries can eventually be answered completely by submitting them only to a subset of these search spaces.

For example, in the used car domain there may be one search space for old cars, i.e. cars built earlier than in the year 2000, whereas another search space contains new cars, i.e. cars built in 2000 or later. While queries for vintage cars can be answered by submitting them to the providers connected to the first search space only, queries for one year old cars can be submitted to only those providers which are connected to the second search space.

Expanding the search space is an iterative process, and each expansion operation selects one search space and then divides this search space into two new search spaces. At the beginning there is only a single search space, i.e. every query belongs to this search space. However, over time the application of the expansion operation provides us with a decision tree for search spaces, which guides the passing of queries down the broker hierarchy to all the connected providers.

2.4 A Decision Tree-Based Data Structure for the Distribution of Queries

The data structure which hands over queries within a given hierarchy from one broker to lower level brokers is a decision tree (for an example see Figure 1 below). Each node of such a decision tree represents one broker. For each node (except the leaf nodes), an attribute-value pair is used in order to divide the search space managed by the current broker into two sub search spaces, managed by the two subsequent brokers. The idea behind the attribute-value pair (A,V) is to use the attribute value V in order to divide the range of attribute values given for the attribute A into two parts. When the expansion operation is carried out, offers are clustered into one of the two new search spaces, depending on their value V2 for the attribute A. If the value V2 for the attribute A is less than or equal to V, the offer belongs to the search space represented by the left successor node of the expanded decision tree node (we say that the *offer is clustered* there). Otherwise, the offer has an attribute value which is larger than V, thus the offer belongs to the search space represented by the right successor node of the expanded decision tree node (and the offer is clustered there).

Each node (A,V) of the decision tree is used to pass queries as follows. Whenever a conjunctive query contains a point query condition "A=V2" or a range query condition "A<=V2" for a constant value V2 which is less than or equal to V, then the query is *not* passed to the right successor node of the actual decision tree node. Similarly, if the query contains a point query condition "A=V2" or a range query condition "A>=V2" for a constant value V2 which is greater than V, then the query is *not* passed to the left successor node of the actual decision tree node. Otherwise, if no further optimizations apply, the query is passed to both successor nodes of the decision tree, i.e. it is handled by both successor brokers. Whenever the decision tree node is a leaf node, the query is passed to all bottom layer brokers that are connected to this leaf node.

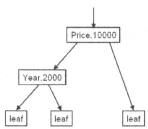

Fig. 1. A (small) decision tree for the distribution of queries

For example, Figure 1 shows a decision tree which contains an initial decision node (price,10000) and a second decision node (year,2000) which only applies for the low cost cars. The first decision node is used to pass queries as follows. Whenever a conjunctive query contains a point query condition "price=Value" or a range query condition "price<=Value" for a constant Value which is less than or equal to 10000, then the query is *not* passed to the right successor node of the actual decision tree node. Similarly, if the query contains a point query condition "price=Value" or a range query condition "price>=Value" for a constant Value which is greater than 10000, then the query is *not* passed to the left successor node of the actual decision tree node. Otherwise, if none of the optimizations which are described in the next section apply, the query is passed to both successor nodes of the decision tree, i.e. it is handled by both successor brokers.

Note that it is possible to keep multiple nodes (or even all nodes) of a decision tree within the same location, such that query passing via multiple brokers can be done at the same location. Therefore, besides the selection of the appropriate brokers, there is no overhead for query passing from one broker to a successor broker.

2.5 Using Aggregated Information
in Order to Reduce the Distribution of Queries

As mentioned within Section 2.1, the brokers use aggregate values for counting the offers and for the storage of minimum and maximum attribute values of the offers of a cluster.

Whenever a query is submitted to a broker that has counted the number of 0 product offers within its cluster (i.e. within the search space which is represented by the broker), query processing is stopped here and returns an empty set of answers.

Furthermore, each broker uses its aggregated minimum and maximum attribute values of all its product offers as follows. Whenever a point query condition

```
attribute=value
```

searches for a value which is less than the aggregated minimum value or greater than the aggregated maximum value of the cluster, then query processing is stopped here, and the empty set is returned. A similar optimization is used for the upper and lower bounds for range query conditions.

2.6 Customers' Local Brokers
and Multiple Entry Points to Clustered Information

Since the user queries may differ from each other, the appropriate clustering technique may vary from query to query. In order to meet this requirement, we allow our system to support multiple entry points, i.e. multiple top-level brokers. These top-level brokers can be distinguished by the sets of attributes which they support. For example, one entry point may support queries within special price ranges whereas another entry point may support queries for a specific car model and year. Depending on the actual query, it may be preferable to use one or the other entry point to the system. Each entry point belongs to a different top-level broker, i.e. starts a new broker hierarchy, which may be connected to a different set of intermediate brokers. In other words, there are multiple clustering hierarchies active in parallel within the whole system. Nevertheless, it is possible that the same intermediate broker is a subbroker of different parent brokers within different broker hierarchies.

Initially a customer query is handed over to the customer's local broker, i.e. a broker that resides at the site of the customer. The purpose of this local broker is to analyse the query and to transform it into a conjunction

    QC and QR

of two queries, where QC is a (possibly empty) conjunction of point or range queries and QR is a (possibly empty) remainder which can not be further transformed into a conjunction of a remainder and a conjunctive point or range query. Then, the attributes found in QC are used in order to select an appropriate hierarchy of brokers in order to answer the query. Whenever there are multiple possible hierarchies which can be used, a hierarchy selection procedure selects the hierarchy which is most appropriate to the given query.

Although our market place supports the efficient evaluation of conjunctive point or range queries, whenever they are currently supported by one of the hierarchies of brokers, our market place is not limited to this class of queries. Note that it is always possible to submit queries Q, the complexity of which goes beyond these conjunctive point or range queries. Whenever it is possible, Q is transformed into an equivalent form QC and QR, where QC is a conjunctive range query and QR is any remainder. In such a case, QC can be used in order to pass the query through the broker hierarchy to a sufficient subset of providers that answer the query completely. Note however that a query Q can also be answered, if it is not possible to transform Q into such an equivalent conjunction QC and QR. In this case, the query Q must be broadcasted to all suppliers, i.e. the query workload in our electronic market for the query Q is not worse than in the broadcast approach to query distribution.

3 Hierarchical Cluster Construction and Dynamic Extension of Cluster Hierarchies

3.1 When to Divide Which Attributes Within Which Search Space?

Expansion operations are only performed on leaf nodes of the decision tree, i.e. on brokers which are direct predecessors of bottom layer brokers. We use the queries passed through such a leaf node in order to decide on which attribute is used in an expansion step to divide the search space. Each expansion decision selects one attribute to be the expansion attribute. An attribute can only be selected as an expansion attribute of a search space, if the search space allows for at least two different attribute values for this attribute.

The decision as to which attribute is chosen as an attribute for an expansion operation depends on the search space, the number of queries submitted to that search space and the number of product offers found for that search space. This means that within different search spaces, the attribute selected for the expansion operation and the time at which the expansion operation is applied will usually be different.

Each attribute which occurs within a query to a certain search space is a candidate for the expansion operation. However, the more frequently an attribute occurs within a query to this current search space, the more likely it will be used for an expansion operation.

In order to decide which attribute is to be used for an expansion operation, we count the frequency by which an attribute is used within a query (called *attribute usage*) for each attribute within each search space. Whenever the attribute usage increases beyond a given threshold and the number of answers within this data cluster is more than 0, we then divide this search space according to the given attribute. The two new leaf node brokers copy the attribute usage values for all attributes from the expanded node[1].

3.2 How Do We Divide the Search Space?

Within the expansion operation, the range of the expansion attribute is divided into two parts which are disjointed but together cover the whole range of the attribute. While in general it is possible to divide an attribute range at any value, we decided to always divide an interval in the middle because this simplifies a possible later recombination of expanded search spaces[2]. Each bottom layer broker which has been previously attached to the cluster, must now be assigned to one of the resulting clusters. Furthermore, after an expansion operation has been applied to a search space, we compute aggregated data for the two new sub-clusters which result from the expansion operation. More specifically, for both sub-clusters, we compute minimum and maximum values of all the attributes and count the number of answers found for the two new clusters. This computation can be done by an upwards propagation of the values found in the provider's proxy clusters that are sub-clusters of these two clusters.

3.3 Managing Multiple Hierarchies

Whenever there are a lot of queries which are not yet supported by the given hierarchy (or hierarchies) of brokers, it may be advantageous to build up one or more new hierarchies of brokers which support these types of queries. In order to explain what

---

[1] In order to avoid that the same attribute is used for expansion operations again and again, we adjust the attribute usage of the expansion attribute to a lower value (50%) after copying it from the expanded node.

[2] Note that we defined the domains of the attributes to contain discrete values. Thus, we are able to divide given intervals of concrete values.

happens, we define *supported attributes* and *supported queries* as follows. Whenever there is a decision tree which has an attribute A_i as the expansion attribute of its root node, then the attribute A_i is said to be a supported attribute. Let QC be the conjunctive point or range query part of a given query Q, and let A_1, ..., A_N be the attributes occurring in QC. If one of the attributes of QC is supported by a broker hierarchy, we call the queries Q and QC *supported*, because we can pass the query Q to this hierarchy. However, if none of the attributes of QC is supported, we call Q *unsupported*.

For each unsupported attribute, we count how many unsupported queries it occurs within. Whenever this number increases over a predefined threshold, the system installs a new top-level broker which supports this attribute. In other words, this new top-level broker performs an expansion operation on this attribute and thereby generates two sub-brokers. Thereafter, the appropriate bottom layer brokers are searched for and connected to both sub-brokers.

3.4   Update, Insertion and Deletion of Product Offers

Whenever a provider changes a product offer, the bottom layer brokers of this provider have to check whether or not this influences the stored aggregated data for minimum and maximum values, and whether or not the changed attribute values of the product offer cross the border of the associated search space of the bottom layer broker.

Whenever minimum or maximum values of a bottom layer broker are changed, the changes must be propagated to the higher level brokers. On the higher level brokers it is again checked as to whether or not the propagated changes modify the minimum and maximum values, and if so the changes are propagated further up the broker hierarchy.

Whenever the change of attribute values of a product offer crosses the border of the search space of a bottom layer broker, then this update of an offer can be treated as an insertion followed by a deletion.

Whenever a new product is offered by a provider which does not belong to a current search space associated with any bottom layer broker of this provider, then a new bottom layer broker for this new product offer has to be established at the interface of the electronic market to this provider. This is basically done be defining a new broker with all minimum and maximum attributes set to the current values found for the new product. Furthermore, this new broker has to be linked into each broker hierarchy, i.e. it has to be connected to that leaf node of each decision tree which represents a search space containing the product description described by this broker. In order to find the correct decision tree leaf node within each broker hierarchy, a point query is submitted to each broker hierarchy, and the data for the new product is used in order to specify the attribute-value pairs of the point query. The same query passing mechanism which is also used for conventional queries is used in order to find the correct leaf node. The only difference is that these queries are not counted in order to find expansion attributes, and that the re-computation of sum and aggregate values is done on the fly.

Whenever a product offer is deleted from a provider's data source, it has to be checked for every bottom level broker, whether or not there are other offers within the same search space. If so, only the minimum and maximum values and the number of offers have to be adjusted and propagated in a similar manner as they are propagated when an expansion operation occurs. If a search space becomes empty via a deletion operation, i.e. there is no product offer found in this search space any more, the number of product offers of this search space is set to 0. Thereby, this search space becomes a candidate search space which may eventually be combined with an adjacent search space. Adjacent search spaces are search spaces which have identical parent search spaces. Combining two adjacent search spaces can be regarded as the opposite operation of expanding a search space. The only purpose of combining two search spaces is to reduce the number of search spaces which have to be handled by the system. When memory is not a bottleneck, the combination of search spaces is not necessary.

4 Performance Evaluation and Results

4.1 Scenario and Data Used for Performance Evaluation

The test scenario that we use to evaluate the proposed solution is the car retail business, with a real-world data set compromising approx. 15500 offers originating from 60 dealers. The data set was retrieved from an existing, centralized internet marketplace. A well-defined filtering was applied to the original data, eliminating small sellers (with less than 10 cars) and also achieving a close-to-normal distribution of the represented dealer inventory sizes. Test runs consist of a number of synthetically generated queries being sent to the system, while workload data is captured. Each test is based on a specific type of query, which is defined by the set of attributes in the query conjunction, and the distribution of values over the ranges specified for these attributes. The query distribution in most tests is equivalent to the data distribution – e.g., the most frequently offered brand would be the one most often asked for. In addition, queries with random attribute value distributions are tested separately (Test 1a in Table 1 at the end of Section 4) in order to see whether this would have any significantly different effect on results. The length of the tests has been chosen so that *broker saturation* is reached: a point at which there are virtually no further modifications to the search space and thus the results remain constant – i.e., the standard deviation of the workload over the last time interval is low.

4.2 Results

As our optimization goal is to reduce the query workload on the provider's data – especially for a high workload of user queries, we vary the number of user queries received at the system entry point of the electronic market. For each dealer, we measure how many queries reach this dealer during an interval of 10 user queries. The sum of these values constitutes the total query workload during the respective interval.

Figure 2 depicts the total query workload over the course of tests 1-3, which are based on a distribution of attribute values equivalent to that of the data set. Up to about the first 500 customer queries, the system load will for short moments exceed the query workload of broadcasting (which we take as the 100% workload comparison value). However, while at saturation, the query workload falls below 25% of the query workload of broadcasting. The final load for Test 3 is particularly low, i.e. approximately 2% of the load of broadcasting, which can be explained by the high selectivity of the underlying query type.

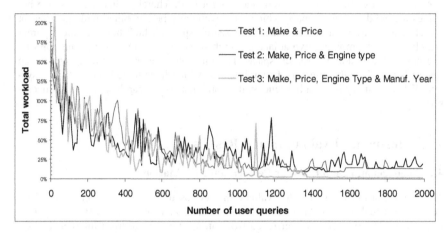

Fig. 2. Total query workload for tests 1-3

In order to better understand the benefits and costs of the system, the total load is further divided into *net load*, i.e. user queries actually routed to dealers, and *overhead*, i.e. queries submitted by the broker while expanding search spaces. To put the load factors into perspective, they are compared to the load of query broadcasting. Figure 3 shows the breakdown of the total query workload for Test 1. The overhead graph (and by implication, the total workload) shows characteristic spikes that correspond to search space adjustments and associated broker-initiated queries - however, the spikes diminish with increasing saturation of the system. At the same time, the net load, which starts at 100% when no routing information is available, decreases continuously.

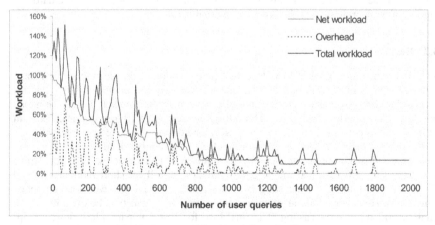

Fig. 3. Query workload breakdown for Test 1

In addition, we capture the total memory usage of the broker as a second load variable. It is measured as a percentage of the total data set size (see Figure 4). At saturation, it is in the range of 7.5% to 10% for the various test cases. These values depend on the broker parameters used, which are equal for all test cases.

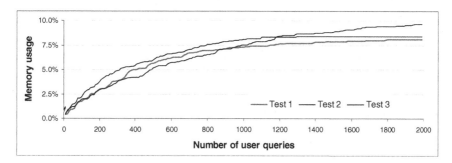

Fig. 4. Memory usage depending on the number of incoming queries

Note however that by tweaking these parameters, a different memory-consumption/query-workload ratio can be achieved. For example, for test case 1, the search space adjustments could be stopped at 5% memory usage (after 420 user queries), in which case the final system load would be 40% (see net workload in Figure 3), which is still a 60% saving compared to broadcasting.

Table 1 shows a snapshot of total query workload and memory usage for all four types of queries that have been run, at a point when saturation was reached (1500 user queries processed). It includes the additional Test 1a, which is a variation of Test 1 that uses equally distributed values for query ranges (e.g., each car make is requested equally as often). The small difference in the workload for Test 1 and Test 1a indicates that query value distribution has a limited effect on workload.

Table 1. Summary of system performance at saturation (1500 user queries)

Test #	Query Attributes	Workload	Memory Usage
1	Make, Price	9.7%	8%
2	Make, Price, Engine Type	10.0%	9%
3	Make, Price, Engine Type, Year of Manufact.	1.7%	8%
1a	Make, Price (equally distributed)	11.3%	7%

5 Summary and Conclusions

We have presented a query distribution system for an electronic market which is to the best of our knowledge the first system which combines the following ideas. Queries are filtered using hierarchically structured routing techniques via decision trees. This enables our system to reduce the amount of "unnecessary" queries, i.e. queries which are sent to a provider which can not contribute to the answer of the query. Furthermore, the decision trees which are used for query routing divide the domains for discrete attributes. They aggregate and store minimum and maximum values for attributes of product offers, as well as the number of found product offers within each cluster, from the values given for its sub-clusters. Compared to the propagation of complex query results, aggregated data can be easily propagated within a hierarchy of brokers. The aggregated data is used in order to pre-select brokers and thereby clusters of product offers to which a given query has to be passed, i.e. this aggregated information helps to identify the providers which can contribute to the answer of the query.

In order to evaluate the query workload saved by our approach, we have used over 15000 product offers originating from 60 used-car dealers. The workload evaluation shows that our approach significantly outperforms the standard (broadcasting) approach, when there is a high workload of queries submitted to the market place. Our approach performs better than the broadcasting approach, when there are more than 1500 queries in total submitted to the market place. Depending on the kind of user queries, we can reduce the number of useless queries in such a scenario by 75% at a minimum and up to 98 % in the best case. Therefore, we consider our approach to be a significant improvement of query management in distributed electronic market places.

References

1. S. Abiteboul, S. Cluet, and T. Milo. Correspondence and translation for heterogeneous data. In Proc. of the 6th ICDT, 1997.
2. Aboulnaga, A and Chaudhuri, S. Self-tuning histograms: Building histograms without looking at data. ACM SIGMOD 1999.
3. Beckmann, N., Kriegel, H., Schneider, R., Seeger, B. The R*-tree: An Efficient and Robust Access Method for Points and Rectangles. *ACM SIGMOD*, 1990.
4. S. Böttcher, S. Groppe, Automated Data Mapping for Cross Enterprise Data Integration. *International Conference of Enterprise Information Systems (ICEIS 2003)*, Angers, France, 2003.
5. Bruno, N., Chaudhuri, S., Gravano, L. Stholes: A Multidimensional Workload-Aware Histogram. *ACM SIGMOD*, 2001.
6. Jaques Calmet, Sebastian Jekutsch, and Joachim Schu: A generic query-translation framework for a mediator architecture. In ICDE, pages 434-443, 1997.
7. Chen-Chuan K. Chang, Hector Garcia-Molina: Approximate Query Translation Across Heterogeneous Information Sources. VLDB 2000.
8. C.-C. K. Chang and H. Garcia-Molina. Mind your vocabulary: Query mapping across heterogeneous information sources. In Proc. of the 1999 ACM SIGMOD Conf., Philadelphia, 1999. ACM Press, NY.
9. Chen, C.M. and Roussopoulos, N. Adaptive Selectivity Estimation Using Query Feedback. ACM SIGMOD 1994.
10. S. Cluet, C. Delobel, J. Simon, and K. Smaga. Your mediators need data conversion! In Proc. of the 1998 ACM SIGMOD Conf.
11. eCl@ss e.V.: eCl@ss - Standard für Materialklassen und Warengruppen. http://www.eClass.de, 2002. eCl@ss e.V. c/o Institut der deutschen Wirtschaft, Köln.
12. Edibatec: Bienvenue sur le site Edibatec. http://www.edibatec.org/, 2002.
13. Electronic Commerce Code Management Association (ECCMA): Universal Standard Products and Services Classification (UNSPSC). http://www.unspsc.org/, 2002.
14. ETIM Deutschland: ETIM. http://etim.de/, 2002.
15. Ganti, V., Lee, M., Ramakrishnan, R. Icicles: Self-Tuning Samples for Approximate Query Answering. *VLDB*, 2000.

16. Groppe, S., Böttcher, S., Birkenheuer, G., Efficient Querying of transformed XML documents, *6th International Conference of Enterprise Information Systems (ICEIS 2004)*, Porto, Portugal, 2004
17. Guttman, A. R-trees: A Dynamic Index Structure for Spatial Searching, ACM SIGMOD, 1984.
18. Haas, P., Swami, A. Sequential Sampling Procedures for Query Size Estimation. *ACM SIGMOD*, 1992.
19. Ioannidis, Y., Poosala, V. Balancing Histogram Optimality and Practicality for Query Result Size Estimation. *ACM SIGMOD*, 1995.
20. Renée J. Miller, Laura M. Haas, and Mauricio A. Hernández: Schema mapping as query discovery. In VLDB 2000, Proceedings of 26th International Conference on Very Large Data Bases, September 10-14, 2000. Cairo, Egypt, pages 77-88, Morgan Kaufmann, 2000.
21. Microsoft Corporation: Microsoft BizTalk Server 2002 Enterprise Edition. Documentation, http://www.microsoft.com/biztalk/, Microsoft Corporation, 2002.
22. E. Sciore, M. Siegel, and A. Rosenthal. Using semantic values to facilitate interoperability among heterogeneous information systems. Trans. on Database Systems, 19(2), 1994.
23. Yufei Tao, Dimitris Papadias. Adaptive Index Structures. VLDB 2002, pp. 418-429
24. Wu, Y., Agrawal, D., El Abbadi, A. Applying the Golden Rule of Sampling for Query Estimation. *ACM SIGMOD*, 2001.
25. L. Yan, R. J. Miller, L. M. Haas, and R. Fagin: Data-driven understanding and refinement of schema mappings. In ACM SIGMOD, Int. Conf., Santa Barbara, 2001.

Uniform Access to Data in Workflows

Johann Eder and Marek Lehmann

University of Klagenfurt
Dep. of Informatics-Systems
{eder,marek}@isys.uni-klu.ac.at

Abstract. Data aspects in workflow systems did not yet receive the
same attention as process aspects. Various kinds of data are processed in
workflow system: from case data to process data, from internal data to access to external databases or document exchanges in inter-organizational
workflows. We propose a uniform treatment of all kinds of data in workflow definition and provide abstraction mechanism which allow transparent access to all kinds of data in a uniform way. We use XML as data
access language in our workflow definition language WDL-X. The concept contributes to transparency of data location and logical and physical
data independence of workflow systems. It facilitates the reuse of predefined activities and subworkflows on different data sets and eases the
interaction of a workflow with its environment by abstracting from the
actual representation of data.

1 Introduction

Data in Workflows. Workflow management systems (WfMSs) are not intended
to provide general data management systems capabilities, although they have to
be able to administer large amounts of data. According to the Workflow Management Coalition (WfMC), which tries to come up with a generally accepted
terminology, we should distinguish three kinds of data in workflows [20]. *Workflow control data* are managed by a WfMS and describe workflow execution
(e.g. control and data flow among activities), relevant internally for a WfMS
and without a long-term impact beyond the scope of the current workflow (e.g.
a termination state of an activity). *Application data* are managed by the applications supporting the process instance and generally are never seen by the
WfMS. *Workflow relevant data* are used by the WfMS to determine the state
transitions of a workflow (e.g. transition conditions) and may be accessed both
by the WfMS and the applications.

There are also other proposals for classifying data in workflows. *Case data*
contain data directly related to an individual case (e.g. insurance claim data in
an insurance claim workflow instance), whereas *master data* contain data not
directly related to an individual case, more general data, used in many different
contexts (e.g. customer data). *Structured data* can be interpreted by a WfMS,
while *unstructured documents* (e.g. pictures) cannot.

These different data categories are not disjoint. For example case data can
be workflow relevant data and master data might be application data. It is also

K. Bauknecht, M. Bichler, and B. Pröll (Eds.): EC-Web 2004, LNCS 3182, pp. 66–75, 2004.
© Springer-Verlag Berlin Heidelberg 2004

possible that some data are required by the WfMS (workflow relevant data) and applications (application data) in the same time.

We generalize all these classes of data into *business data* and *workflow control data* (or *control data* for short). Business data describe persistent business information necessary to run an enterprise. These data may be accessed by a WfMS, invoked applications and other systems independent from the WfMS. Control data has the same interpretation as in [20].

Data used within a workflow by a WfMS may be in different types and formats. Basically each product uses different solutions varying from the minimal set of built-in primitive types (number, string, date) [2] to user defined types (e.g HTML forms in Panta Rhei [7] or ER-diagrams in LEU [11]).

Workflow Repositories and External Data Sources. Workflow repositories are used practically by every WfMS to store their data. A *process model repository* stores information about process models (e.g. activity types, data types etc.) and a *process repository* stores all process specific information (control data and part of the business data) [11]. As a repository could be used a file system managed by a WfMS (e.g. Staffware classic [18]), a RDBMS (e.g. Panta Rhei [7]) or an OODBMS [13]. The authors of the system Meteor [15] proposed the XML repository RepoX [17] for storing definitions of workflow processes in the form of XML documents.

Control data are usually stored in a repository. Business data may be either controlled by a WfMS and stored in the repository or may be managed in external systems (e.g. corporate database) and the WfMS maintains references to these data in the external systems. Access to these external data is frequently provided by automatic activities or other means which are not a part of the WfMS (e.g. Automatic Steps and Scripts in Staffware [18], system invoked activities in Panta Rhei [7]). In this case most of the activity programming will be related to updating external databases. An important drawback of this approach is that these WfMS-external data can only be used indirectly as workflow relevant data, e.g. be queried for control decisions, because the WfMS needs a direct data access to determine the state transitions.

We propose to provide a WfMS with a uniform and transparent access method to all business data stored in any data source. The WfMS should be able to use data coming from external and independent systems to determine a state transition or to pass it between activities as parameters.

XML and Workflows. The importance of XML technology is increasing tremendously for workflow management. The WfMC presented two standards based on XML. The Wf-XML [21] supports interoperability between multiple workflow enactment services. XPDL [22] is designed to exchange workflow process definitions between different WfMSs. It allows the use within workflow definition data typed with XML Schema. However, it does not state how complex XML documents can be tested in expressions. Moreover, XPDL does not specify how one can access environmental data within a process definition.

A fully XML based approach to workflow processing is presented in [14]. Participants of a workflow exchange messages described in XML language X-MSG.

The workflow itself is defined in another XML language X-IBP. The process control logic called XS-PCL is written in XSL.

Another approach for processing XML documents in WfMSs is presented in [3]. The authors proposed to partition a single XML document into several meaningful segments. A segment is a unit of work that can be performed by an activity in a workflow process.

XML is the main data format in many B2B standards (e.g. ebXML [5]). Also web services extensively use XML (e.g. BPEL4WS [1]). Methods for integrating WfMSs with standards for web services are becoming more important [16].

We propose to use XML as the main business data format at every stage of workflow processing. A WfMS should be able to test conditions on XML data to determine the state transitions, regardless of where these data are stored and maintained. Data-passing between activities should also rely on XML-standards, independent of whether these activities are internal to a workflow or external. Both goals aim at a seamless integration of intra-organizational and trans-organisational workflow and on location transparency of data.

The remainder of this paper is organized as follows: In Section 2 we present the idea of uniform access to XML data in workflows with an example. Section 3 contains a metamodel for describing XML data and data access plug-ins. In Section 4 we present an architecture for providing a WfMS with transparent access to XML documents stored in different data sources. Section 5 describes the mechanism of data access plug-ins. We draw some conclusions in Section 6.

2   Uniform XML Based Data Access

The work we present here is a continuation of our work in workflow systems. Our workflow system *Panta Rhei* [7] used a form-flow metaphor to provide access to workflow specific data. For interorganizational workflows [6] we saw the necessity to define adaptors to accommodate to different document definitions of partner organizations (clients, suppliers, etc.) and we then represented case data in XML [9] for interacting with other workflow or application systems. Now we propose XML as data representation and access methodology everywhere in the workflow definition where data is accessed.

In a nutshell our approach is as follows:

- We use XML schema to describe the structure of all data.
- Activity and workflow definitions use XML-types for characterizing input and output parameter. These types are views on the actual data storage.
- XPath is used for accessing data and evaluating conditions.
- Access methods link the parameters to the actual data stores.
- Access methods may be associated with parameters and variables at runtime.

We illustrate the main concepts of our approach with an example. First we propose to use XML Schema types [10] to describe all kinds of data. XML Schema types describing business data are used in many workflows within an enterprise

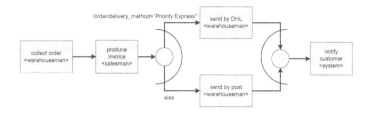

Fig. 1. Example workflow definition as a workflow graph

```
1     process processOrder(IN order : orderType, IN plugIn : dataAccessPlugIn)
2        documents invoice        : invoiceType accessedBy plugIn,
3                  notification    : notificationType;
4        begin
5          warehouseman collectOrder(order, notification);
6          salesman produceInvoice(order, invoice);
7          if (order./order/deliveryMethod = "Priority Expres")
8                warehouseman sendByDHL(order);
9          else
10               warehouseman sendByPost(order);
11         endif;
12         system notifyCustomer(notification);
13    end;
```

Fig. 2. Example workflow definition in WDL-X

(e.g. the same XML Schema type describing an invoice in all workflow definitions). The enterprise accesses several data sources (within or outside its organization) of business data required in many workflow definitions.

A workflow graph with an example workflow describing the shipment of an
order is presented in Fig. 1.

The workflow definition may be also represented in a script language called
WDL-X. It extends the Workflow Definition Language (WDL) [7] by replacing
all data definition and data access with XML technology. A script corresponding
to the example is presented in Fig. 2.

A document describing the order is passed to the process as an input parameter (line 1). The parameter comes from the outside of the workflow. E.g. it may
be passed by a business partner activating the workflow as a web-service, or the
workflow is invoked as a subworkflow in some more complex process.

Apart from the *order* two other documents (*invoice* and *notification* declared
in lines 2 and 3) are passed between the activities. All documents are typed with
XML Schema (e.g. *orderType*). The definition of the simplified XML Schema
type and an example of the order are in Fig. 3.

Processes and activities can accept parameters in one of the following modes:
IN - as an input parameter (read only), *OUT* - as an output parameter (write
only) and *INOUT* - as an in- and output parameter (read/write). In the example are several activities, which accept as parameters XML documents in the
described modes, e.g.: notifyCustomer (*INOUT* notification : notificationType)
or produceInvoice (*IN* order : orderType, *OUT* invoice : invoiceType).

70   Johann Eder and Marek Lehmann

```
1 <xs:complexType name="orderType">
2   <xs:sequence>
3     <xs:element name="dispatchAddress" type="addressType"/>
4     <xs:element name="invoiceAddress" type="addressType"
5       minOccurs="0"/>
6     <xs:element name="e-mail" type="xs:string"/>
7     <xs:element name="deliveryMethod">
8       <xs:simpleType name="deliveryType">
9         <xs:restriction base="xs:string">
10          <xs:enumeration value="Priority Express"/>
11          <xs:enumeration value="Air Mail"/>
12        </xs:restriction>
13      </xs:simpleType>
14    </xs:element>
15    <xs:element name="items">
16      <xs:complexType>
17        <xs:sequence>
18          <xs:element name="item" type="itemType"
19            maxOccurs="unbounded"/>
20        </xs:sequence>
21      </xs:complexType>
22    </xs:element>
23    <xs:element name="subtotal" type="xs:float"/>
24    <xs:element name="postage" type="xs:float"/>
25    <xs:element name="totalBeforeVAT" type="xs:float"/>
26    <xs:element name="VAT" type="xs:float"/>
27    <xs:element name="total" type="xs:float"/>
28  </xs:sequence>
29  <xs:attribute name="orderNo" type="xs:string"/>
30 </xs:complexType>
```

```
1 <order orderNo="026-6462982">
2   <dispatchAddress>
3     <name>John Doe</name>
4     <street>Anystreet 7</street>
5     <city>Anycity</city>
6     <ZIP>A-007</ZIP>
7     <country>Neverland</country>
8   </dispatchAddress>
9   <e-mail>john@any.org</e-mail>
10  <deliveryMethod>Priority Express</deliveryMethod>
10  <items>
11    <item>
12      <name>Krzysztof Penderecki - Orchestral Works</name>
13      <price>4.99</price>
14      <orderedQuantity>1</orderedQuantity>
15    </item>
16    <item>
17      <name>Henryk Sienkiewicz - Quo Vadis?</name>
18      <price>24.50</price>
19      <orderedQuantity>1</orderedQuantity>
20    </item>
21  </items>
22  <subtotal>29.49</subtotal>
23  <postage>8.19</postage>
24  <totalBeforeVAT>30.89</totalBeforeVAT>
25  <VAT>6.79</VAT>
26  <total>37.68</total>
27 </order>
```

Fig. 3. XML Schema type definition and an example XML document instance

First a human actor *warehouseman* executes the manual activity *collectOrder*. This activity produces a new *notification* instance. Afterwards a *salesman* has to produce an invoice. Depending on the delivery method indicated in the order it is shipped by DHL or by post. At the end the system automatically notifies the customer per e-mail about the shipment.

The example in Fig. 2 illustrates the new concepts of our approach. The WfMS works with valid XML documents typed with XML Schema. These data are accessed in a uniform way regardless of where they are stored. This is achieved by special, replaceable and reusable wrappers of external data sources called data access plug-ins (see sec. 5). A data access plug-in is passed to the example workflow definition in line 1 as an input parameter *plugIn*. This plug-in is later used to access an XML document of type *invoiceType* (line 2). Documents may also be stored locally in a process repository. In such a way the document *notification* is accessed (line 3).

Data access plug-ins increase productivity and flexibility of the WfMS. We are able to specify a workflow definition and say where the data come from during the instantiation of this definition. Data access plug-ins may also be declared as constants in WDL-X, passed as elements of any document the process receives, or predefined during the instantiation in a process control sheet, which includes control data of the process.

To control the flow of the workflow an XPath expression may be evaluated on XML documents as in the line 7 of the example. Documents tested in this way can be accessed by a data access plug-in. Thus workflow relevant data do not have to be stored in the process repository anymore.

3   Metamodel

We propose a new metamodel (Fig. 4) for static workflow schema aspects. It describes a *workflow* and related actors, activities and data. It focusses on data aspects by describing XML documents, XML Schema types, data access plug-ins and forms. XML Schema types describe XML documents passed between activities and accessed by various data access plug-ins. XSLT transformations provide transformations between various types. Simple data items of XML documents can be addressed with XPath expressions and be used to define conditions.

Activities are either *(external) workflows, elementary* or *complex activities.* Elementary activities are either *automated* or *manual activities.* Complex activities are composed of other activities. The type of a complex activity describes its control structure (*seq* for a sequential, *par* for parallel and *cond* for conditional). *Agents* are responsible for executing activities. An agent may be a *user*, or a *role.*

Activities can accept parameters in one of the *access modes.* The *XML documents* are passed as parameters between activities. Each XML document has one root *element* of one XML Schema *type.* Types are either *simple* or *complex.* A complex type can have *attributes* and *elements.* A new type can be derived from an other type. Attributes are always of a simple type, elements can be either of a simple or a complex type. XML documents can be accessed by *data access plug-ins.* Each plug-in is capable of accessing XML documents of one or more XML Schema types. A document of one type can be transformed to a document of another type by a *transformation* between the source and the target XML Schema type [8, 12].

A *simple data item* is an attribute or an element of a simple type. The simple data item can be addressed within an XML document with an XPath expression. The simple data item (or a combination of several items) is used to uniquely identify the XML document in a collection of many documents of the same type. Simple data items are also used in conditional complex activities

Manual activities need some way of presenting XML data to a human actor. We propose to use *forms* defined in XForms [4]. XForms can be parameterized and accept XML documents as input and produce XML documents as output.

4   Proposed Architecture

We propose a new architecture of a WfMS which supports the usage of XML documents at every stage of workflow processing and allows the WfMS to transparently access many sources of business data via data access plug-ins. The architecture is presented in Fig. 5. It includes new modules responsible for storing information about XML Schemas, managing data access plug-ins and for transforming between XML documents.

The *Data Schema Manager* registers XML Schemas according to the metamodel presented in section 3. A workflow designer may use registered types in a workflow specification. This part of the WfMS manages also the information about relations between types and the transformations between different types.

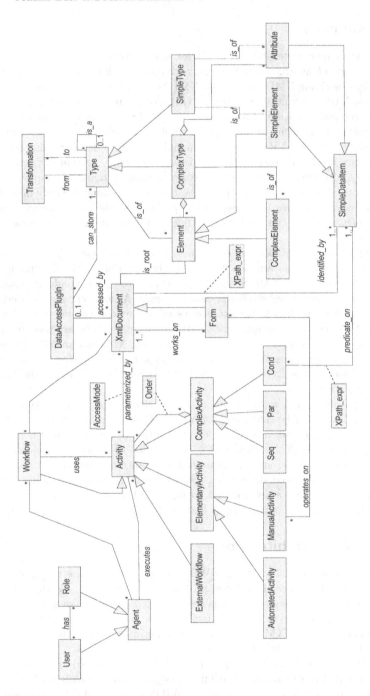

Fig. 4. Workflow metamodel

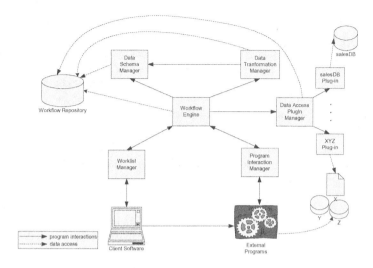

Fig. 5. Proposed architecture

The *Data Transformation Manager* uses information about the registered XML Schema types and the transformations provided by the Data Schema Manager and transforms XML documents when necessary in workflow execution (e.g. to accept XML documents from business partners).

The *Worklist Manager* is responsible for worklists of the human actors and for the interaction with the client software (worklist handlers). The *Program Interaction Manager* calls programs implementing automated activities. It may also accept calls from the external systems e.g. Wf-XML messages. The *Workflow Engine* provides operational functions to support the execution of instances of business process, based on the process definitions [20]. The Plug-in Manager is described in section 5.

5   Data Access Plug-Ins

The Data Plug-in Manager controls *data access plug-ins*. A data access plug-in is a replaceable and reusable wrapper of an external and independent data source. Each plug-in must be registered with the manager together with it's applicable XML Schema types. The requirements for the data access plug-in are:

- Creation, selection, update, and deletion of an XML document in a collection of many documents of the same XML Schema type.
- Evaluation of an XPath expression on a selected XML document.

The data access plug-in can be wrapped around any data source if it provides the described functionality, e.g. files from a file system, XML views over relational or object-relational databases, or native XML databases. Thus the WfMS can access legacy databases easily.

Consider the following frequent scenario: an enterprise has a large database with the customer data which are used in many processes. In our approach the company defines a XML Schema type describing customer data and implements a plug-in, which wraps this database and retrieves and stores customer data in XML format. The XML type has to be registered in the Data Schema Manager and the plug-in in the Data Plug-in Manager. From now on in all workflow definition the plug-in can be used for accessing customer data. This approach has many advantages:

– Business data from external systems are directly accessible by the WfMS. Thus these data can be also used as workflow relevant data.
– Both XML Schema type and the data access plug-in are reusable. They can be used in many workflow definitions.
– This solution is easily evolvable and maintainable. If the customer data have to be moved to a different data source, it is sufficient to use another plug-in (see sec. 2). The workflow definition and activities remain basically unchanged.
– All data in the workflow are in XML form. This simplifies data transformations with many technologies developed for XML. Thus the seamless integration with other partners and B2B standards is much easier.

With improved technology for XML-views over relational data, which allows not only retrieving but also updating data [19], the implementation of plug-ins will become easier. Modern type system will also allow for the creation of generic plug-ins on the definition level which are then adaptive to the actual sources in the implementation.

6   Conclusions

The main contributions of the presented approach for uniform access to data in workflows are:

– All data in workflows (application data, process data, external data sources, etc.) are described, represented and processed in a uniform way.
– We offer a simple and transparent mechanism for accessing data stored in many different data sources (workflow repository, external systems).
– Seamless integration with external systems can an be achieved by exchange of process and application data in XML format.
– XML data types and data access plug-ins can be reused in many workflow definitions.
– Reuse of subworkflows and activities is made easier and is no longer prohibited by differences in data representation.

The concept and the architecture we propose strives for achieving true physical and logical independence of process and data. The abstraction represented in exchangeable plug-ins for data access frees workflow definitions from the accidentiality of representation formats. Besides the obvious advantages for intra- and interorganizational exchange of data and documents, maintenance and evolution of workflow systems will benefit considerably.

References

1. T. Andrews, F. Curbera, H. Dholakia et al.: *Business Process Execution Language for Web Services (BPEL4WS), Version 1.1.* http://ifr.sap.com/bpel4ws/
2. M. Ader: *Workflow and Business Process Management Comparative Study. Volume 2.* Workflow & Groupware Stratégies, June 2003
3. H. Bae, Y. Kim: *A document-process associacion model for workflow management.* Computers in Industry 47, pp. 139-154, Elsevier, 2002
4. M. Dubinko, L. L. Klotz, R. Merrick, T. V. Raman: *XForms 1.0.* W3C Recom.
5. ebXML Technical Architecture Project Team *ebXML Technical Architecture Specification v1.0.4.* http://www.ebxml.org/
6. H. Groiss and J. Eder. *Workflow systems for inter-organizational business processes.* ACM SIGGROUP Bulletin, Dec. 1997.
7. J. Eder, H. Groiss, W. Liebhart: *The Workflow Management System Panta Rhei.* In: A. Dogac, L. Kalinichenko, T. Öszu, A. Sheth (Eds.): *Workflow Management Systems and Interoperability,* Springer-Verlag 1998
8. J. Eder, M. Lehmann: *Composition of Transformations for XML Schema Based Documents.* Short paper at ADBIS 2003
9. J. Eder, W. Strametz: *Composition of XML-Transformations.* EC-Web 2001
10. D. C. Fallside: *XML Schema Part 0: Primer.* W3C Recommendation
11. V. Gruhn, M. Schneider: *Workflow Management based on Process Model Repositories.* IEEE Conference on Software Engineering 1998
12. M. Lehmann: *Exploiting Generalization for the Composition of Transformations of XML Schema Based Documents.* CAiSE Forum 2003, in CEUR-WS.org/Vol-74/
13. C. Liu, X. Lin, X. Zhou, M. Orlowska: *Building a Repository for Workflow Systems.* 31th Conference on Technology of Object-Oriented Languages and Systems, 1999
14. M. Lee, S.-H. Kang: *XML-based Automatic Workflow Control for Integrated Business Process.* Submitted for publication.
15. J. A. Miller, D. Palaniswami, A. Sheth, K. Koschut, H. Singh: *WebWork: Meteor$_2$'s Web Based Workflow Management System.* JIIS (10), Kluwer 1998
16. M. Sayal, F. Casati, U. Dayal, M.-Ch. Shan: *Integrating Workflow Management Systems with Business-to-Business Interaction Standards.* ICDE 2002
17. M. Song, J. A. Miller, I. B. Arpinar: *RepoX: An XML Repository for Workflow Design and Specifications.* Technical Report at University of Georgia, 2001
18. Staffware plc: *Staffware Technical Overview. Issue 1.* October 2001
19. L. Wang, M. Mulchandani, E.A. Rundensteiner: *Updating XQuery Views Published over Relational Data: A Round-trip case study.* XML Database Symposium, 2003
20. Workflow Management Coal.: *Terminology and Glossary.* 1999, WFMC-TC-1001
21. Workflow Mngt. Coal.: *Interoperability Wf-XML Binding.* 2001, WFMC-TC-1023
22. Workflow Mngt. Coal.: *Workflow Process Definition Interface - XML Process Definition Language (XPDL).* 2002, WFMC-TC-1025

Formal Verification
of BPEL4WS Business Collaborations

Jesús Arias Fisteus, Luis Sánchez Fernández, and Carlos Delgado Kloos

Telematic Engineering Department
Carlos III University of Madrid
Avda. Universidad, 30
28911 Leganés, Madrid, Spain
{jaf,luis,cdk}@it.uc3m.es

Abstract. Web services are a very appropriate communication mechanism to perform distributed business processes among several organisations. These processes should be reliable, because a failure in them can cause high economic losses. To increase their reliability at design time, we have developed VERBUS, a framework for the formal verification of business processes. VERBUS can automatically translate business process definitions to specifications verifiable in several available tools. It is based on a modular and extensible architecture: new process definition languages and verification tools can be added easily to the framework. The prototype of VERBUS presented in this work can verify BPEL4WS process specifications, by translating them to Promela. The Promela specifications are verified with the well known model checker Spin. In this paper we describe the general architecture of VERBUS and how BPEL4WS specifications are translated and verified. The explanation is completed by describing what types of properties can be verified and providing an overview of the implementation.

1   Introduction

Inter–organisational business processes are a key technology for business to business collaborations. Nowadays many enterprises have automated their internal business processes with workflow technologies. They have now a new challenge: the automation of their collaborations with partner enterprises, in open and very dynamic environments, to accelerate their business in a cost–effective manner. Web services are a promising technology to support these type of collaborations [1, 2]. It is an XML–based middleware technology that provides RPC–like remote communication, using in most cases SOAP over HTTP.

Web services provide a state–less communication mechanism: WSDL can specify remote operations and their input and output parameters, but not the relations between several operations. Business processes have a state. Therefore, new languages are necessary to execute business processes on top of Web services. Several languages have been used to model these business processes [2]. They are often called *choreography languages*, because they specify the order in

K. Bauknecht, M. Bichler, and B. Pröll (Eds.): EC-Web 2004, LNCS 3182, pp. 76–85, 2004.

which the activities of the process must be executed. The most important are BPEL4WS [3], BPML [4] and ebXML BPSS [5]. Among them, only BPEL4WS is specific for Web services. The Web Services Choreography Working Group of the World Wide Web Consortium (W3C) is also currently developing a new Web services choreography language.

Complex business collaborations require the specification of complex business processes. Specificating complex processes is error prone, due to concurrency in the execution of activities, the possibility of communication errors, faults in remote systems, etc. Enterprises can only trust in this technology if the correctness of the processes can be ensured, because a failure in them can cause high economic losses. In this work we present VERBUS (*VERification for BUSiness processes*), a system for automatic verification of business processes using model–checking. Its main objective is to help process designers to ensure the correctness of the defined processes. The current prototype receives an input BPEL4WS process specification and a set of properties that the designer wants to verify. Then the system automatically translates the specification to a formal specification language and verifies it using a model–checker. If a property is found to be false, the system gives a counter–example to the designer. VERBUS is modular and extensible: new process definition languages and verification tools can be easily added to the framework.

Several works have been done previously on business processes verification. Woflan [6] is a Petri–Net based verification tool. It can perform verifications on workflow definitions, and was integrated with several commercial workflow management systems. In [7] formal semantics are defined for UML activity diagrams to allow the verification of workflow processes defined with these formalisms. It uses the SMV model checker. A framework for the verification of Web services is proposed in [8]. It can perform analysis on a Web service described with DAML-S by translating the description to a Petri–Net based model.

None of these works can be applied to BPEL4WS processes. The results of these works are specific, both in terms of process modelling language and verification tool. However, VERBUS proposes a framework in which several process definitions languages and verification tools can be integrated, based on a common intermediate formal model. This formal model is very simple, but can represent complex semantics like the fault handling mechanism of BPEL4WS in a straightforward way, as showed in the next sections.

This paper is organised as follows. Section 2 makes a brief introduction to BPEL4WS. Section 3 describes the main architecture of VERBUS. Section 4 explains how VERBUS translates BPEL4WS processes to its formal model. Section 5 explains the possibilities that VERBUS offers for performing verifications. Finally, the main conclusions of this work are summarised.

2   Modelling Business Processes with BPEL4WS

Business Process Execution Language for Web Services (BPEL4WS) [3] is an XML notation for specifying business process behaviour based on Web services.

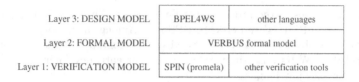

Layer 3: DESIGN MODEL	BPEL4WS	other languages
Layer 2: FORMAL MODEL	VERBUS formal model	
Layer 1: VERIFICATION MODEL	SPIN (promela)	other verification tools

Fig. 1. Architecture of the VERBUS framework

It was developed by Microsoft, IBM, BEA, Siebel Systems and SAP. It allows the specification of executable processes and business protocols. An executable process defines the behaviour of a participant in a collaboration. A business protocol defines the message exchange of all the participants involved in a collaboration.

BPEL4WS provides basic activity structuring (sequential and parallel composition, conditional execution and loops), variables, hierarchical activity composition with scopes, Web services based communication (invocation of remote Web services operations and providing Web services operations to remote systems), event handling and fault and compensation handling mechanisms.

Activities are executed in the context provided by a *scope*. Each scope contains activities and data. All the activities contained in a scope share the same context. Scopes can be hierarchically nested. The root of the hierarchy is the process, that can be viewed as a special scope. It can contain any number of children scopes. Each scope can contain also children scopes, and so on. Scopes store data in variables, that can be accessed by any activity contained by this scope, or any scope nested in it.

Scopes are also important for fault and compensation handling. The fault handling mechanism is very similar to the Java exception handling mechanism. An activity can throw *faults* to notify an error in its execution. Faults can be handled by a scope or, if not, they are re–thrown to the next enclosing scope. Section 4.4 explains this in detail. The compensation mechanism allows the specification of transactional behaviour for business processes. Each scope can define a compensation handler to make the rollback of the actions that were executed by the scope. This handler is executed when the scope has successfully completed but it must be compensated due to faults that occurred in other scopes.

3   The VERBUS Framework

VERBUS is a modular and extensible framework for the verification of business processes. It proposes an architecture with three layers, as showed in Fig. 1. The *design model* (layer 3) deals with the design of business processes, using specification languages like BPEL4WS or BPML, for example. The *formal model* (layer 2) deals with the specification of processes using a formal model. VERBUS defines its own formal model for this layer, based on Finite State Machines (FSMs). The *verification model* (layer 1) deals with the verification of business processes. Several general–purpose verification tools can be placed in this layer, such as Spin [9] or SMV [10].

Layer 3 specifications are translated to formal (layer 2) specifications using automatic translation tools. There is one tool for each layer 3 language. Layer 2 specifications are also translated to verification languages using automatic translation tools. There is one tool for each verification language, because each verification tool has normally a specific input language. Layer 2 is an intermediate layer that increases the modularity and extensibility of the system, by disconnecting the design and verification layers. Thus, only one translation tool is needed when introducing a new verification tool in the framework, and it will be available to specifications defined in any language in the design layer. The same applies to the introduction of new layer 3 languages.

The current prototype of VERBUS implements two translation tools. One of them translates a BPEL4WS process specification to a formal specification. The other translates a layer 2 specification to a Promela [9] specification, that can be verified with the model–checker Spin.

3.1   The VERBUS Formal Model

The formal model used in the layer 2 of VERBUS is based on FSMs. It is briefly presented here. Its formal definition is given in [11].

A process is composed by a set of attributes and a set of transitions. At a given moment, each attribute has a value within a set of possible values. The value of all the attributes of the process at a given moment establishes its state. The process progresses from one state to another by means of transitions. A transition is a pair of states (origin and destination) that defines a possible progress of the process. The process starts at an initial state. Then it fires transitions, until it reaches a state that is not in the origin of any transition. This state implies the completion of the process and is called a *final state*.

The FSM of a business process has normally many transitions. In order to avoid defining them explicitly, VERBUS represents them with *functional transitions*. A functional transition is defined by two predicates: *domain* and *action*. The domain defines a set of states that are origin of transitions. The action defines how these origin states change to obtain the final states. Therefore a functional transition represents a set of transitions that share a similar behaviour.

The concepts of entity, entity type and activity are introduced as notational elements, to make specifications more readable. However, they do not affect the basic formalism. An entity type is a group of typed fields (boolean, enumerated or integer types). An entity is an instance of an entity type. Each field of an entity type generates as many attributes as times its data type is instantiated. An activity is a logical unit for grouping related functional transitions.

4   Translating BPEL4WS to the VERBUS Formal Model

The translation of BPEL4WS specifications to the formal model is the most complex functionality of VERBUS. This section summarises how it is done. The translation of *sequences* and the *fault–handling* mechanism were selected

```
<xsd:complexType name="Order">              enttype OrderMessage {
  <xsd:sequence>                              urgent: boolean;
    <xsd:element name="productId"             order__productId: abstract;
               type="xsd:string" />           order__colour: enum (white, red, blue,
    <xsd:element name="colour">                              black);
      <xsd:simpleType>                       }
        <xsd:restriction base="xsd:string">  entity order: OrderMessage;
          <xsd:enumeration value="white"/>
          <xsd:enumeration value="red"/>
          <xsd:enumeration value="blue"/>
          <xsd:enumeration value="black"/>
  (...)
</xsd:complexType>
<message name="OrderMessage">
  <part name="urgent" type="xsd:boolean"/>
  <part name="order" type="tns:Order"/>
</message>
<variable name="order"
          messageType="tns:OrderMessage"/>
```

Fig. 2. Mapping between BPEL4WS variables and VERBUS entities

as representative examples of how the translation is performed. The current prototype of VERBUS can translate also any of the other activities. In the web page of the VERBUS project (http://www.it.uc3m.es/jaf/verbus) there are several examples that show how VERBUS translates these other activities.

4.1 Variables

BPEL4WS variables are mapped to VERBUS entities. Each variable is an instance of a data type defined by a WSDL message, an XML element or an XML Schema type. First, the data type is transformed to an entity type. Then it is instantiated as an entity. Simple data types are transformed to VERBUS data types if possible (boolean, enumerated and integer), or declared as *abstract* otherwise. Complex data types are transformed by recursively transforming their components. Fig. 2 shows an example. The message type OrderMessage has two parts: urgent and order. The part urgent is a simple type and so it is translated to a boolean field in the VERBUS entity type. The part order is a complex type: the sequence of the elements productId (string) and colour (enumerated data type). It is translated to two fields, one for each element.

4.2 Activities

The execution of each BPEL4WS activity instance is controlled by a life–cycle. Depending on the type of activity two different life–cycle types were identified in this work. The *general life–cycle* is used for activities that can have handlers (process, scope and invoke). The *simple life–cycle* is used for the other activities. Both life–cycle types are represented in Fig. 3.

Each activity is mapped to an entity and several functional transitions. The entity represents the state of the activity in its life–cycle. The functional transitions represent the way the activity can progress through its life–cycle and how

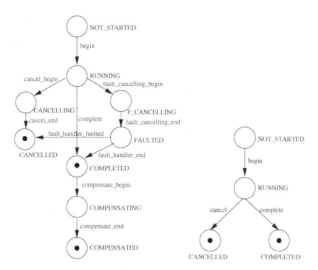

Fig. 3. Life–cycle for activities. The general life–cycle is on the left and the simple life–cycle is on the right. States are labelled with uppercase letters and transitions with lowercase letters. States containing a black dot can be final states of the life–cycle

it affects to the attributes of the process. The concrete functional transitions of each activity depend on its activity type. However, there are several rules that are common to almost all activities.

Activity instances have always a *begin* transition, that represents the beginning of their execution. Its domain represents the preconditions of the activity. Normally it is a condition that checks the state of other activities (depending on the type of its parent activity), and its own state (it must be **not_started**). Its action changes the state of the activity to **running**.

Activity instances have normally a **complete** transition also, that represents the end of their execution. Its domain checks that the activity is in **running** state. Depending on the activity type, it may include other conditions. Its action puts the activity in **complete** state, and can change also attributes of the process to represent the effects of the activity execution.

If an activity has a non–deterministic behaviour then it is normally modelled with several mutually–exclusive functional transitions. Each of them represents a different behaviour of the activity. Examples of non–deterministic behaviour are **pick** activities, activities that can throw faults, **receive** or **invoke** activities that can receive messages with different data, etc.

4.3 Sequence Activity

The BPEL4WS sequence activity can contain one or more inner activities, that must be executed in sequential order. Given an activity in the sequence, it can begin its execution only if its preceding activity has been completed. The sequence itself is completed when its last inner activity has been completed.

```
<sequence name="main">            activity main_act_2 {
 <receive name="init" .../>        transition begin {
 <switch name="switch">...</switch>   domain: {main_act_2_lc__.state=not_started}
 <scope name="end">...</scope>        action: {main_act_2_lc__.state=running}}
</sequence>                        transition complete {
                                    domain: {(main_act_2_lc__.state=running &
                                            end_act_11_lc__.state=completed)}
                                    action: {main_act_2_lc__.state=completed}}
                                  }
                                  activity init_act_3 {
                                   transition begin {
                                    domain: {(main_act_2_lc__.state=running &
                                            init_act_3_lc__.state=not_started)}
                                    action: {init_act_3_lc__.state=running}}
                                   transition complete {...}
                                  }
                                  activity switch_act_4 {
                                   transition begin {
                                    domain: {(init_act_3_lc__.state=completed & ...)}
                                    action: {(switch_act_4_lc__.state=running & ...)}}
                                   ... }
                                  activity end_act_11 {
                                   transition begin {
                                    domain: {(switch_act_4_lc__.state=completed & ...)}
                                    action: {end_act_11_lc__.state=running}}
                                   ... }
```

Fig. 4. Mapping a BPEL4WS sequence. The examples is abbreviated to highlight the most important conditions and transitions

This behaviour is modelled by adding a condition to the domain of the `begin` transition of each inner activity and a condition to the domain of the `complete` transition of the sequence activity. The condition added to the first inner activity states that the sequence activity must be in `running` state. The condition added to the other inner activities states that the previous activity must be in `completed` state. The condition added to the `complete` transition of the sequence activity states that the last inner activity must be in `completed` state. Fig. 4 shows an example.

4.4 Fault Handling

BPEL4WS has a powerful fault–handling mechanism. The `process`, `scope` and `invoke` activities can contain fault handlers. When a fault is thrown in a given activity, a handler in the immediately enclosing `scope`, `process` or `invoke` is selected, based on the fault name and variable type. Before the handler is executed, all the running inner activities of this scope are cancelled. If no handler is appropriate, then the whole scope is cancelled, and the fault is re–thrown to the next enclosing scope. A fault that reaches the `process` level causes the cancellation of the whole process.

To manage the fault–handling mechanism, several attributes are added to the general life–cycle entity type. One of them is boolean and its value is `true` when a fault has occurred in the activity. The other is enumerated, and its value specifies which is the selected handler when a fault has occurred. The activity contained in each fault handler checks these variables as a precondition for its execution.

The cancellation mechanism is needed to implement fault–handling. It is implemented in VERBUS in this way: a scope that must be cancelled puts itself in `fault-cancelling` state. Its inner activity has a transition that cancels itself if the scope is in `fault-cancelling` state. In a similar way, if this activity has inner activities, they detect this cancellation and cancel themselves, and so on. The scope has a transition that puts itself in `faulted` state when none of its inner activities is running. At this moment the activity of the fault handler is allowed to start its execution. When this activity completes its execution, the scope puts itself in `completed` state.

4.5   Prototype Implementation

The current prototype of VERBUS is mainly composed by a BPEL4WS to VERBUS translator and a VERBUS to Promela translator. It is based on the BPEL4WS specification version 1.1 [3]. It was developed in Java and uses the open source libraries Xerces, Xalan and WSDL4J. The prototype works in command line, but a graphical user interface is currently under development. It will incorporate a graphical editor of BPEL4WS processes.

The main lack of the current prototype is the *compensation* mechanism, because of the complexity associated with it: a copy of all the variables must be saved for each completed activity instance, because they must be compensated using the value that variables had when they were completed. `While` loops even make this more complex, because multiple instances of each inner activity can be created. This feature will be handled in future versions of VERBUS, by storing a copy of attributes for each completed activity. This will increase the complexity of the verification, and therefore a configurable parameter will be added to limit the maximum number of activity instances.

5   Verification of Processes

The main goal of VERBUS is the verification of business process specifications. VERBUS allows the modeller to state properties that must be true for a given process specification, and checks whether these properties are true or false for it. If some property is found to be false, VERBUS gives a counterexample. From the point of view of the formal layer, properties are expressed with boolean predicates about the value of the attributes of the process. The current prototype of VERBUS can verify several types of *safety* and *liveness* properties:

- *Invariants*: an invariant is a predicate that must be true in every reachable state. From the point of view of the BPEL4WS process, invariants look like *for every state if the activity named "init" is running, the part "urgent" of the global variable "order" must have a false value.* The counterpart property in the formal model layer is: `!(init_act_3.state=running & order)`.

- *Goals*: a goal is a predicate that must be true in every reachable final state. I.e. the predicate must be true whenever the process stops its execution. VERBUS adds automatically one goal to ensure that the process and all the activities are in a valid final state of their life–cycle (not_started, completed, cancelled or compensated) when the process reaches a final state. Thus any dead–lock or process block is detected. Goals like *when the process completes its execution the part "urgent" of the global variable "order" must have a false value* can detect functional errors in specifications.
- *Transition pre and post–conditions*: given a transition, a pre–condition (post–condition) is a predicate that must be true always immediately before (after) the execution of the transition. An example is: *immediately before the activity named "init" completes its execution the part "urgent" of the global variable "order" must have a true value.*
- *Activity reachability analysis*: VERBUS can detect transitions that can not be executed in any trace of the process. Thus activities that can never be started are detected, for example.
- *Properties defined with LTL*: VERBUS can check properties expressed in LTL (*Linear Temporal Logic*). Using LTL the modeller can specify temporal causalities like *if the part "urgent" of the global variable "order" has a true value, then sometime in the future it must have a false value.*

Formal layer specifications can be translated to Promela in a very straightforward way. The generated Promela specifications have a main do loop, in which all the transitions of the process are defined. The domain of each transition acts as a guard, and appears before the action. There is an else statement that breaks the loop when no transition can be selected (process completion). After the loop, there is an assertion for each goal property. Assertions for invariants are placed in a concurrent Promela process. Assertions for pre and post–conditions are placed before or after the action of each transition. In [11] this translation is explained in more detail.

6   Conclusions

This work presents VERBUS, a modular and extensible framework for automatic business process verification. It proposes an architecture with three layers: the design layer, the formal layer and the verification layer. The formal layer is a business process specification model based on the FSMs formalism. It disconnects process description languages and verification languages. Process definitions (design layer) can be automatically translated to specifications in the formal layer. These specifications can be automatically translated to specifications in the verification layer and verified using verification tools.

Works had been done previously on business processes verification, but they can not be applied directly to BPEL4WS compositions. They use specific process description languages and verification tools. On the contrary, VERBUS provides an open framework in which several process description languages and verification tools can be integrated.

The implementation of a prototype of VERBUS has demonstrated the feasibility of the framework. The prototype is mainly composed by two translation tools. The first one translates BPEL4WS specifications to the formal model. The second one translates formal model specifications to Promela specifications, that can be verified using Spin. The VERBUS formal layer can model the flow control primitives commonly used in business processes. It is even expressive enough to model the complex fault handling and cancellation mechanisms of BPEL4WS.

As future work, this first prototype will be completed by implementing the BPEL4WS compensation mechanism. Support for new process specification languages like BPML and verification tools like SMV will be added to VERBUS.

Acknowledgements

This work is partially supported by the Spanish Science and Technology Ministry, in the project TIC2003-07208 "Infoflex".

References

1. Jae-yoon Jung, W.H., Kang, S.H.: Business Process Choreography for B2B Collaboration. IEEE Internet Computing **8** (2004) 37–45
2. Aissi, S., Malu, P., Srinivasan, K.: E-business process modeling: the next big step. IEEE Computer **35** (2002) 55–62
3. Andrews, T., Curbera, F., Dholakia, H., et al.: Business Process Execution Language for Web Services. Version 1.1 Specification. (2003) Available at http://www-106.ibm.com/developerworks/webservices/library/ws-bpel.
4. Arkin, A.: Business Process Modelling Language. Business Process Management Initiative. (2002)
5. ebXML Business Process Team: ebXML Business Process Specification Schema. Version 1.01. (2001) Available at http://www.ebxml.org/specs/ebBPSS.pdf.
6. Aalst, W.M.P.: Woflan: A petri-net-based workflow analyzer. Systems Analysis – Modelling – Simulation **35** (1999) 345–357
7. Eshuis, R.: Semantics and Verification of UML Activity Diagrams for Workflow Modelling. PhD thesis, University of Twente (2002)
8. Narayanan, S., McIlraith, S.: Simulation, Verification and Automated Composition of Web Services. In: Proceedings of the Eleventh International World Wide Web Conference, Budapest, Hungary (2002)
9. Holzmann, G.J.: The Spin model checker. Addison-Wesley (2003)
10. Clarke, E.M., Grumberg, O., Peled, D.A.: Model Checking. MIT Press (1999)
11. Fisteus, J.A., Marin, A., Delgado, C.: VERBUS: A Formal Model for Business Process Verification. In: Proceedings of the 2004 IRMA International Conference, New Orleans, USA (2004)

Seamless Federation of Heterogeneous Service Registries

Thomi Pilioura[1], Georgios-Dimitrios Kapos[2], and Aphrodite Tsalgatidou[1]

[1] University of Athens, Dept. of Informatics and Telecommunications
TYPA Buildings, Panepistimioupolis
Ilisia, 157 84, Athens, Greece
{thomi,atsalga}@di.uoa.gr
[2] Harokopio University of Athens, NOC
70, El. Venizelou Str, 176 71, Athens, Greece
gdkapos@hua.gr

Abstract. Web service technology extends the existing web infrastructure by transforming it from a repository of documents to a source of services. As the number of web services increases, the provision of the appropriate service publication and discovery framework is of paramount importance for exploiting the full potential of the web service technology. This paper presents the principles, the functionality and the design of PYRAMID-S, a scalable framework for unified publication and discovery of semantically enhanced services scattered around heterogeneous Registries. It uses a hybrid peer-to-peer topology to organize Registries based on domains. In such a topology, each Registry retains its autonomy, meaning that it can use the publication and discovery mechanisms as well as the ontology of its choice. Furthermore, the discovery of services is based on QoS characteristics in order to enable service selection.

1 Introduction

Web service (WS) technology is a collection of emerging standards, tools and platforms that extend the existing web infrastructure to a business-oriented, transactional platform, where multiple web services may interoperate to provide information, transact business and generally take action for users or agents, dynamically and on demand. Web services may be published in various registries with incompatible publishing and discovery mechanisms (e.g. UDDI Registries [12], DAML-S Registries [7][8], ebXML Registries [5]) resulting in cumbersome service publication and discovery. This situation is being aggravated by the increasing number of services. Therefore, the location and selection of suitable services becomes a critical issue and the provision of the appropriate service publication and discovery framework is of paramount importance for exploiting the full potential of the web service technology.

At present, the most prevalent standard for WS publication and discovery is the UDDI [12] specification. However, the effectiveness of UDDI is limited due to a number of shortcomings that are related to the following issues:

Service Description and Matchmaking: UDDI is mainly used in combination with WSDL [11]. WSDL is an XML grammar for specifying the syntactic aspects of a web service such as what it does, where it is located and how it is invoked. The only semantic information about services is provided by using the various standard UDDI taxonomies (related industry, products or services offered and geographical region). However, this semantic information cannot be used for inferring relationships during

K. Bauknecht, M. Bichler, and B. Pröll (Eds.): EC-Web 2004, LNCS 3182, pp. 86–95, 2004.

searching; this is due to the fact that the UDDI search services are limited to keyword search on certain fields such as name, identifier or taxonomy. Furthermore, the current UDDI model limits the discovery of a service to functional requirements and thus it cannot address questions related to non-functional requirements such as: "will the web service meet my performance requirements such as 2 ms response time?"

Scalability: UDDI partially addresses the scalability issue through the use of multiple replicated nodes in the same UDDI registry. Apart from fault tolerance, the use of multiple nodes decreases the number of publication/discovery requests per node. However, this scheme does not reduce the number of entries per node, thus resulting in limited scalability and high cost for the operators of the UDDI nodes. UDDI Version 3 introduces the notion of multiple registries that may share data among themselves with the knowledge that keys (unique identifiers of each entity within a registry) remain unique. In this way, entities in a private registry, for instance, can now be copied into another private registry for broader exposure or into a public registry, for public consumption. However, this entails the following disadvantages: (a) further increase of the number of service entries in each registry and (b) further communication overhead for keeping consistent all copies of the shared entities.

In this paper we propose a framework (PYRAMID-S hereinafter), which addresses the above limitations and in addition it supports *seamless federation of heterogeneous registries*. PYRAMID-S could be considered as an improvement to UDDI and as a contribution to the ongoing evolution of web service technology. The rest of the paper is organized as follows: Section 2 gives an overview of PYRAMID-S, while Section 3 describes the PYRAMID-S functionality and design. Finally, we conclude with a discussion section.

2 Overview of PYRAMID-S

PYRAMID-S is a framework that addresses the existence of heterogeneous service description and discovery mechanisms as well as the lack of semantics and the scalability issue of UDDI. The lack of semantics is tackled by using a number of ontologies which are presented in the following section. The heterogeneity and scalability issue are addressed by the adoption of a layered architecture presented in section 2.2.

2.1 PYRAMID-S Ontologies

In PYRAMID-S we address the challenge of semantics by using four different types of ontologies: the Standard Domain Ontology (SDO), the Registry Domain Ontology (RDO), the Domain Classification Ontology (DCO) and the QoS Ontology.

Standard Domain Ontology (SDO): This ontology reflects abstract concepts and relationships in a particular application domain. It has two parts: the *Operation* part and the *Data* part. The *Operation* part models major action types and thus helps to determine the type of operations that each web service performs. For example the *Operation* part of an SDO for the Loans Services domain may include concepts such as CreditScoreCalculation and CreditProfileCheck. The *Data* part incorporates concepts, their properties, and relations among concepts in a particular application domain. For example an SDO for the Loans Services domain (gray part of Fig. 1) may include concepts such as Loan, Bank, LoanAmount, ServiceFee and InterestRate. The SDO of a specific domain is the default ontology of the PYRAMID-S framework for that domain. The Registries conforming to that SDO use this ontology for the semantic publication and querying of the web services they hold.

Registry Domain Ontology (RDO): Registries may either adopt the SDO or use their own domain ontology (RDO). In the second case the Registry operator has to provide a *mapping* from its own ontology to the SDO. *Ontology Mapping* is the alignment of entities (concepts, attributes, relations etc.) in one ontology with those of another ontology, so as to capture shared meaning (Fig. 1). The necessity of having RDOs and the mapping from RDO to SDO stems from the fact that no global enforcement on the use of ontologies is possible in highly autonomous environments.

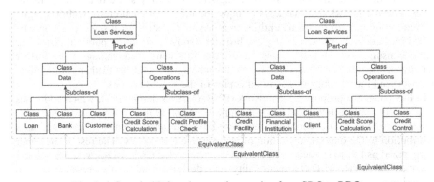

Fig. 1. A Sample SDO and a sample mapping from SDO to RDO.

Domain Classification Ontology (DCO): It maintains relationships among domains and mappings of each Registry of the PYRAMID-S to one or more domains. In addition, it stores properties of Registries, such as the access URL, the Registry provider details, the access URL of the RDO and the mapping from RDO to SDO (in case of non-conformance to SDO), as well as the constraints in accessing that Registry. It also stores the relationships between domains and SDOs. Fig. 2 shows a sample DCO in the form of a tree. Information regarding the Registries in a DCO may be expressed as a set of tuples $T_i = <R_i, D_i, A_i>$, where R_i is the access URL of a Registry, D_i is a domain, and A_i are the properties of the Registry. The tuples are identified by the combination of R_i and D_i, since a Registry may be mapped to more than one domains. This means that for any x, y $(T_x \neq T_y \Rightarrow R_x \neq R_y \vee D_x \neq D_y)$. Information regarding the domains in the DCO may be expressed as a set of tuples $V_i = <D_i, SDO_i>$.

QoS Ontology: Based on previous studies [9][10] and our experience in the WS area, we have constructed a QoS ontology composed of the following dimensions: response time, cost, availability and security. This ontology is used in combination with SDO for the semantic publication and querying of web services.

2.2 The PYRAMID-S Layered Architecture

One of the main goals of our work is to provide a scalable framework for seamless federation of heterogeneous registries. Scalability can be attained by distributing services in domain specific Registries. This enables more pertinent service discovery as the selection of a domain Registry works as a first filter in the discovery process. For example, if a Registry is related to the "Loan Services" and "Insurance Services" domains, it will maintain web services specific to those domains and queries for such type of services can be routed to it. The seamless federation can be achieved by adding a layer of unification over the heterogeneous registries.

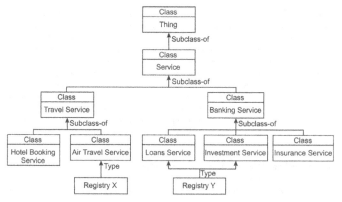

Fig. 2. A Sample DCO.

On the basis of the above considerations we propose a framework, which consists of three layers depicted in the right part of Fig. 3. The bottom layer, i.e. the Registries Layer, already exists while the two other layers (in gray background), namely the Gateways and the Routers Layer, are introduced by us in order to achieve our goal.

The *Registries Layer* consists of a number of Registries provided by diverse Registry operators. Each Registry retains its autonomy and the two other layers of PYRAMID-S act as a meta-Registry that controls and supports access to the Registries. PYRAMID-S accommodates any kind of web service Registry such as DAML-S [7][8] based Registries, UDDI Registries and ebXML Registries [5].

The *Gateways Layer* consists of a number of servers that are known a priori to the clients. The servers of this layer function as entry points to the PYRAMID-S system and provide to the users a single unified view over heterogeneous Registries.

The *Routers Layer* consists of a number of servers that provide routing service to the Gateways in order to forward the queries/advertisements entered in the Gateways to the appropriate domain Registries.

PYRAMID-S is based on a peer-to-peer network, which provides the infrastructure for the distributed nodes of PYRAMID-S to communicate with each other. The peer-to-peer topology renders PYRAMID-S scalable as it allows Routers to easily advertise and unadvertise themselves to the Gateways. More importantly, this topology ensures that there is not a single point of failure in the Routers layer.

Each node, depending on the layer it belongs, plays a particular role in the peer-to-peer network. Each peer of the Routers Layer plays a role similar to that of an index server in a semi-centralized peer-to-peer network where the peers communicate with the index server in order to obtain a reference to the data/processing that is available on the network. This implies a hybrid peer-to-peer network. In the following, we present in detail the functionalities provided by each layer of PYRAMID-S framework.

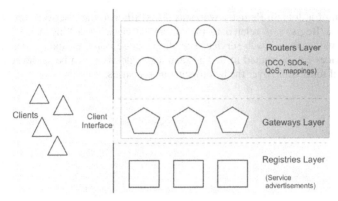

Fig. 3. The PYRAMID-S Architecture.

3 Detailed Description of PYRAMID-S

3.1 PYRAMID-S Functionality

Gateways Layer. As mentioned before the peers of this layer function as entry points to the PYRAMID-S framework. User actions are directed to any peer of this layer, which then, depending on the user action, interacts with either a Router peer or both a Router peer and one or more Registry peers and returns a reply. User actions may vary from service queries or advertisements to modifications of the DCO, depending on the role of the user. PYRAMID-S distinguishes three different types of users:

- Simple users, who publish and discover web services
- Registry operators, who, in addition to publishing and discovering web services, can add/remove Registries from PYRAMID-S and update Registry information
- Domain administrators, who can update the DCO and the SDOs, besides publishing and discovering web services

Browsing and searching through the DCO and SDOs is available to all types of users and greatly facilitates most of their actions presented in the following paragraphs.

Service Publication. When a user wishes to register a service in PYRAMID-S, s/he searches for the desirable Registries using the appropriate interface provided by the Gateways. The Registries can be found using various criteria, such as the Registry Provider, the Domain or combination of them. Then s/he selects the desired Registries from a list of Registries conforming to her/his criteria. The Gateway provides the user an interface for entering the Service Advertisement (SA), the structure of which is described later. The SA is then converted to a form understandable by each Registry and is forwarded to it. Finally, the user is informed about the result of his/her request.

When users publish a service they provide the WSDL document describing it (we assume that all types of Registries use the WSDL as a basis for service description, as it is the most widely accepted standard) and semantically annotate each operation and its I/O parameters with the corresponding concepts found in the SDO. These semantic annotations accompanied with the QoS metrics and the service provider information constitute the Semantic Service Description (SSD). Thus, the Service Advertisement

(SA) consists of two parts, the SSD and the WSDL document, where SSD = <SP, OPs, Is, Os, QoS> (SP: service provider information, OPs: set of service operations specified using concepts found in the Operation part of the SDO, Is/Os: set of input/output parameters specified using concepts found in the Data part of the SDO, QoS: quality of service metrics).

Service Discovery. Service discovery is based on a Service Query (SQ) that specifies the requirements about a service to discover: SQ = <SN, SD, SP, OP, Is, Os, QoS>, (SN: service name, SD: service textual description, SP: service provider information, OP: requested operation specified using concepts found in the Operation part of the SDO, Is/Os: set of input/output parameters of the requested operation specified using concepts found in the Data part of the SDO, QoS: quality of service metrics).

Service discovery may be performed either on a specific Registry or on all the Registries of a specific domain. This is accomplished through an appropriate user interface, provided by the Gateway Layer, which enables the service requestor to specify the SQ describing his/her needs. The SQ is built by using concepts of the SDO that the Gateway peer retrieves from a Router. The service requestor may also specify relative weights corresponding to the QoS characteristics. The SQ is submitted to the selected Registries after it has been properly translated. Each Registry uses its own matchmaking algorithms. The results of the Registries are returned to the Gateway which consolidates and ranks the results based on the user's predefined weights.

Registry Management. Registry operators may use the respective interface provided by a Gateway in order to insert/update or delete a Registry and its associated properties in the PYRAMID-S system. The DCO is presented to the Registry operator in order to associate his/her Registry to the appropriate domain. The user input is translated into one of the following operations on the DCO:

- Insert(T_x): Registry R_x is stated to be related to domain D_x and to provide its services with A_x properties (T_x=<R_x, D_x, A_x>). This operation is valid only if there is no $T_y \in$ DCO: $R_y = R_x \wedge D_y = D_x$. After the completion of the operation, DCO is DCO+$\{T_x\}$.

- Delete(T_x): Registry R_x is no longer related to domain D_x. This operation is valid only if $T_x \in$ DCO. After the completion of the operation DCO is DCO−$\{T_x\}$.

- Update(T_x,A_x'): The properties of Registry R_x for domain D_x are updated to A_x'. This operation is valid only if $T_x \in$ DCO. After the completion of the operation DCO is DCO−$\{T_x\}$+$\{(R_x,D_x, A_x')\}$.

If a mapping from RDO to SDO is needed, the registry operator provides it by using the appropriate Gateway interface. In this interface, the RDO and SDO are retrieved from a Router and represented as taxonomy of concepts in a tree structure.

Domain Administration. Domain administrators may update the DCO with the addition of new domains or renaming of existing ones. Also, new SDOs may be created and existing ones may be modified with the addition of new concepts. Domain deletion in the DCO and concept renaming or deletion in the SDOs are not allowed, as they would introduce inconsistency regarding registered Registries and services.

Routers Layer. This layer consists of a number of peers, each holding a copy of the DCO, SDOs, RDO to SDO mappings, as well as a copy of the QoS ontology.

Through the use of the DCO, the Routers provide routing service to the Gateways in order to forward the queries/advertisements entered in the Gateways to the appropriate domain Registries. The peers of this layer ensure high availability, protection and consistency of the routing information, which is information regarding Registries and their mapping to domains. If any Router is disconnected from the network, the routing service is not affected unless this peer is the last Router of the peer network.

Registries Layer. This layer consists of a number of Registries that may be heterogeneous due to different choices at the physical level (different DBMSs), logical level (different data models) and conceptual level (different ontologies). The peers of this layer are responsible for getting the service advertisement (SA) or the service request (SQ) from the Gateway and for performing the necessary actions.

3.2 PYRAMID-S Design

In this subsection we present the design of PYRAMID-S Gateways and Routers and describe how the aforementioned functionality is offered. We do not present the design of Registries since they are autonomous entities participating in PYRAMID-S.

Gateway Design. There are two ways of accessing PYRAMID-S: through a Web Server GUI or through a web service (WS interface). Each Gateway peer provides both interfaces (Fig. 4). By using the Web Server GUI end-users may perform service queries/publications or administration tasks. The Web Server GUI interacts with the WS interface of a Gateway peer, through which the overall functionality of PYRAMID-S becomes available.

Actions requested by end users are translated into the appropriate SOAP messages, which are sent to the WS interface of a Gateway. The Web Server GUI is enhanced with additional facilities, such as visual navigation of the DCO and SDOs and automatic generation of GUIs for web service invocation. Furthermore, the Gateway WS interface is publicly available and may be accessed by other client applications.

A Gateway peer is a composite web service utilizing four constituent web services, namely the *Ontology Accessor*, the *Mediator*, the *Publisher* and the *Finder*. Fig. 4 depicts the interdependencies among these services, as well as external communications.

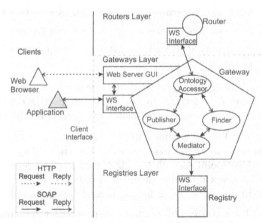

Fig. 4. Detailed design view of PYRAMID-S.

The *Ontology Accessor* communicates with Router peers in order to create, retrieve or update the DCO and SDOs.

The *Mediator* is a utility service that transforms service queries/advertisements from PYRAMID-S representations to Registry specific representations. Service discovery results, deriving from Registries, are also transformed reversely. Implementation of the transformation operations depends on syntactic and semantic conventions used by the Registry, as well as the support for QoS characteristics. Therefore, a distinct Mediator service is needed for every type of Registry incorporated in PYRAMID-S, which may result in having more than one Mediators in each Gateway.

The *Publisher* performs a service publication given the Service Advertisement, the domain(s) where the service is to be published and optionally a set of selected Registry peers for the publication. If no Registries are specified, the most appropriate ones are located by the Publisher through the DCO (provided by the Ontology Accessor) and used. The appropriate Mediators are then used for translating the service advertisement to Registry interpretable forms.

In a similar manner, the *Finder* accepts Service Queries, the domain(s) to search for the service and optionally a set of selected Registry peers for the discovery. If this optional parameter is omitted, the Finder uses the DCO (retrieved by the Ontology Accessor) to locate the Registries that belong to the specified domain(s). Discovery requests are sent to the selected Registries, after the necessary transformations performed by Mediators. Discovery results are reversely transformed by the Mediators and forwarded to the Finder which ranks them according to the weighted value of their QoS characteristics, according to user preferences.

Router Design. Each Router has a web service interface that allows building, retrieving and updating the DCO and SDOs. Insertions, deletions and updates of the DCO (actions hereinafter) may be performed by any Router (upon request by a Gateway) and are propagated to all other Routers. Therefore consistency of the DCO should be assured during conflicting operations, performed by the same or distinct Routers within a short time-frame (i.e. the time needed for an operation to be propagated to the whole peer group). There are two cases of having conflicting operations:

- when two or more Routers attempt to rename the same domain of the DCO
- when insertions, deletions and updates are performed on the same couple of Rx and Dx, i.e. on the same Tx

Our conflict resolution mechanism uses a request/reply/notify scheme incorporated by the Routers, as described in [14]. This may be seen as a distributed lock management scheme, where each requesting Router requests permission, by the Routers peer group, to perform an operation on a specific part of the DCO. In case of a conflict, the resolution mechanism allows at most one Router to proceed with its requested operation.

4   Discussion

In this paper we have presented PYRAMID-S, a framework that enables seamless federation of heterogeneous Registries. More specifically, PYRAMID-S entails the following advantages:

- It is an open platform as it integrates various types of WS Registries achieving thereby better interoperation without affecting their specifications and autonomy.
- The introduction of Gateways as an entry point to PYRAMID-S abstracts the interface of heterogeneous Registries into a single unified view. Thus, users are alleviated from the burden of handling the diversion between various technologies since they can uniformly publish or discover web services.
- The use of syntactic, semantic as well as QoS information about a service enables higher recall, improved precision and better result ranking.
- The accommodation of a great number of Registries, Routers and Gateways solves the scalability problem. Registry categorization according to DCO helps in narrowing the search context and improves performance. Besides, in PYRAMID-S the exposure of private Registries to public consumption is much simpler in comparison to the copying mechanism proposed in UDDI version 3. Overall system performance may be tuned by adapting the number of Routers and according to business requirements.
- The service-oriented design and implementation of PYRAMID-S allows the use of its modules for building other applications.

The most relevant work to ours is the METEOR-S system [6]. It uses an ontology-based approach to organize Registries, enabling domain based semantic classification of WS. The main differences between the two approaches are the following: (a) although both approaches use a peer-to-peer architecture, in PYRAMID-S we exclude the clients from the peer-to-peer network. The advantage of this is that we do not require service requestors and providers to download and install any software; this results in zero deployment and maintenance cost, (b) whereas in METEOR-S approach the client selects the domain ontology it prefers and sends the advertisement or query to a single Registry, our system supports publication and discovery across multiple Registries thanks to the use of RDOs and mediators, (c) whereas in METEOR-S the editing of the domain classification and registry information is performed only in a single peer resulting in a single point of failure, in PYRAMID-S we allow editing in a number of peers making provision for data consistency.

A prototype implementation of PYRAMID-S is under way. After the completion and the performance analysis of the current implementation, we are considering extending PYRAMID-S functionality to support service composition whenever no direct matches are available to fulfill a request. Furthermore, we plan to use Content Distribution Networks (CDN) [13] to improve load balancing and performance in the Gateways layer of PYRAMID-S.

References

1. DAML-S 0.9. http://www.daml.org/services/DAML-S/0.9/
2. DAML+OIL. http://www.daml.org/2001/03/daml+oil-index.html
3. DAML Services Coalition: DAML-S: Web Service Description for the Semantic Web. Proceedings of The First International Semantic Web Conference (ISWC), Sardinia (Italy), June, 2002
4. DAML Services Coalition: DAML-S: Semantic Markup for Web Services. Proceedings of the International Semantic Web Working Symposium (SWWS), July 30-August 1, 2001
5. ebXML Registry. http://www.oasis-open.org/committees/tc_home.php?wg_abbrev=regrep

6. Verma, K., Sivashanmugam, K., Sheth, A., Patil, A., Oundhakar, S. and Miller, J.: METEOR–S WSDI: A Scalable Infrastructure of Registries for Semantic Publication and Discovery of Web Services. Journal of Information Technology and Management (to appear)
7. Paolucci, M. and Kawamura, T. and Payne, T.R. and Sycara, K.: Importing the Semantic Web in UDDI. Proceedings of Web Services, E-Business and Semantic Web Workshop, CaiSE 2002., pages 225-236, Toronto, Canada
8. Paolucci, M., Kawamura, T., Payne, T.R., Sycara, K.: Semantic Matching of Web Services Capabilities. Proceedings of the 1st International Semantic Web Conference (ISWC), 2002
9. Cardoso J., Miller J., Sheth A. and Arnold J.: Modeling Quality of Service for Workflows and Web Service Processes. Technical Report UGA-CS-TR-02-002, LSDIS Lab, Computer Science Department, University of Georgia
10. Sheth A., Cardoso J., Miller J., Kochut K. and Kang M.: QoS for Service-Oriented Middleware. Proceedings of 6th World Multiconference on Systemics, Cybernetics and Informatics, Proceedings Vol. 8, Orlando, July 14-18, 2002, pp. 528-534
11. Web Services Description Language. http://www.w3.org/TR/2002/WD-wsdl12-20020709/
12. Universal Description, Discovery and Integration. http://www.uddi.org
13. Rabinovich, M. and Spatsheck, O.: Web Caching and Replication , Addison-Wesley 2001
14. Pilioura, T., Kapos, and G.-D., Tsalgatidou, A.: PYRAMID-S: A Scalable Infrastructure for Semantic Web Service Publication and Discovery. Proceedings of RIDE 2004, Boston, March 2004

A Survey of Public Web Services

Su Myeon Kim[1] and Marcel-Catalin Rosu[2]

[1] KAIST. EECS Dept. Yusung-Gu Gusung-dong 373-1,
Taejon, Korea
smkim@nclab.kaist.ac.kr
[2] IBM T.J. Watson Research Center 19 Skyline Drive,
NY, USA
rosu@us.ibm.com

Abstract. Enterprise IT infrastructures and their interfaces are migrating toward a service-oriented architecture, using Web Services (WS) as a de-facto implementation protocol. As a result, WS-generated traffic is expected to have a considerable impact on the Internet. Despite the high amount of interest in WS, there have been few studies regarding their characteristics. In this survey, we analyze publicly-accessible WS over a 9 month period. We study the evolution and distributions of the WS population, and message characteristics and response times of each WS. We also closely analyze two popular WS sites: Amazon and Google. Some of our initial results contradict common intuition. The number of public WS has not increased dramatically, although there are signs which indicate intensive ongoing activities in the WS domain. The geographic distribution of public WS is largely skewed. Most importantly, the sizes of WS responses and their variation are smaller than those of the existing Web objects.

1 Introduction

Enterprise IT infrastructures are currently migrating toward a service-oriented architecture, using Web Services (WS) as a de-facto implementation protocol. By supporting service-oriented and component-based application architectures, WS provide a distributed computing technology for revealing the business services of applications on the Intranet as well as on the Internet using open and standard-based XML protocols and formats. The use of standard XML-based protocols makes WS platform-, language-, and vendor-independent, and so an ideal protocol for a service-oriented architecture. In spite of the wide acceptance of WS in computing infrastructures, there have been few studies on WS characteristics.

In this paper, we analyze public WS in various ways, retrieving all the WS entries of a UDDI [1] Business Registry (UBR). It should be noted here that we believe most of publicly available WS information are found in the UBR since it is proposed as a global registry for every type of business services. First, we study the evolution of the WS population and its distribution by domain and geographic location. Second, we develop a methodology for estimating WS message sizes. Towards this goal, we determine the distributions of several WS characteristics, such as message styles, and usage of complex and elementary types. Third, we examine the liveness and response times of the available public WS. Lastly, using our methodology, we analyze the WS of two popular sites - Amazon and Google – and compare the message sizes predicted by our methodology with the message sizes observed during interactions with the two sites.

K. Bauknecht, M. Bichler, and B. Pröll (Eds.): EC-Web 2004, LNCS 3182, pp. 96–105, 2004.
© Springer-Verlag Berlin Heidelberg 2004

Our initial results contradict common intuition. First, the number of public WS has not increased dramatically, although there are certain signs which indicate that many intensive activities are ongoing in the WS domain. Second, the geographic distribution of public WS is largely skewed with about three fifths of public WS located in US. Third, response and request message sizes are comparable, and WS response messages are smaller than existing Web objects. We expect these results to benefit WS applications and tools developers. This survey is part of an ongoing research and upcoming analysis results will be published on our web site [2].

The remainder of this paper is organized as follows. Section 2 describes our methodology for data collection and for estimation of WS message sizes, and the results of our analysis and experiments. Section 3 applies the techniques previously developed to the Amazon and Google WS. Section 4 is a brief overview of the related work. Section 5 is dedicated to conclusion and future work.

2   Data Collection and Analysis

The analysis in this section is based on the data that we collected weekly, between 8 Aug. 2003 and 7 May. 2004, from a UBR. Only a fraction of the retrieved UBR entries are relevant to Web Services, i.e., include a reference to a Web Services Description Language (WSDL) file.

2.1   Population and Geographic Distribution

Currently, about 1200 WS are registered in a UBR. Fig. 1 summarizes the data collected during the 9 month period. The number of 'valid' WS – WSDL file is retrievable - is substantially smaller than the total number of WS: approximately 67% of the WS are not valid, which is similar to the findings of a previous UDDI integrity study [6]. Furthermore, many of the downloaded WSDL files are incomplete. The most common errors are syntax errors and omission of mandatory elements. During the 9 month interval, the number of valid WS decreases a little, which is contrary to the slight increase in the number of WSDL files published. Note that there is a small but noticeable decrease in the number of valid WS on 10 Oct. 2003 due to a server hosting 54 web services becoming unavailable[1]. Finally, we found that very few organizations update their WSDL files after publication.

The distributions of valid WS by top level domain and geographic location on 7 Nov. 2003 are shown in Fig. 2 (a) and (b), respectively. As shown in the figure, 49% of WS is hosted by the .com domain and 63% of the WS are hosted in the United States. Our further analysis of the distribution of WS hosting sites shows that the portion of sites hosted by the .net domain, and in US shrink in Fig. 2 (a) and (b), respectively. From this fact, we infer that a larger number of WS is hosted by the same .net domain and/or US-resident sites.

---

[1] Microsoft's .Net WS contest server (http://www.contest.eraserver.net) hosts Web Services which receive Microsoft's Best of the .NET Awards.

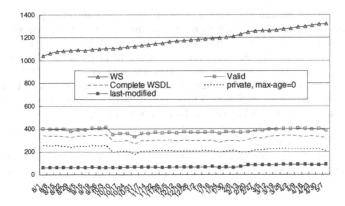

Fig. 1. Web Services in UBR.

Fig. 2. The Distribution of valid WS by (a) top level domain, (b) geographic location.

2.2 Styles and Structures

By design, a WSDL file includes a comprehensive description of the associated WS. WSDL file analysis, thus, exposes many of the WS characteristics, such as encoding type, message style, and number of operations for each WS. In Section 2.3, we use this information to estimate the size of WS request and response messages.

By inspecting the collected WSDL files, we found that there are many more document-style WS than RPC-style WS; the argument about which style is better is still an ongoing debate. Among the 294 valid WSDL files collected on 7 Nov. 2003, 70% define document-style WS and 30% define RPC-style WS. All of the document-style WS adopt the literal encoding and all of the RPC-style WS adopt the soap encoding. HTTPS is used by only 4% of these services, while the others use HTTP. 89% of WS have less than 10 operations. Lastly, more than 78% of the WSDL files were generated with the Microsoft toolkit.

We also analyze the WSDL files to determine the frequency of elementary, array, and compound types in WS messages. We found that responses use more arrays and compound variables than requests do. Fig. 3 shows the distribution of elementary types, with array and compound types expanded into elementary types. As most WS definitions do not specify array lengths, we had to select lengths for these arrays. The figure shows type distributions for array lengths 2 and 16. The results show that the string and string array types are very common.

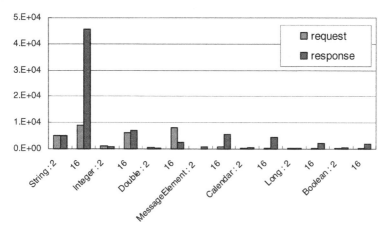

Fig. 3. Frequency of Elementary Types.

2.3 SOAP Message Size

Characterizing the size of SOAP messages [3] is important since WS traffic is expected to become a prevailing traffic on the Internet. In this section, we first describe how we estimate SOAP message sizes using the information in the WSDL files. Then, we explain some meaningful characteristics of the SOAP message sizes.

A SOAP message can be divided into four parts – HTTP header, essential tag, namespaces, and payload. Below is the formula used to estimate the size of a SOAP message:

SOAP message size = HTTP header + essential tag (SOAP envelope tag + SOAP body tag) + namespaces + payload (payload tag + summation of (type tag + XML representation of the type) for each elementary type field in parameters)

In this equation, 'essential tag' represents the SOAP envelope and body tags, and 'namespaces' represents the aggregation of all occurrences of namespace attributes in a message. The namespace attribute can occur in the SOAP envelope tag, SOAP body tag, payload tag, etc. The 'payload' consists of parameters and the payload tag.

We determine the size of each message component by examining real SOAP messages. We investigate messages of several WS, including Amazon and Google WS (see Section 3). We observe that there are small variations in HTTP header and essential tag and that most messages use 5 ~ 7 namespaces. Four of these namespaces - SOAP envelope, XML schema, XML instance and encoding style - are present in most SOAP messages.

In order to determine the payload size, we use the following methodology. First, we determine the size of the payload and type tags. The payload tag is used to wrap up a list of parameters (RPC-style) or a XML tree (document-style) and its size has a small variation. The type tag is used to declare the parameter names and types, and its size has a small variation, as well. Second, we estimate the number of elementary type fields as shown in Section 2.2. Lastly, we determine the average size of the XML representations for the fields of each elementary type. For most numeric types, we assume the sizes to be as small as realistically possible. Thus, the resulting message size estimate is a practical lower-bound. Detailed description on average size determination is omitted due to the space limitation. Note that string is the most frequently used type and its size is highly variable. Therefore, we assume that the lengths of the string type fields are distributed uniformly between a minimum and a maximum range. Similarly, we selected a small value for the lengths of arrays.

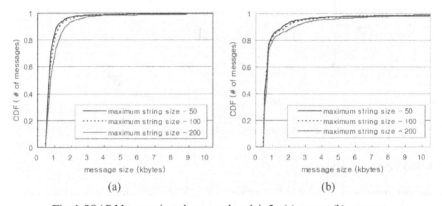

Fig. 4. SOAP Message size when array length is 2 - (a) request (b) response.

Fig. 4 (a) and (b) shows the CDFs of WS request and response message sizes, respectively; the minimum string size is always 5, the maximum string size is 50, 100, 200 characters, and array length is 2. Even when maximum string size is 200, 93% of request messages are smaller than 2KB. In contrast, most HTTP requests are known to be smaller than 500bytes [7]. Fig. 4 (b) shows that 88% of response messages are smaller than 2KB, even when the maximum string size is 200. String size has little impact on small messages, as these messages use few parameters.

We also investigate the sensitivity of the message size distribution varying the selected array length. (The results are not reported here due to space limitation.) The results show very little variation in the message size distributions, especially when the message size is small. This suggests that a small number of WS use a large number of arrays.

Lastly, we compare the distributions of SOAP messages to that of existing Web content. For Web content, we use the model presented in [8], which screens out the population factor of unique files; this approach is compatible with our analysis of WS message sizes. Contrary to the common expectation that SOAP messages are larger than existing Web objects due to XML formatting, most SOAP messages are smaller (see Fig. 5 (a)). For instance, while 92% of SOAP messages are smaller than 2KB, only 45% of the existing Web objects are smaller than 2KB.

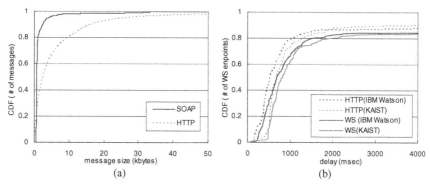

Fig. 5. (a) SOAP message vs. Web objects: array length is 2 and the maximum string size is 200 characters, (b) WS and HTTP response delay.

2.4   Liveness and Invocation Delay

The server providing the WSDL file is typically unrelated to the server hosting the WS. Therefore the liveness of the WS has to be verified directly. We wrote a small program called Web Services Ping (WSPing), which accesses the endpoints specified in the WSDL files using http/https.

```
<?xml version="1.0" encoding="UTF-8"?>
<soapenv:Envelope xmlns:soapenv="http://schemas.xmlsoap.org/soap/envelope/"
xmlns:xsd="http://www.w3.org/2001/XMLSchema"
xmlns:xsi="http://www.w3.org/2001/XMLSchema-instance">
  <soapenv:Body>
   <Request soapenv:encodingStyle="http://schemas.xmlsoap.org/soap/encoding/">
     <dummy xsi:type="xsd:string"> This request is sent for an academic research purpose. Please send
an e-mail to smkim@nclab.kaist.ac.kr if any problem. Thanks </dummy>
   <Request>
   </soapenv:Body>
  </soapenv:Envelope>
```

Fig. 6. WS probing message.

WSPing sends a simple SOAP message which has a valid HTTP header and a SOAP envelope. The message is shown in Fig. 6. It has only one field which is a message to indicate that it is not a malicious attack along with our e-mail address. Since the message does not conform to the expected message format, the response is a SOAP fault: the server cannot understand our request message. If the response conforms to a valid SOAP fault message format, the WS is considered alive.

Our weekly experiments show that approximately 16% of the valid WS are down and that 96% of the live WS respond in two seconds or less. Fig. 5 (b) shows the CDF of response times for WS as well as Web servers, as measured on 13 Nov. 2003; measurements performed on other dates show similar results. When probed from IBM Watson in US and KAIST in Korea, about 85% of WS servers are alive, and about 2~3% more Web servers are alive. Our attempts to measure ping delays do not show any meaningful results, as most sites block ICMP ping messages.

3   Case Studies

Using the proposed methodology, we closely analyze two popular WS: Amazon and Google. Both WS offer the same functionality as their Web sites.

3.1   Amazon

Amazon provides their WS for associates, suppliers, or developers. The 'associates' program is a business model enabling 3rd party web site operators to link their web sites to Amazon and earn referral fees for the sales made through their links. Amazon actively supports their WS: version 1.0 was released in July 2002 with basic shopping capabilities; version 2.0 was released in October 2002; lastly, version 3.0 was released in April 2003 with an expanded API for 3rd party suppliers and shopping cart handling. In addition to the main US Amazon site, the WS API is supported for the Amazon sites in UK, Japan, and Germany. The WS Toolkit, including examples, can be downloaded from the Amazon WS home [4].

The main Amazon WS site is located in US and it is operated by Amazon itself, i.e., not outsourced. Their WS operations use only string types: 279 elementary strings, 778 one-dimensional, 702 two-dimensional, and 40 three-dimensional string arrays. Most of these strings and string arrays are used in response messages, as only 179 elementary strings and 9 string arrays are used in request messages.

Amazon WS v3.0 API has 20 operations, shown in Fig. 7. We classify the operations according to their functionality into Product Browse operations and Shopping Cart operations. First-level operations are classified according to their response message type. These types are shown as ovals. Second-level operations are classified according to request message type. As a result, operations in the same leaf node have the same request and response message types. HTTP and WS response delays are 327 and 502msec when measured from IBM Watson, and 501 and 510msec from KAIST.

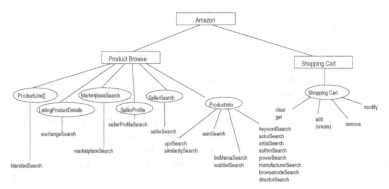

Fig. 7. Operation Tree of Amazon Web Services.

Fig. 8 (a) and (b) show the message sizes, both real and estimated, for requests and responses, respectively. We assume array length of 2 or 16. Note that browse operations have two kinds of responses: lite and heavy. A lite response delivers the summary of the selected items, while a heavy response delivers all the available information. The fixed size components are identical but the payload varies widely.

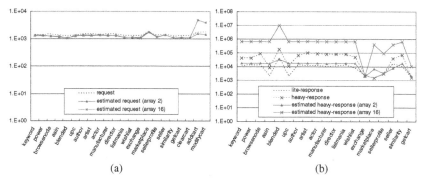

Fig. 8. Amazon WS Message Size (a) request (b) response.

Fig. 8 (a) shows that our estimation of request sizes is accurate, especially when the array length is 2. The only large gaps, when array length is 16, are due to the fact that the addcart and modifycart operations use string arrays. Fig. 8 (b) shows the response message sizes; estimations are less accurate. Note that only the sizes of heavy type messages are estimated. The pattern of lines is almost identical and the line for heavy-response is between estimated lines. To improve accuracy, application specific information is needed.

3.2 Google

Google provides a WS API to their Web search engine in order for developers to embed Google search functions into their programs [5]. The Google WS API was launched in April 2002 and is still at the beta version. The Google API has only three operations: doGetCachedPage, doSpellingSuggestion, and doGoogleSearch. These operations use 14 elementary strings, 11 one-dimensional string arrays, 5 Booleans, and 5 Integers. HTTP and WS response delays are 292 and 329msec when measured from IBM Watson, and 841 and 1046msec from KAIST.

Fig. 9 shows the message sizes of Google WS. We assume maximum string size of 50 characters and array length of 2 or 16. The figure shows that our estimation of message sizes is accurate except for the response message size of doGetCachedPage. In this case, as Google returns a cached Web page as a single parameter of byte[] type, array length should be much larger than 16.

4 Related Work

To the best of our knowledge, this is the first survey of public WS. Although there have been many studies on Web evolution [14,15] and Web site evaluation [16], they do not study WS sites.

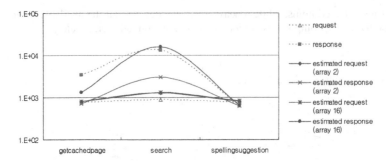

Fig. 9. Google WS message size.

Mapping and analysis of the Internet geography have been studied in detail [9]. These studies focus on the geographic location of Internet components such as end nodes and routers. Our investigation considers a geographic distribution of WS endpoints, not just IP-level internet nodes.

WS portals [10,11,12,13] provide information about useful WS, including category, rate, price, and service explanation. Most of this information targets WS consumers. We investigate the evolution, internal structures, and message characteristics to improve the understanding of WS technology.

5 Conclusion

In this survey, we study several aspects of public WS using the information that we collected weekly over the past 9 months from an UBR. First, we determine the WS population and its distributions. Second, we develop a methodology for estimating WS message sizes. Towards this goal, we determine the distributions of several WS characteristics, such as message styles, and usage of complex and elementary types. Third, we examine the liveness and response time of each WS. Lastly, using our methodology, we analyze the WS of two popular sites in detail.

Our initial results show that the number of public WS does not increase dramatically and that about three fifths of the current WS population is based in US. In addition, our results indicate that there are substantial differences between the sizes of request/response messages for public WS and current Web traffic. Lastly, string type is much more frequently used than the other types.

We expect these results to be beneficial in various ways. For instance, WS tool developers may optimize their products for the preferred message style and frequently used variable types in SOAP messages. In addition, the proposed message size estimation methodology helps WS server or network administrator to perform resource planning and configuration easily without analysis on actual usage log.

We plan to extend our survey by collecting more WSDL information from other sources. We also plan to refine our methodology for WSDL analysis as well as message size estimation. For instance, we plan to use the semantics of the WS operations to estimate string and arrays lengths. This survey on public WS is part of an ongoing project and upcoming analysis results will be published on our web site [2].

References

1. Universal Description, Discovery and Integration (UDDI),
   www.oasis-open.org/committees/uddi-spec/faq.php
2. http://nclab.kaist.ac.kr/~smkim/ws_survey/index.html
3. WSDL and SOAP specs at http://www.w3.org/2002/ws
4. http://www.amazon.com/webservices, Amazon web services home
5. http://www.google.com/apis/, Google web APIs home
6. Mike Clark, UDDI – The Weather Report (The outlook is missed),
   http://www.webservicesarchitect.com/content/articles/clark04.asp
7. Bruce A. Mah, An Empirical Model of HTTP Network Traffic, INFOCOM '97. Sixteenth
   Annual Joint Conference of the IEEE Computer and Communications Societies. Proceedings IEEE , Volume: 2 , 7-11 April 1997, Page(s): 592 -600 vol.2
8. Paul Barford and Azer Bestavros and Adam Bradley and Mark Crovella", Changes in Web
   Client Access Patterns: Characteristics and Caching Implications, special Issue on Characterization and Performance Evaluation, 1999
9. http://www.cybergeography.org/atlas/geographic.html, An atlas of cyberspaces
10. http://www.xmethods.net, Xmethods
11. http://www.salcentral.com/salnet/webserviceswsdl.asp, salcentral
12. http://www.remotemethods.com/, remotemethods
13. http://www.bindingpoint.com/, BindingPoint
14. Junghoo Cho and Hector Garcia-Molina, "The evolution of the web and implications for
   an incremental crawler", Proc. Of VLDB 2000, Cairo, Egypt
15. Dennis Fetterly, Mark Manasse, Mark Najork, and Janet Wiener, "A Large-Scale Study of
   the Evolution of Web Pages", Proc. of WWW 2003, May 20-24, Budapest, Hungary
16. Luis Olsina, Guillermo Lafuente, and Gustavo Rossi, "E-commerce Site Evaluation: a
   Case Study", Proc. of EC-Web 2000, Sep. 4-6, London, UK

Protocols for Electronic Negotiation Systems: Theoretical Foundations and Design Issues*

Gregory E. Kersten[1,2], Stefan E. Strecker[1], and Ka Pong Law[1]

[1] John Molson School of Business, Concordia University, Montreal
{gregory,strecker,kplaw}@jmsb.concordia.ca
[2] School of Management, University of Ottawa, Ottawa

Abstract. Existing electronic negotiation systems (ENSs) typically implement a single, fixed negotiation protocol, which restricts their use to negotiation problems that were anticipated and established a priori by the system's designers. The single-protocol restriction limits ENSs' applicability in experiments and in many real-life negotiation situations. ENSs that allow for the use of different protocols also allow for the customization to users' needs and abilities. We present theoretical foundations for the design of flexible and highly customizable protocol-driven ENSs.

1 Introduction

The term *e-negotiation systems* has been used to describe software that employs Internet technologies, is deployed on the World Wide Web, and capable of supporting, aiding or replacing one or more negotiators, mediators or facilitators [1]. A number of ENSs have been designed, implemented and applied to various negotiation problems. Some systems facilitate negotiation of documents and their joint preparation, e.g., contract negotiations [2], others use email, chat and streaming video software [3]. An overview of different ENSs can be found in Shim and Hsiao [4] and Neumann et al. [5].

With few exceptions - notably SilkRoad [6] and INSS [7] - existing ENSs implement only one fixed negotiation protocol [8]. This restricts the use of ENSs to types of problems and interactions that were assumed and established a priori by their designers. This, in turn, imposes limitation on the behavioural research of the ENSs' use and their efficiency and efficacy, on the ENSs' applicability to support evolving negotiations, and those conducted by users who have different needs, cognitive abilities, and cultural and professional backgrounds.

Ongoing behavioural research on ENS focuses on (i) technology adoption by negotiators, and (ii) the impact of different systems on the negotiation process and negotiated outcomes [9, 10]. Both research directions utilize experimental and empirical methodologies. From this perspective (in particular in experimental studies of ENSs' use and adoption), the assessment of the impact of different system features on the process and outcomes of negotiations requires the use of systems, whose differences and similarities can be easily controlled by the researcher. From a negotiator's point

---

* This work was supported with grants from the Initiative for New Economy of the Social Sciences and Humanities Research Council Canada, and the Natural Science and Engineering Research Council Canada.

K. Bauknecht, M. Bichler, and B. Pröll (Eds.): EC-Web 2004, LNCS 3182, pp. 106–115, 2004.

of view, the limitation to a single fixed protocol restricts the use of a particular ENS to the supported class of negotiation problems, which may not include their problem at hand. If, on the other hand, ENSs implement negotiation protocols, which apply to a large class of negotiation problems, i.e. are very general, they impose significant cognitive and informational demands on the users who need to make decisions about the selection of tools and features. Negotiators who use a system to negotiate need to concentrate on the problem and process, and make decision about the concessions rather than compare different tools and decide about system features. It is thus advantageous that: (1) a protocol be constructed for the negotiators based on their characteristics and the negotiation problem and context, or (2) the negotiators decide on a negotiation agenda, which sets a particular formal protocol.

The purpose of this paper is to present the theoretical foundations of negotiation protocols[1]. These protocols can be implemented in a software platform and then used for the construction of various ENSs. The remainder of this contribution is organized as follows. Section 2 briefly reviews vital elements of a negotiation methodology. Section 3 introduces the theoretical foundations of negotiation protocols and their properties, and Section 4 presents ongoing and future work.

2 Negotiation Methodology

Negotiation methodology describes the methods, procedures, and techniques used to collect and analyze information used in negotiation, the process of communication, exchange of offers and concessions, and arrival at an agreement or deadlock. It is important that these methods and techniques match the negotiator's capabilities, complement each other, do not produce contradictory information and – when used – contribute to the negotiation effectiveness.

2.1 Negotiation Process and Activities

The use of a methodology has been advocated by negotiation experts, but this advice is often neglected in unstructured negotiations (e.g. face-to-face or via e-mail). One of the important contributions of an ENS is to provide a methodology, which matches the negotiators' requirements and is appropriate to their problem. The use of a methodology in an ENS is also required for the tractability of the process and its ease of use.

For the purpose of this work, we consider only two key components of the negotiation methodology: (1) the *negotiation process model*, and (2) the *negotiation protocol*. The process model provides a framework for negotiations; it organizes the activities undertaken by negotiators by grouping them into negotiation phases and by assigning different activities to each phase. It serves as a starting point for the software design and draws its significance from imposing a methodologically sound approach to negotiators [12]. The protocol is a formal model, often represented by a set of rules, which govern software processing, decision-making and communication tasks, and imposes restrictions on activities through the specification of permissible inputs and actions [13, 14]. Negotiation protocols are further discussed in the next section. To our

---

[1] This paper is a revised and short version of Kersten, G.E., S. Strecker, and K.P. Law (2004). Protocols for Electronic Negotiation Systems: Theoretical Foundations and Design Issues, InterNeg Working Paper 06/04: Ottawa, Canada. 1-16.

knowledge, there are no behavioural studies on e-negotiations and, therefore, no process model specific to e-negotiation has been developed. For the purpose of designing and implementing an ENS, we use a five-phase model based on Gulliver's eight-phase model [15], which allows for the consideration of a wide range of negotiations, including those supported by ENSs. The five phases are planning, agenda setting, exchanging offers and arguments, reaching an agreement and concluding a negotiation. Each negotiation phase has its own purpose and set of activities, which are concrete actions undertaken by each negotiator. The purpose of the different negotiation phases is to provide the participants with a framework and rationale for activities conducted in each phase. The consideration of phases helps to specify negotiation activities undertaken and the relationships among them.

The negotiation process model provides a framework, but it does not impose any restrictions on the negotiators concerning the sequencing of phases. In any given phase, the negotiators may revisit previous phases and then return to initial phase. Moreover, it often occurs in real-life negotiation that negotiators skip or ignore one or more phases. Although negotiation experts suggest that all phases should be considered, we leave this issue to the protocol designer as there may be specific situation, in which one or more phases should be bypassed.

2.2 Negotiation Protocols and Activity Types

Any negotiation supported by an ENS requires that the software designers precisely define the activities and their sequence using a negotiation protocol [10, 13]. The negotiation protocol defines the activities that are permissible in every state of the negotiation, their sequence as well as input and output requirements. The key concepts used to define the activities and to specify their sequencing are presented in Figure 1.

Behavioural theory posits that activities depend on the negotiators' characteristics and the negotiation context (e.g. power distribution, and the relative importance of outcomes). These characteristics determine the negotiators' approaches, their strategies and tactics leading to the selection of specific activities from the negotiation phases. Behavioural research cannot provide sufficiently precise insights regarding sequencing of activities within each negotiation phase.

This is because of the number of possible combinations of the negotiator's characteristics, interdependencies between characteristics of the negotiators, dependence of the negotiators' behaviour on external factors (e.g. the relationship with other stakeholders), and the complexity of the problem and process. With the exception of well-defined and highly structured negotiations, such as those taking place in procurement of standardized goods, the negotiators cannot follow a strict set of rules defining the activity's sequence.

The above mentioned complexities introduce the requirement for providing the negotiators with some degrees of freedom in the selection of activities. During the process, the negotiators may wish to review the problem, modify their preferences, add or remove issues etc, which imposes the requirement of some activities to be optional and/or exchangeable for other activities. Also, the negotiators may be forced to undertake certain activities in order to move to the next activity. For example, they should learn about the negotiation problem, consider their own objectives and preferences and evaluate the counterpart's offer before making their own offers. To accommodate these requirements, we distinguish between *mandatory activities* and *optional activities* (see Figure 1).

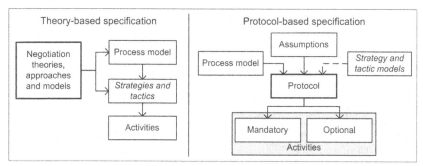

Fig. 1. Theory- and protocol-based activity specification.

The distinction between mandatory and optional activities is necessarily context-dependent; the same activity may be mandatory in one state of the negotiation and optional in another. For example, when the user enters the system for the first time, he is required to learn about the negotiation problem; at this time this activity is mandatory. When he logs in the second and subsequent times, learning about the problem should not be a mandatory but an optional activity. It is the negotiation protocol that, based on the process model and the assumptions of the protocol designer, categorizes some activities as mandatory or as optional, and modifies this categorization as the negotiation progresses. The assumptions underlying a specific protocol may reflect the negotiators characteristics (e.g. culture and profession), the type of negotiations (e.g., distributive, integrative, and mixed), and the complexity of the negotiation problem (e.g. one or more issues). In the research environment, these assumptions may also reflect the needs of the researcher studying the users' behaviour and the system's efficacy.

Different negotiators and negotiation situations require that different protocols be used. The protocols may differ in the sequencing of the same set of activities. Conversely, the same set of activities may be (re-)used in the construction of many different protocols. Negotiation strategies and tactics also may require the use of different protocols. Moreover, different types of negotiations, e.g. single or multiple issues, and different roles of the negotiators, e.g. buyer or seller, require different protocols. Another need for different negotiation protocols derives from the requirements and demands that different stakeholders have regarding their use of an ENS. To meet the requirements of negotiators and researchers, it is essential to equip an ENS with the flexibility to carry out several different protocols and to provide the user or researcher with the possibility of designing new negotiation protocols.

2.3 Process Model and Negotiation States

The framework provided by the process model is implemented in the negotiation protocol, which is represented by a sequence of activities and rules imposed on the execution of the sequence. Additionally, the execution of a protocol depends on the context of a negotiation, or more precisely, on the current state of a negotiation a user is currently involved in and on the user's earlier actions in that negotiation. The process model reflects the progression of a negotiation as it tracks the completion of phases and activities. An example of the process model, and its phases and activities is given in Table 1. We use these phases and activities to illustrate, in Section 3, formal protocol construction and manipulation.

Table 1. Example of the process model, activities and states.

Negotiation phase and activity	State	Abbr.
1. Planning		
– Negotiation problem	Negotiation case	*NC*
2. Agenda setting		
– Preferences and rating	Utility construction	*UC*
– Assessment of alternatives	Alternative construction	*AC*
3. Exchanging offers and arguments		
– Offer and/or message construction	Offer message	*OM*
– Counter-offer assessment	Counterpart's offer	*CO*
4. Reaching agreement		
– Agreement	Agreement reached	*AR*
	Agreement assessment	*AS*
– Closing negotiation	End	*EN*
5. Concluding negotiation		
– Agreement improvement	Agreement improvement	*AI*
– Offer and/or message	Offer message	*OM*
– Counter-offer assessment	Counterpart's offer	*CO*
– Closing negotiation	End	*EN*

Each negotiation activity is associated with an ENS state (see Table 1); however the reverse is not true: The system may be in a state that does not correspond to any negotiation activity. For instance, state *AS* involves agreement efficiency analysis and does not correspond to any activity. The difference between a negotiation activity and an ENS state is that the former describes a user action, while the latter denotes a user and/or a system action.

3   Negotiation Protocols

Every ENS implements a negotiation protocol – even though some system designers do not specify the protocol explicitly – the protocol can be derived from the required and possible interactions between the negotiators and the system. It is sensible to formulate the negotiation protocol explicitly, because it specifies the users' interactions and thus the users need to determine if the system conforms to their requirements. In addition to the interaction transparency introduced by explicit protocols, it also allows for mapping protocols onto negotiation processes. Furthermore, it is also possible to assess the protocols' underlying assumptions. Various formalisms have been applied to represent negotiation protocols, e.g. Petri nets [16] and state chart diagrams [17]. Our approach is based on set theory mainly for its flexibility and readability.

3.1   Preliminaries and Conditions

Following the distinction between mandatory and optional activities (see Figure 1), we distinguish two types of ENS states: *mandatory* or *optional*. Let:

$S = \{s_1, ..., s_N\}$ be the set of all possible states;

M be the set of mandatory states ($M \subset S$);

O be the set of optional states ($O \subset S$);

$s_{start} \in S$ be the first state of the protocol; and

$s_{end} \in S$ be the last state of the protocol; it is the protocol termination state.

We assume that $s_1 = s_{start}$ and $s_N = s_{end}$. Every state is associated with at most one mandatory state, which defines a partial protocol sequence, i.e. a sequence is a *pair* of two states:

$$s_i \rightarrow s_j, s_i \neq s_j \text{ with } i, j \in I, \tag{1}$$

where $s_i \in S$; $s_j \in M$; and $|I| = N$ is the number of states.

Using the states given in Table 1, we can formulate several sequences, including the following two sequences: $NC \rightarrow UC$, $UC \rightarrow AC$. State UC is mandatory for NC; the user can move to state AC only after completing activity associated with UC. Similarly, AC is mandatory for UC. Optional states allow the user (or system) conducting activities within a sequence prior to moving to the next sequence.

$$s_i \rightarrow s_j \text{ } opt \text{ } O_i, \text{ with } s_i \neq s_j, s_i \in S, s_j \in M, O_i \subset O, \tag{2}$$

where *opt* is the operator of state association and O_i is the set of optional states associated with state s_i.

Formula (2) is interpreted as follows: The user who is in state s_i can visit states $s_l \in O_i$ multiple times and return from these states to s_i, but he cannot move to any state s_k ($s_k \neq s_j, s_j \in S \setminus O_i$), before he visits state $s_j \in M$. For example, the user who assesses alternatives (AC) can return to the description of the negotiation problem (NC) and revise his preferences (UC), but he cannot move to any other state listed in Table 1, unless he formulates an offer, that is: $AC \rightarrow OM \text{ } opt \text{ } \{NC, UC\}$.

A state may have a null state associated as mandatory state as long as the set of optional states is non-empty. The resulting sequence with a mandatory null state is denoted as:

$$s_i \rightarrow 0 \text{ } opt \text{ } O_i \text{ with } s_i \in S, M = 0, O_i \subset O, \tag{3}$$

where 0 is the null state. Similarly, a state may have a mandatory state with an empty set of optional states ($O_i = \varnothing$):

$$s_i \rightarrow s_j \text{ } opt \text{ } 0 \text{ with } s_j \in M. \tag{4}$$

Based upon these preliminaries, negotiation protocols are required to meet certain general conditions.

Condition 1: If state s_i has null mandatory state, then at least one optional states has to be associated with s_i, i.e.

$$s_i \rightarrow 0 \text{ } opt \text{ } O_i \Rightarrow O_i \neq \varnothing. \tag{5}$$

Condition 1 is required in order for the user to be able to move from the state with which no mandatory state is associated to one or more optional states. Moves between optional states are not considered sequences. Assume that set O_i in (5) has three elements $O_i = \{ s_j, s_l, s_k \}$. The user can move from any optional state to any other optional state, e.g., he can move from s_j to s_l to s_j. One implication is that all optional states in (5) are elements of O_i. The second implication of (5) is that to move from s_i or one of its optional states to a state, which is not an element of O_i, is possible only if there is a state in O_i, which is a part of another sequence of type (2) or (3). This requirement is formulated in the following condition.

Condition 2: With every state s_i, which has a null mandatory state, at least one optional state has to be associated, which is part of another sequence, that is:

$$\forall \ s_i : s_i \to 0 \ opt \ O_i : \exists \ s_l, s_l \in O_i \ \text{and} \ (s_l \to s_j, s_j \in M \ \text{or} \ s_l = s_{end}).$$

This condition assures that the user can move from any state to either a state with which a mandatory state is associated or to the termination state s_{end}. Condition 1 and 2 do not assure that every state can be accessed by the user; this is achieved if the following condition is met.

Condition 3: With the exception of the starting state (s_{start}), every state $s_i \in S$ is mandatory and/or optional, i.e.

$$\forall \ s_i, s_i \neq s_{start}, s_i \in S : s_i \in M \cup O.$$

Condition 4: A mandatory state may appear only in one sequence of the protocol,

$$\forall \ s_i, s_j, s_l \in S, \ s_i \to s_j \Rightarrow \neg \exists \ s_l \to s_j, s_i \neq s_l, s_j \in M.$$

The above four conditions define the *required* characteristics of every protocol.

Definition 1: $q(i,k)$ is the *list* of k sequences that begin with state s_i and end with the mandatory state s_{i+k}, such that:

1. s_i is an optional state for s_{i-1};
2. The mandatory state for s_{i+k} is the null state.
3. No state, other than s_{i+k}, in $q(i,k)$ has mandatory null state; and
4. With the exception of s_{i+k} every mandatory state is the first state in *one* other sequence in $q(i,k)$.

The sequence $q(i,k)$ is:

$$q(i,k) : s_i \to s_{i+1}, s_{i+1} \to s_{i+2}, \ldots, s_{i+k-1} \to s_{i+k} \wedge s_i \notin M \wedge s_{i+k} \to 0. \qquad (6)$$

The list $q(i,k)$ can be represented as a graph starting at state s_i and ending at s_{i+k}. Every state starting a sequence has a mandatory state which starts another sequence, with the exception of the last state s_k. The sequences in the list may or may not have associated with optional states (see Figure 2). Let:

J be the index set of lists of sequences; $q(i_j, k_j)$ denotes the j-th list in the protocol;

$Q = \{q(i_j, k_j), (j \in J)\}$ is the set of all lists of sequences of the type given by (6) in the protocol;

$P = \{s_i \to 0 \ opt \ O_i, i \in I\}$ be the set of all sequences in which the mandatory state is the null state;

S_i ($S_i \subset S$) be the set of states that are elements of the mandatory and optional sets associated with s_i and the states preceding s_i, i.e., $S_i = \{s_{start}, s_2, ..., s_i; O_{start}, O_2, ..., O_i\}$; S_{i+} ($S_{i+} \subset S$) the set of states that are elements of the mandatory and optional sets associated with s_{i+1} and states following s_{i+1}, i.e. $s_{i+2}, ..., s_{end}$.

Note that $S_{i+} \cap S_i$ is not necessarily an empty set because some states may appear in more than one optional sets both preceding, including and following s_i.

<u>Definition 2:</u> Negotiation protocol $\wp$ is the 5-tuple:

$$\wp = (S, O, M, P, Q) \tag{7}$$

3.2 Protocol Completeness and Modifications

Given the definition of a negotiation protocol $\wp$, we are able to establish a completeness theorem of negotiation protocols and proof the completeness of a protocol in the sense that all states of the protocol can be visited. The theorem and proof are available in the companion working paper [11]. The discussion of different protocol states and their relationships in Section 3.1 does not take into account the dynamics of the negotiation process. We formulated Conditions 1-4, which specify protocol properties required to introduce, in particular, the concept of a complete protocol. This is not to say that there may not be situations in which the protocol designer may want to violate one or more of these properties. One such example is that termination state s_{end} occurs only once in the protocol. For practical reasons this condition may be purposefully violated, so that the user has an option to terminate the negotiation at every state rather than be forced to follow the protocol until he reaches state s_{end}.

The distinction between mandatory and optional states partially takes into account context-dependency; it only allows to access different optional states before moving to a mandatory state. Protocol $\wp$ defined with (7) may be used in highly structured protocols, which follow the rules implemented in $\wp$. The rules governing the moves between states are static; they do not depend on the states visited. A stronger requirement reflecting protocol context-dependency is to allow for the states' rearrangement during the negotiation. In many negotiations, the permissible states depend on states previously visited. The dynamics of the negotiation process are reflected in context-dependent modifications of the negotiation protocol at run-time, which means that some mandatory states may became optional, some optional states may be added and others removed depending on the user and system actions.

3.3 Intervening States

The characteristic that distinguishes negotiations from individual decision making is exchange of information between the negotiators (e.g., offers, messages and offer acceptance). Information sent by one negotiator affects his counterpart's activities. Therefore, the system has to display this information at the earliest possible time and irrespectively of the state he wants to visit. The states which contain and process information sent by the counterpart are called *intervening states*.

In face-to-face negotiations, the negotiators may exchange messages even during the planning phase. The synchronous aspect of these negotiations causes that they rarely formulate offers before both sides are ready to negotiate. Asynchronicity of negotiations conducted via an ENS causes that one party may learn about the problem and be ready to exchange offers and messages, while the other party does not yet know the negotiation problem. This may require that the user be moved from some states to an intervening state, but not from other states. For example, if the user is in state *NC* and his counterpart makes an offer, this offer should not be displayed to the user prior to his specification of preferences in state *UC*. We therefore associate with every intervening state a set of *permissible states*; these are the states from which the user can be moved to the intervening states.

4   Summary and Future Work

In this paper, we lay out theoretical foundations for negotiation protocols based on a negotiation methodology derived from behavioural research. The foundations facilitate the design and implementation of negotiation protocols and allow for the construction of ENSs based on these protocols. The construction of negotiation protocols may be a highly complex task. The theory in Section 3 will allow for the implementation of a software tool that supports protocol designers and automatically verifies, if the particular protocol meets the formulated conditions.

We are currently designing and implementing the software platform Invite, which will serve as a run-time environment for multi-protocol ENSs on the one hand and as a host for software tools for protocol design and verification. Our approach strives to achieve a level of genericity for the platform that enables the construction of multi-protocol ENSs from existing parts and thus allows for reusability of predefined components. The software platform will execute different negotiation protocols in different ENSs and thus will simplify the adoption of e-negotiations in real-world and in research environments. Our future work includes the implementation of components for several bilateral negotiation protocols, and a respective protocol designer support tool. We also plan to extend the Invite platform to multi-bilateral and multilateral e-negotiations.

References

1. Ehtamo, H., R.P. Hämäläinen, and V. Koskinen (2004). An e-learning module on negotiation analysis. *Hawai'i International Conference on System Sciences*. Hawai'i: IEEE Computer Society Press.
2. Schoop, M. and C. Quix, (2001). DOC.COM: A Framework for Effective Negotiation Support in Electronic Marketplaces. *Computer Networks*, **37**(2): 153-170.
3. Lempereur, A., (2004). Updating Negotiation Teaching Through The Use of Multimedia Tolls. *International Negotiations Journal*, **9**(1): (to appear).
4. Shim, J. and N. Hsiao (1999). A Literature Review on Web-Based Negotiation Support System. Documentation for Web-based Negotiation Training System (WNTS): cpol.albany.edu/wnts/WNSS_Literature_Reivew.pdf. Accessed: April 23, 2002.
5. Neumann, D., et al., (2003). Applying the Montreal Taxonomy to State of the Art E-Negotiation Systems. *Group Decision and Negotiation*, **12**(4): 287-310.
6. Ströbel, M. (2003). *Engineering Electronic Negotiations*, New York: Kluwer.
7. InterNeg (1997). InterNeg Support System. http://interneg.org/interneg/tools/inss/. Accessed: April 1, 2004.
8. Ströbel, M., (2001). Design of Roles and Protocols for Electronic Negotiations. *Electronic Commerce Research Journal*, **1**(3): 335-353.

9. Starke, K. and A. Rangaswamy (1999). *Computer-Mediated Negotiations: Review and Research Opportunities*, eBusiness Research Centre: University Park. 37.
10. Bichler, M., G. Kersten, and S. Strecker, (2003). Towards the Structured Design of Electronic Negotiation Media. *Group Decision and Negotiation*, **12**(4): 311-335.
11. Kersten, G.E., S. Strecker, and K.P. Law (2004). *Protocols for Electronic Negotiation Systems: Theoretical Foundations and Design Issues*, Interneg Working Paper 06/04: Ottawa, Canada. 1-16.
12. Lewicki, R.J., D.M. Saunders, and J.W. Minton (1999). *Negotiation*. 3 ed, Boston, MA: McGraw-Hill.
13. Kim, J. and A. Segev (2003). A Framework for Dynamic eBusiness Negotiation Processes. *IEEE Conference on E-Commerce*: CITM. http://groups.haas.berkeley.edu/citm/citm-home.htm.
14. Kersten, G.E. and G. Lo, (2003). Aspire: Integration of Negotiation Support System and Software Agents for E-Business Negotiation. *International Journal of Internet and Enterprise Management (IJIEM)*, **1**(3): 293-315.
15. Gulliver, P.H. (1979). *Disputes and Negotiations: A Cross-Cultural Perspective*, Orlando, FL: Academic Press.
16. Hung, P. and J.-Y. Mao (2002). Modeling of E-negotiation Activities with Petri Nets. *35th International Conference on System Sciences (HICSS'02*. Hawaii: Computer Society Press. http://csdl.computer.org/comp/proceedings/hicss/2002/1435/01/14350026.pdf.
17. Benyoucef, M. and R.K. Keller (2000). An Evaluation of Formalisms for Negotiations in E-Commerce. *Proceedings of the Workshop on Distributed Computing on the Web*. Quebec City, Quebec, Canada: Springer. 45-54.

Implementing Complex Market Structures with MetaMarkets

Juho Mäkiö and Ilka Weber

Karlsruhe University (TH), Department of Economics and Business Engineering
Information Management and Systems, Englerstr. 14
76131 Karlsruhe, Germany
{maekioe,weber}@iw.uni-karlsruhe.de

Abstract. One theoretical approach to designing and constructing complex market structures is the concept of Cascading Dynamic Market Models (cDMMs). CDMMs allow the configuration and combination of multiple market models. MetaMarkets is presented here as an implementation concept for complex market structures. MetaMarkets form a concatenation of a set of markets and rules that represent relations between single market structures and their environment. Various market model combinations and their representation are discussed, and a communication method with the environment presented. MetaMarkets lead to a layered software architecture that we briefly depict.

1 Introduction

Electronic marketplaces facilitate the exchange of goods, services, information, and payments and create economic value for buyers, sellers, market intermediaries, and for society [2]. Bakos states that the main functions of markets are matching buyers and sellers, facilitating market transactions, and providing an institutional infrastructure enabling the efficient functioning of the market. Thus, market design focuses on the design of "efficient markets" providing "precise and accurate information to all participants and giving them the ability to identify and exploit all advantageous trades" [1]. The institutional rules that make the electronic market work, and the process that installs these rules, have to be analysed on the basis of market participants' requirements, economic efficiency, and social justice.

Market participants have various - and to some extent - contradictory requirements. Thus, it would appear desirable to have many electronic markets, each fulfilling the participants' requirements concerning the traded goods and the trading rules. This would lead to many different markets, and consequently to a split of liquidity between all markets. As this dilemma of liquidity versus adaptability cannot be resolved in conventional electronic trading systems, a new market concept is needed in order to fulfil investors' requirements and to avoid the splitting of marketplace liquidity. One way would be to combine markets, which not only implies the integration of markets based on identical market models, but also the combination of different market models. Alternatively, the integration of markets leads to the synchronous existence of orders within two or more markets that, for their part, raise economic and technical questions concerning the feasibility and reasonability of such concepts.

This paper does not discuss the economic reasonability of market integration with reference to the corresponding literature [7]. Instead it demonstrates a novel compo-

K. Bauknecht, M. Bichler, and B. Pröll (Eds.): EC-Web 2004, LNCS 3182, pp. 116–125, 2004.

nent based concept for the implementation of market integration. In this concept, the market structures are concateneted with the information for their management. From this concatenation, questions arise such as: "Which kind of combinations of market models are possible?"; "How can MetaMarkets communicate with their environment?", and "What does the software architecture for MetaMarkets look like?". Because this concept joins market structures that belong together with their management information we call it *MetaMarket*.

The remainder of this paper is organized as follows. Section 2 introduces Cascading Dynamic Market Models as a solution for the liquidity versus adaptability dilemma mentioned above. Section 3 briefly presents components that are used for component based market modelling. Section 4 introduces the MetaMarket concept as an extension of component based modelling and presents some key issues surrounding it. The implementation of MetaMarkets is then discussed in Section 5. Finally, the paper concludes in Section 6 with remarks and discussion about our future research.

2 Cascading Dynamic Market Models (cDMMs)

The individual preferences and requirements of market participants concerning the trading rules raise a challenge for the market designer because their fulfillment appears to be impossible using traditional concepts of market models. This section focuses on the market microstructure (one perspective of the market engineering concept) and proposes a complex market structure (in this paper we use the terms "market structure" and "market model" synonymously) mapping the requirements of the traded product as well as the needs and demands of the market participants. These needs and demands require a market design that induces market efficiency and, in particular, provides precise and accurate information to all participants, efficient and reliable communication with one or several markets simultaneously, safe and trustworthy exchanges and ensures the correctness and efficient computation of market decisions [1]. Therefore, we propose a new market concept that provides the integration of markets within one market model – that is to say, multiple market models combined on one trading platform fulfilling the requirements listed above.

[3] introduce the concept of *"Dynamic Market Models (DMMs)"*. Market participants themselves are given the opportunity to choose market microstructures' characteristics according to their preferences in a DMM. This idea of dynamic market models fulfils the postulated characteristic of more individual market design, but does not provide much more flexibility than traditional market models: the market participant just chooses one set of market parameters and therefore one market he wants to place the order in.

[7] extend the concept of DMM to *"cascading Dynamic Market Models (cDMMs)"*, considering the integration of single market models within one order book. We suggest a more comprehensive interpretation of this concept of cDMMs. The cascading concept supports the configuration and combination of multiple market models and is, thus, an extension of the concepts presented by [3] as well as [7]. For a comprehensive definition and description of cDMMs, the following two perspectives must be considered: (1) the market designer's view and (2) the order's view.

Form the market designer's point of view, cDMMs allow the market designer to determine the market structure, that is the parameters of the market mechanism and the trading rules, as well as a combination of multiple market models within the trading platform. This combination can either be parallel (parallel market models) or sequential (sequence of market models). From the order's perspective, cDMMs allow the market participant not only to choose more than one market to place the order in simultaneously, but also to define preferences for the sequence of markets the order has to pass through.

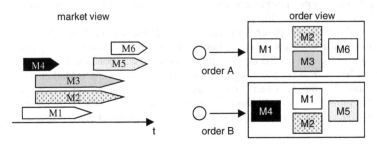

Fig. 1. Cascading Dynamic Market Model – market's and order's perspective.

This is depicted in Figure 1. As shown in the market view, six markets exist, M1 to M6, each market individually designed, e.g. by different trading rules and matching algorithms, and combined either in parallel or sequentially to a cDMM. The orders A and B, illustrated in the order view, choose a sequence of markets to be traded in. Order A has the preference of first being traded in market M1, then, if not executed in this market, moving on simultaneously to the parallel markets M2 and M3, and finally, being traded in market M6. A second example is given for order B. Order B first goes into market M4. If not executed here, order B exists simultaneously in M1 and M2 and afterwards, if not executed, enters market M5.

In a first step, we have suggest the idea of cDMMs as an integration of multiple market models within one trading platform. The market microstructure, e.g. the trading rules and matching algorithms, has to be defined. As we postulate a generic approach to define the market structure depending on the product specifications and the demands of the market participants, we propose, in a second step, a component based approach.

3 Components

The central questions for the implementation of electronic markets are 1) which trading rules are needed? and 2) how can they be implemented and finally composed to a concrete market model? In [6] a component based approach for the definition of market models is given. The authors define components as rules and algorithms that build the fundamental criteria for the market structure and for the definition of its characteristics in following way:

Definition: Component
Given a set of rules $R = \{R_1, R_2, ..., R_k\}$ with R_i, $i \in \{1, ..., k\}$, k mutual independent rules, and a set of algorithms $A = \{A_1, A_2, ..., A_l\}$ with A_j, $j \in \{1, ..., l\}$, l mutual independent algorithms. Then C is a component defined as a set of rules R and a set of algorithms A that is $C = \{R, A\}$.

For the concatenation of these components to new components and finally to new market structures, the authors define a logic composition operation for two or more components as follows:

Definition: Compositon

A composition is a logic operation of two or more components.
Given two components C_1 and C2, each component defined by a rule and an algorithm, a new component is achieved by the logical combination of C_1 and C_2, that is C $= C_1 \, o \, C_2 = C_2 \, o \, C_1$. In this case, C_1 and C_2 are subcomponents of C.

Having determined components and the composition of components, a definition for a component based market structure can be given in following way:

Definition: Component based market structure

Given a set of rules R, a set of algorithms A, and n components $C_i = \{R^i, A^i\}$ for i = 1,...,n with $R^i \subseteq R$ a subset of R and $A^i \subseteq A$ a subset of A we define a market structure based on components as a composition of n Components, that is a component based market structure

$$M = C_1 \, o \, C_2 \, o \, ... \, o \, C_n = \{R^1, A^1\} \, o \, \{ R^2, A^2\} \, o \, ... \, o \, \{R^n, A^n\}.$$

These definitions propose an abstract way to support the design and configuration of complex market structures in an easy manner. According to these definitions, a market structure can be built up from components using composition.

These criteria, or parameters, have been discussed for example by Wurman et al. [9], by Lomuscio et al. [5], by Ströbel and Weinhard [8]. In particular, the Montreal Taxonomy [8] gives a comprehensive overview of the criteria, parameters, rules, and algorithms necessary to define a market structure. These criteria are independent and orthogonal and form an n-dimensional criteria space, where "n" is the number of all criteria necessary to define a market structure.

Following sections present an approach analogous to the component based composition of market models for the definition and implementation of complex market structures.

4 MetaMarket

This section focuses various aspects of the implementation and realization of multiple markets. Thus, the concept of *MetaMarkets* is presented as one approach to the implementation of cDMMs.

CDMMs can be generated in two ways: by a market designer, or by an investor. In the first case, the market designer configures each market model individually and creates a complex market structure by combining two or more (individually configured) market models to one logical unit. This was mentioned above as the "market designer's view". In this case, the market designer joins two or more markets running simultaneously or sequentially in such a unit. Although the internal structure of each logical unit (that is the setting of the market structures' parameters of each market model and the combination of these market models) is visible to the market participants, each unit can be treated as one single market. Thus, it is characteristic for cDMMs that the market designer fixes their internal structure as well as additional rules.

In the second case, an investor can generate cDMMs ad hoc (on the fly). The investor inserts the information about the markets into the order which the order should enter simultaneously or sequentially. Focussing on the market models the order has to pass through, we get a cDMM that exists only from the order's point of view. This case is mentioned above as the "order's view". Accordingly, each order potentially contains a cDMM of its own. The implications of both ways for the definition of a cDMM are discussed below.

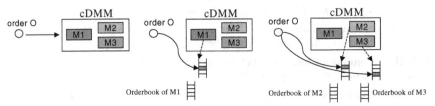

Fig. 2. Order books in cDMMs.

As mentioned above, our concept of cDMMs is an extension of Neumann et al. (2002). The authors consider the integration of single market models within one order book. Due to the necessity to integrate any kind of market structures, the integration cannot be based on one order book. Consider the example of mutual different matching rules: each matching rule requires a separate and differently organized order book. This problem is particularly obvious from the order's point of view: each market participant is able to define a virtual cDMM with an individual order book for each order. Referring to this, it seems impossible to define a common order book. Thus, we propose a more general concept of market integration. In our approach, each market has its own order book and every single order may register itself in the multiple order books synchronously, according to the rules that the investor has defined for the order. Figure 2 illustrates the situation described above. The order, O, that is first entering a cDMM, registers itself in (the order book of) M1 and can be matched in M1. If no matching occurs, O cancels its registration in M1 and registers synchronously in M2 and M3.

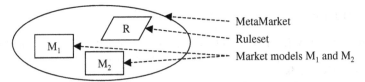

Fig. 3. Markets and internal rules of a MetaMarket.

In this context, new problems arise: the synchronization of accesses and deadlocks. These cases are deeply discussed in Czernohous et al. (2003) [4] and do not fall within the ambit of this paper.

Analogous to the definition of market structures by rules and algorithms, a market designer defines cDMMs as a combination of multiple markets. This combination of the markets is based on rules between these markets. The concept of *MetaMarkets* we propose is one way to manage the combination of multiple markets and the rules between the markets.

Definition: MetaMarket

A *MetaMarket* is defined as a set of markets and rules representing relations between markets (intern rules R^i) and their environment (extern rules R^e). Let *MM* be a MetaMarket, $M := \{M_1, M_2, ..., M_k\}$ a set of markets, and $R := \{R_1, R_2, ..., R_n\}$ a set of rules. Then we can define *MM* as a composition of markets and rules with

$$MM := M_1 \, o \, M_2 \, o \, ... \, o \, M_k \, o \, R_1 \, o \, R_2 \, o... \, o \, R_n, \; k, n \in \mathbb{N}, \; R_j \in \{R^i_x, R^e_y\}, \; x, y \in \mathbb{N}.$$

Note that defining the MetaMarkt as a composition we consider both markets and rules as components that are combined to complex market structures by the composition. Internal rules of the MetaMarket define, for example, the sequence of the markets and their validity over time, e.g. discrete time points for starting and stopping markets. External rules define, for example, the sequence of markets an order has to pass through within a MetaMarket. Figure 3 sketches the setting of a MetaMarket with two markets M_1 and M_2 and rule set R.

As already mentioned, rules are necessary to combine multiple markets to a cDMM as a complex market structure (market designer's view) or to define the sequence of markets an order has to pass through (order's view). The markets and the rules are managed together and coordinated by MetaMarkets. Nevertheless, each market contains trading rules and algorithms that are defined by market structure parameters (cf. Section 3). Such rules can either be time based (e.g. fixed or relative starting and stopping rules) or event based (e.g. market will be cancelled due to a high price volatility). The rules of a MetaMarket analogously control the coordination of the multiple markets it contains. Thus, the concept of MetaMarkets is a promising approach to managing the rules for cDMMs and provides the coordination of the markets within a cDMM.

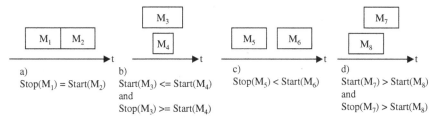

Fig. 4. Combinations of market models.

As described above, cDMMs are defined by a set of market models and the coordination of the market models by rules. In all probability, the most intuitive rule between market models is based on the time. Time-based rules dictate, e.g. the starting and stopping times of markets, and thus formulate time-based relations between the markets. Let $Start(M_i)$ be the starting time of market M_i and $Stop(M_i)$ the stopping time of it and let $Start(M_i) \leq Stop(M_i)$ for $i=1,...,8$.

Figure 4 presents, in four cases, different possible combinations of two market models with different starting and stopping times. The case a) shows markets M_1 and M_2 being valid one by one. In case b) market M_3 starts before market M_4 and ends after it. In case c) the situation in which Market M_5 stops before M_6 starts: $Stop(M_5) < Start(M_6)$ is focused. The case of overlapping markets is shown in d).

The example mentioned can be extended to event-based starting and stopping rules. In that case, the starting and stopping times are not fixed but flexible, depending on events, that trigger the starting and the stopping of markets. To specify the case of event-based rules, consider a market structure such as an English Auction. The English Auction can be stopped 10 minutes after the last order has been inserted. In this case, the stopping time is relative to the event "last order inserted" and thus the stopping rule of the English Auction is event based.

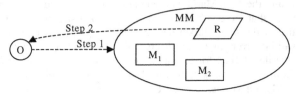

Fig. 5. Communication between an order and a MetaMarket.

MetaMarket is a concept to manage cDMMs especially to coordinate multiple market models throughout rules. In addition to this, MetaMarkets also have to "communicate" their internal structure to its environment. Consider the case of an investor choosing a *cascading dynamic market (cDM)* for his order to be traded in (cDM is an instance of cDMM). Thus, the order has to register in the cDM and with its registration the order receives information about the internal structure of the cDM i.e. the sequence of markets and their coordination. Figure 5 (cf. also Figure 2) describes this situation. An order O is entering a MetaMarket MM. First, O communicates MM its interest to be traded in MM (Step 1). Then MM communicates to O the sequence of markets it has to pass through (Step 2). According to this information, O initialises its own rules and can be traded in MM.

5   Implementation of MetaMarkets

As described above, a MetaMarket is a coherent combination of markets and rules. The description of MetaMarkets enables the integration of multiple market models and rules between them. This section briefly presents the description of MetaMarkets in XML. In the XML-file, the markets belonging together are managed as a single unit. Figure 6 presents a draft of an XML-structure for the description of MetaMarkets.

The area `<Relationships>` ... `</Relationships>` contains information about all relationships between market structures.

The information between the tags `<Relationship>` ... `</Relationship>` describe the relationship of a single market structure with the whole MetaMarket or paired relationships between market models. The relationships are defined by events (as in time-based instances) that regulate the starting or stopping of concrete markets within the MetaMarket. We define the following syntax for the definition of events: *Market[Market_Name(StartEvent(Entry);StopEvent(Exit)],* whereby specifications combined by logical operations for both events are allowed. For example, if the market model "StockMarket" should be activated at 12:00 am and finished at 16:00 pm we can specify it as follows:

Market[StockMarket(clocked(12:00);clocked(16:00)].

```
<MetaMarket>
    <Relationships>
        <Relationship>...</Relationship>
        <Relationship>...</Relationship>
        ...
    </Relationships>
    <OrderSequenceInformation>…</OrderSequenceInformation>
  <!--contains links to all markets that are included into this
    MetaMarket-->
    <MarketList>
        <Market> ... </Market>
        <Market> ... </Market>
        ...
    </MarketList>
</MetaMarket>
```

Fig. 6. An XML-draft for a MetaMarket.

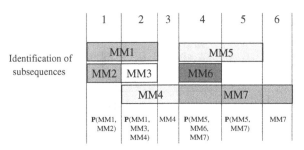

S(P(MM1,MM2), P(MM1,MM3,MM4), MM4, P(MM5,MM6,MM7), P(MM5,MM7), MM7)

Fig. 7. Order sequence information in the MetaMarket.

The area `<OrderSequenceInformation>` ... `</OrderSequenceInformation>` contains information that a MetaMarket has to "communicate" to an entering order (cf. Figure 6). From the order point of the view, the information submitted from the MetaMarket describes any combination of market conceivable in a MetaMarket. The principle idea is that any combination of market models is imaginable as a sequence of parallel and sequential market models. Therefore, we use a grammar to describe a sequence of parallel (P) and sequential (S) market models. With this grammar, we are able to define any combination of market models. In the concrete implementation of this grammar, additional information are used to describe events that are used to trigger the state of the order.

Figure 7 clarifies the grammar described above. The chart represents the information an order receives at the moment it enters a MetaMarket. In this example, the order has to visit seven markets in six subsequences. In the first subsequence, the order enters market MM1 and MM2 synchronously. After exiting market MM2, the order enters markets MM3, MM4, and so on. As already mentioned, the events that trigger entry or exit can be time based, or specifically defined in the order, in the market model, or in the MetaMarket.

The definition of the market models used in a MetaMarket is given between the tags <MarketList> ... </MarketList>. These tags isolate a group of objects that define the concrete market models in the current MetaMarket.

To keep a single market model independently usable in any MetaMarket, it is not physically included into the MetaMarket definition, but linked. This leads to the layered architecture of MetaMarkets presented in Figure 8.

The order layer contains four orders and three MetaMarkets in the MetaMarket layer. The market layer contains the available markets - M1, M2, M3, and M4. MetaMarket1 contains three markets - M1, M2, and M3; MetaMarket2 contains markets M3 and M4; and MetaMarket3 contains only market M4.

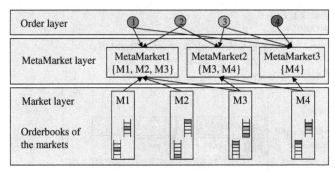

Fig. 8. Layered Architecture of MetaMarkets.

MetaMarkets enable the insertion of a single instance of a market into any number of MetaMarkets. Consequently, orders that are inserted into different MetaMarkets can meet in one market instance common to both of the MetaMarkets. For example, in Figure 8 the same instance of M4 is present in both MetaMarket2 and MetaMarket3. Order 3 is inserted into MetaMarket2 and MetaMarket3 and order 4 is inserted into MetaMarket3. In this instance, order 3 and order 4 can be traded, although they are originally inserted into different MetaMarkets. Additionally, order 3 can be traded with order 1, which is inserted into MetaMarket1 and MetaMarket3, hence, MetaMarket1 and MetaMarket2 have a common instance of market model M3.

6 Concluding Remarks and Future Work

The main problem in fulfilling the requirements of market participants at the level of market modelling is that they are, to some extent, contradictory, and therefore not resolvable in conventional electronic trading systems. The concept of MetaMarkets offers a practical approach for new kinds of electronic markets. We propose that MetaMarkets eliminate some of the problems that arise from the dilemma of liquidity versus adaptability because it combines multiple market models in one complex market model, and supports a larger volume of market participants' requirements. It is fair to say that this dilemma does not vanish solely with MetaMarkets. The MetaMarket concept provides promising possibilities for market modelling. It transfers the problems generated by the dilemma from the level of asking: "What can be done to fulfil market participants' requirements?" to the more concrete question: "How can available concepts be used to fulfil these requirements?"

Further research about market integration with MetaMarkets is needed, as well as research about their effects on market quality. Moreover, a rigorous definition of economically meaningfully events that trigger the entry or exit of an order into a market is required. After implementation of the MetaMarket concept in the near future, more detailed information about its economic effects and usability are needed. As a consequence, experiments involving students and simulations are imminent.

References

1. Babin, G., Crainic, T., Gendreau, M., Keller, R., Kropf, P.G., Robert J.: Towards Electronic Market-places: A Progress Report, ICECR-4, Dallas, Texas, November (2001) 637-648
2. Bakos, J. Y.: The Emerging Role of EM on the Internet. In: Communications of the ACM, Vol. 41, No. 8, (1998) 35-42
3. Budimir, M., and Gomber, P.: Dynamische Marktmodelle im elektronischen Wertpapierhandel. In: Scheer, A.-W. and Nüttgens, M. (eds.): Electronic Business Engineering: Vierte Internationale Tagung Wirtschaftsinformatik, Heidelberg, Physica, (1999) 251-169
4. Czernohous C., Kolitz K., Mäkiö J., Weber I., Weinhardt Ch.: Integrating Electronic Market Models - Problems and Solutions of Parallel Markets. 10th Research Symposium on Emerging Electronic Markets RSEEM (2003)
5. Lomuscio, A. R., Wooldridge, M., Jennings, N. R.: A Classification Scheme for Negotiation in Electronic Commerce. In: Dignum, F. and Sierra, C. Springer (eds.), Agent Mediated Electronic Commerce, LNAI 1991, (2001) 19–33
6. Mäkiö, J., Weber, I.: Component-based Specification and Composition of Market Structures. In: Bichler M. et al. (eds.), Coordination and Agent Technology in Value Networks, GITO, Berlin, (2004) 127-137
7. Neumann, D., Holtmann, C., Weltzien, H., Lattemann Ch., Weinhardt Ch.: Towards A Generic E-Market Design. In: Towards the Knowledge Society: e-Commerce, e-Business and e-Government. eds. J. Monteiro, P. M. C. Swatman, and L. V. Tavares. Lisboa, Kluwer Academic Publishers (2002) 289-305
8. Ströbel, M. and Weinhardt, Ch.: The Montreal Taxonomy for Electronic Negotiations", Journal of Group Decision and Negotiation, 12(2), (2003) 143-164
9. Wurman, P.R., Wellman, M.P., and Walsh, W.E.: A Parametrization of the Auction Design Space Games and Economic Behavior, vol. 35, no. 1-2, (2001) 304-338

Evaluation of an Online Multidimensional Auction System: A Computer Simulation Investigation

Sungwon Cho[1], Kyoung Jun Lee[1,*], Martha E. Crosby[3], and David N. Chin[3]

[1] Service Development Laboratory, Korea Telecom, 17 Woomyeon-dong,
Seocho-gu, Seoul 137-792, Korea
sungwonc@kt.co.kr
[2] School of Business, Kyung Hee University, Hoegi-Dong, Dongdaemun-Ku, Seoul, Korea
klee@khu.ac.kr
[3] Department of Information and Computer Sciences, University of Hawaii at Manoa,
Honolulu, HI 96822, USA
{crosby,chin}@hawaii.edu

Abstract. Through computer simulations, this paper evaluates the performance of an online multidimensional auction system with negotiation support and especially focuses on investigating the efficacy of two design features of online multidimensional auction system on its performance: sellers' feedback and post-utility scoring method. The performance of the auction system is measured by joint gain and speed of convergence. The simulation results demonstrate that the use of sellers' feedback and post-utility scoring method lead to better bargaining outcomes as measured by the buyer's total utility and the number of auction rounds. The research results provide important theoretical implications about the role of information feedback in auction design.

1 Introduction

Although auctions have been studied by economists for a long time, only recently has the online multidimensional auction mechanism received attention from researchers as an efficient way of resolving one-to-many bargaining problems [Bichler 2000]. Among the early studies on multidimensional auctions [McAfee & McMillan 1988], Che [1993] studied design competition in government procurement by developing a model of two-dimensional auctions, where firms bid on both price and quality, and bids are evaluated by a scoring rule set by a buyer. Branco [1997] further extended Che's model by incorporating the impact of costs' correlations on the design of multidimensional auction mechanisms. According to his analysis, when the costs of the several bidders are not independent, the buyer has to use a two-stage auction; in the first stage the buyer selects one firm, and in the second stage, he or she bargains to readjust the level of quality to be provided. Bichler [2000] provided the first experimental analysis of multidimensional auctions. He showed that the utility scores achieved in multidimensional auctions were significantly higher than those in conventional auctions. Strecker and Seifert [2002] report on a computer-based laboratory

---

* Corresponding Author.

K. Bauknecht, M. Bichler, and B. Pröll (Eds.): EC-Web 2004, LNCS 3182, pp. 126–134, 2004.
© Springer-Verlag Berlin Heidelberg 2004

experiment in a sole sourcing scenario of a single, indivisible object and investigate whether a multi-attribute reverse English and a multi-attribute reverse Vickrey auction institution lead to identical outcomes with respect to the buyer's utility, suppliers' profits and allocational efficiency. The results show no significant difference in suppliers' profits.

This research focuses on investigating the efficacy of two design features of online multidimensional auction system on its performance: sellers' feedback and post-utility scoring method. The performance of the auction system is measured by joint gain and speed of convergence. The joint gain is operationalized by a utility score achieved by the buyer and/or seller [Bichler 2000] and the speed of convergence can be measured by the number of rounds taken in the multi-round auction.

The remainder of this paper is organized as follows. Section 2 explains the use of sellers' feedback and the post utility scoring. Section 3, 4, and 5 proposes the hypotheses, experimental design, and experiment setting respectively, Section 6 gives the results of simulation and the final section discusses the conclusions and future research issues.

2   Multidimensional Auction with Seller's Feedback and Post-utility Scoring

2.1   Use of Sellers' Feedback

In the conventional procurement auction, buyers search current market conditions (i.e., product feature and price) and create Request for Quotes (RFQs) to initiate the auction. Therefore, the buyers' aspiration levels are determined by the search results. In case the buyers fail to properly assess the market conditions when they initiate auctions (e.g., the buyers' requirement is set too high for a given budget), the auctions lead to failure, causing extra cost and time. Furthermore, the buyers do not receive any useful information to adjust their RFQs when the auctions fail. Therefore, the buyers must initiate another round without knowing which requirement is set too high within a given budget. Such a situation occurs due to incomplete information inherent in the auction process. Economists have argued that incomplete information leads to less efficient bargaining outcomes [Strecker & Seifert 2003].

We argue that this can be resolved by providing the buyers with information on market conditions. Our system is designed to foster more efficient outcomes by providing sellers' cost information to buyers. However, exposing detailed cost information can be a sensitive issue for sellers. Therefore, revealing sellers' cost information should be minimized to provide just enough information so that the buyers can initiate the next round of the auction with a more reasonable RFQ.

2.2   Post-utility Scoring Method

Buyers sometimes do not have perfect knowledge on their utility functions before they see the alternatives from sellers. Our system allows buyers to determine their preference structure after alternatives for all the issues have been determined, that is, after collecting offers from all the sellers. Buyers evaluate offers based on their utility functions, and utility functions are composed of the relative importance of issues and individual utility scores for each issue.

3 Hypotheses

We hypothesize that a buyer using MAMENS would achieve better bargaining outcomes than those using a conventional multidimensional auction system (Note: Throughout this paper, conventional multidimensional auction systems refer to the multidimensional auction systems built based on the proposed multidimensional auction mechanism but not having the two unique design features of MAMENS). It is also hypothesized that an increased number of sellers will lead to better bargaining outcomes for the buyers regardless of the trading mechanism. More specifically, the following formal hypotheses are proposed.

H1: Using the post-utility scoring method of the MAMENS system will lead to more joint gain than not using it.

H2: An increased number of sellers will lead to more joint gain regardless of utility scoring method.

H3: Providing buyers with sellers' cost information in the MAMENS system will lead to a quicker speed of convergence.

H4: An increased number of sellers will lead to quicker speed of convergence regardless of the existence of sellers' cost information.

H5: Providing buyers with sellers' cost information in the MAMENS system will lead to more joint gain than not providing it.

H6: An increased number of sellers will lead to more joint gain regardless of existence of the sellers' cost information.

4 Experimental Design

In order to test the hypotheses, two independent experiments were conducted using computer simulation as in Bichler [2001]. Details of the computational platform used for the simulation is presented in the following sections. While holding other variables constant, each experiment employed two independent variables: the treatment and number of sellers. In each experiment, there were three groups with a different number of sellers (3, 5, and 7). The computer simulation ran 30 sessions for each group under the two conditions: one with treatment and the control group without treatment. Except for the treatment, all the parameter values were the same within the experiment.

Experiment I

Hypotheses 1 and 2 (the effect of the post-utility scoring method) were tested in Experiment I. A buyer initiated the multidimensional auction with a maximum level of price threshold (i.e., 100) in order to avoid the failure of first round bargaining due to a tight budget. Sellers were assigned randomly to the two conditions: MAMENS (with the post-utility scoring method) and conventional multidimensional auction system (without the post-utility scoring method). To investigate the effect of the post-utility scoring method, the mean values of the buyer's total utility (i.e., joint gain) from both conditions were compared using ANOVA test.

Experiment II

In Experiment II, hypotheses 3, 4, 5, and 6 (i.e., the effect of sellers' feedback) were tested. In this experiment, unlike in Experiment I, a buyer initiated the multidimensional auction in each trading session with an unreasonably low level of price threshold (i.e., 68), purposefully causing the failure of first round bargaining. After the failures of each round, the buyer relaxed one requirement per round in order to increase the chances of receiving a satisfactory offer in the next round. The auction continued to run new rounds until the buyer found a satisfactory offer.

There were two treatments in Experiment II to illustrate relaxing requirements: MAMENS (with sellers' feedback) and conventional multidimensional auction system (without sellers' feedback). The buyer using MAMENS relaxed the requirement that was most cost-causing to the majority of sellers. On the other hand, the buyer using the conventional multidimensional auction system relaxed the requirement that was personally least important.

Investigating the effect of sellers' feedback is more complex than investigating the effect of the post-utility scoring method. The number of rounds taken to reach agreement as well as the mean value of the buyer's total utility is used as a measure of effectiveness of the two systems. The number of rounds would reveal the efficiency of the negotiation support capability whereas the buyer's total utility value would show the quality of the final bargaining outcomes. These two dependent variables were compared using ANOVA test.

5 Experiment Setting

5.1 Task

The task used in the experiments is digital camera trading. The hypothetical digital camera trading game involves two issues in addition to the price: resolution (number of pixels) and delivery time (number of days). The total cost of a camera depends on only two factors: the cost of resolution and delivery time. Each trading session involved one computer-simulated buyer and various numbers of computer-simulated sellers (3, 7, and 11). To investigate the research questions in Experiment I, we run the computational platform with two different modes to calculate the overall utility to the buyer: *MAMENS mode* (with post-utility scoring) and *conventional auction mode* (without post-utility scoring). In Experiment I, the winning offers determined by the two different modes are compared. In Experiment II, only MAMENS mode is used because the experiment's focus is not the effect of different utility scoring methods.

5.2 Parameters

The computational platform involves a number of parameters that are considered to affect the bargaining outcomes. In order to focus on testing the research questions, some of the parameters are intentionally manipulated or held constant by the researcher, while others are randomly assigned by the computer (Table 1).

Table 1. Parameters used in the computer simulation.

Parameter name	Parameter value used in the simulation
Number of sellers	3,7,11
Number of issues	3
Number of trading session runs	30
Buyer's price threshold	100 in Experiment I , 68 in Experiment II
Value weight	54:23:23 (Price: Resolution: Delivery time)
Cost weight	Random number between 0.2 and 0.8

Number of Sellers
Most previous bargaining experiments used a fixed number of bidders because of the cost for human subjects. Bichler [2000] used four sellers in his multidimensional auction experiment. We, however, use different numbers of sellers for each experiment in order to investigate the effect on the bargaining outcome of a changing the number of sellers. For each experiment the computational platform runs the same simulation with three different group sizes: 3, 7, and 11 respectively.

Number of Issues
A multidimensional auction can involve many issues, although price is the main concern for the buyer. Throughout the simulation the number of issues is being held to three - price, delivery time, and resolution - in order to focus specifically on the current research questions.

Number of Trading Sessions
For each study, the computational platform runs 30 trading sessions in order to provide sufficient data for the statistical analysis. Each session might include several trading rounds if the buyer cannot find the winning offer in the first round. Otherwise, one session of bargaining will include only one trading round.

Buyer's Price Threshold
In the simulation, the buyer has a price threshold or a budget limit that the sellers' offers cannot exceed in order to be accepted. Therefore, it can be assumed that the lower the price threshold the less the chance of finding an offer that fulfills the RFQ. Different buyers' price thresholds are used for each experiment. In Experiment I, the purpose is to examine the effect of the utility scoring method and therefore subsequent bargaining rounds are not performed. Therefore, buyers hold the highest possible threshold (100) in order to avoid impasse in the first round. In Experiment II, on the other hand, the threshold is set significantly lower (68), in order to make it harder for sellers to fulfill the RFQ within the price threshold. The threshold of 68 was chosen because it was the value that led to impasse in the first round of bargaining in the pilot

testing of the simulation. However, as the buyer keeps relaxing requirements in subsequent rounds, sellers can also reduce the total cost, increasing the chance of fulfilling the RFQ within the price threshold.

Value Weight

The relative importance of issues can affect the bargaining outcomes of multidimensional auctions [Bichler 2000]. Therefore, it is important to balance the weight distributions and keep them constant. The pilot experiments of this study sought to use perfectly balanced weight distribution (e.g., 34:33:33). However, it was determined that there was a difference between the weight for price and the other two issues. Price is a *continuous attribute* in terms of determining utility score while the other two issues are *discrete attributes*. The pilot experiments showed that the weight on the price tends to be under-represented compared to the other weights due to the different utility scoring method. In other words, if all three issues have the same weight, the impact of price change is less than those of the other two. This simulation, therefore, put more weight on the price. However, the same weight distribution, (54:23:23), is used throughout the entire simulation.

Cost Weight

Unlike the buyer who has three value weights, sellers have only two cost weights: one for resolution and the other for delivery time. The cost weight is randomly determined by the computer within the range of 0.2 and 0.8 adding up to 1.

6 Simulation Results

6.1 Experiment I: The Effect of the Post-utility Scoring Method

In Experiment I, for all groups, the utility scores achieved by the buyer in the post-utility selection treatment were significantly above those achieved by the conventional method. Using a two-way ANOVA ($\alpha=0.05$), the null hypothesis of revenue equivalence between the post-utility scoring method and the conventional method was rejected, and the hypothesis 1 that MAMENS's post-utility scoring method would achieve higher utility scores than the conventional method was supported. Also, the number of sellers had a significant effect on the outcome. Therefore, hypothesis 2 was also supported. Although there was not a specific hypothesis related to the interaction effect, it was investigated using a two-way ANOVA test and no significant interaction effect was found. Table 2 shows the results of Experiment I.

Table 2. The results of Experiment I: Hypotheses 1 and 2 (ANOVA).

ANOVA test results (hypotheses 1and 2)			
Source of Variation	Df	F	P-value
Number of sellers	2	3.12	0.047
Treatment (post-utility scoring vs. conventional)	1	19.37	< 0.0005
Interaction	2	1.17	0.312

The buyer's total utility values achieved in the treatment of the post-utility scoring method were, on average, 3.27% in group 1(group size 3), 4.86 % in group 2 (size 7), and 7.62% in group 3 (size 11) higher than those achieved by the conventional method. Figure 1 shows the buyer's total utility value on average for each group.

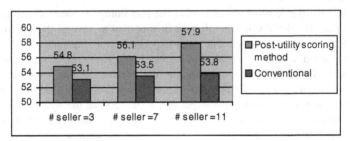

Fig. 1. Average buyer's total utility value.

6.2 Experiment II: The Effect of Sellers' Feedback

In Experiment II, for all groups, the number of rounds taken by the buyer to determine the winner in the MAMENS system was significantly smaller than that of the conventional system. Using a two-way ANOVA test ($\alpha = 0.05$), hypothesis 3 was supported: MAMENS leads to quicker agreement than the conventional system. The effect of the number of sellers was also significant. Therefore, hypothesis 4 was also supported. The interaction effect was not significant. Table 3 summarizes the results and Figure 2 shows the average number of rounds taken for each group and treatment.

Table 3. The results of Experiment II: Hypotheses 3 and 4 (ANOVA).

ANOVA test results (hypotheses 3 and 4)			
Source of Variation	df	F	P-value
Number of sellers	2	15.41	< 0.0005
Treatment (MAMENS vs. conventional system)	1	13.25	< 0.0005
Interaction	2	1.19	0.306

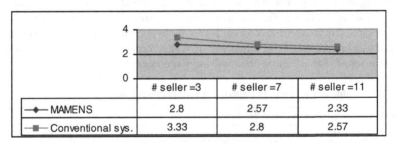

Fig. 2. The average number of rounds taken for each group and treatment.

For all the groups, the utility scores achieved by the buyer in the MAMENS system were also significantly above those of conventional system. Using an ANOVA test

($\alpha = 0.05$), the null hypothesis of revenue equivalence between the MAMENS system and conventional system was rejected, and hypothesis 5 was supported: MAMENS achieved higher utility scores than the conventional system. The effect of the number of sellers was also significant. The interaction effect was not significant. The results are shown in Table 4 and Figure 3 shows the buyer's total utility value for each group in Experiment II.

Table 4. The results of Experiment II: Hypotheses 5 and 6 (ANOVA).

ANOVA test results (hypotheses 5 and 6)			
Source of Variation	Df	F	P-value
Number of sellers	2	3.39	0.036
Treatment (MAMENS vs. conventional system)	1	17.20	< 0.0005
Interaction	2	1.24	0.291

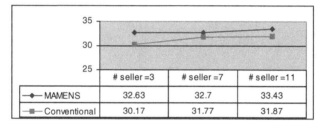

Fig. 3. Buyer's total utility value in Experiment II.

7 Discussions and Conclusion

The research results provide important theoretical implications about the role of information feedback in auction design. Koppius et al. [2000] argue that information feedback during an auction might have a significant impact on the performance of the auction mechanism and their proposition was made regarding the information feedback on improving a bid from a seller's perspective like in [Bodendorf et al. 1997; David et al. 2002]. Parkes [2002] considers auction design in a setting with costly preference elicitation and motivates the role of proxy agents situated between bidders and the auction, and maintain partial information about agent preferences and compute equilibrium bidding strategies based on the available information. The proxy agents can also elicit additional preference information incrementally during an auction. Parkes [2002] shows that indirect mechanisms, such as proxied ascending-price auctions, can achieve better allocative efficiency with less preference elicitation than direct mechanisms, such as sealed-bid auctions.

The simulation results presented in this paper validate the proposition from the buyer's perspective. Revealing information by a party can also tilt the information balance of power [Koppius et al. 2000]. Although this paper did not investigate this issue in depth, it is suggested that a trusted third party can help the participants maintain a balance of power by regulating the degree of information feedback.

The research has several limitations. First, the computer simulation was conducted in a controlled environment to examine the effect of a limited number of factors. Therefore, the research results may turn out differently in real auction situations where various unexamined factors are involved that interact with each other. Second, although this study simulated realistic bargaining situations, some of the parameters were necessarily arbitrary. These limitations are inherent in computer simulation and can be overcome by a field study.

In addition to field experiments, there are several promising areas for future research. There needs to be further investigation on the impact of other variables on the performance of multidimensional auction mechanisms. Although this study investigates the effect of changing the number of bidders in the analysis of multidimensional auctions, there are still more variables that might affect the bargaining outcome in these multidimensional auctions. For example, the effect of the number of issues on the bargaining outcomes has not been thoroughly studied. Future studies need to look at such variables and their interactions by extending the simulation model presented in this study.

References

1. Bichler, M., An Experimental Analysis of Multi-Attribute Auctions, Decision Support Systems 29:249-268, 2000.
2. Bichler, M., The Future of e-Markets, Cambridge University Press, 2001.
3. Bodendorf, F., Bui, T., Reinheimer, S., A Software-Agent-Based DSS for Supporting an Electronic Air Cargo Market, Proceedings of the International Society for Decision Support Systems (ISDSS97), Lausanne, Schweiz, 1997.
4. Branco, F., The Design of Multidimensional Auctions, RAND Journal of Economics, 28(1):63-81, 1997.
5. Che, Y., Design Competition Through Multidimensional Auctions, RAND Journal of Economics, 24(4):668-680, 1993.
6. David, E., Azoulay-Schwartz, R., and Kraus, S., Protocols and strategies for automated multi-attribute auctions, Proceedings of the first international joint conference on Autonomous agents and multiagent systems, 77 - 85, 2002
7. Koppius, O., Kumar, M., Heck, E., Electronic Multidimensional Auctions and the Role of Information Feedback, Proceedings of the 8th European Conference on Information Systems, Vienna, Austria. 2000.
8. McAfee, R. and McMillan, J., Multidimensional Incentive Compatibility and Mechanism Design, Journal of Economic Theory 46:335-54, 1988.
9. Parkes, D., Price-Based Information Certificates for Minimal-Revelation Combinatorial Auctions, Lecture notes in computer science, 2531:103-122, 2002.
10. Strecker, S. and Seifert, S., Electronic sourcing with multi-attribute auctions, Proceedings of the 37th Hawaii International Conference on System Sciences, 2004
11. Strecker, S. and Seifert, S., Preference Revelation in Multi-Attribute Bidding Procedures: An Experimental Analysis, 14th International Workshop on Database and Expert Systems Applications, DEXA'03, September 1-5, Prague, Czech Republic, pp. 850-854, 2003.

Electronic Negotiations –
A Generic Approach with Action Systems

Juho Mäkiö[1], Ilka Weber[1], and Christof Weinhardt[1]

University of Karlsruhe, Information Management and Systems
Englerstrasse 14, 76131 Karlsruhe, Germany
{maekioe,weber,weinhardt}@iw.uka.de

Abstract. This paper proposes a domain-independent generic trading platform
that provides various auction and negotiation types. Requirements of the platform
in the "generic" context, e.g. domain-independency, reusability, and flexibility,
are identified and characterised. We propose two comprehensive concepts provided by the generic platform: (i) a basic order structure, and (ii) a basic transaction process. The generic order presents a domain-independent structure defined
by multiple attributes. The basic transaction process is modelled at a high level
of abstraction respectively various auction and negotiation protocols. Considering the basic transaction process as an action system leads to a finite sequence of
states. Hence, the sequence of states is not fixed, and each state can be individually parameterised. These characteristics enable an individual configuration of an
abstract execution model for negotiation processes and thus provides genericity
in electronic negotiations.

1 Introduction

The intention of our research work is to develop and implement the concept of a generic
platform for electronic markets. The platform is the core, or market server of our generic
system and supports all facets of electronic markets. Ranging form bilateral negotiations
like chatting, to auction mechanisms, or even more complex negotiation protocols, the
generic platform is the basic system that enables the automation of trading and negotiation processes. The platform provides the infrastructure and all necessary services to
set up electronic markets for electronic negotiations. Basic functions that are common
to all electronic markets, and thus provided by the market server, are (1) input functions
that accept input data from outside the system, (2) storage functions that retain input
data and retrieve stored data, (3) processing functions that calculate, and manipulate in
other ways, the input and stored data, and (4) output functions that produce processing
results for use outside the system.

According to these aspects, the trading platform, or market server, can be defined as
a run-time environment for electronic markets. Hence, a market is commonly defined
as a physical, or virtual, location where price is determined and buy and sell orders are
matched to create trades according to a set of rules that govern the processing of these
orders. The definition given in [1] states that "electronic markets are based on technology and are highly automated, providing different types of services for investors".

K. Bauknecht, M. Bichler, and B. Pröll (Eds.): EC-Web 2004, LNCS 3182, pp. 135–143, 2004.
© Springer-Verlag Berlin Heidelberg 2004

Bakos [2] describes electronic markets as "inter-organizational information systems that allow buyers and vendors to exchange information about prices and product offerings". Common to these definitions is that an electronic market carries out a market with technical aids to fulfil the needs of buyers, sellers and other information carriers in respect of information dissemination and exchange. In this context, trading describes the interaction and coordination between buyers and sellers to exchange information, goods, services, and payments. The interaction and coordination process comprises standardised as well as complex transaction processes, e.g. auctions and negotiations. However, electronic markets support the transaction processes mentioned above, enabling multiple buyers and sellers to interact, and provide additional services and tools. Most traditional electronic markets or negotiation systems provide coordination mechanisms, ergo one pricing mechanism.

Since all auctions are negotiations, (but not vice versa, cf. [3]) we consider works from both fields of research in this section. McAffee and McMillan [4] define an auction as "a market institution with an explicit set of rules determining resource allocation and prices on the basis of bids from the market participants". According to Smith [5], an institution, together with an economic environment, defines a microeconomic system.

1. The institution I defines M the language of the market and g, the communication rules for agents as well as the rules governing the communication process (c.f. [5], [6]). Besides this, an institution defines allocation rules h to determine the (provisional or final) allocation of the commodities, and cost imputation rules c, the payment to be made by the agents. The individual property rights of each agent i are defined by $I_i = (M_i, h_i, c_i, g_i)$ specifying the space of possible messages M_i agent i may sent, agent i's allocation h_i, agent's payment c_i, and agent's message exchange rules g_i. The collection of all agents' property rules results in the institutions of the microeconomic system $I = (I_1, \ldots, I_N)$.

2. An economic environment $e = (e_1, \ldots, e_N)$ is defined by the characteristics e_i of economic agents $i \in \{1, \ldots, N\}$ (market participants). Agent's i characteristic e_i is defined over a $K + 1$ dimensional commodity space specifying the agent's utility function, a technology (endowment), and a commodity endowment. Hence, the environment e is defined as a "set of initial circumstances which can not be altered by the agents or the institutions within which they interact" [5]. Furthermore, each characteristic of an agent is private and not publicly observable.

Bringing together both the institution I and the microeconomic environment e, a microeconomic system S can be defined: $S = (e, I)$. Thus, considering each agent i, the microeconomic system S is given by $S = (e, I) = (e_1, \ldots, e_N, I_1, \ldots, I_N)$.

This paper focuses a dynamic view on the phases of the transaction process and its activities of the institution I. The proposed action based approach on the transaction process leans on the media reference model (MRM) [7].

The MRM proposes a comprehensive concept for electronic negotiations contributing to a structured and methodological approach in engineering electronic negotiations. The MRM analyses the transaction process that is the interaction of agents on a (electronic) medium, e.g. a platform or electronic market, and identifies several phases of interaction. Based on the MRM, the contribution of this paper is manifold. We set out to: (1) identify requirements of a generic electronic platform, providing various auction types, e.g. a generic order structure and the generic transaction process, and (2) propose a basic transaction process on a high level of abstraction. Requirements on the generic platform towards the order structure and the transaction process are identified in section 2. Hence, the order structure is not into the scope of this paper and thus we briefly sketch the idea of the generic order type. Section 3 focus on the aspects of a generic platform and present a basic framework for the generic transaction process. The main contribution of this paper is the modelling of the basic transaction process with action systems (cf. Section 3). Section 4 gives an example of an English auction, e.g. matching and allocation, modelled by an action system. In Section 5 we briefly summarise the main contributions of our research work.

2   Platform Requirements

To focus the genericity of the electronic trading system, the aim is to conceptualise and implement a basic system that provides various transaction protocols[1]. Concerning electronic trading systems, the generic characteristic has various facets:

1. *Order-Structure (Request-Structure):* As the electronic trading system is not determined for a specific application domain, the transaction object has to be defined by a flexible and generic order structure (*generic order*). A generic order is constructed to serve various applications - the domain-independent structure is defined by multiple attributes, not limited to a certain number of attributes. For example in a stock market, the order is determined by a ISIN-number, the volume, and the price. In an automobile market, a car is specified by the colour, the horsepower, the type, the driven kilometres, and the price. The number of the attributes is not limited.
A generic order can be seen as a framework, seeking to capture much of the complexity of the transaction objects by encompassing several variables, here attributes. Note that a framework identifies and structures the relevant variables. Furthermore, it also reveals the interactions between the variables. As such, the theory, the framework is based upon, comprises the variables, their organization, their interactions and finally their relationships. Thus, in our context of the generic order, the framework has to provide the characteristics of (1) the transaction object and (2) the market characteristics. To accomplish these prerequisites, the framework provides the dynamic definition and specification of the attributes. As a consequence of this, the framework or the generic order is a powerful concept enabling a generic application to various domains.

2. *Reusability of the transaction process:* The transaction process has to be defined and structured as a reusable process. Here, "reusability" means that the basic structure of the process can be used for similar transaction processes, such as auction (and later, negotiation) processes. Thus, identical or common activities of auctions have to be identified, building a basic structure of the transaction process. The basic activities and the basic process are defined within the core in a domain independent and flexible manner.

---

[1] In this context, "generic" is defined as something that is applicable to an entire class or group.

- *Domain-Independency*: The basic transaction process has to be detached from the domain and its specific transaction object as well as domain-specific behaviour of market participants. The basic process should be adaptable for different domains.
- *Flexibility:* The basic transaction process has to be easily configured and implemented in new domains. Specifying the values of the basic activities within the transaction process results in a new auction type. Thus, a great flexibility in the design and creation of new auction types is achieved.

In a first step focussing on auction processes, our goal is to define and to validate a collection of various auction types. Analysing various auction types shows that all auctions have the process of matching, allocation and pricing in common. The reusability of such a common process allows the platform to run various auction types. Consider a finite number l of auction or negotiation types represented by their institutions $I_{Auction} = \{I^1, \ldots, I^l\}$. Each auction type I^i has its own individual transaction process P_i. Thus, genericity means (here) standardising the individual process to one reusable process. Let P_G be this basic standardised generic transaction process. Then, the standardisation can be expressed by a function π on P_i with $\pi : P_i \to P_G \, \forall i = 1, \ldots, l$. The function π is the standardisation of the auction transaction processes or to say in other words - the mapping of the auction specific transaction processes into one basic transaction process P_G.

Note: The economic environment e can be assumed as given. As e contains e.g. preferences of the agents, which are not commonly known, or the number of market participants, the economic environment is not relevant for modelling the transaction process in an abstract way.

Hence, the basic transaction process can be decomposed in its functional elements or components, which on their elementary level depends on parameters. Thus, we have to distinguish between two views on a generic process: (i) a static view and (ii) a dynamic view. From the static view the generic process depends on the identified parameters and the basic rules (c.f. [8], [9]) - from a dynamic view, it depends on activities that determine the process. Even these activities are controlled by parameters. From a dynamic point of view, the generic transaction process and its characteristics fall within the scope of Section 3.

3   Transaction Process

As mentioned in Section 2, a basic transaction process within the generic platform should fulfil the prerequisites of reusability, e.g. domain-independency and flexibility. The Montreal Taxonomy (MT) [10] focuses on auction and negotiation processes, presenting one common taxonomy. One contribution of the MT is the identification of four transaction phases (cf. [11]) and its sub-phases, as well as phase-relevant parameters common to all auction and negotiation protocols. The four main transaction phases are:

1. the *knowledge phase*, gathering information concerning products, market participants etc.,
2. the *intention phase*, specifying supply and demand with offers to sell and offers to buy,

3. the *agreement phase*, identifying the terms/conditions of the transaction and signing the contract, and

4. the *settlement phase*, executing the agreed-upon contract, determining the payments, supporting post sales etc.

All auction or negotiation protocols have these phases in common; they can differ in the setting of specific processes (rules and algorithms), e.g. different matching and pricing rules in the agreement phase, as well as in the sequence or repetition of the phases, e.g. multi-round negotiation processes . Even complex auction protocols like combinatorial or multi-attribute auctions follow these transaction phases. Thus, one challenge of the generic approach is to provide various negotiation mechanisms in one system.

The definition of P_G focuses on the operational perspectives of markets. Operational perspectives common to all markets embrace the handling of orders. Therefore, processes common to all electronic markets, and respectively order-handling, need to be identified and separated from those unique to each electronic market. We consider these phases as action systems for the abstract description of the negotiation process phases. Originally, action systems were introduced for the "modelling of distributed systems at a high level of abstraction and for rigorous refinement of such models" [12]. Action systems offer a simple execution model where the whole program is considered as a guarded iteration statement [13]. The execution model has the form:

loop
$$A : g \rightarrow S(x)$$
end loop

In this model action A is a statement. The execution of this statement is guarded by the guard g. Each action has a set of participant processes x and a multiple assignment statement $S(x)$ that has read-write-access to the local variables of the process x only. This model consists of atomic units of execution. The sequence of the execution is not definite: the execution of any statement $S(x)$ is allowed if g is *true*. $S(x)$ is a single guarded iteration statement, noted by "**loop**" and "**end loop**", that is repeated and executed as long as g is true.

Considering the negotiation process at the high abstraction level, it consists of four phases: the information phase (*Inf*), the intention phase (*Int*), the agreement phase (*Agr*), and the settlement phase (*Set*). In addition to the negotiation process phases, we introduce an action (*Env*) for the setting of phase independent criteria[2] in the abstract execution model. Thus, adapting the idea of an action system to the negotiation process phases leads to an action system with a limited set of abstract actions. In this instance the basic transaction process P_G can be considered as a sequence of statements as follows:

---

[2] Phase independent criteria do not influence the transaction process and its phases directly. These criteria are determined e.g. by the business structure (e.g. fees) or infrastructure. As noted before the action *Env* does not model the economic environment - the economic environment is assumed as given (e.g. the preferences of agents or the number of market participants).

$$A^{Env} : g^{Env} \rightarrow S^{Env}(x^{Env})$$
$$A^{Inf} : g^{Inf} \rightarrow S^{Inf}(x^{Inf})$$

loop

$$A^{Int} : g^{Int} \rightarrow S^{Int}(x^{Int})$$
$$A^{Agr} : g^{Agr} \rightarrow S^{Agr}(x^{Agr})$$

end loop

$$A^{Set} : g^{Set} \rightarrow S^{Set}(x^{Set})$$

Note that the loop characterizes the iterative character of negotiations. The abstract execution model is not meant as an absolute sequence of executed actions - actions can be repeated, e.g. processes of the intention and agreement phase. The necessity of loops is motivated by, e.g. multi-round negotiation processes, allowing agents or bidders to modify their own offers or to cause a change to the offer of the bid-taker. Hence, revising offers and generating counteroffers leads to an alternating process between the intention and agreement phase [10].

The determination of the process parameters and participant processes requires a closer view on each phase of the negotiation process. According to the MT, this paper concerns the intention phase and the agreement phase of electronic transactions making the following distinction: "an agreement process represents the complete agent interaction in the intention and agreement phase for the coordination of one or more transactions" [10]. Both of these phases can be subdivided in tasks related to the offer exchange in the electronic negotiation. The intention phase (A^{Int}) consists of three subtasks or sub-phases (i) offer specification (A^{Int_1}), (ii) offer submission A^{Int_2}, and (iii) offer analysis A^{Int_3}. The agreement phase (A^{Agr}) can be subdivided in the three phases of (i) offer matching (A^{Agr_1}), (ii) offer allocation (A^{Agr_2}), and (iii) offer acceptance (A^{Agr_3}). Hence, the intention phase is defined by $A^{Int} = (A^{Int_1}, A^{Int_2}, A^{Int_3})$ and the agreement phase by $A^{Agr} = (A^{Agr_1}, A^{Agr_2}, A^{Agr_3})$.

Since auctions vary on the allocation mechanism, on the rules that determine the participation, and on the stopping and starting rules, the simple execution model needs to be enriched by additional process parameters. Considering an action A_k with two classes X_k and Y_k. To each class, participant processes x_k and y_k are defined. Let ω_{x_k} be a process parameter for the process x_k and ω_{y_k} be a process parameter for the process y_k. Then the action A_k has the form:

$$A_k((x_k : X_k, \omega_{x_k}), (y_k : Y_k, \omega_{y_k})) : g_k((x_k, \omega_{x_k}), (y_k, \omega_{y_k})) \rightarrow S_k((x_k, \omega_{x_k}), (y_k, \omega_{y_k}))$$

A_k is enabled if the guard $g_k((x_k, \omega_{x_k}), (y_k, \omega_{y_k}))$ is true, and its execution modifies the local states of x_k and y_k to S_k. Note that the local variables of an object can only be modified in actions in which they participate. The two-process action model is an extension of the action model, enhanced by an additional process and parameterised actions. As such, the extension to multi-process actions, determined by its process parameters is enabled within the nature of the execution model.

Let $X = \{x_0, x_1, \ldots\}$ be a set of all participant processes of the negotiation process and let $\Omega = \{\omega_0, \omega_1, \ldots\}$ be a set of all suitable process parameters. Additionally, a set of transaction phase specific processes $X^{Env}, X^{Inf}, X^{Int_i}, X^{Agr_i}, X^{Set} \subseteq X$ as well as a set of transaction phase specific process parameters $\Omega^{Env}, \Omega^{Inf}, \Omega^{Int_i}, \Omega^{Agr_i},$

$\Omega^{Set} \subseteq \Omega$, $i = 1, 2, 3$ can be specified. Each of these processes belongs to a well-defined class (note, these classes are not further specified here) and the process-specific parameters to a defined type. Focussing one action A^k out of this action model we get:

$$A^k(X^k, \Omega^k) : g^k(X^k, \Omega^k) \to S^k(X^k, \Omega^k)$$

Here the action A^k with $k \in \{Env, Inf, Int_1, Int_2, Int_3, Agr_1, Agr_2, Agr_3, Set\}$ models one of the phases of the transaction processes already mentioned. If the guard $g(X^k, \Omega^k)$ is true, then for any processes of X^k and process-parameters Ω^k an action instantiation $A^k(X^k, \Omega^k)$ is enabled. The execution-task of the action is given by statement S^k.

For instance, applying these actions to the action model of the generic transaction process already mentioned, and substituting the subtasks, a more detailed abstract execution model for electronic negotiations is attained. This more detailed execution model is enriched by additional process parameters and thus offers a new approach towards the basic negotiation process P_G (see execution model below).

Depending on the underlying mechanism determined by rules, some actions need not be specified and can be substituted by empty actions: element x_0 is defined as an empty process and element ω_0 as an empty process-parameter.

It is notable that each concrete execution of a negotiation according to this abstract execution model varies on its particular parameterisation. It enlarges the consideration of Ströbel and Weinhardt [10] by giving a more abstract, as well as precise execution model for electronic negotiations, connecting action systems with the field of research of electronic negotiations.

Execution model of the generic transaction process P_G

$A^{Env}(X^{Env}, \Omega^{Env}) : g^{Env}(X^{Env}, \Omega^{Env}) \to S^{Env}(X^{Env}, \Omega^{Env})$

$A^{Inf}(X^{Inf}, \Omega^{Inf}) : g^{Inf}(X^{Inf}, \Omega^{Inf}) \to S^{Inf}(X^{Inf}, \Omega^{Inf})$

loop

$A^{Int_1}(X^{Int_1}, \Omega^{Int_1}) : g^{Int_1}(X^{Int_1}, \Omega^{Int_1}) \to S^{Int_1}(X^{Int_1})$

$A^{Int_2}(X^{Int_2}, \Omega^{Int_2}) : g^{Int_2}(X^{Int_2}, \Omega^{Int_2}) \to S^{Int_2}(X^{Int_2})$

$A^{Int_3}(X^{Int_3}, \Omega^{Int_3}) : g^{Int_3}(X^{Int_3}, \Omega^{Int_3}) \to S^{Int_3}(X^{Int_3})$

$A^{Agr_1}(X^{Agr_1}, \Omega^{Agr_1}) : g^{Agr_1}(X^{Agr_1}, \Omega^{Agr_1}) \to S^{Agr_1}(X^{Agr_1})$

$A^{Agr_2}(X^{Agr_2}, \Omega^{Agr_2}) : g^{Agr_2}(X^{Agr_2}, \Omega^{Agr_2}) \to S^{Agr_2}(X^{Agr_2})$

$A^{Agr_3}(X^{Agr_3}, \Omega^{Agr_3}) : g^{Agr_3}(X^{Agr_3}, \Omega^{Agr_3}) \to S^{Agr_3}(X^{Agr_3})$

end loop

$A^{Set}(X^{Set}, \Omega^{Set}) : g^{Set}(X^{Set}, \Omega^{Set}) \to S^{Set}(X^{Set})$

4   Example

This section demonstrates how the abstract execution process can be used to define an English auction. The English auction is a sequential price-based auction where the price is tracked by a clock. The English auction constructs a single-sided market with many buyers and one seller, typically used to sell wine, art and antiques, where the supply is a single unit [14].

A small example will be utilized in this paper to illustrate the generic execution model for electronic negotiations. This example models actions A^{Agr_1} (matching) and A^{Agr_2} (allocation) for the execution model of an English auction. The platform software receives parameters for these actions as they are input. These parameters are joined to the platform with the abstract execution model. This combination results in a concrete instance of an English auction that is executable on the generic platform.

In this example "Matcher" is a class and "match" a participant process that is parameterised by a double value "price". The Boolean parameter "exec" provides a control mechanism for the execution of the auction. Note, that this parameter is for an English auction always set "true". This means that the matching will be executed after each buy order inserted into the auction. Setting the value of "exec" to false turns the English auction into a sealed bid auction. In that case, the matching must be triggered separately.

As the "Matcher", the "EnglishAllocator" is also a class, and "allocate" is a participant process of that class. The parameter "triggerType" defines what the allocation will be triggered by, e.g. by the period of time elapsed since the entrance of the last buy order. The "interval" defines the duration of this period. The meaning of the parameter "exec" is analogous to that given for "Matcher". The parameterisation for both actions A^{Agr_1} (matching) and A^{Agr_2} (allocation) is illustrated below:

A^{Agr_1}: $A(match : Matcher, price : double, exec : boolean)$:

$\quad g(match, price, exec) \rightarrow S(match, price, exec)$

A^{Agr_2}: $A(allocate : EnglishAllocator, triggerType : String, interval : integer,$

$\quad exec : boolean)$:

$\quad g(allocate, triggerType, interval, exec)$

$\quad\quad \rightarrow S(allocate, triggerType, interval, exec)$

5   Conclusion

This paper presented an approach to define genericity for electronic negotiation platforms. It suggests defining both order structure and transaction process in a generic way. Integrating these into the platform results in the genericity of the platform. The genericity of the order structure is enhanced by the dynamic definition and specification of order attributes. The genericity of the transaction process is reached by identifying common activities for all negotiations and by defining an abstract execution model based on these common activities. These activities are finally used as parameterisable actions for the definition of the interaction phases of electronic transactions.

The implementation of the generic process and the generic order type into one platform is part of our current work. This platform, the *electronic financial trading platform (e-FITS)*, is a client-server based platform supporting various auction types. These auction types range from single-sided to double-sided auctions and can be combined either sequentially or parallel to complex mechanisms. All these auction types are mapped into one generic process, which is based on action systems as it is presented in this paper. Due to the parametrization of the process, each of these auctions types can individually be configured. Beside, the concept of the generic order structure is implemented in e-FITS. Thus, single- as well as multi-attribute products or even product bundles can be mapped within e-FITS. Future work will focus on complex auction types such as multi-attribute auctions or bundle trading (combinatorial auctions) as well as an extension to electronic negotiations. The implementation of the market structure of these complex auction types is still work in progress.

References

1. Levecq, H., Weber, B.: Electronic trading systems : Strategic implications of market design choices. Journal of Organizational Computing and Electronic Commerce **12** (2002) 85–103
2. Bakos, J.Y.: A strategic analysis of electronic marketplaces. MIS Quarterly **15** (1991) 295–310
3. Kersten, G.E., Teich, J.: Are all e-commerce negotiations auctions? In: Fourth International Conference on the Design of Cooperative Systems, Sophia-Antipolis, France. (2000)
4. McAffee, R., McMillan, J.: Auctions and bidding. Journal of Economic Literature **25** (1987) 699–738
5. Smith, V.L.: Microeconomic systems as an experimental science. The American Economic Review **72** (1982) 923–955
6. Smith, V.L.: Markets, institutions and experiments. Encyclopedia of Cognitive Science (2001)
7. Schmid, B.: Elektronische Märkte - Merkmale, Organisation, Potentiale. In: Handbuch Electronic Commerce. Vahlen Verlag (1999)
8. Wurman, P.R., Wellman, M.P., Walsh, W.E.: A parametrization of the auction design space. Games and Economic Behavior **35** (2001) 304–338
9. Mäkiö, J., Weber, I.: Component-based specification and composition of market structures. In: Procceedings of the MKWI 2004, Coordination and Agent Technology in Value Networks. (2004) 127–137
10. Ströbel, M., Weinhardt, C.: The montreal taxonomy for electronic negotiations. Group Decision and Negotiation Journal **12** (2003) 143–164
11. Schmid, B.: Was ist neu an der digitalen ökonomie? In Belz, C., Bieger, T., eds.: Dienstleistungskompetenz und innovative Geschftsmodelle; Forschungsgespräche der Universitt St. Gallen, Thexis Verlag St. Gallen (1999)
12. Kurki-Suonio, R.: Action systems in incremental and aspect-oriented modeling. Group Decision and Negotiation Journal **16** (2003) 201–217
13. Dijkstra, E.W.: Guarded commands, nondeterminacy and the formal derivation of programs. Communications of the ACM **18** (1975) 453–457
14. Ashenfelter, O.: How auctions work for wine and art. Journal of Economic Perspectives **3** (1989) 23–36

Interaction Trust Evaluation
in Decentralized Environments

Yan Wang and Vijay Varadharajan

Department of Computing
Macquarie University
Sydney, NSW 2109
Australia
{yanwang,vijay}@ics.mq.edu.au

Abstract. In decentralized environments, such as P2P, as lack of central
management, the trust issue is prominently important for interactions
between unfamiliar peers. This paper first presents a probabilistic approach for evaluating the interaction trust of unfamiliar peers according
to their interaction history. In addition, after an interaction, peers can
evaluate each other and modify the trust status. Based on it, this paper
presents an approach for trust value modification after interactions.

1 Introduction

Recent years, P2P and Grid technologies have widely obtained attentions in both
research and industry communities. Some successful systems emerged, such as
GNutella [1], Kazaa [2], SETI@home [3] and Globus [4]. These systems enable
the share of resources in a loosely-coupled network consisting of a large number
of peers. Each peer contributes its information and even CPU resource to the
network. Tasks, such as exchanging a set of large volume or large partition
information, or completing a complex and partitioned task, could be achieved
through the interaction and collaboration of all involved peers.

As lack of the central management in most P2P systems, the dynamic status
of each peer as well as the network causes trust evaluation a very important issue. Before interacting with an unfamiliar (strange) peer, it is rational to doubt
its trustworthiness. Therefore, to enable the trust evaluation prior to interacting with a set of unfamiliar peers makes the transaction securer. In particular,
when P2P network is used for e-commerce applications, the trust evaluation
prominently becomes a more important issue.

To evaluate the trustworthiness of a peer, some methods can be adopted.
Generally there are two categories for these methods. One is based on the mechanism of security certificate authentication. A registered peer should apply a
certificate from a Certificate Authority (CA) that can be used for identifying
the peer to other peers. This is useful to authenticate a new peer which may
newly join the community or it has no interaction history with other peers. And
thus the initial trust can be established if the authentication process is successful.

K. Bauknecht, M. Bichler, and B. Pröll (Eds.): EC-Web 2004, LNCS 3182, pp. 144–153, 2004.

The other category is to investigate a peer with which the end-peer has no interaction history but others do [5]. By collecting the feedbacks from other peers about their comments on the previous interactions, the end-peer may analyze and thereafter determine the trust value of the peer being investigated.

In this paper we propose a novel model that evaluates the trust values of peers. In our method, the trustworthiness of a certain peer can be determined by investigating the interaction history of other peers if the end-peer has no previous interaction with it. Meanwhile a method is also proposed for modifying the trust value of a peer after the interaction with it is completed.

2 Related Work

There are numerous notions of trust and different kinds of trust that satisfy different properties that can be established differently [5].

In terms of computer security, trust is considered as a fundamental concept. An entity is trustworthy if there is sufficient credible evidence leading to believe that the system will meet a set of given requirements. Trust is a measure of trustworthiness, relying on the evidence provided [6]. For instance, in traditional client/server systems, a client should pass the authentication verification by the server before obtaining any privilege for accessing the data from the server. Far from that, a more complex mechanism is proposed in [7] as the process of trust negotiation, where the two parties need to open the respective authentication policy to each other and exchange their required certificates (i.e. credentials in [7]). The outcome of credential exchange depends on if each party accepts the autointoxication policy of the other side and if they have sufficient evidence and credentials to meet the requirement of the other party. These work is generally based on existing standards such as X.509 [8] or PGP [9] and provides various extensions. They are valuable for initial trust establishment for two strangers.

But these methods only take into account the authentication and authority of a peer that may ask certain level access privilege or intend to involve a specific interaction. The outcome after authentication is simply 'Yes' or 'No' where 'Yes' means the authentication is successful and 'No' means unsuccessful. No previous interaction histories are evaluated. In terms of calculation, this is a non-calculative trust [10].

On the other hand, trust can be defined in terms of trust belief and trust behavior [11]. Trust belief between two parties is the extent to which a party believes that the other party is trustworthy in a certain situation. Trustworthy means one is willing and able to act in the other party's interests. Trust behavior between two parties is the extent to which a party depends on the other in a given situation with a feeling of relative security, even though negative consequences are possible. If a trust belief means "party A believes that party B is trustworthy", then it will lead to a trust behavior as "A trusts B" [5].

[5] proposed a PeerTrust model considering the trust belief between two peers in a P2P environment. In this model, each peer will give an evaluation as Satisfaction (S) or Complaint (C) to another peer after their interaction. Any

peer can collect these information about a given unfamiliar peer so as to evaluate the peer in terms of the degree of satisfaction it receives in providing services to other peers in the past. Anyway, we would like to argue that it is a bit simple for more exact trust evaluation if a peer assigns just satisfaction or complaint after it receives the service of the other peer. Moreover, how to evaluate the trust value of a peer if the end-peer has at least one interaction already is not mentioned in the literature.

3   Trust Evaluation

In this section, we will propose our model that evaluates the trust values of peers by investigating other peers. In our method, the trustworthiness of a certain peer can be determined by investigating the interaction history of other peers if the end-peer has no previous interaction with it. After the investigation, the probability of a given threshold of trust value for a peer can be calculated. With these collected results, a set of peers can be chosen that satisfy the requirement of the end-peer. After that, the end-peer can choose some of them to collaborate for completing specific tasks. Meanwhile a method is also proposed for modifying the trust value of a peer after the interaction with it is completed. In the following context, for the sake of simplicity, we assume that feedbacks are collected from a large number of honest peers after the process of filtering malicious complaining peer. A method for identifying malicious complaining peers can be found in [12].

3.1   Trust Metrics

In P2P environments, a peer can be client and server anytime providing shared resources and services to the open community. The trust of a given peer is the existing cumulative degree of satisfaction from other peers based on the services and their quality it ever provided to these peers.

1. For an individual peer, its degree of satisfaction with another peer which is a service provider in an interaction can be a real number among a predefined scope (e.g. a real number among $[0,1]$), not just simply 1 or 0. The value may result from the service quality, the recognition by the end-peer.
   For example, end-peer A broadcasts a set of tasks to a set of remote peers. After the results are returned, A could compare the quality of services performed by different peers. If a peer frequently misbehaved, it will constantly get low evaluation by most other peers. The final trust value is the cumulative sum of feedbacks from a large number peers for a relative long period.
2. Regarding a certain peer, suppose the initial trust value is a very low value (e.g., $0.1 \in [0,1]$), constant good behaviors should be able to upgrade its trust value. Anyway, constant good behaviors in a short period (with only a few interactions) should promote less than that in a relatively longer period (with many interactions). Meanwhile, a positive high value should affect less to a peer with high trust value. For example, suppose the trust value is a

real number among [0,1], if peer A has got its cumulative trust value of 0.9, a new higher value 0.95 can only give a minor positive affect (e.g., +0.001) to A's trust value. The positive increment of A's trust value should result from constant good behaviors. Likewise, in such a case, a new lower value also brings minor negative affect to a high value peer since the high value is established through long-term interactions with good behaviors.

3.2   Trust Evaluation Method

Now suppose an end-peer A hopes to have a transaction with a peer X, with whom A has no previous interaction history. To evaluate the trust status of X, A will have to investigate the trust value through other peers which have transaction histories with X.

Now we assume that each peer gives a trust value (a real value) between 0 and 1 over the other after a transaction. That is if peer Y just has a transaction with peer Z, the trust value given by Y over Z is denoted as $T_{Y \to Z} \in [0, 1]$. "1" means the highest satisfaction degree while "0" means the lowest one. After having collected a set of feedbacks from other peers, A could analyze the data and make the estimation on the trust status of peer X based on Gauss Distribution in Probability Theory [13].

Suppose peer A has sent requests to a set of intermediate peers $\{M_1, M_2, \ldots, M_k\}$ from which A will collect feedbacks

$$\{T_{M_1 \to X}, T_{M_2 \to X}, \ldots, T_{M_k \to X}\}$$

The *mean trust value* $\bar{T}$ can be calculated as

$$\bar{T} = \frac{1}{k} \sum_{i=1}^{k} T_{M_i \to X} \tag{1}$$

Accordingly, the *sample variance* is

$$S^2 = \frac{1}{k-1} \sum_{i=1}^{k} (T_{M_i \to X} - \bar{T})^2 \tag{2}$$

Let $\mu = \bar{T}$, $\sigma^2 = S^2$. Since $T \sim N(\mu, \sigma^2)$, for any random variable T and a given value v, according to the theory of Gauss Distribution [13], we have the distribution function as follows

$$F(v) = P(T \le v) = \frac{1}{\sqrt{2\pi}\sigma} \int_{-\infty}^{\frac{v-\mu}{\sigma}} e^{-\frac{x^2}{2}} dx \tag{3}$$

Likewise, we have

$$P(T > v) = \frac{1}{\sqrt{2\pi}\sigma} \int_{\frac{v-\mu}{\sigma}}^{\infty} e^{-\frac{x^2}{2}} dx \tag{4}$$

Definition 1: After having collected $\{T_{M_1 \to X}, T_{M_2 \to X}, \ldots, T_{M_n \to X}\}$ from a set of intermediate peers $\{M_1, M_2, \ldots, M_n\}$ and calculated $\bar{T}$ and S^2, $P(v_1 < T \le$

v_2), the probability of X's trust value in a given scope $(v_1, v_2]$ $(v_1 < v_2, v_1, v_2 \in [0, 1])$, is

$$P_\alpha^X(v_1, v_2) = P(v_1 < T \le v_2) = \frac{1}{\sqrt{2\pi}\sigma} \int_{\frac{v_1-\mu}{\sigma}}^{\frac{v_2-\mu}{\sigma}} e^{-\frac{x^2}{2}} dx \qquad (5)$$

Definition 2: From definition 1, end peer A could calculate *the probability that peer X's trust value is better than a given value* $v \in [0, 1]$.

$$P_\beta^X(v) = P(T > v | T \in (0, 1]) = \frac{P(v < T \le 1)}{P(0 < T \le 1)} = \frac{\int_{\frac{v-\mu}{\sigma}}^{\frac{1-\mu}{\sigma}} e^{-\frac{x^2}{2}} dx}{\int_{-\frac{\mu}{\sigma}}^{\frac{1-\mu}{\sigma}} e^{-\frac{x^2}{2}} dx} \qquad (6)$$

If there are a number of potential peers $\{X_1, X_2, \ldots, X_n\}$ that peer A can complete transactions with, the request sent by A will ask other peers to reply their feedbacks about the trust value over there peers. Given a trust value threshold φ, the final best peer B can be chosen as

$$\exists B \in \{X_1, X_2, \ldots, X_n\}, \quad P_a^B(\varphi) = \max_{1 \le i \le n} \{P_a^{X_i}(\varphi)\} \qquad (7)$$

3.3   Trust Modification After Interactions

In this section, we will discuss the method for trust modification after interactions.

In addition to the trust metrics in section 3.1, some principles on trust value computation are as follows:

1. Incremental number of ratings taken into account in an evaluation reduces the level of modification applied over the trust rating until a certain level of confidence is archived. Then the modification applied becomes constant.
2. A larger difference of the existing trust value and the newly given trust value should certainly cause more changes in the trust evaluation. In contrast, a smaller difference will have less affect.

A Possible Solution. Here we suppose that after an interaction, a satisfaction degree $s_i \in [0, 1]$ at time t_i can be given. With s_i, the corresponding trust value is

$$T_i = s_i^m \qquad (8)$$

where m is an integer and $m \ge 1$

We call m a *strictness factor*. For example, suppose a satisfaction degree is $s_i = 0.9$, then $T_i = 0.9$ if $m = 1$ or $T_i = 0.81$ if $m = 2$. The larger m is, the lower T_i is. The larger m is, the stricter it is.

But equation (8) cannot reflect the relationship between current trust value T_i and previous trust value T_{i-1}.

If T_{i-1} is the trust value at time t_{i-1}, s_i is the satisfaction degree obtained at time t_i, then the trust value at time t_i is

$$T_i = T_{i-1} + \theta_i \cdot (s_i - T_{i-1}^{\frac{1}{m}})^m \qquad (9)$$

where $m=1, 2, 3, \ldots$; θ_i is the *impact factor* determining the impact of recent change on the trust value.

Here, we define θ_i as

$$\theta_i = \frac{e^{1-T_{i-1}} - 1}{e + 1} \qquad (10)$$

Analyzing the above equations, we can observe that

1. If $T_{i-1} = 1$ then $\theta_i = 0$. So $T_i = T_{i-1}$. Namely if $\lim_{i \to \infty} T_{i-1} = 1$, then $\lim_{i \to \infty} \theta_i = 0$ and $\lim_{i \to \infty} T_i = T_{i-1}$
   From this property, we can know that if the trust value of a peer is very high (e.g. 1) after many interactions, the new trust value will have minor affect (refer to principle (2) in section 3.1).
2. If $T_{i-1} = 0$, then according to equation (10),

$$\theta_i = \frac{e - 1}{e + 1} \approx 0.46 = \theta_{max}$$

Hence from equation (9), we have

$$T_i = \frac{e - 1}{e + 1} \cdot s_i^m$$

From this property we could know that for a new peer with no interaction history, its initial value is 0. In its first interaction, if the satisfaction degree is 1, the new trust value will be about 0.46, extremely better than the previous value 0. But it is still far from 1. This is because of principle (2) of trust metrics in section 3.1. The cumulative trust value should result from constant interactions with positive feedback. If the peer continues obtaining positive high values, its trust value can move further toward 1.

Anyway, the problem with equations (10) and (9) exists when a peer X has gained very high trust value (e.g. 1) after sufficient $i-1$ interactions with another peer Y. If in the ith interaction, Y was cheated or something serious occurred. How to assign a new trust value?

Now consider a typical case: Suppose $T_{i-1} = 1$ and $v_i = 0$. According to equation (10), $\theta_i = 0$. So the trust value of peer X will not be affected. Therefore, equation (10) only considers the case of positive increment. The case of negative increment should also be taken into account.

A Corrected Solution. Now let's discuss the correctness of the above solution.

Definition 3: If T_{i-1} is the trust value at time t_{i-1}, s_i is the satisfaction degree obtained at time t_i, then *the trust value at time t_i is*

$$T_i = T_{i-1} + \theta_i \cdot (s_i^m - T_{i-1}) \qquad (11)$$

where $m=1, 2, 3, \ldots$; θ_i is the impact factor determining the impact of recent change on the trust value.

Definition 4: Now, we define the *impact factor* as

$$\theta_i = \frac{e^{|s_i^m - T_{i-1}|} - 1}{e + 1} \tag{12}$$

The properties of equation (11) and (12) are discussed as follows.

Property 1: If $\lim_{i \to \infty} |s_i^m - T_{i-1}| = 1$, then $\lim_{i \to \infty} \theta_i = \theta_{max}$. From equation (12), it is easy to have

$$\text{if } \lim_{i \to \infty} |s_i^m - T_{i-1}| = 1, \text{ then } \lim_{i \to \infty} \theta_i = \frac{e-1}{e+1} = \theta_{max}$$

From this property, we could observe that in the two cases discussed in section 3.3, $|s_i^m - T_{i-1}| = 1$. So no matter what the peer gets, a positive or a negative feedback, the weight will be the maximum. If peer X was assigned a new satisfaction degree as 0 while its previous trust value is 1, according to equation (12) and (11), its new trust value will become 0.54, which is in an intermediate level (relatively low level).

Meanwhile, for a new peer with no interaction history, its initial value is 0. In its first interaction, if the satisfaction degree is 1, the new trust value will be about 0.46, extremely better than the previous value 0. But it is still far from 1. This is because of principle (2) of trust metrics in section 3.1. The cumulative trust value should result from constant interactions with positive feedback. If the peer continues obtaining positive high values, its trust value can move further toward 1.

Property 2: If $\lim_{i \to \infty} |s_i^m - T_{i-1}| = 0$, then $\lim_{i \to \infty} \theta_i = 0$.

In this property, when $\lim_{i \to \infty} T_{i-1} = 1$, if s_i is very close to T_{i-1}, namely $\lim_{i \to \infty} s_i = 1$, then $\lim_{i \to \infty} |s_i^m - T_{i-1}| = 0$ and hence $\lim_{i \to \infty} \theta_i = 0$. This means that if a peer's trust value is very high, a new high value of satisfaction degree will not affect the trust value too much.

Property 3: For any $s_i \in [0,1]$ and $T_i \in [0,1]$, $\theta_i \in [0, 0.46]$. According to definition 4, the more the difference of T_{i-1} and s_i^m is, the larger θ_i is. This is consistent to principle (2) in section 3.3.

Principle (1) in section 3.3 will be examined in our experiments.

4   Simulation

4.1   Experiment 1

This experiment compares the impact of different values of strictness factor m on the trust evaluation (see equation (11) and (12)). We set m to 1, 2, and 3 respectively. With static $s_i = 0.9$, the trust value variations are illustrated in Fig. 1. We can observe that with the same T_0 and s_i, the higher the m is, the lower the T_i is.

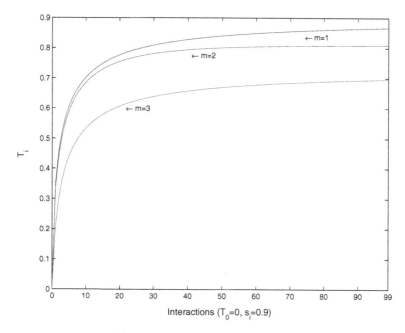

Fig. 1. T_i variations in experiment 1

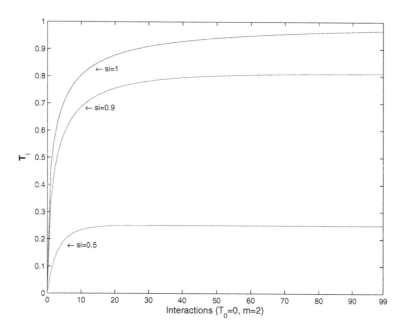

Fig. 2. T_i variations in experiment 2

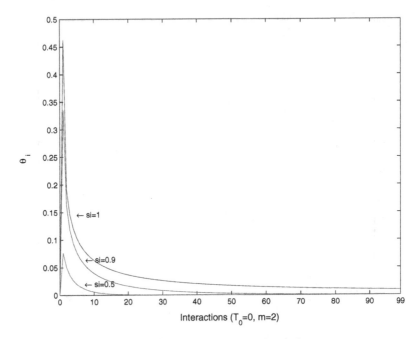

Fig. 3. θ_i variations in experiment 2

4.2 Experiment 2

In this experiment, we set $m = 2$ and set static s_i in different values aiming at observing the variation of trust value (see Fig. 2). Meanwhile the wight variations are illustrated in Fig. 3. The performances in Fig. 2 are consistent to principle (2) in section 3.1 and principle (1) in section 3.3.

In this experiment, the initial trust value is set as 0. We can observe that when having sufficient interactions with stable s_i, the final trust value is approximately s_i^m, namely $\lim_{i \to \infty} T_i = s_i^m$.

From Fig. 3, we can observe that with static s_i, θ_i becomes less and less soon. The performance is consistent to principle (2) in section 3.1.

5 Conclusions

In this paper, we have discussed the approach for evaluating the interaction trust in P2P environment. We also proposed an approach for trust modification after interactions. They are valuable for peers to collect other peers' interaction history to the trust evaluation or identify each other's service satisfactory degree for trust modification. The property analysis and simulation have examined that the trust metrics and principles are basically followed.

Moreover, we envisage that trust and security are two prominent dimensions in P2P environments where lacks central management. We will continue working on the security and trust framework incorporating the interaction trust evaluation approach. Meanwhile, the interaction trust evaluation can be combined with certificate and security based trust evaluation/establishment before any interaction occurs between two unfamiliar peers. Furthermore the method to eliminate the negative effect of malicious peers which evaluate very low values to other peers will be explored in our future work.

References

1. *GNutella.* http://www.GNutella.com/.
2. *Kazaa.* http://www.Kazaa.com/.
3. *SETI@home.* http://www.SETI@home.com/.
4. *Globus.* http://www.Globus.com/.
5. L. Xiong and L. Liu, "PeerTrust: A trust mechanism for an open peer-to-peer information system," Tech. Rep. GIT-CC-02-29, Georgia Institute of Technology, 2002.
6. M. Bishop, *Computer Security: Art and Science.* Addition-Wesley Press, 2003.
7. T. Yu, M. Winslett, and K. E. Seamons, "Interoperable strategies in automated trust negotiation," in *Proceedings of ACM Conference on Computer and Communications Security 2001*, pp. 146–155, 2001.
8. International Telecommunication Union, *Rec. X.509-Information Technology-Open Systems Interconnection-The Directory: Authentication Framework*, August 1997.
9. P. Zimmerman, PGP *User's Guide, MIT Press.* 1994.
10. B. Nooteboom, *Trust: Foundations, Functions, Failure and Figures.* Edward Elgar Publishing Inc., 2002.
11. D. H. Knight and N. L. Chervany, "The meaning of trust," Tech. Rep. WP9604, Universoty of Minnesota, Management Information Systems Research Center, 1996.
12. K. Aberer and Z. Despotovic, "Managing trust in a peer-2-peer information system," in *Proceedings of CIKM 2001*, pp. 310–317.
13. G. Grimmett, *Probability: An Introduction.* Oxford University Press, 1986.

Towards a Privacy Preserving e-Commerce Protocol

Indrajit Ray and Mike Geisterfer

Department of Computer Science
Colorado State University
Fort Collins, CO 80523, USA
{indrajit,mgeister}@cs.colostate.edu

Abstract. Every time a user performs a transaction over the Internet, a wealth of personal information is revealed, either voluntarily or involuntarily. This causes serious breach of privacy for the user, in particular, if the personally identifying information is misused by the different players involved in the transaction. Ideally, therefore, the user would like to have a considerable degree of control over what personal information to reveal and to whom. In this paper we propose a new e-commerce protocol that helps the user protect her privacy while purchasing products over the Internet. The proposed scheme provides a flexible and powerful approach for the secure handling of private data and offers the user considerable control over how she wishes to disseminate her personal data.

1 Introduction

Researchers are increasingly getting concerned about protecting the user's privacy during an e-commerce transaction session. Unfortunately, efforts to define and develop technologies that support the specification of consumer privacy requirements as well as help protect them, are evolving at a considerably slow pace. Efforts like the Platform for Privacy Preferences (P3P) Project of the World Wide Web consortium [9] and others, provide solutions to some facets of electronic consumer privacy. Majority of such efforts attempt to define mechanisms by which the user can understand how a site, with which the user is planning to undertake an e-commerce transaction, handles personal information. Proponents argue that these efforts enable the users to act on what they see. However, currently there does not exist a working definition of what constitutes a violation of consumer privacy in the electronic arena. Technology does not exist that allows a customer to selectively disseminate personally identifying information during an e-commerce transaction.

There has been work done in the past on enabling technologies, like the use of anonymity and pseudonymity models, secure transmission protocols and use of third parties and identity repositories for preserving privacy. While these works contribute to a great extent towards protecting private information from prying eyes, they do little towards the misuse of information by players who have access to such information. Used separately, these models, tools and technologies solve only parts of the problem. Used together in a co-operative manner, these existing and emerging resources can provide the consumer with techniques that allow them more control over how they want to share private information. This way, we believe, the consumer will have her own level

K. Bauknecht, M. Bichler, and B. Pröll (Eds.): EC-Web 2004, LNCS 3182, pp. 154–163, 2004.

of electronic privacy protection. In this work, we first attempt to provide a working definition of electronic privacy from the point of view of consumers. We then propose a new protocol for e-commerce transactions that helps protect consumer privacy in the light of our definition.

The rest of the paper is organized as follows. Section 2 describes our proposed privacy preserving protocol. We begin the section by providing a working definition of what constitutes consumer privacy. We look into the literature to determine what others have said about privacy and then formulate our own (section 2.1). Then in section 2.2 we summarize the assumptions that we make for the proper functioning of the protocol. This is followed in section 2.3 with a description of the protocol. The protocol is analyized in section 2.4. Fially we conclude in section 3.

2   Proposed Privacy Preserving Protocol

2.1   Consumer Privacy – A Working Definition

Privacy has been defined in many, sometimes radically different, ways. There are those that think of privacy as a right, equating it to some absolute standard. There are others that believe that privacy is merely an alleged benefit that can be revoked or nullified at a whim under the guise of societal priorities. As individuals, we each have different needs and views of what constitutes personal and private information [2]. This task is a bit more difficult when we have to define what privacy means to us as we use the Internet, mainly because the average Internet user has very little idea as to what the information profile they present on the Internet [2], and how easily that information can be observed and captured. The literature provides us with several attempts to define privacy on the Internet. Each of these definitions of privacy is either based on some static categorization of data or deals with privacy from a single viewpoint of a specific type of user within a system [4, 3, 8, 16]. Unfortunately, most of these definitions have been proposed by entities that have little at stake in that privacy, namely, the web sites where the consumer transacts business. These web sites have most of the control and power when they deal with consumers [2, 8, 10]. Thus their definitions do little to help the consumer.

We adapt the definition of privacy from [15]. We define consumer information privacy as follows.

Definition 1. *Consumer information privacy is an interest that the Internet consumer has in maintaining her personal information including data and knowledge about themselves, their actions and activities, securely in her control without that control being compromised by other individuals end entities.*

Definition 2. *A consumer information privacy policy is a set of specifications that control the capture, use and dissemination of all information that is subject to that consumer's definition of information privacy.*

The implication of this definition of consumer privacy is that it now allows the consumer some say over how to and what to reveal about their personal information. We are now ready to give our protocol, which allows the consumer to explicitly specify what information can be shared.

2.2 Protocol Prelude and Assumptions

Our protocol relies on a trusted third party, TP, which is a trusted repository of select personal and private information of the consumer. A TP is expected to work only
for the customer and is expected not to behave in any manner that is detrimental to
the customer. The TP can, without revealing the personal and private information of
the customer to a second party, complete a transaction on behalf of the consumer. Our
protocol also relies on anonymizing networks [7, 1, 4, 5, 11, 6, 12–14] between the customer and the different players who stand to gain by linking the current transaction
to the consumer. We assume that the anonymizing network also provides protection
against message coding attacks, message volume attacks, timing attacks and replay attacks.

A consumer C wishes to make purchases over the internet, knowing that she will
have to release some of her private information to complete such transactions. To facilitate such purchases, C registers her private data with the trusted third party TP. C sends
TP a set of personal and private information that she anticipates will be needed to complete various transactions. She also establishes a privacy policy PC that describes the
minimum exposure restrictions for her data stored with TP. C stores with TP the following information: her name, two aliases, two separate mailing addresses, two credit card
numbers, and an email address. As part of registration process with TP, C also provides
enough personal information so that TP can authenticate her to its satisfaction. It is the
responsibility of TP to protect this data from entities other then C.

We assume that the following players, besides the customer C and the merchant M,
are involved in the transaction – the trusted third part TP, the bank, B and the shipper,
S. C does not directly distribute any of her personal information to any business entity
during a transaction. She relies on TP to distribute necessary information in exactly
the manner that she directs. This gives C the maximum control over that portion of her
private data that is typically needed to complete e-commerce transactions. However,
we need to be careful about collusions among the various players in the protocol. Although each player by itself may not have sufficient information about a consumer they
can share this information and link one with the other to jeopardize the privacy of the
consumer. We do not overrule such collusion other than one involving TP and the bank.

The following activities are assumed to be done before the actual protocol starts.

1. The consumer C and the trusted third party TP have successfully exchanged a
   shared secret key K_{CTP}.
2. C creates a one time public/private key pair (C_{ipub}, C_{iprv}) that is valid only for the
   duration of the current transaction. The certificate for this public key is self signed.
   The key is shared with the merchant. The merchant optionally (if the merchant
   also wants anonymity for its participation in the transaction) generates a one-time
   publi/private key pair (M_{ipub}, M_{iprv}). The merchant shares this key with the customer.
3. C and M completes policy (trust) negotiation, resulting in a transaction policy P.
   This policy P includes the designation of recipients of individual items of C's private data.

We assume that each time a player needs access to some private information of
the customer, the player approaches TP with a ticket that bears authorization from the

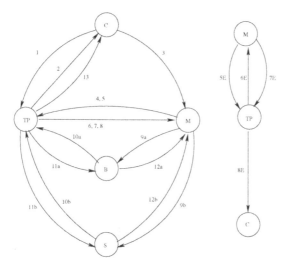

Fig. 1. Messages exchanged in protocol execution

customer for the release of relevant information. We also assume the communication between the customer and the merchant is over an anonymizing network.

2.3 Protocol Description

Figure 1 summarizes the messages exchanged in the privacy preserving e-commerce protocol. We discuss the protocol in details in the following.

Message 1 $C \Longrightarrow TP$: $[(C_{id-auth}, M_{id}, 2, n, C_{ipub}), K_{CTP}]$

C starts the transaction by sending TP the following items: (i) a true self-identifier, C_{auth}, (ii) an identifier for the merchant, M_{id}, (iii) the number (2 in this case) of ticket granting tickets, TGTs, that will be issued in this transaction, and (iv) a nonce, n, all encrypted with a secret key, K_{CTP}, shared by C and TP. By sending this message to TP, C is actually requesting a unique transaction id and a session public key for subsequent communications with TP. $C_{id-auth}$ is a value that authenticates C to TP. For a given transaction T_i, C can send any number of TGTs. This depends on the number of additional players that are involved in the transaction besides the merchant. In our case, C is sending 2. A nonce is used to authenticate the receipt from TP and prevent replay. C_{ipub} is the one-time public key of C unique to this transaction.

Message 2 $TP \Longrightarrow C$: $[(T_i, ň, TP_{ipub}), K_{CTP}]$

Upon receiving the initial request from C, TP generates a unique transaction id, T_i, and a unique public/private key pair (TP_{ipub}/TP_{iprv}) to be used for the duration of the transaction. TP sends C these items together with a response nonce $ň$. TP_{ipub} should be used by all participants that wish to communicate with TP during this transaction.

Message 3 $C \Longrightarrow M$: $[G_1, M_{ipub}]$, $[(T_i, TP_{ipub}, C_{nym}), M_{ipub}]$, $[([(T_i, [KD(G_1), K_{CTP}],$
instruct$), TP_{ipub}]), M_{ipub}]$
where $G_1 =$ uselimit,expiry,$P, (d_{name}, M), (d_{pay}, B), (d_{addr}, S)$ instruct $= \{\}$
Now that it has acquired T_i and TP_{ipub}, C can issue TGTs to M. C sends the following as the first TGT: (i) the grant list, G_1, (ii) the transaction id , Ti, (iii) the public
key of TP, TPipub, (iv) identification of C as known to M, Cnym, (v) and a special
section that must be passed on to TP. The entire message 3 is considered a TGT.
The grant list G_1 consists of:
  - *uselimit*, the number of times this TGT may be submitted to TP. For this example, this value is 1, allowing M to submit this TGT just once.
  - *expiry TP*, a time indicating the time when this TGT is no longer valid.
  - the transaction policy P, and
  - a list of paired values: the id of the private data belonging to C to which M will
    gain access, and the recipient of the actual value of the data represented by the
    id. In the second pair in G of message 3, d_{pay} is the id of C's payment information, and B indicates that M's bank B will receive the actual data associated to
    d_{pay}.
T_i is the transaction id. TP_{ipub} is the public key of TP for T_i. C_{nym} is the 'name' by
which M knows C. This value allows C to remain anonymous to M if it so chooses.
If C has no need to be anonymous, then C would use a known identity as the value
of C_{nym}.
The special section is there specifically to ensure the integrity of the TGT arriving
at TP. This section, encrypted in TP_{ipub}, contains a repeat of the transaction id, T_i,
a signed keyed digest of the grant list G_1, and a fixed length field that could contain
special instructs for TP concerning this TGT.

Message 4 $C \Longrightarrow M$: $[G_2, M_{ipub}]$, $[(T_i, TP_{ipub}, C_{nym}), M_{ipub}]$, $[([(T_i, [KD(G_2), K_{CTP}],$
instruct$), TP_{ipub}]), M_{ipub}]$
where $G_2 = 7,6$ months,$P, (d_{email}, M)$instruct $= \{$"$d_{email} : blind forward$"$\}$
C sends another TGT, with different *uselimit* and *expiry* values.
The grant list G_2 consists of:
  - an *uselimit* of 7, allowing M to submit this TGT a maximum of 7 times.
  - an *expiry* of 6 months.
  - the transaction policy P, and
  - a list of paired (id, recipient) values.
For this TGT, C has placed special instructions for TP in the special section. C will
indicate that TP should provide a redirect for C's email address instead of handing
the actual email address to M. In this case, when M requests uses a ticket to request
an email address of C, TP will return an address that will eventually forward any
email sent to that address to the actual email address of C. In this manner, C retains
full control on this private data.

Message 5 $M \Longrightarrow TP$: $[(G_1, T_i, M_{ipub}, [(T_i, [KD(G_1), K_{CTP}],$ instruct$), TP_{ipub}]), TP_{ipub}]$
Now that M has received the TGTs from C, it can proceed with its part of the
transaction. Its first task is to submit the first TGT to TP, as a request for tickets
granting access to the data items listing in G_1. It sends TP: (i) the grant list, (ii)
the transaction id, (iii) it's own transaction specific public key, and (iv) the special
section created by C for TP.

Messages 6, 7, 8 $TP \Longrightarrow M$: $[(Denied, reason), M_{ipub}]$ {Message 6}
OR
$TP \Longrightarrow M$: $[(t_{pay}, B, T_i), M_{ipub}]$ {Message 6}
$TP \Longrightarrow M$: $[(t_{addr}, B, T_i), M_{ipub}]$ {Message 7}
$TP \Longrightarrow M$: $[[name, TP_{iprv}], M_{ipub}]$ {Message 8}
A triple of the form (t_i, R_j, T_k) is termed a 'ticket'; t_i is the token for data i, R_j is the recipient of the data, and T_k is the transaction specific id.
Upon receiving message 5 from M, TP must first satisfy itself that the integrity of G_1 has been maintained. If not, TP sends M a reply stating the request was denied and the reason why (integrity violation). At this point, the transaction is over. From here, we go to message 13, where TP will ack to C the status of the transaction.
If TP accepts message 5, then it has to make sure that the specific requests for access to C's private data are allowed under P and the installed default policy for C, P_C. P_C, created sometime earlier by C, is stored at TP, and describes the minimum confidentiality limits for C's data stored at TP. Any request to access data submitted to TP by any other party must meet at least these policies. P, the transaction policy, contains the agreed upon policies for the accesses granted in the grant list, in this case G_1.
Seeing that the requests have met the policies in P, TP sends tickets to M, each containing a token for the access, the recipient of that data, and the transaction id.
Message 6 is a ticket for the payment information for this transaction. It consists of a token to access the payment information (d_{pay}), t_{pay}, the designation of the recipient, in this case B, and the transaction id, T_i.
Message 7 consists of a token to access daddr, t_{addr}, its recipient, S, and T_i.
Message 8 shows a short cut. Since TP sees that M is the recipient of the dname information, it does not need to send it a ticket for access. Since G_1 granted a single time access to this data, TP can send the data directly (name) to M, without having the extra handshake involved with a ticket.
Now, here it seems that C is providing M with some of its private data, namely C's name. Actually, C supplied M with a name, which may have just been an acceptable alias or pseudonym for C.

Message 9A $M \Longrightarrow B$: $[([(t_{pay}, B, T_i), M_{prv}], TP, TP_{ipub}), B_{cpub}]$
The merchant M wants payment for the product he is providing C, so he sends to his bank the information necessary to secure that payment. M sends B: (i) the ticket necessary to access C's private payment information, (ii) the id of the trusted party holding that data, TP, and (ii) the transaction specific public key for TP, TP_{ipub}.
B interprets the receipt of message 9A as a request by M of B to complete a transfer of payment into M's account using the information in the ticket.

Message 10A $B \Longrightarrow TP$: $[((t_{pay}, B, T_i), [(B_{auth}, T_i), B_{cprv}]), TP_{ipub}]$
For B to obtain any useful data from TP, it must be able to specify the data and demonstrate the authority to retrieve it; moreover it needs to authenticate itself to TP. To do this, B sends TP: (i) the ticket for the payment data, and (ii) a digitally signed authentication code, B_{auth}, and transaction id.
Bauth is a unique code that has been pre-established between B and TP. Use of this code in conjunction with T_i establishes B as the authentic recipient of the data specified in the ticket (t_{pay}, B, T_i).

160 Indrajit Ray and Mike Geisterfer

Message 11A $TP \Longrightarrow B$: $[(Denied, reason), B_{cpub}]$

OR

$TP \Longrightarrow B$: $[([(F_C, KD(F_C)), TP_{iprv}], [[(t_{pay}, B, T_i), TP_{iprv}], M_{ipub}]), B_{cpub}]$

When TP receives a ticket (as in message 10A) is must do several things. It must first check to see that it is a valid ticket. To be valid, (t_{pay}, B, T_i) must match the signature of a ticket that has been issued by TP, but not redeemed. A signature is the three values as a related triple, and each of these fields must be valid. If the ticket signature is valid, then it checks to see if the ticket has expired. The ticket expiry and use limit were set by the granting TGT (in this case G_1 from message 5) and stored at TP when the ticket was created. The entity requesting data with the ticket must also be verified as the authentic recipient of that data. The code B_{auth} is used for this authentication.

If TP determines that the ticket is invalid, it sends B a message indicating that the request was denied, and a reason why it was denied (expired, uses depleted, mismatch on signature, or invalid recipient).

If TP determines that the ticket is valid, then it sends back to B: (i) the actual payment data for this transaction, F_C, (ii) a keyed digest of F_C, and (iii) an a special message to be passed back to M.

In this example, F_C is the amount of the transaction and the appropriate credit card information for C. B will run a typical credit card swipe payment transaction to credit M's account for the amount indicated from the credit card account of C. A keyed digest of F_C is included as extra confidence that the information supplied in F_C is correct.

Because a ticket issued by T_p to M was redeemed by someone other than M, TP will send an acknowledgement of that redemption through the redeemer back to M.

Message 12A $B \Longrightarrow M$: $[([Unsuccessful, B_{cprv}], (Denied, reason)), M_{ipub}]$

OR

$B \Longrightarrow M$: $[[XferInfo, B_{cprv}], M_{ipub}], [[(t_{pay}, B, T_i), TP_{iprv}], M_{ipub}]$

If the ticket request made by B to TP was denied, it will send a similar message back to M, stating that the funds transfer was unsuccessful.

If B has successfully completed the funds transfer, it will acknowledge this to M, as well as send the acknowledgment message send to it by TP. B sends M: (i) a digitally signed acknowledgement of a completed funds transfer, including any transaction processing information important to B and M, and (ii) the block of message from TP for M.

Messages 9B, 10B, 11B, 12B $M \Longrightarrow S$: $[([(t_addr, S, T_i), M_{prv}], TP, TP_{ipub}), S_{pub}]$

$S \Longrightarrow TP$: $[((t_addr, S, T_i), S_{auth}, T_i), S_{prv}]), TP_{ipub}]$

$TP \Longrightarrow S$: $[([(A_C, KD(A_C), TP_{iprv}], [[(t_{addr}, S, T_i), TP_{iprv}], M_{ipub}]), S_{pub}]$

$S \Longrightarrow M$: $[[XferInfo, S_{prv}, M_{ipub}], [[(t_{addr}, S, T_i), TP_{iprv}], M_{ipub}]$

Message 9B - 12B follow a similar course as 9A- 12A.

Now that M has received payment for the product from C, he needs to know where to ship the product. M will now follow the same protocol as in message 9A- 12A to get the shipping address of C to the shipping company S. In this way, when S retrieves (or receives) the package from M it has an address to which to send the product.

In message 9B, M sends S the ticket necessary to access C's private shipping address, and where S can get that address, TP.

In response to receiving message 9 from M, S sends message 10B to TP: (i) the ticket for the payment data, and (ii) a digitally signed authentication code, Sauth, and transaction id.

As with B, Sauth is a unique code that has been pre-established between S and TP. It is used to authenticate S as the recipient of the data specified in the ticket (t_{addr}, S, T_i). Upon determining that ticket is valid, TP sends back to B message 11B: (i) the actual address for this transaction, A_C, (ii) a keyed digest of A_C, and (iii) the ack for M.

In this example, A_C is the shipping address that C has chosen to use for this purchase. She may or may not have included a name to go with that address. In any case, A_C contains exactly what S needs, as this was determined in the establishment of P during the initial policy negotiation between C and M. Again, a keyed digest of A_C is included as extra confidence that the information supplied is A_C is correct.

Now that S has successfully acquired the shipping address, it will acknowledge this to M, as well as send on the ack message send to it by TP. S sends message 12B to M: (i) a digitally signed acknowledgement of a completed address acquisition, and (ii) the block of message from TP for M.

Message 13 $TP \Longrightarrow C$: $[[(G_j, T_i, Status), TP_{iprv}], C_{ipub}]$

When a TGT that is sent by C is exhausted or consumed, TP sends a status message to C, to allow C to close accounting on that TGT. The TGT is identified by its grant list and transaction id, G_j and T_i respectively.

Ticket Granting Ticket #2

With the second TGT sent to M, C grants M access to her email address for up to seven uses over the next six months. As we see in the description of Message 4, C places special instruction in that message that instructs TP to provide redirect service for that email. Figure 1B and the following message description briefly details M's usage of this TGT.

Message 5E

$M \Longrightarrow TP$: $[(G_2, T_i, M_{ipub}, [(, T_i, [KD(G_2), K_{CTP}], instruct), TP_{ipub}]), TP_{ipub}]$

When M initially wants to use the email address of C, it must request a ticket for access to that data. Using the information from TGT #2, M sends TP: (i) the grant list, (ii) the transaction id, (iii) it's own transaction specific public key, and (iv) the special section created by C for TP.

Message 6E $TP \Longrightarrow M$: $[(Denied, reason), M_{ipub}]$

OR

$TP \Longrightarrow M$: $[(t_{email}, M, T_i), M_{ipub}]$

Upon receiving message 5E from M, TP must first satisfy itself that the integrity of G_2 has been maintained. If not, TP sends M a reply stating the request was denied and the reason why (integrity violation). At this point, the transaction is over. From here, we go to message 13, where TP will ack to C the status of the transaction.

TP accepts message 5B, and seeing that the requests have met the policies in P, TP sends a ticket to M, containing a token for access to C's email address, the designation of the recipient of that data, and the transaction id.

Unlike in message 8, now TP cannot use a short cut and return C's email address directly to M. TP has been instructed to provide a redirect for her email address. Therefore, TP sends a ticket instead.

Message 7E $M \Longrightarrow TP:$ $[((t_email, M, T_i), [(M, T_i), M_{iprv}]),$
$TP_{ipub}], [(EMsg, [KD(EMsg), M_{iprv}]), TP_{ipub}]$

Sometime later (remember, C granted M six months access to her email address), the merchant M wants to send C an email message with new catalog items and a sale promotion. M sends TP: (i) the ticket for C's email address, (ii) the id of the trusted party holding that data, TP, (ii) a digitally signed id, M, and transaction id, and (iii) the email message $EMsg$ that M wishes to send to C.

Message 8E $TP \Longrightarrow C:$ $EMsg$ {via normal electronic mail}

TP receives this message, verifies the ticket, and forwards $EMsg$ onto C. TP increments the uses count for this ticket by one. M is free to reuse this ticket another five times within the next six months.

2.4   Analysis of the Protocol

It is easy to see that because we use an anonymizing network for communication between the merchant and the consumer; most of the potential privacy breaches outlined in 2.1 can be prevented. Using this protocol, the personal and private data of C (other than what C has intentionally exposed) can be exposed in only one of three ways. The first is if an attacker is able to capture the messages containing any of C's private data *and* that attacker is able to break the encryption wrapping that data. We have already assumed that an attacker would not be able to break the cryptographic functions involved. Besides, the only time that actual private data is transmitted is in messages involving the bank and shipping company, whose communication lines would already have to be very secure.

The second method would involve the release of the information in d_{pay}. This could only happen if M and B colluded. As we have already discussed, banks define trust concerning financial information, so it is very unlikely that this will happen.

That leaves the possible exposure of d_{addr}, which involves trust in S. There is no inherent trust in this part of the model yet. S by itself has only an address for a package containing some unknown product. S could infer the contents of the package (because it would know M's business, and therefore would likely have a general idea of the contents of the package). Collusion between M and S, would only garner exact knowledge of the contents of the package, since C never supplied her real name. This type of information would be useful in the same way as that of internet action profiling information. One way to overcome this would be for C to instruct M to send the package to TP first, who would, for an additional fee, forward it on to C's shipping address. Even if C chose to trust S, the availability of this extension to the protocol would allow more choices to the internet consumer.

3   Conclusions and Future Work

In this paper we proposed a new e-commerce protocol that allows the consumer to have more control over their privacy needs. The scheme proposed provides a flexible, yet powerful, approach for the secure handling of private data. The protocol prevents the unauthorized re-use and re-distribution of private in all cases where the target player does not really need access to the consumer's private data. Moreover, by virtue of using an anonymizing network, most privacy breaches can be prevented in our protocol. We are currently in the process of implementing the protocol using COTS components. We have investigated the J2EE technology towards this end. We plan to have an implementation shortly.

References

1. The anonymizer. http://anonymizer.com.
2. M.S. Ackerman, L.F. Cranor, and J. Reagle. Privacy in e-commerce: Examining user scenarios and privacy preferences. In *Proceedings of the 1st ACM Conference on Electronic Commerce, Denver, Colorado*, pages 1–8, 1999.
3. A.Kobsa and J.Schreck. Privacy through pseudonymity in user-adaptive systems. *ACM Transactions on Internet Technology*, 3(2):149–183, May 2003.
4. O. Berthold, H. Federrath, and M. Kohntopp. Project anonymity and unobservability in the internet. In *Proceedings of the Workshop on Freedom and Privacy by Design / Conference on Freedom and Privacy 2000 CFPI*, pages 57–65, Toronto, Canada, April 4-7 2000.
5. P. Boucher, A. Shostack, and I. Goldberg. Freedom systems 2.0 architecture. http://www.freedom.net/info/whitepapers/Freedom_System_2_Architecture.pdf, December 2000.
6. C.Molina-Jimenez and L.Marshall. True anonymity without mixes. In *Proceedings of the Second Annual Workshop on Internet Applications, 2001, WIAPP'01*, pages 32–40, July 2001.
7. D.L.Chaum. Untraceable electronic mail, return address, and digital pseudonyms. *Communications of the ACM*, 24(2):84–88, February 1981.
8. D.M.Kristol. Http cookies: Standards, privacy, and policies. *ACM Transactions on Internet Technology*, 1(2):151–198, November 2001.
9. L.F.Cranor et al. The platform for privacy preferences 1.1(p3p 1.1) specification. W3C Consortium, http://www.w3.org/TR/2004/WD-P3P11-20040210, February 2004.
10. L.I. Millet, B. Friedman, and E. Felton. Cookies and web browser design: Toward realizing informed consent online. In *Proccedings of the ACM SIGCHI Conference on Human Factors In Computing Systems*, pages 46–52, March 2001.
11. M.J.Freedman and R.Morris. Tarzan: A peer-to-peer anonymizing network layer. In *Proceedings of the Ninth ACM Conference on Computer and Communications Security (CCS 2002)*, pages 193–206, November 2002.
12. M.K.Reiter and A.D.Rubin. Crowds: Anonymity for web transactions. *ACM Transactions on Information and Systems Security*, 1(1):66–92, November 1998.
13. M.Rennhard et al. An architecture for an anonymity network. In *Proceedings of the 10th IEEE International. Workshops on Enabling Technologies: Infrastructure for Collaborative Enterprises (WET ICE 2001)*, pages 165–170, June 2001.
14. M.Rennhard et al. Analysis of an anonymity network for web browsing. In *Proceedings of the 11th IEEE International. Workshops on Enabling Technologies: Infrastructure for Collaborative Enterprises (WET ICE 2002)*, pages 49–54, June 2002.
15. R.Clarke. Introduction to dataveillance and information privacy, and definition of terms. Web Page, http://www.anu.edu.au/people/Roger.Clarke/DV/Intro.html, September 1999.
16. S.Srinivasan. On piracy and privacy. *IEEE: Computer*, pages 36–38, July 2003.

Using Recoverable Key Commitment to Defend Against Truncation Attacks in Mobile Agents

Ming Yao, Kun Peng, Matt Henricksen, Ernest Foo, and Ed Dawson

Information Security Research Centre
Queensland University of Technology
Brisbane, QLD, 4000, Australia
{m.yao,k.peng,m.henricksen,e.foo,e.dawson}@qut.edu.au

Abstract. Protection of data integrity in mobile agents has drawn much attention in recent years. Various degrees of agent data integrity have been achieved by a number of proposed schemes. A known vulnerability of these published techniques is the truncation attack. In the truncation attack, either two visited hosts collude to discard the partial results collected between their respective visits, or one revisited server deletes all entries between its two visits. In this paper we propose a "recoverable key commitment" technique to effectively defend against the truncation attack. It also prevents other known attacks such as modification, insertion and deletion.

1 Introduction

Mobile agents are small threads of execution that migrate from machine to machine, performing operations locally [1, 6, 5]. They have great potential for electronic commerce applications. A shopping agent can travel the Internet in order to buy a specific product on behalf of the user at the most convenient price. The agent migrates to multiple servers, collects price quotes and is free to choose its next move dynamically based on the data it acquired from its journey.

There are however some security issues concerning mobile software agents. In particular, if a mobile agent is capable of finding the best price among various vendors of a particular item, it is important to ensure the collected price data is not tampered with.

Karjoth *et al.* [3] published a family of protocols, which are referred to as the KAG protocols, to ensure the integrity of the offers acquired from the visited hosts. A common vulnerability of the KAG protocols is that they cannot resist the "truncation" attack. In this attack, a server containing the agent colludes with a previously visited server to discard all the offers between their respective visits or a server that is revisited by the agent discards all the offers between its two visits. A *stemming attack* is an extension of the truncation attack where one or more faked offers are inserted in place of the truncated data.

K. Bauknecht, M. Bichler, and B. Pröll (Eds.): EC-Web 2004, LNCS 3182, pp. 164–173, 2004.
© Springer-Verlag Berlin Heidelberg 2004

Aimed at preserving the integrity of a sequence of data segments, a number of techniques by Loureiro *et al.* [4] and Cheng *et al.* [1] have been published. However, they can only prevent the truncation attack from either an intruder, or colluding servers.

Contribution. The main purpose of this paper is to propose a solution to defend against the truncation and stemming attacks for mobile agents. We have devised a "recoverable key commitment" technique to detect "double operations", which are required by the truncation, stemming as well as other known attacks, when a server S_m recomputes existing data collected by the agent, regardless of whether the data was provided by other servers or by itself. We assume that, for fairness, every server can provide one and only one offer. In this paper we assume that the proposed technique is implemented in an electronic market environment where a trusted third party plays a role of judge to settle any dispute.

Organisation. The rest of the paper is organised as follows: Section 2 details the truncation and stemming attacks. Section 3 proposes a new scheme to detect the truncation attack. We conclude the paper in Sect. 4.

(An extended version of this paper is available upon request from the authors.)

2   Truncation and Stemming Attacks

Assume S_m and S_i ($m < i$) are colluding servers. We depict the truncation and stemming attacks as following:

Truncation attack. Assume the agent arrive at S_i. S_i captures the agent with encapsulated offers O_0, O_1,... O_{i-1}, and sends the agent to the previously visited server S_m. S_m is able to delete the offers between S_m and S_i from the agent. After the truncation, S_m sends the agent back to S_i, and S_i can then carry on the agent's execution. A special case is that S_m sends the agent back to the originator after the attack. In this case, S_m and S_i both have to agree to sacrifice S_i's interest, since S_i's offer will not be included in the agent.

Stemming attack. This attack often occurs in conjunction with the truncation attack: S_m inserts a series of fake offers under the names of victim hosts S'_{m+1}, S'_{m+2}...until S_i or the originator S_0. S_m can first replace its previous offer with O'_m using its own identity and a fake server S'_{m+1} as its successor. The offer O'_m is then signed using S_m's long term private key. For constructing the other fake offers O'_{m+1}, O'_{m+2}, ...,O'_{i-1} (or O'_{0-1}), S_m can arbitrarily choose fake private keys and signs for S'_{m+1}, S'_{m+2}..., S'_{i-1} (or S'_{0-1}). After the agent returns to its originator, the originator would find out that the keys used for signing O'_{m+1}, O'_{m+2}...,O'_{i-1} (or O'_{0-1}) are not legitimate private keys (by verifying with the CA). Therefore O'_{m+1}, O'_{m+2}...,O'_{i-1} (or O'_{0-1}) are not signed by their corresponding signers S'_{m+1}, S'_{m+2}...,S'_{i-1} (or S'_{0-1}). However, it turns out that there could be two possibilities: (1) the hosts S'_{m+1}, S'_{m+2}...,S'_{i-1} (or S'_{0-1}) intentionally inserted offers without honestly signing on it, (2) the server S_m inserted fake offers under the names of S'_{m+1}, S'_{m+2}...,S'_{i-1} (or S'_{0-1}). The originator cannot accuse anyone because of the above uncertainties.

3   The Proposed Scheme

This section first depicts an architectural environment - an electronic market, in which the proposed mechanism and its application can be designed and implemented. A new "recoverable key commitment" mechanism is then introduced and applied in a simple digital signature scheme to detect and prevent "truncation" and "stemming" attacks as well as other attacks against integrity. This section will detail the scheme.

3.1   Participants and an Electronic Market

The participants in the e-market in our setting include: (1) a buyer (the mobile agent's originator), (2) a number of vendors' servers and (3) a trusted third party that can be designated by authorities. A buyer's mobile agent enters the e-market through the trusted third party which may provide yellow-page like services. The agent then travels from server to server and collects offers. After completing its journey, the agent returns to the trusted third party to verify its collected results and finally travels back to its originator.

The trusted third party plays an important role in the proposed new scheme. The trusted third party registers the vendors' servers and manages the commitments from the registered servers. In case of a dispute between an e-market member and a customer or another member, the trusted third party serves as an arbitration board. In our architecture, the behaviour of the trusted third party can be publicly verified by a prover. The prover can be shared among multiple servers to distribute the needed trust and strengthen the robustness of the system.

3.2   Recoverable Key Commitment

The idea of "recoverable key commitment" is to split the private key for signing into a number of pairs of shares. Gathering any pair of the shares can reveal the private key. In normal cases, any party other than the key owner knows at most one share in each pair. Once committed, the owner of all pairs of the shares can not change these shares in the same protocol run, but can choose new pairs after the run has completed. This technique attempts to achieve *conditional anonymity* [2] in which the identity of any dishonest server will be revealed, while the honest servers remain anonymous.

The "recoverable key commitment" mechanism is based on a technique called "secret splitting" [2] where a message M is divided into pieces so that all the pieces must be put together to reconstruct M. In the proposed "recoverable key commitment" mechanism, a secret S possessed by each server is split into many pairs (s_{e_i}, s_{o_i}) so that S can be discovered as:

$S = s_{e_i} + s_{o_i}$, for $i = 1, 2, \cdots, n$,
where s_{e_i} and s_{o_i} denote partial shares in S with even and odd number subscripts respectively.

The "recoverable key commitment" technique involves a protocol of four phases **Split**, **Commit**, **Choose and share** and **Unveil**. The protocol is run between two parties: a secret holder and a secret sharer. Assume p, q and g are system parameters for all the servers in the e-market such that p and q are large primes, where q is a factor of $p-1$, and g is a generator of the subgroup of order q in $\mathbb{Z}_p^*$. Before the new protocol run, these two parties perform:

Split. The secret holder chooses its secret $S = \log_g y$ to be used in the new protocol run and publishes y. The secret holder splits S, finding n equations such that:

$s_{e_1} + s_{o_1} = S \bmod q$ (1)

$s_{e_2} + s_{o_2} = S \bmod q$ (2)

...

$s_{e_n} + s_{o_n} = S \bmod q$ (n)

Commit. The secret holder computes and publishes $2n$ commitments to the corresponding partial shares $y_{e_1} = g^{s_{e_1}} \bmod p$, $y_{o_1} = g^{s_{o_1}} \bmod p$, ..., $y_{e_n} = g^{s_{e_n}} \bmod p$, $y_{o_n} = g^{s_{o_n}} \bmod p$. This commitment mechanism is unconditionally binding, therefore at the end of the **Commit** phase the secret holder is unable to change its chosen shares. The commitments can be verified by anyone against y. Anyone can verify the commitments by testing:

$y_{e_1} \times y_{o_1} = y$ (1)

$y_{e_2} \times y_{o_2} = y$ (2)

...

$y_{e_n} \times y_{o_n} = y$ (n)

where $y_{e_i} \times y_{o_i} \equiv g^{s_{e_i}} \times g^{s_{o_i}} = g^{s_{e_i}+s_{o_i}} = g^s = y$

During a protocol run, the secret holder and the secret sharer conduct the following processes:

Choose and Share. The secret holder must use a hash function to select a set of n shares in secret S and their corresponding commitments. One of the shares is from one equation in the **Split** phase above. Let $\{s_{c1}, s_{c2}, ..., s_{cn}\}$ represent n chosen shares and s_{cj} can be either s_{ej} or s_{oj} $(1 \leq j \leq n)$. The secret holder then sends these n shares to the secret sharer. These selected shares do not reveal the secret S used by the sender, since they provide only half of the secret to the secret sharer.

Unveil. A dispute often takes place when the secret holder (for example, a malicious server) attempts to operate more than once in the same protocol run after having conducted a certain computation. For instance, a malicious server tampers with existing computed data from other servers or itself collected by a mobile agent after having made offers to the agent previously. As discussed in the **Choose and share** phase, the server (the secret holder) is forced to choose a set of n shares to be sent to its next server (the secret sharer). As a consequence, the malicious server will produce two sets of shares to be received by the secret sharers (the secret sharers could be same or different). The probability of producing two identical sets of shares is $\frac{1}{2^n}$.

In the **Unveil** phase, if there is any suspicious secret holder, the recipient servers are able to reveal the secret by combining different sets of shares from the same secret holder. For instance, assume a secret sharer S_i receives $\{s_{c_1}, ..., s_{c_n}\}$ from a secret holder, S_m, and another secret sharer, S_j, receives $\{s'_{c_1}, ..., s'_{c_n}\}$ from S_m as well. S_i and S_j can examine these two sets of shares. If any share s_{c_i} $(1 \leq i \leq n)$ is different from the corresponding share s'_{c_i}, S_i and S_j are able to reveal S_m's secret S by performing the following computation: $S = s_{c_i} + s'_{c_i}$.

3.3 Application of Recoverable Key Commitment Against Truncation Attack in Mobile Agents

We employ the "recoverable key commitment" technique in mobile agent applications to defend against truncation attacks. The application is implemented in an e-market environment.

The protocol using "recoverable key commitment" is illustrated in Fig. 1.

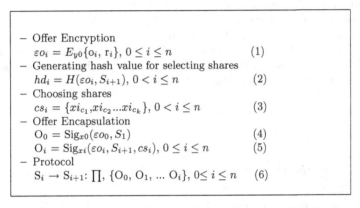

$$- \text{ Offer Encryption}$$
$$\varepsilon o_i = E_{y0}\{o_i, r_i\}, 0 \leq i \leq n \qquad (1)$$
$$- \text{ Generating hash value for selecting shares}$$
$$hd_i = H(\varepsilon o_i, S_{i+1}), 0 < i \leq n \qquad (2)$$
$$- \text{ Choosing shares}$$
$$cs_i = \{xi_{c_1}, xi_{c_2}...xi_{c_k}\}, 0 < i \leq n \qquad (3)$$
$$- \text{ Offer Encapsulation}$$
$$O_0 = \text{Sig}_{x0}(\varepsilon o_0, S_1) \qquad (4)$$
$$O_i = \text{Sig}_{xi}(\varepsilon o_i, S_{i+1}, cs_i), 0 \leq i \leq n \qquad (5)$$
$$- \text{ Protocol}$$
$$S_i \rightarrow S_{i+1}: \textstyle\prod, \{O_0, O_1, ... O_i\}, 0 \leq i \leq n \qquad (6)$$

Fig. 1. The protocol using "recoverable key commitment" mechanism

There are seven stages involved in the preparation, execution and finishing phases of the protocol: **Setup, Offer encryption, Choose and Share, Sign, Verify, Update** and **Reveal**. All the stages except the **Reveal** stage will be always performed in each protocol run. The **Reveal** stage will be conducted only when a malicious action is detected. Any invalid data will be detected in the **Verify** stage. The application contains three parties: the sending server, the receiving server and the trusted third party.

Before the protocol starts, all the participant servers and the trusted third party have to conduct a **Setup** process.

Setup. This stage involves an interactive protocol that performs the *"split"* and *"commit"* phases of the "recoverable key commitment" between the trusted third party and n servers.

For $i = 1, 2, \cdots, n$, we use notations xi_{e_j} and xi_{o_j} to denote partial shares in the long-term private key xi (the secret S in Sect. 3.2) of the server S_i, and yi_{e_j} and yi_{o_j} to denote the corresponding commitments to xi_{e_j} and xi_{o_j}. Assume each server chooses k sets of shares. Hence, the result of this stage consists of:

1. a number of sets of shares $\{(x1_{e_1}, x1_{o_1}), ..., (x1_{e_k}, x1_{o_k})\}$, $\{(x2_{e_1}, x2_{o_1}), ...,$ $(x2_{e_k}, x2_{o_k})\}, ..., \{(xn_{e_1}, xn_{o_1}), ..., (xn_{e_k}, xn_{o_k})\}$ chosen by hosts $S_1, S_2, ...,$ S_n are known only to the respective hosts, and

2. the same number of sets of commitments to their corresponding shares $\{(y1_{e_1},$ $y1_{o_2}), ..., (y1_{e_k}, y1_{o_k})\}$, $\{(y2_{e_1}, y2_{o_1}), ..., (y2_{e_k}, y2_{o_k})\}, ..., \{(yn_{e_1}, yn_{o_1}), ...,$ $(yn_{e_k}, yn_{o_k})\}$ where $yi_{e_1} = g^{xi_{e_1}}$, $yi_{o_1} = g^{xi_{o_2}}$ and so on.

The shares are chosen in the following way:

$xi_{e_1} + xi_{o_1} = xi$ (1)

$xi_{e_2} + xi_{o_2} = xi$ (2)

...

$xi_{e_k} + xi_{o_k} = xi$ (k) where xi is the long term private key of S_i.

The commitments are published by the trusted third party.

After the **Setup** stage is completed, the agent starts to visit a sequence of servers. Let us assume the agent will visit n servers. The originator S_0 initialises the protocol in Fig. 1 by randomly generating r_0. S_0 then encrypts a secret token o_0 and r_0 with its own public key y_0. S_0 signs this encrypted value together with the identity of S_1 to construct a dummy encapsulated offer O_0. Finally S_0 sends O_0 to the first server S_1.

From S_1 onwards, each server S_i will perform the following four stages:

1. Offer encryption. Assume the agent arrives at a server S_i. S_i makes an offer o_i and also computes its next server S_{i+1}. Then S_i constructs εo_i by encrypting o_i and a random value r_i using y_0.

2. Choose and Share. Before the agent is sent to S_{i+1}, S_i chooses k shares and sends these shares to S_{i+1} with the other data.

To ensure the shares are bound to each computation result, they are chosen using the following algorithm:

– S_i takes its encrypted offer εo_i and identity of the next server S_{i+1} as inputs to a one-way hash function $hd_i = H(\varepsilon o_i, S_{i+1})$ that returns k bits output. We choose hd_i to be a string of bits $b_1 b_2 ... b_k$ since we have k sets of shares.

– S_i chooses one share xi_{e_j} or xi_{o_j} out of the set (xi_{e_j}, xi_{o_j}) ($0 \leq j \leq k$) in the equations above according to the value of each bit in $b_1 b_2 ... b_k$. For example, S_i can choose the first share in equation (1) with even number subscript xi_{e_1} if $b_1 = 0$; xi_{o_2} if $b_1 = 1$. For convenience, we use a notation xi_{c_1} to indicate a chosen share. xi_{c_j} is either xi_{e_j} or xi_{o_j} ($1 \leq j \leq k$). As such, k shares $cs_i = \{xi_{c_1}, xi_{c_2}...xi_{c_k}\}$ are selected. The probability of producing two identical sets of shares in this case is $\frac{1}{2^k}$.

Note the same set of shares cannot be reused in different protocol runs. Otherwise the long-term private keys of the revisited servers will be revealed. At the end of a protocol run, an **Update** stage must be conducted. If multiple agents are allowed to participate in the same protocol run, a server must provide different sets of shares for different agents; otherwise an "interleaving" attack can take place, which will be discussed in Sect. 3.4.

3. Sign. Finally S_i constructs an encapsulated offer O_i by signing the encrypted offer εo_i, the identity of its next server S_{i+1} and cs_i.

4. Verify. During the agent's execution, a list of public keys of the participant servers should be published and/or carried with the agent. All the commitments of the servers can be stored locally in each server's database. When these public keys and commitments are available to all the servers in the agent's itinerary, at server S_{i+1}, partial results obtained at any previous servers can be verified.

When the agent arrives at S_{i+1}, carrying $\{O_0, O_1, \dots O_i\}$, S_{i+1} can conduct:

- S_{i+1} obtains O_i from the chain and searches for the corresponding public key y_i from the key list. If $Ver_{y_i}(O_i) = true$, S_{i+1} can ensure that the signature is authentic. S_{i+1} recovers $\{o_i, r_i\}_{y_0}$, the identity of S_{i+1} and cs_i. S_{i+1} can not view o_i since it was encrypted using y_0. Only the originator is able to decrypt the offer o_i, hence it provides data confidentiality. S_{i+1} can verify the identity of itself. Finally S_{i+1} verifies the shares in cs_i.
- S_{i+1} gains shares $\{xi_{c_1}, xi_{c_2} \dots xi_{c_k}\}$ from cs_i. S_{i+1} computes $yi'_{c_1} = g^{xi_{c_1}}$, $yi'_{c_2} = g^{xi_{c_2}} \dots yi'_{c_k} = g^{xi_{c_k}}$. S_{i+1} also computes $hd_i = H(\varepsilon o_i, S_{i+1})$ and gains $b_1 b_2 \dots b_k$ of hd_i. It searches the corresponding commitments in its own database and checks whether these equations are satisfied: If $b_j = 0$ $(1 \leq j \leq k)$, $yi'_{c_j} \overset{?}{=} yi_{e_j}$; else $b_j = 1$, $yi'_{c_j} \overset{?}{=} yi_{o_j}$. If this correspondence does not exist, S_{i+1} can be sure that S_i did not correctly choose the set of secret shares and should report this action to the trusted third party. As such S_{i+1} is able to verify $cs_1, cs_2, \dots cs_{i-1}$.

Following the same line of reasoning, $O_0, O_1, \dots O_{i-1}$ can be verified. If no integrity violation is detected and the shares are matched with the commitments, the agent continues its execution; otherwise, the agent's computation aborts early. In the latter case, S_{i+1} reports the abnormality to the trusted third party and sends the identity of the suspicious server to the trusted party.

Once the agent completes its journey, it returns to the trusted third party before going back to the originator. The trusted third party also verifies all the offers and shares carried by the agent. To detect if any suspicious *double operations* have taken place, the trusted third party can publish $O_1, \dots O_n$ and their associated shares $\{x1'_{c_1}, x1'_{c_2} \dots x1'_{c_k}\}, \dots \{xn'_{c_1}, xn'_{c_2} \dots xn'_{c_k}\}$. If a visited server S_i ($1 < i \leq n$) discovers any mismatch between the published shares and its received shares, for instance, $\{xj'_{c_1}, xj'_{c_2} \dots xj'_{c_k}\} \neq \{xj_{c_1}, xj_{c_2} \dots xj_{c_k}\}$ $(1 \leq j < n)$, it can contact the trusted third party and send the mismatched shares. We assume that only the trusted third party has the authority to reveal a dishonest server's long-term private key. The **Reveal** stage then will be conducted.

Reveal. The trusted third party compares $\{xj'_{c_1}, xj'_{c_2}, \dots, xj'_{c_k}\}$ with $\{xj_{c_1}, xj_{c_2}, \dots, xj_{c_k}\}$. If at any position two bits are not matched, the long term private key of S_i can be obtained by simply computing the addition of those bits. For instance, if $xj'_{c_2} \neq xj_{c_2}$, then $xj = xj'_{c_2} + xj_{c_2}$.

After these stages are completed, the trusted third party will dispatch the agent back to the originator (the buyer) with all the collected data.

Update. At the beginning of *each* protocol execution, the trusted third party informs all the participant servers to choose a new set of shares and compute their commitments. It erases the old commitments and publishes the new commitments. The hosts must make sure that they will not use the same set of shares in two protocol runs. Otherwise their long-term private keys will be revealed.

The protocol discussed above prevents a malicious server from corrupting collected data chain in such a way that the malicious server's long-term private key will be exposed with high probability. The long-term private key exposure imposes a significant impact on the malicious server which makes conditional anonymity a sufficient deterrent in a shopping mobile agent system.

3.4 Security Analysis

Theorem 1. *If a server S_m computes hd_m more than once using different εo_m or S_{m+1} as inputs, S_m's long term private key can be reconstructed with an overwhelmingly large probability.*

Proof. Let $H()$ be a collision-resistant hash function. Suppose a malicious server S_m launches a truncation attack by replacing its successor server S_{m+1} and its own data εo_m with S'_{m+1} and $\varepsilon o_m'$ where $(\varepsilon o_m, S_{m+1}) \neq (\varepsilon o_m', S'_{m+1})$, then $hd_m \neq hd'_m$ is satisfied with a overwhelmingly large probability where $hd_m = H(\varepsilon o_m, S_{m+1})$ and $hd'_m = H(\varepsilon o_m', S'_{m+1})$ as $H()$ is collision-resistant. So two different sets of shares $\{xm_{c_1}, xm_{c_2}, \ldots, xm_{c_k}\}$ and $\{xm_{c'_1}, xm_{c'_2}, \ldots, xm_{c'_k}\}$ determined by hd_m and hd'_m respectively are revealed and there exists $\{c_\alpha, c'_\alpha\} = \{e_\alpha, o_\alpha\}$, $1 \leq \alpha \leq k$, with the same probability. Therefore, S_m's private key $xm = xm_{e_\alpha} + xm_{o_\alpha}$ can be reconstructed with the same probability. $\square$

The new protocol can effectively prevent the truncation and stemming attacks, and some other attacks.

– **Truncation and Stemming Attacks.** In the protocol in Fig. 1, any encapsulated offer $O_j = \mathrm{Sig}_{xj}(E_{y0}\{o_j, r_j\}, S_{j+1})$ $(1 \leq j \leq n)$ includes a signature over the encrypted offer and the identity of the next intended server. To successfully launch the truncation attack, the malicious server has to change the identity of the successor server S_{j+1} to the colluding server or a newly chosen successor server. Therefore S_j can only recompute $O'_j = \mathrm{Sig}_{xj}(\{o_j, r_j\}_{y0}, S'_{j+1})$ and replace O_j with O'_j, and also choose a set of shares using $hd_j = H(O_j, S'_{j+1})$. Theorem 1 shows that the probability of generating two identical sets of shares using different parameters by the same server is negligible. So long as S_j has produced two different sets of shares in the same protocol run, its long term private key will be discovered in the **Unveil** stage (see Sect. 3.3).

The stemming attack can also be detected, as the malicious server has to recompute the encapsulated offer to include the servers's identities which would not have been included without intervention of the malicious server. In addition, the malicious server S_m in the this attack (discussed in Sect. 2) can be discovered: (1) during the **Verify** stage when S_{m+1} checks S_m's digital signature if S_m deliberately inserted an offer but did not honestly sign it, or (2) during the **Reveal** stage, after the trusted third party publishes all the offers, if S_m truncated a string of data and inserted fake offers under the victim servers' names.

– **Modification, Deletion and Insertion Attacks.** These three attacks are addressed by the literature [3, 6, 5], and occur when an entity maliciously alters or deletes previously generated partial results, or inserts offers which would not have been included without the intervention of the malicious entity. Re-computation is required to launch these attacks. Following the same argument in the truncation attack above, these three attacks will be identified in the **Unveil** stage.

– *Interleaving Attack.* To launch this attack, a malicious server participates in two or more previous protocol executions (parallel sessions), including the possible origination of one or more protocol executions by the malicious server itself. The impact of this attack on the "recoverable key commitment" protocol is that the malicious server is able to disclose an innocent server's long term private key by obtaining more than one set of shares from the same server which are carried by different agents in different parallel protocol runs. To avoid this attack, each server has to maintain a number of sets of shares, each of which is tightly bound to one agent.

Defense against other attacks is described in the extended paper. The proposed scheme relies on the fact that each server will honestly utilise the hash-based algorithm to choose its secret shares. This can be checked at the **"Verify"** stage when a verifier checks the correspondence between the commitments calculated from a server's chosen shares and the same server's published commitments, based on each bit of the hash value.

Computation Efficiency. Compared to the schemes using simple key encryption, the proposed "recoverable key commitment" mechanism has additional computation and communication cost.

Suppose each server chooses t sets of shares and the agent visits n servers. DSA is used for digital signatures and ElGamal algorithm is used for shares' commitments. The communication cost only occurs when all the participant servers send their commitments to the trusted third party and when the agent is dispatched from one server to another. Referring to Table 1 (RKC indicates the "recoverable key commitment"), we count the average computational cost for each server in terms of the number of modular exponentiations required by DSA signatures as an example.

Table 1. Comparison of computational and communication cost of the protocol

Average Computational Cost			Maximum Communication Cost		
Stages	Without RKC	With RKC	Stages	Without RKC	With RKC
Setup	-	$1 \times 2t$	Setup	-	$2t \times 128bytes$
Offer Encryption	2	2	Dispatch $(S_{n-1} \to S_n)$	$\sum_{i=0}^{n-1} size(\varepsilon o_i)$ $+ \sum_{i=0}^{n-1} size(S_i)$ $+n \times 40\ bytes$	$\sum_{i=0}^{n-1} size(\varepsilon o_i)$ $+ \sum_{i=0}^{n-1} size(S_i)$ $+n \times 40\ bytes$ $+n \times t \times 128\ bytes$
Choose and Share	-	-			
Sign	1	1			
Verify	n	$n + \frac{tn}{2}$			
Update	-	$1 \times 2t$			
Reveal	-	-			

From the analysis above, some additional computation and communication cost can be observed. The computation complexity relies on the number of the shares chosen. The greater the number of shares chosen, the greater the computation cost and also the larger the payload of the agent as the shares have to be sent with the agent. However the system is more secure with a larger number of shares. Therefore there is a tradeoff between the computation complexity and the security requirements.

However, the extra cost does not impact a great deal in the performance of the protocol, since all the additional computation can be done off-line. Communication cost grows linearly on the number of the servers to be visited.

4   Conclusion and Future Work

A number of published protocols [3, 6, 5] for data integrity in mobile agents have been vulnerable to truncation attacks where a sequence of data are deleted by malicious hosts. In this paper, we proposed a robust defense against the truncation and stemming attacks for mobile agents. The proposed "recoverable key commitment" technique attempts to achieve "conditional anonymity" where the identity of a malicious server who attempts "double operations" will be revealed. The proposed new technique "recoverable key commitment" can also effectively detect and prevent other attacks.

However, in the proposed technique the sets of the shares grow in size as the mobile agent travels. Therefore the future work will be focused on how to improve the performance of the proposed technique.

References

1. Cheng, Jeff S.L., Wei, Victor K.: Defenses against the Truncation of Computation Results of Free-Roaming Agents. In: Deng, R., Qing, S., Bao, F., Zhou, J. (eds.): Proceedings of the 4th International Conference (ICICS 2002). Information and Communications Security, Lecture Notes in Computer Science, Vol. 2513. Springer-Verlag, Berlin Heidelberg New York (2002) 1–12.
2. Hassler, V.: Security Fundamentals for E-Commerce. Artech House, INC.
3. Karjoth, G., Asokan, N., Gülcü, C.: Protecting the Computation Results of Free-Roaming Agents. In: Rothermel, K., Hohl, F.. (eds.): Proceedings of the 2nd International Workshop on Mobile Agents (MA '98). Lecture Notes in Computer Science, Vol. 1477. Springer-Verlag, Berlin Heidelberg New York (1998) 195–207.
4. Loureiro, S., Molva, R., and Pannetrat, A.: Secure Data Collection with Updates. Electronic Commerce Research Journal, Vol. 1/2. Kluwer Academic Publishers (2001) 119–130.
5. Yao, M., Foo, E., Peng, K., Dawson, E.: An Improved Forward Integrity Protocol for Mobile Agents. To appear in Proceeding of the 4th International Workshop on Information Security Applications (WISA 2003), Jeju Island, Korea. Springer-Verlag, Berlin Heidelberg (2003).
6. Yee, B. S.. : A Sanctuary for Mobile Agents. Secure Internet Programming. Lecture Notes in Computer Science, Vol. 1603. Springer-Verlag, Berlin Heidelberg (1999) 261–273.

OCL-Constraints for UMM Business Collaborations

Birgit Hofreiter, Christian Huemer, and Werner Winiwarter

Department of Computer Science and Business Informatics
University of Vienna, Liebiggasse 4, 1010 Vienna, Austria
{birgit.hofreiter,christian.huemer,werner.winiwarter}
@univie.ac.at

Abstract. Recently, a trend towards business processes in Business-to-Business e-Commerce (B2B) is apparent. One of the most promising approaches is UN/CEFACT's modeling methodology (UMM) based on UML. However, developing a new UMM model for each small variation in a business process would lead in a multitude of "similar" business processes. Thus, a more generic UMM model together with well-defined constraints for different business environments is a better approach to ensure unambiguity. In this paper we develop templates for such constraints based on an extended version of OCL.

1 Motivation

For a long time standardization in Business-to-Business e-Commerce (B2B) followed a pure data centric approach. Recent standardization approaches take business processes into account. The most prominent examples include: Business Process Execution Language (BPEL) [2], Business Process Modeling Language (BPML) [1], and ebXML Business Process Specification Schema (BPSS) [13]. Since all of them are XML-based, software tools are able to process the choreography and execute the business process. In contrast, UN/CEFACT's modeling methodology (UMM) [16] starts from the business requirements in order to define a choreography that meets the business needs. UMM uses the Unified Modeling Language (UML) for describing the business aspects of the business processes and the information exchanged. The resulting choreography provides semantics to be expressed in the XML languages mentioned above.

Usually, a UML diagram does not provide all relevant aspects of a specification. There exist additional constraints that cannot be expressed in the graphical syntax. The preferred language for specifying these constraints in UML is the Object Constraint Language (OCL) [12]. Since UMM is based on UML it seems to be straight forward to specify constraints in OCL. The current Revision 12 of the UMM User Guide references and even mandates the use of OCL for specifying pre- and postconditions, rules, guards, etc. However, it does not show in any instance how to use OCL in UMM.

The goal of this paper is to define how to use OCL in UMM. UMM does not make use of all existing UML features. It defines a very strict UML Profile for the specific purpose of modeling B2B business processes, so-called business collaborations. Inasmuch UMM puts UML into a very small corset, which needs only a limited set of

K. Bauknecht, M. Bichler, and B. Pröll (Eds.): EC-Web 2004, LNCS 3182, pp. 174–185, 2004.
© Springer-Verlag Berlin Heidelberg 2004

constraint types. Consequently, UMM requires only a small subset of OCL. There-fore, we develop OCL-based templates that reflect all useful constraints for UMM business collaborations. Since OCL originally does not focus on activity graphs and does not mention access to tagged values, we make some necessary extensions to OCL.

The remainder of this paper is structured as follows: Section 2 concentrates on re-lated work in the area of business processes for B2B environments. In Section 3 we introduce the core concepts of UMM. We keep them to a minimum necessary to un-derstand how our OCL-based templates will fit into. Section 4 defines OCL-based templates for the UMM artefacts business collaboration protocol and business trans-action. The notation of our templates is an extended Backus Naur. Form A short sum-mary in Section 5 concludes the paper.

2 Related Work

Today different approaches exist for choreographing atomic Web Services to complex business processes. Microsoft based XLANG [11] on the pi-calculus, whereas IBM developed the Web Services Flow Language (WSFL) [8] on the foundation of petri nets. The first organization to combine these two approaches was BPMI with their Business Process Modeling Language (BPML) [1]. Later on BEA, IBM and Micro-soft started a unification of XLANG and WSFL that became known as Business Proc-ess Execution Language (BPEL) [2,9]. Currently this approach seems to be the win-ner among the competing standards. Another well know approach is W3C's Web Services Choreography Interface (WSCI) [18] that describes only one partner's par-ticipation in a business process. Similarly to Web Services, ebXML provides a stack of protocols to standardize B2B on top of XML. The protocol for describing the cho-reography of message exchanges between business partners is ebXML Business Proc-ess Specification Schema (BPSS) [13].

All protocols mentioned above describe the behavior between Web Services and/or the execution side of a business process. They do not consider the design of a busi-ness process by a business process analyst. For this purpose BPMI is developing the Business Process Modeling Notation (BPMN) [17]. This notation presents the amal-gamation of best practices in the business process modeling community. Another option for a graphical syntax is UML. RosettaNet uses a UML-based methodology to develop their Partner Interface Processes (PIPs) [10]. UN/CEFACT started the devel-opment of its methodology on top of UML. During the ebXML initiative the company EDIFECS - that owned copyright of the methodology used in RosettaNet - transferred these copyrights to UN/CEFACT. Inasmuch the current version 12 of UMM [16] represents also a successor of RosettaNet's methodology.

UN/CEFACT's vision is developing business process models for global e-business. These business process models must not include any ambiguity. In practice, one and the same business process varies a little bit with respect to the business environment. Developing a new model for each variation will result in a multitude of models. Thus, a generic model together with constraints for different business environments is a much more effective approach to ensure unambiguity. This results in a key difference between UMM and the XML-based approaches. The XML-based approaches describe an executable process. Consequently, this process must be defined in a specific business environment. In UMM a business process model is valid in more business environments. The semantics of an executable process are derived by applying the constraints defined for a specific business environment to the generic model. In the future, transformation rules from UMM to BPEL, BPSS, etc., will enable to derive executable business process from a common generic basis. This transformation goes beyond the scope of this paper. In our paper [6] we demonstrate the transformation from UMM to ebXML BPSS.

One option for specifying constraints is natural language which results in ambiguity. Another option is formal languages which are often hard to understand by businessexperts or system modelers. There exist rule based languages which have been developed for e-business in a Web environment, e.g. Business Rules Markup Language (BRML) [3]. Nevertheless, UMM needs a constraint language that reflects its meta-model. Since UMM is UML-based, the preferred language for specifying constraints is the Object Constraint Language (OCL) [12]. OCL has been developed by IBM as a business modeling language. Later it became part of OMG's set of UML specifications. It is a formal language that is said to be easy to read and write by modelers.

3 UN/CEFACT's Modeling Methodology (UMM)

UMM consists of 4 views, corresponding patterns, as well as a well-formed meta-model which defines the syntax and semantics for each view. Due to space limitations we will not go into the details of each view. The interested reader is referred to the UMM Meta Model [15] and the UMM User Guide [16]. In this Section we briefly describe those concepts of UMM needed to understand the proposed OCL-based templates. Fig. 1.presents an overview of the most basic concepts. The diagram does not present the UMM meta-model nor is it a class diagram. The graph is used to explain the UMM on-tology and each box represents a concept in the UMM ontology.

A *business process* is defined as an organized group of related activities that together create customer value [4]. If all the activities are performed by one organization this leads to an intra-organizational business process. In B2B the activities are executed by different organizations which collaborate to create value. UMM concentrates on the unambiguous definition of an inter-organizational business processes and calls it *business collaboration*.

A business collaboration is performed by two (= binary collaboration) or more (multi-party collaboration) business partners. A business collaboration might be complex involving a lot of activities between business partners. However, the most basic business collaboration is a binary collaboration realized by a request from one side and an optional response from the other side. This simple collaboration is a unit of work that allows roll back to a defined state before it was initiated. Therefore, this special type of collaboration is called *business transaction.*

Since UMM is based on UML, it uses the concept of use cases to capture requirements. In case of a complex business collaboration the requirements are described in a so-called *business collaboration protocol use case.* These requirements lead to a choreography of activities in order to create the customer value. The activity graph representing this choreography is called *business collaboration protocol* (c.f. Fig. 2). Each activity shown in a business collaboration protocol refers to exactly one business transaction. Therefore, each activity of the business collaboration protocol is called a *business transaction activity.* Each of these activities is characterized by the tagged values *timeToPerform* and *isConcurrent.*

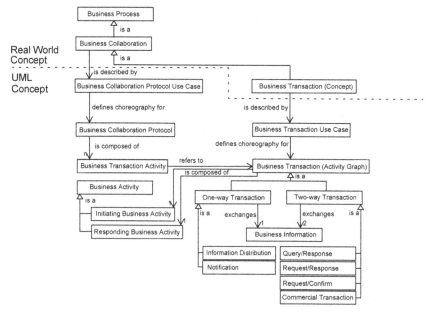

Fig. 1. UMM in a Nutshell

The requirements of a business transaction are described by a *business transaction use case.* Again, the requirements lead to a choreography of the business transaction. The resulting activity graph is what is really called *business transaction* in UMM (c.f. Fig. 3). One might argue, that business transaction activity and business transaction present the same concept. Since different UML elements - an activity and an activity graph - are required in the UML notation, these concepts are distinguished in UMM.

The activity graph of a business transaction is always composed of two *business activities,* an *initiating business activity* performed by the initiator and *reacting business activity* performed by the other business partner. In a *one-way transaction* business information is exchanged only from the *initiating business activity* to the *reacting business activity.* In case of *two-way transaction* the reacting business activity returns business information to the initiating business activity. The UML notation of an object flow is used to show the exchange of business information.

In UMM we distinguish two one-way transactions - *notification* and *information distribution* - and four two-way transactions - *query/reponse, request/confirm, request/response* and *commercial transaction.* These types of business transactions cover all known legally binding interactions between two decision making applications as defined in Open-edi [7]. Furthermore, the type of business transaction is manifested in the defaults for the tagged values of the initiating/requesting business activity: *isAuthorizationRequired, isNonRepudiationRequired, timeToPerform, timeToAcknowledgeAcceptance, isNonRepudiationOfReceiptRequired,* and *recurrence.*

4 OCL-Based Templates for UMM

Having introduced the basic concepts of UMM, it becomes evident that OCL-based templates are useful only for certain artefacts. Use Cases capture the requirements which result in OCL constraints. Constraints do not apply to use cases themselves. Consequently, candidates for OCL-based templates are activity graphs for business collaboration protocols and business transactions as well as class diagrams for business information exchanged. In this paper, we concentrate on the choreography of the activity graphs. Constraints on business information exchanged cannot be explained within the page limit and will be a topic of another paper.

The following two subsections present the OCL-based templates for business collaboration protocols and business transactions. Each template is demonstrated by an example. These examples refer to two very simple case studies. The first one is order management of books and the second one is order management of tourism products. For more details on this case study we refer to our paper introducing business context variations in UMM [5].

4.1 Constraints for Business Collaboration Protocols

The choreography of a business collaboration protocol follows a description provided in the corresponding use case description. Fig. 2. shows the business collaboration protocol of our example. The order management either begins by a search for product or by the query for the reservation list. After a search it is possible to order or reserve a product. Both activities require the customer to be registered. If the result of a search was not satisfying another search is performed or the reserved products are queried. After a reservation was performed the next activity is either a new search or the query for the reserved products. Note that querying products requires customers to be registered, because otherwise they were not able to make a reservation. After querying the reserved products, a product might be ordered. The other choice is to perform a new search. The business collaboration always ends after ordering a product. However, the search for product, the reservation, and the presentation of the reserved products might also be the last activity with the consequence that no book is ordered.

A business collaboration is valid in one or more business environments. Thus, the business environments are specified in a tagged value of the business collaboration. The best way to describe a business environment is by the concept of business context as introduced by ebXML core components [14]. In this specification business context is defined as a mechanism for qualifying and refining core components according to their use under particular business circumstances. We enlarge the scope of this definition to apply the mechanism not only to core components but also to any UMM artifact. The business context in which the business collaboration takes place is specified by a set of categories and their associated values. In ebXML eight categories have been identified: business process, product classification, industry classification, geopolitical, official constraints, business process role, supporting role, and system capabilities. We split the category business process into the two categories business collaboration and business transaction, because both exist in a UMM model and must be distinguished. The context categories are not limited to the ones identified, but we do not recommend the use of other categories.

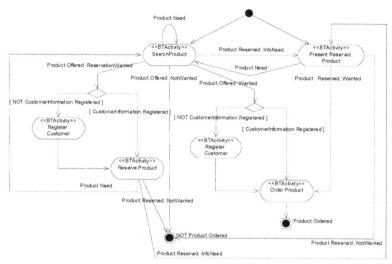

Fig. 2. Business Collaboration Protocol for Order Management

The definition of a business environment is nothing else then a constraint on the activity graph of a business collaboration protocol. Thus, the definition of an OCL constraint seems to be straight forward. However, OCL was designed to specify invariants of classes and pre- and post-conditions for methods. We need access to the tagged values of an activity graph (and other UML elements). The OCL specification [12] does not consider this type of access. OCL allows invariants for classifiers only. In our approach, we apply invariants to other UML elements as well. The syntax is similar to that of invariants for classifiers. In case of defining the business environment of the business collaboration protocol, we specify the corresponding business collaboration protocol after the OCL keyword *context* and followed by the keyword *inv* for invariants. Instead of defining constraints on attributes of a classifier, we assign constraints to the tagged values describing the business environment. The business environment is defined as name-value-pairs for the context categories connected by boolean operators.

The template for defining invariants of a business collaboration protocol is defined in BNF further below. The template is followed by an example constraint. Although our order management collaboration seems to be rather general, we restrict it to two business environments for demonstration purposes. The example constraint restricts our business collaboration protocol to the book order management case and the tourism product order management case.

BusinessCollaborationProtocolInvariant ::=

context *<BusinessCollaborationProtocol>* **inv:** <BusinessContextStatement>

BusinessContextStatement :: =
    [<BusinessContext> [<BooleanOperator> <BusinessContextStatement>]? |
    [(<BusinessContext> <BooleanOperator> <BusinessContextStatement>)]

BusinessContext ::= <BusinessContextDriver> <relationalOperator> "<literal>"

BusinessContextDriver ::= **BusinessCollaboration** | **BusinessTransaction** |
  ProductClassification | **IndustryClassification** | **Geopolitical** |
  Official Constraints | **BusinessProcessRole** | **SupportingRole** |
  SystemCapabilities | <OtherBusinessContextDriver>

```
OtherBusinessContextDriver ::= <literal>

BooleanOperator ::= AND | OR | XOR
relationalOperator ::= = | > | < | >= | <= | <>
```

Example:
```
context OrderManagementBusinessCollaborationProtocol inv:
    BusinessCollaboration = "OrderManagement"
    AND (Product Classification = "Book" OR Product Classification = "Tourism Product")
    AND (IndustryClassification = "PrintMedia" OR IndustryClassification = "Tourism")
```

A business collaboration protocol choreographs business transaction activities. The business environment for each business transaction is identical to the one of the business collaboration protocol. The tagged values of one and the same business transaction activity - which are the concurrency flag and the time to perform - might vary for mutually exclusive subsets of the overall business environment. In the example below *search product* can happen concurrently and must be completed in 24 hours by default. The default applies to the tourism case, whereas searching for books cannot be concurrent and must be completed in 12 hours.

The variations in the tagged values are constraints on the business transaction activity. Thus, we define invariants of business transaction activities. If no variations for the tagged values exist, we simply define the values for *isConcurrent* and *timeToPerform*. Otherwise, we use an if-statement to check the tagged value of the business environment and set the other tagged values if appropriate. The else-clause contains the default values. Unfortunately, OCL does not include an elsif-clause in the if-statement. In reality there exist many different business environments resulting in different combinations of default values. To avoid nested if statements and for reasons of readability we have extended the OCL statement to include an elsif-clause.

```
BusinessTransactionActivityInvariant ::=
context  <BusinessTransactionActivity> inv:
    <MultipleBusinessTransactionActivityTaggedValueStatement>
    [if <BusinessContextStatement> then
    <MultipleBusinessTransactionActivityTaggedValueStatement>
    [elsif <BusinessContextStatement>
    then <MultipleBusinessTransactionActivityTaggedValueStatement>
    ]*
    [else <MultipleBusinessTransactionActivityTaggedValueStatement> ]?
    endif]

MultipleBusinessTransactionActivityTaggedValueStatement ::=
    <BusinessTransactionActivityTaggedValueStatement>
    [AND <MultipleBusinessTransactionActivityTaggedValueStatement>]?

BusinessTransactionActivityTaggedValueStatement ::= <BusineesTransactionActivityTagged-
    Value>="<literal>"

BusinessTransactionActivityTaggedValue ::= isConcurrent | timeToPerform
```

Example:
```
context SearchProduct inv:
if ProductClassification = "Book" AND IndustryClassification= "PrintMedia"
then timeToPerform = "12 hrs" AND isConcurrent = "false"
else timeToPerform = "24 hrs" AND isConcurrent = "true"
```

Each business transaction activity requires some preconditions to be met before execution and results in some post-conditions. OCL supports the definition of pre- and post-conditions. According to the UMM User Guide pre- and post-conditions reflect well-defined states in the life-cycle of business entities. For checking the state of an object OCL provides the method *oclInState* which returns a boolean. In our example, *order product* requires that the business entity *product* is either in state *offered* or *reserved* as well as business entity *customer information* is in state *registered*. After executing *order product* a product will be either in state *ordered* or *order failed*. However, the pre- and post-conditions might vary again with respect to the business environment. This fact is accomplished by using an if-clause similar to the one above for tagged value variations. In our example, we suppose that a tourism product might not be ordered without prior reservation. Consequently, the business entity *product* must be in state *reserved* for *order product*. This fact is shown in the if-statement of the example below.

```
BusinessTransactionActivityPreAndPostConditions ::=
context  <BusinessTransactionActivity>
     [    [pre: <MultipleBusinessEntityStateConditions>] ?
          [post: <MultipleBusinessEntityStateConditions>] ? ] |
     [if <BusinessContextStatement>
     then
          [pre: <MultipleBusinessEntityStateConditions>] ?
          [post: <MultipleBusinessEntityStateConditions>] ?
     ### rest of if-clause is truncated ###
     endif]

MultipleBusinessEntityStateConditions ::=
     [<BusinessEntityStateCondition> [<BooleanOperator> <MultipleBusinessEntityStateConditions>] ?] |
     [(<BusinessEntityStateCondition> <BooleanOperator> <MultipleBusinessEntityStateConditions>)]

BusinessEntityStateCondition ::=
     [ NOT ]? <BusinessEntity>.oclInState(<BusinessEntityState>)

BusinessTransactionActivity ::= <literal>
BusinessEntity ::= <literal>
BusinessEntityState ::= <literal>
```

Example:
```
context OrderProduct
     if ProductClassification = "TourismProduct" AND IndustryClassification = "Tourism"
     then
          pre: Product.oclInState(Reserved)
          AND CustomerInformation.oclInState(Registered)
          post: Product.oclInState(Ordered) XOR Product.oclInState(OrderFailed)
     elsif ProductClassification = "Book" AND IndustryClassification = "PrintMedia"
     then
          pre: (Product.oclInState(Offered) OR Product.oclInState(Reserved))
          AND CustomerInformation.oclInState(Registered)
          post: Product.oclInState(Ordered) XOR Product.oclInState(OrderFailed)
     endif
```

The last template for the business collaboration protocol specifies constraints on the transitions between business transaction activities. The transition from one business transaction activity to another requires not only the completion of the first activity, but also the occurrence of an event on the initiator's side of the next activity. For example, the transition from *search product* to *order product* requires the completion of *search product* that, hopefully, results in the state *offered*. However, this does not mean that the buyer must order the product. First, the buyer has to decide that he/she wants the offered product. This decision is modeled as an event that results in the sub-state *wanted* of the parent state *offered*. Furthermore, an optional guard applies to transitions. Valid guards are the context of the business environment and business entity states. In our example the transition from *search product* to *order product* is limited to the book case, because in tourism a reservation is required prior to ordering. Furthermore, the state of *customer information* guards the transition.

```
BusinessTransactionAcitivityTransition ::=
context from <BusinessTransactionActivity> to <BusininessTransactionActivity>
Event: <MultipleBusinessEntityStateConditions>
Guard: <GuardStatement>
```

GuardStatement ::=
    [<Guard> [<BooleanOperator> <GuardStatement>]? | [(<Guard> <BooleanOperator> <GuardStatement>)]
Guard :: = <BusinessContextStatement> | <MultipleBusinessEntityStateConditions>

Example:
context from SearchProduct to OrderProduct
    Event: Product.oclInState(Offered::Wanted)
    Guard:ProductClassification = "Book" AND IndustryClassification = "PrintMedia"
                                   AND CustomerInformation.InOclState(Registered)

4.2 Constraints for Business Transactions

Each business transaction activity of the business collaboration protocol is refined by a separate activity graph called a business transaction. Fig. 3 depicts the business transaction *search product*. The customer performs *request a search* as initiating activity that produces a *search request* document. This document is input to the reacting activity *perform search* which is executed by the seller. The reacting activity outputs the *search result* document that is returned to the initiating activity. Since there is a response that does not immediately result in a contractual obligation and the responder has the information (about the product) already available, the transaction is of type *query/response*. The initiating activity is stereotyped accordingly.

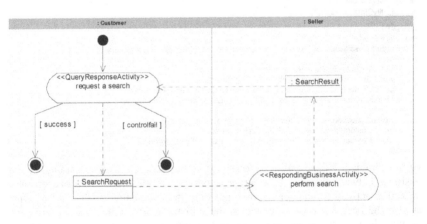

Fig. 3. Business Transaction "Search Product"

First, we define the business environment for the business transaction, which covers both of our example cases. The constraint statement is similar to that for the business collaboration protocol. The business environment is defined as a string of name-value-pairs for the context categories connected by boolean operators.

BusinessTransactionContextConstraint ::=
context <*BusinessTransaction*> **inv:**<BusinessContextStatement>

Example:
context SearchProduct inv:
    BusinessCollaboration = "OrderManagement" AND BusinessTransaction = "SearchProduct"
    AND (Product Classification = "Book" OR Product Classification = "Tourism Product")
    AND (IndustryClassification = "PrintMedia" OR IndustryClassification = "Tourism")

Both the initiating business activity and the responding business activity are characterized by a well-defined set of tagged values. Again the instances of the tagged values might vary for different subsets of the overall business environment. The code fragments below refer to constraints for tagged values on the initiating business activity. The ones for the responding business activity are quite similar. In our example we define that for the book case the maximum time to perform is 4 hours. There is no need for acknowledgments, authorization and non-repudiation. In case of control failures the initiating activities restarts the transaction 3 times before giving up.

```
InitiatingBusinessActivityTaggedValuesConstraint ::=
context <InitiatingBusinessActivity> inv:
    <MultipleInitiatingBusinessActivityTaggedValueStatement> |
    [if <BusinessContextStatement>
    then <MultipleInitiatingBusinessActivityTaggedValueStatement>
    ### rest of if-clause is truncated ###
    endif]
MultipleInitiatingBusinessActivityTaggedValueStatement ::=
<InitiatingBusinessActivityTaggedValueStatement>
[AND <MultipleInitiatingBusinessActivityTaggedValueStatement>]?
InitiatingBusinessActivityTaggedValueStatement ::=
    <InitiatingBusinessActivityTaggedValue> = <literal>
InitiatingBusinessActivityTaggedValue ::= TimeToAcknowledgeReceipt |
    TimeToAcknowledgeAcceptance | TimeToPerform | AuthorizationRequired |
    NonRepudiationOfOriginAndContent | NonRepudiationOfReceipt | Recurrence
```

Example:
```
context RequestASearch inv:
if ProductClassification = "Book" AND IndustryClassification = "PrintMedia"
then TimeToAcknowledgeReceipt = "Null" AND TimeToAcknowledgeAcceptance = "Null" AND
TimeToPerform = "4 hrs" AND AuthorizationRequired = "false" AND NonRepudiationOfOriginAndContent =
    "false"
AND NonRepudiationOfReceipt = "false" AND Recurrence = "3"
else ... endif
```

Finally, there might exist variations in the business transaction type according to the business environment. As mentioned above search product is by default a query/response transaction, since there are no contractual obligations involved and the responder has the information already available. Imagine that in tourism the information is not already available, but must be calculated by the responder. Accordingly, the transaction type changes to request/response. This is shown in the example below. A more radical variation can happen in case of tacit approval when a commercial transaction (two-way) changes to a notification (one-way).

```
context <BusinessTransaction> inv:
    if <BusinessContextStatement>
    then BusinessTransactionType = <BusinessTransactionType>
    ### rest of if-clause truncated ###
    endif
BusinessTransactionType ::= InformationDistribution | Notification | QueryResponse |
RequestConfirm | RequestResponse | CommercialTransaction
```

Example:
```
context SearchProduct inv:
if ProductClassification = "TourismProduct" AND IndustryClassification = "Tourism"
then BusinessTransactionType = "RequestResponse"
else BusinessTransactionType = "QueryResponse"
```

5 Summary

B2B e-Commerce standardization is more and more directed towards business processes. Most approaches are in the area of Web Services. Their goal is to describe a
choreography for an executable business process that is assembled from a set of Web
Services. For this purpose the process must be defined in a specific business environment. In contrary, UMM is a methodology that starts from gathering user requirements and develops business process and information models that are independent of
the underlying B2B technology (Web Services, ebXML, EDI, etc.). UMM's goal are
unambiguous business process models for global e-business. For the sake of reusability, a business process model must be generic enough to adopt to different business
environments. Nevertheless, it must be specific enough to unambiguously describe a
business process execution in a given business environment.

In order to fulfill this pretension UMM must deliver generic models that exactly
define the constraints for adopting to a certain business environment. This requires a
constraint language that is adjusted to the UMM meta-model. Since UMM is UML-
based it seems to be straight forward to use OCL for this purpose. In the same way as
UMM restricts the UML meta-model, we must restrict the flexibility of OCL. Thus,
this paper defines OCL templates specially designed for UMM artefacts. The constraints for business collaboration protocols are: (1) definitions of applicable business
environments, (2) invariants for tagged values of business transaction activities, (3)
pre- and post-conditions of business transaction activities, and (4) invariants for transitions. The templates for business transactions are: (1) definitions of applicable business environments, (2) invariants of tagged values for initiating and reacting business
activities (3) invariants for business transaction types.

We also started to develop OCL templates for adopting the business information
exchanged in a business transaction to different business environments. We plan to
summarize this complex topic in the near future. In our paper [6] we map UMM models (developed for a specific business environment) to ebXML BPSS. It is our goal to
demonstrate mapping for other choreography languages as well. Moreover, we want
to show how a generic UMM model including constraint statements for multiple
business environments will map to different choreographies in the same choreography
language.

References

1. Arkin, A.; Business Process Modeling Language (Version 1.0); November 2002;
   http://www.bpmi.org/bpml-spec.esp
2. Andrews, T., Curbera, F., Dholakia, H., Goland Y., Klein, J., Leymann, F., Liu, K., Roller,
   D., Smith, D., Thatte, S., Trickovic, I., Weerawarana, S.; Business Process Execution
   Language for Web Services, Version 1.1, May 2003
   http://msdn.microsoft.com/library/default.asp?url=/library/en-us/dnbizspec/html/bpel1-
   1.asp
3. Grosof, B.N., Labrou, Y.; An Approach to using XML and a Rule-based Content Language with an Agent Communication Language"; Proceedings of the IJCAI-99 Workshop
   on Agent Communication Languages (ACL-99); Stockholm (Sweden), August 1999
4. Hammer, M., Champy, J.; Reengineering the Corporation: Manifesto for Business Revolution; Harper Business; 1993

5. Hofreiter, B., Huemer, C.; Modeling Business Collaborations in Context; Proceedings of On The Move to Meaningful Internet Systems 2003: OTM 2003 Workshops; Springer; November 2003
6. Hofreiter, B., Huemer; Transformation of UMM Models to ebXML BPSS; to appear in: Proceedings of XML4BPM Workshop, Marburg (Germany) March 2003; http://www.ifs.univie.ac.at/~ch/UMM2BPSS.pdf
7. ISO; Open-edi Reference Model; ISO/IEC JTC 1/SC30 ISO Standard 14662; 1995
8. Leymann, F.; Web Services Flow Language (WSFL 1.0); May 2001 http://www-306.ibm.com/software/solutions/webservices/pdf/WSFL.pdf
9. Leymann, F., Roller, D., Schmidt, M.-T.; Web Services and Business Process Management; IBM Systems Journal, Vol. 41, No. 2, 2002
10. RosettaNet; RosettaNet Implementation Framework: Core Specification V02.00.01; March 2002; http://www.rosettanet.org/rnif
11. Thatte, S.; XLANG - Web Services for Business Process Design; June 2001; http://www.gotdotnet.com/team/xml_wsspecs/xlang-c/default.htm
12. OMG; Object Constraint Language Specification; http://www.omg.org/cgi-bin/doc?formal/03-03-13
13. UN/CEFACT; ebXML - Business Process Specification Schema v1.10; October 2003; http://www.untmg.org/downloads/General/approved/ebBPSS-v1pt10.zip
14. UN/CEFACT; Core Components Technical Specification V2.01; November 2003; http://www.untmg.org/downloads/General/approved/CEFACT-CCTS-Version-2pt01.zip
15. UN/CEFACT; UMM Meta Model, Revision 12; January 2003; http://www.untmg.org/downloads/General/approved/UMM-MM-V20030117.zip
16. UN/CEFACT; UMM User Guide, Revision 12; September 2003; http://www.untmg.org/downloads/General/approved/UMM-UG-V20030922.zip
17. White, S; Business Process Modeling Notation Working Draft (1.0); August 2003; http://www.bpmi.org/bpmn-spec.esp
18. W3C; Web Service Choreography Interface (WSCI) 1.0; August 2002; http://www.w3.org/TR/wsci/

Use and Extension of ebXML Business Profiles for Textile/Clothing Firms

Nicola Gessa[1], Cristiano Novelli[1], Massimo Busuoli[2], and Fabio Vitali[1]

[1] Dipartimento di Scienze dell'Informazione, Università di Bologna,
Mura Anteo Zamboni 7, 40127, Italy
{gessa,novelli,fabio}@cs.unibo.it
[2] Enea UDA-PMI, Laboratorio XML, via Don Fiammelli 2, 40129, Bologna, Italy
massimo.busuoli@bologna.enea.it

Abstract. Managing business workflow can benefit from the adoption of new solutions proposed by different initiatives of ICT. MODA-ML project defined an interoperability framework, based on ebXML standard, to enhance collaboration and interaction inside the Textile/Clothing supply chain. In this paper we briefly give an overview of the architecture of MODA-ML and we present our approach to generate automatically BPSS documents to provide a common formal description of the business process supported. Because of the requirements of the T/C sector, we have also studied some improvements to obtain more flexibility in defining partner profiles with CPP documents.

1 Introduction

Electronic business surely represents the new development perspective for the worldwide trade. Together with the idea of the ebusiness, and the exigency to exchange business messages between trading partners, the concept of business-to- business (B2B) integration arouse. B2B integration is becoming necessary to allow partners to communicate and exchange business documents, as catalogues, purchase orders, reports and invoices, overcoming architectural, applicative, and semantic differences, according to the business processes implemented by each enterprise.

Business relationships can be very heterogeneous, and consequently there are various ways to integrate enterprises with each other. Moreover nowadays not only large enterprises, but also the small- and medium- enterprises are moving towards ebusiness: more than two-thirds of SME use the Internet as a business tool [7]. One of the business areas which is actively facing the interoperability problem is that related with the supply chain management.

In general two distinct supply chains that look alike do not exist: depending on the enterprise, the same concept of a supply chain can be very different; in some cases what is called supply chain is not a really supply chain at all. In [4] 16 types of supply chain are listed, each of them characterised mainly for the intended output companies are seeking to obtain.

SCM solutions concern not only new technologies to manage the processes, but also the designing of new processes well-suited for the new kind of market that is now arising [2]; in this article is highlighted as many companies, despite the high cost of SCM products they bought, they can't use them successful because of two main prob-

K. Bauknecht, M. Bichler, and B. Pröll (Eds.): EC-Web 2004, LNCS 3182, pp. 186–195, 2004.
© Springer-Verlag Berlin Heidelberg 2004

lems: the understanding how their existing supply chain processes work really and the conflicts between different silos in the same enterprise. These problems require developing a real SCM process to cut across the divisional boundaries and· in which to use the new technology. The central point is to understand the change management issue that will need to be addressed. In the new era of the Web and considering the new communication means, many companies must consider to deconstruct their conventional supply chains and to build an interactive ebusiness network to gain flexibility [14].

Surely e-business has conditioned supply chain management: [10] focuses on the role of e-business in supply chain integration. Improving interoperability can lead to a more successful management of the supply chain: [1] lists seven principles that would drive the efforts improving SCM. These principles aim to enhance revenue, cost control, asset utilisation and customer satisfaction exploiting ICT to obtain more flexibility and to balance customers' demands with the company's needs for a growth.

But what can we expect from a solution and architecture for supply chain management and integration? Which are the goals of a truly integrated supply chain? In some cases it is no clear which are the advantages in implementing and using software for SCM. At the beginning the companies viewed SCM software as part of their business architecture that would bring to "cost saving" advantages. Actually proper platform for SCM can not only streamline production processes, but also create value for the enterprises. [9] discusses the meaning of "value" of supply chain software: this paper highlights that software creates value when it brings to ROI (Return Of Investment), and examines how application can create value for supply chain. ROI occurs when the investment returns exceed the cost of the capital, but the value of supply chain software could vary depending on the perspective. [11] asserts that an integrated supply chain does more than reduce cost, but also creates value for the enterprises, the partners and the shareholders. In [15] the real leverage of a lean supply chain is in creating capacity of growth. This paper argues that the companies must realise that instead of expense reduction or profit enhancement, the main benefits of architectures and software for SCM consist in a new capacity to match with customer demands.

The content of this paper is based on the experience of development of a sectoral framework for the Textile Clothing sector, MODA-ML (Middleware tools and Documents to enhance the Textile/Clothing supply chain through XML) [5], and its first steps in analysing and formalize the business processes in the T/C supply chain.

2   The Workflow Management Scenario

Each activity within an enterprise, whether it is a production or a management one, is inserted in an enterprise business process that in general involves different actors and sectors of the same enterprise or requires the co-operation among different companies. A business process can then be defined as a collection of activities (performed by human personnel or by automatic mechanisms like software systems) to achieve a particular business object. Some examples can be the hiring of new employees or the definition of a purchase order. These business processes must be represented is some manner. A workflow, or workflow process, is a formal executable description of a business process.

Workflow management is done using Workflow Management System (WfMS): a WfMS is a framework and a set of tools to facilitate the definition and the maintenance of the integration logic and to control how to dispatch information among (human) participants of an administrative process. It also defines the business logic necessary to integrate heterogeneous and distributed systems.

During the last 10 years many initiatives have faced the management workflow problem. The Workflow Management Coalition (WfMC), founded in August 1993, is an international non-profit organisation composed of over 285 members and embraces software vendors, research groups, university, and customers. The basic result consists in the definition of the Workflow Reference Model [8], a description of a workflow system architecture that attempts to construct an abstract view of the core characteristics of business processes, separated from the technologies.

BPMI is another initiative that promotes and develops the use of Business Process Management. It aims, like WfMC, to establish standards for process design, development, management, maintenance. BPMI initiative stems from a non-profit corporation within the state of California.

WfMC and BPMI are only two of the major protagonists in the scenario of the Enterprise Modelling, that is in truth composed of many other languages and frameworks.

In order to contribute (partially) to solve the problem of multiple enterprise modeling languages, the European Commission funded the Semantic Network Project called UEML (Unified Enterprises Modelling Language) [16]. The main object of UEML is to provide industry with a unified and expandable modelling language, which should serve as an interlingua between EM tools and applications.

There are several commercial products available for those enterprises that aim to manage their business processes using a WfMS. Among them are WebSphere MQ Worklow, from IBM, BEA Weblogic Integration and Microsoft Biztalk Orchestration. We will talk about ebXML approach to model workflows in section 4.

Besides WfMS, a new approach is now being diffused in the ICT research field: Web services represent a future perspective for the development of interoperability web-based solutions that can leverage on new emerging technologies.

Nevertheless the real challenges that Web Services framework are facing, is to provide a way not only to advertise a single web service allowing its usage for a specific task, but to provide a way to compose and connect different services together, providing more and more powerful and flexible services [13].

Considering Web services as a framework to define, advertise and connect business processes, making them accessible within the same enterprise or across different ones, and the new efforts to develop service composition languages, it becomes necessary to focus the relationship between Web services and business process management [12].

3   MODA-ML, a Framework to Integrate Business Processes in the Textile/Clothing Sector

The MODA-ML project (Middleware tOols and Documents to enhAnce the Textile/Clothing supply chain through xML) was born to build an architecture to provide an interoperability framework among the enterprises in the Textile/Clothing sector and aims at contributing to establish an European standard for the sector. This project collected various research organisations (ENEA, Politecnico di Milano, Domina, Gruppo SOI, Institut Francais Textil Habillement - IFTH) together with a representative set of leading Italian Textile/Clothing manufacturers. It has been supported by the Fifth Framework programme of the European Commission within the IST (Information Society Technology) initiative (more information can be found in http://www.moda-ml.org) and took part in the cluster of project about Agents and Middleware Technologies (EUTIST-AMI) (IST-2000-28221).

The project has adopted the guidelines published by the ebXML initiative: ebXML (Electronic Business using XML) is a set of specifications from UN/CEFACT and OASIS that defines a collaboration framework over the Internet to enhance interoperability between enterprises. We have chosen ebXML because of it resulted to be the more general methodology that completely faces the issues raised in the B2B field; it was one of the first initiatives providing complete specifications, especially to manage transport, security and reliability aspects; it combines the Edifact experience with the novel solutions introduced along with the XML technologies and appears to be technological implementation independent. Being general, public and free, the ebXML framework allows anyone who wants to develop a sectoral B2B integration solution for a well-defined business scenario. Finally, considering our needs, the framework proposes a peer-to peer exchange model that is well-suited for the real enterprise collaboration in the Textile/Clothing scenario.

The main aim of ebXML is to support two different aspects of the interoperability processes:

- The semantic definition of the documents: ebXML proposes a set of "core components" used to define the semantic value of a document. Differently from the traditional EDI approach, ebXML emphasises the importance of these components on the entire document structure, and this aspect gives ebXML more flexibility with respect to EDI.
- Several technical specifications on the communication protocols: MODA-ML follows completely ebXML transport specifications.

The basic structure of the architecture is a vocabulary (the Moda-ML vocabulary) of well defined terms. The definition of the terms comes out from the integration of the Editex experience (European standardisation initiative for the Textile/Clothing sector which has not spread enough because of its rigidity and complexity) with the assessments and needs realised along with pilot users, industry trade associations, and focus groups. Our results have then been weighed up by the CEN, leading to the specification document "CEN workshop agreement" of the standardisation initiative TEXSPIN. In the same way the business processes of the Moda-ML framework have been defined.

The terms represent the basic business components and are defined as XML elements. Some components of these documents are specialized for particular needs, but many components are shared by all the documents: each component of the dictionary represents in fact a well-defined concept that can be specified in the messages. This organization of the dictionary makes it possible to perform the necessary distinction between the syntactical model, the semantic model and the transport model of the messages being exchanged. Public business document types can then be built starting from this set of business elements and upon them in a modular manner, defining rules and constraints to express the interrelations existing among the concepts they represent. Also the structure of these document templates is contained in the vocabulary.

The effective implementation of the vocabulary is done using a database application that provides a sophisticated description of the defined basic components. This database collects any information on the semantic blocks needed to build the document types. Such information include the name of the XML elements, their description and the associated properties such as data format, length, range of permitted values and so on. The vocabulary further specifies a root element for each document type and all the relations existing among the elements such as sequence, cardinality and so on. A simple application will then re-create the complete set of rules (an XML Schema) for each document type by starting from the root element and following the defined relations.

MODA-ML also provides a set of XSLT style sheets to create HTML pages off the XML instances so that the document content can be visualised in a readable manner even if using a simple Web browser. The Vocabulary represents the core of the management of every aspect related to the MODA-ML document types, schemas and instances. We call this approach the XML document factory.

Together with the vocabulary, the framework provides the necessary tools to exchange MODA-ML documents. These tools are collectively called the message switching system.

The message switching system implements a transport protocol based on ebXML messaging service specifications; since the Textile/Clothing sector is composed of various kinds of enterprises, each characterised by a different level of technological sophistication in its information systems, it becomes fundamental to create simple software modules that can be made publicly available, providing an easy and low-cost integration with complex legacy information systems within skilled companies.

The main component of the MODA-ML message switching system is the Message Service Handler (MSH), that acts as an email client, sending and receiving MODA-ML documents as attachments to email messages: it takes care to validate MODA-ML documents and it uses SMTP as its transport protocol.

In order to enhance the functionalities of the MSH, we have considered:

- Security aspects for authentication and non-repudiation of MODA-ML messages.
- Integration of user guides and XML schemas as automatically generated products of the MODA-ML vocabulary.

MODA-ML staff and the pilot users can automatically generate the XML schema and the user guide on every message, even in course of definition; generating XML schemas or user guides produces documents that can be immediately downloaded. A generic user seeking information about the message usage can only download all the developed versions of the schemas and the users guides. These operations are all ASP applications executable from the web.

4   Partner Collaboration Profiles Within the MODA-ML Framework

Besides the semantic definition of the documents and the transport specification, ebXML defines a standard mechanism to describe business processes. In this way ebXML aims to increase the interoperability among the enterprises easing the spreading and the interchange of the different business processes. This mechanism is the

Business Process Specification Schema (BPSS)[3] that, by formally defining the business processes, integrates the modelling of the e-business processes together with the software components meant to implement them. This specification is used as an input for the definition of the company profiles and the successive collaboration agreement between commercial partners in an ebXML scenario (respectively Collaboration Protocol Profile, CPP, and Collaboration Protocol Agreement, CPA).

Inside the MODA-ML initiative we have faced the definition and management of inter-enterprise collaborations. The proposed framework defines both business messages and the way to exchange them, but aims to provide also a mechanism to improve the workflow management, the integration and the interoperability among different partner of the Textile/Clothing supply chain, and the agreement about interaction mechanism. In order to achieve this aim, it is necessary a standard formal definition to describe business processes. This definition can eases inter-enterprises collaboration and commercial transactions, overall spreading information about business processes.

MODA-ML business processes are specified using BPSS documents. Every BPSS is generated directly from the MODA-ML dictionary. Using a web interface and an HTML form it is possible to select a process and build, from the implicit definition contained in the vocabulary, the corresponding BPSS.

During the development of the tool to create BPSS document we have found two different DTD to validate our BPSS: one found on www.ebxml.org, and the second on www.oasis-open.org. Also the examples we have found on the web sites to understand the correct use of the BPSS were not coherent: these examples propose different ways to structure the XML elements and adopt differently a XML schema or a DTD to validate the BPSS. Finally we decided to adopt the DTD for the version 1.01 of BPSS provided by the official web site of ebXML.

MODA-ML process definition is not completely compliant with ebXML specification: MODA-ML processes are composed of one or more activities each of which can consist in the exchange of one or more MODA-ML messages. Differently from ebXML, MODA-ML message exchange is not subdivided into a "request-response" atomic activities to better fit with really situations.

ebXML uses the BPSS as the starting point to generate a CPP document. As defined in [6] a CPP (Collaboration Protocol Profile) "defines the capabilities of a *Party* to engage in electronic *Business* with other *Parties*. These capabilities include both technology capabilities, such as supported communication and messaging protocols, and *Business* capabilities in terms of what *Business Collaborations* it supports". A CPP document describes an enterprise and the role it can carry out inside a business process, but does not allow to define more specifically the information that can be managed by the enterprise itself. The ebXML definition of CPP results to be not flexible enough to tackle the requirements of the T/C supply chain.

Together with the generation of BPSS documents, the MODA-ML project takes care to produce CPP documents to describe the collaboration profile of the MODA-ML users. MODA-ML refers to 2.0 version of the CCP, available on the official site of ebXML (www.ebxml.org).

On the other hand MODA-ML approach to define enterprise profile aims to be more flexible than ebXML one. As we have highlighted in section three, the Textile/Clothing sector is composed of a large set of very different and heterogeneous companies that establish very dynamic collaborations with their sectoral partners. These collaborations can change depending on the final product that has to be realised. Moreover the enterprises in general are not well disposed towards sudden and drastic changes of their "well-proved" management systems. They surely prefer a gradual approach in adopting new mechanisms to manage business processes, to exchange documents and contact their partners. It is not feasible to impose completely new transport mechanism or to propose absolutely unusual and unfamiliar documents.

These practical issues conditioned the way to compose CPP documents: in defining their profile, MODA-ML users require:

1. To choose a specific sub set of documents to manage for a particular business process. The real scenario of the T/C supply chain is composed of a large variety of partners that want to interact according to MODA-ML process, but can implement only a sub set of the exchange activity inside the process. In general, there are many enterprises that, depending on their internal organisation, do not know how to manage a certain kind of information, and how to insert the related electronic business documents inside their internal workflow.

2. To specify which part of the business document they can manage. MODA-ML messages contain different kinds of information. Depending on the enterprise, this information can result as absolutely indispensable, optional or instead not required. MODA-ML document schemas provide a flexible structure of business documents to reflect enterprise requirements, providing a mechanism to produce business messages customized for each situation.

In order to provide a mechanism to solve the first issue, we have considered three possible approach: modify the CPP DTD for an enhanced version of CPP documents, use of the "SimplePart" element to specify the message type to be sent for a particular activity as a "completely arbitrary type", or use the "CanSend", and "CanReceive" elements to specify the transport method to deliver business documents. Finally we have chosen to use the CanSend and CanReceive elements to point out different way from MSH to exchange MODA-ML messages. In this way a partner of the supply chain, that does not want to use the MODA-ML framework (i.e. MSH) to exchange a particular business message, can point out, using these two elements, an alternative mechanism to deliver the message (i.e. phone or fax or whatever). Using ebXML terminology, in our CPP a MODA-ML user can specify inside a Binary Collaboration the supported sub set of Binary Transaction Activity, avoiding the constrain to manage the whole Binary Collaboration (that represents the business process) defined.

To solve the second issue, we decided to modify the DTD of the CPP introducing a new element to allow the users to specify how she/he considers determined parts of the message. In this way a MODA-ML user editing its own CPP can define which information she/he judges to be binding, optional or rejected inside the business message that have to be exchanged. A brief example of the use of this new element is depicted in fig. 1.

```
<tp:DocumentOptionalElements tp:partyId="IT0987654321"
         tp:bpssuuid="v2003-1_FabricProduction">
         <tp:Doc tp:name="Textile Darn Order" tp:position="0">
    <tp:Entity tp:name="msgfunction" tp:count="0" tp:state="Required"
    tp:xpath="Textiles Darn Order/@msgfunction"/>
    <tp:Entity tp:name="MOtotals" tp:count="1" tp:state="Rejected"
             tp:xpath="Textiles Darn Order/MOtotals"/>
         </tp:Doc>
    </tp:DocumentOptionalElements>
```

Fig. 1. A brief example of the new element.

This information will become fundamental for a successive definition of the Collaboration Protocol Agreement (CPA) document: the table 1 can be used as a reference to match those message parts that are customisable to define a final message.

Table 1. Possible matches between different requirements on same part of the message.

Definition of user 1	Definition of user 2	Final definition
Binding	Binding	Binding
Binding	Optional	Binding
Binding	Rejected	*To contract*
Optional	Optional	Binding/Rejected
Optional	Rejected	Rejected
Rejected	Rejected	Rejected

Following the guidelines of the project, that developed all of its services like web applications, the tool to generate the BPSS has been implemented as a set of VBScript dynamic web pages. Once that every element concerning the new business processes and the relative business documents has been specified and its description has been included in the vocabulary, it is possible to automatically generate the related BPSS starting from such description. Using an appropriate web interface the MODA-ML staff can select a particular process and then, by a simple click, generate the XML files. The BPSS documents are then stored in a directory publicly available via web for MODA-ML partners (Fig. 2).

The two main aims of this tool are:

- to have a standard-formal definition of the processes supported by the MODA-ML framework.
- to maintain the vocabulary as the only central component of the framework to update during its growth.

Besides the BPSS generator tool, we have implemented an on line editor for CPP documents. In fact, starting from the BPSS it will be possible for each actor to edit his own Collaboration Protocol Profile (CPP), that will be used as reference for the role of the actor in the relevant process. The possibility for every enterprise to tailor the message set defined in the BPSS and to customize interaction parameters on its own capabilities is related with the basic requirement of the MODA-ML project that aims to face the heterogeneity of the Textile/Clothing sector.

From the user's point of view, BPSS and CPP implementation can enhance the understanding of the services provided by each enterprises, and the analysis of possible interaction mechanisms.

Naturally the work in implementing BPSS and CPP documents targets to a future definition of CPA documents. As explained in ebXML specification, CPA documents represents the agreement achieved by two different partners in the supply chain to do electronic business. This agreement stem out from the possible matching between the enterprise profiles expressed in CPP. The future step will be the analysis of (semi-automatic) tools to build CPA documents.

5   Results of the MODA-ML Project

The MODA-ML project involved some industrial pilot users (five leading firms), that experienced the result of the project. In the first phase the pilot users began to check the documents' capabilities to fit their information flows that were already managed via phone or fax. Then they began to insert the MODA-ML documents in their real workflow with customers and suppliers.

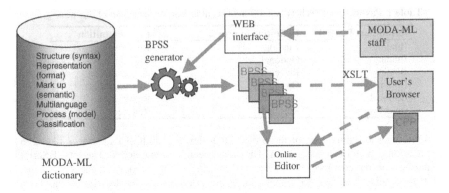

Fig. 2. MODA-ML architecture for BPSS and CPP management.

The introduction of MODA-ML suggested evolutions of the internal information systems and new services to be offered to the customers. Moreover the adoption of the (pure) data exchange framework has resulted very inexpensive (in terms of both licence and human resources) for the industry.

The project has demonstrated a good capacity to attract new potential users: 3 consortia (110 firms) in the industrial textile districts of Biella and Prato and also four technology providers are going to MODA-ML. Nevertheless, we still haven't got a critical mass for a fast spreading of the MODA-ML results. Presently they support further developments to extend the supply chain coverage and to improve the usability and flexibility of the framework.

But the most important result obtained by the MODA-ML is that its results have been absorbed in the final document of the CEN/ISSS TEXSPIN Workshop. Promoted by Euratex (European association of national industry trading association of the T/C) and supported by CEN/ISSS *(European Committee for Normalisation/Information Society Standardisation System)* TEXSPIN aimed "to provide a framework for the (B2B) integration of the European Textile/Clothing/Distribution chain". This initiative ended in July 2003, and the final CWA was published in autumn 2003.

Bibliography

1. Anderson, D., Britt, F., Favre, D., The Seven Principles of Supply Chain Management, From the Spring 1997 issue of Supply Chain Management Review
2. Bermudez, J., Supply Chain Management: More Than Just Technology, from the March/April 2002 issue of Supply Chain Management Review
3. [BPSS] http://www.ebxml.org/specs/ebBPSS.dtd
4. Cavinato, J., What's Your Supply Chain Type?, Supply Chain Management Review - May 1, 2002

5. P.G. Censoni, P. De Sabbata, G. Cucchiara, F. Vitali, L. Mainetti, T.Imolesi , "MODA-ML, a vertical framework for the Textile-Clothing sector based on XML and SOAP", in "Challenges and achievements in e e-business and e-work"; Prague 15-18 October 2002, ISBN IOS Press 58603 284 4/ISBN Ohmsha 4 274 90541 1 C3055
6. [CPP] http://www.ebxml.org/specs/ebcpp-2.0.pdf
7. European e-business Showcase, European Communities, 2003. ISBN 92-894-5057-6
8. Hollingsworh, The Workflow Reference Model: 10 Years On, http://www.wfmc.org/standards/docs/Ref_Model_10_years_on_Hollingsworth.pdf
9. Kahl, S., What's the "Value" of Supply Chain Software? , Supply Chain Management Review - January 1, 1999
10. Lee, H., Seungjin, W., E-Business and Supply Chain Integration, November 2001, http://www.stanford.edu/group/scforum/Welcome/EB_SCI.pdf
11. Lee, H., Creating Value Through Supply Chain Integration, From the September/October 2000 issue of Supply Chain Management Review
12. Leymann, Roller, Schmidt, Web services and business process management, IBM Systems Journal, Volume 42, n° 2, July 2002
13. Peltz, C., Web Service Orchestration and Choreography, Web Services Journal, 7- 2003
14. Radjou, N., Deconstruction of the Supply Chain, Supply Chain Management Review - November 1, 2000
15. Reeve, J., The Financial Advantages of the Lean Supply Chain, 3/1/2002, from the March/April 2002 issue of Supply Chain Management Review
16. [UEML project]: http://www.ueml.org

A Framework
for Multilingual Electronic Data Interchange

Rouzbeh Maani and Saeed Parsa

Computer Department, Iran University of Science and Technology, Narmak, Tehran, Iran
`rouzbeh_maani@yahoo.com, parsa@iust.ac.ir`

Abstract. In The restriction of using English in B2B conversations has always been a big barrier for eCommerce globalization. In this paper, the design of an environment to support B2B electronic data interchange in any language set by the users is presented. After some basic checks, XML messages can be translated into the user defined language. This translation is conducted by the use of a local dictionary. In addition, to verify the messages, there is a compiler in our proposed framework that checks the data types, syntax and semantics of any exchanging message.

Keywords: B2B, non-English, eCommerce

1 Introduction

English is not the native language of 64.4% of internet users and this number will grow up to 70.8% by the end of 2004 [1]. Hence, English language has become a major barrier against the development of eCommerce amongst the non English speaking nations. It is difficult for non English speaking parties around the world to communicate in English.

To resolve the difficulty, some big companies such as Rosetta net [2] and ebXML [3] that use XML for passing messages in eCommerce, have provided global repositories of standard XML tags to determine the semantics of messages [4] [5] [6]. Using these repositories, companies can be sure that their messages are correct and understandable. A major difficulty with using these tags is the large number of references to the repositories. In addition, the problem of preparing messages in English still remains.

DTD[1] files have been used to control the structure of XML messages. The problem is the weakness of DTD files for defining the number of elements and the type of data items appearing in XML messages [7]. To resolve the difficulty, some suggestions have been made by Growley and Webber [8]. In this article, a new scheme based on the XML Schema, is proposed. The remaining parts of this article are organized as follows: in Section 2 a brief history of the B2B technology and its problems is presented. Section 3, provides an overview of our new scheme for preparing XML messages in any desired language. In Section 4, our proposed scheme is elaborated in more details. The conclusion and future extension of this article is presented in Section 5.

---

[1] Document Type Definition

K. Bauknecht, M. Bichler, and B. Pröll (Eds.): EC-Web 2004, LNCS 3182, pp. 196–205, 2004.
© Springer-Verlag Berlin Heidelberg 2004

2 Background and Related Works

Generally, B2B is based upon electronic data interchange. In the first years of the B2B evolution, EDI[2] was used. EDI is described as the interchange of structured data according to agreed message standards between computer systems, by electronic means [9]. Since the pioneers of EDI tried to cover all parts of the electronic commerce, EDI standards are numerous and difficult to use. To resolve this difficulty, the idea of SIMPL-EDI was proposed. The purpose of SIMPL-EDI was to reduce extra messages and make EDI more efficient [10]. However, despite the relative efficiency, SIMPL-EDI messages can not be easily understood. There is a need for EDI experts to interpret EDI messages. Therefore, SIMPL-EDI has not been useful for most of the small and medium size companies. To resolve the difficulty, the idea of using XML messages was emerged.

XML messages have been effectively used in B2B interactions. The XML's ability to separate structure from meaning is expected to contribute to the emergence of open markets with non-proprietary XML interfaces being the foundation of B2B communication [11]. The full potential of using XML as a data format lies in its ability to empower millions of Web users to participate in and create new dynamic networks. With XML being the basis of information networks, the definition of flexible, open interfaces outside of applications becomes possible, opening networks to a large number of users and enhancing the life span of data. This is why many initiatives striving to make electronic commerce "Easy, trusted, and ubiquitous" are XML-based [11]. Another reason is System and vendor independence and Low entry costs [12]. On the other hand the easiness of using XML and readability of XML messages for non-expert users makes it easy for small and medium sized companies to use.

Despite all these advantages, there is a big problem with XML based solutions. The problem is the interpretation of the tags used in XML messages. To resolve the problem, some big companies such as Rosetta net [2] and ebXML [3] have provided comprehensive dictionaries of XML tag definitions. These dictionaries can be accessed via global repositories [14].

There has been a big debate among industry and Government experts for meaningful nomination of XML tags used in EDI. One issue is whether to have both human and machine-readable tags. Additional issues are how to build a data dictionary from the time-tested X12 and EDIFACT data dictionaries and whether the data dictionary should be language-neutral. If this neutral data dictionary could be built for use on the Internet, XML could be used as the neutral conveyance format for exchanging business data for Internet Electronic Commerce applications. XML will not relieve the requirement for mapping to this neutral data dictionary, but it will alleviate some of the pain of using complex framework to map to other applications. In addition, this would enable small-to-medium-sized businesses to take advantage of EDI, but at a much lower cost and commitment of resources. Figure 1 illustrates the basic concept of a semantic repository [13].

As illustrated in Figure 1, in the first step a user or agent in Organization 1 queries a Global Repository for common business objects to be passed to a trading partner (Organization 2). In Step 2, references to the queried objects are passed as a transac-

---

[2] Electronic Data Interchange

tion to the trading partner. In Step 3, the references are used to map the data into the organization's application system [13].

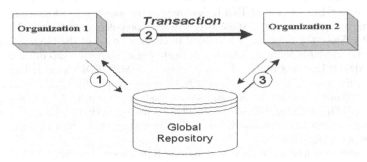

Fig. 1. Extensible Markup Language Repository Conceptual Architecture.

One of the main problems of today's technologies based on XML is the use of DTD files to explain the structure of XML messages. Despite the advantages of DTD files to explain the type and structure of XML elements, they have some weaknesses. These weaknesses are:

- Limitation of data types.
- The number of elements is not clear.
- Name Spaces are not supported.

Another problem of XML based technologies is the lack of appropriate security system for exchanging business messages [15].

One of the big problems of traditional EDI is to handle B2B scenarios. The underlying principle must be that the trading relationship must be understood and defined before EDI starts, rather than expecting EDI to sort it out [10]. In other words, the two companies that want to have a transaction have to determine the scenario previously [16]. They can not create new scenarios when they need. In the next sections we will propone our approach to solve the problems mentioned in this section.

3 Suggested Framework

In this section by referring to the above mentioned problems, we will clarify our suggestions. Our suggested framework is based upon a compiler for syntax and semantics checking. The characteristics of the framework are as follows:

- Syntax and semantics checking of XML messages.
- Possibility of defining XML tags name by the user.
- Checking the order of XML messages considering the B2B scenario.
- Possibility of defining XML elements and new messages and scenarios.
- Possibility of message encryption by a symmetric key.

In the next sections these characteristics are explained. In each case the problems and suggested solutions are proponed.

3.1 Syntax and Semantics Checking

Fortunately, syntax checking is so easy with regards to XML structure. The compiler embedded within our suggested framework, checks all messages according to the XML standard format. As mentioned before one of the main problems of XML messages is the lack of a specified standard to manage the underlying semantics for XML tags. Some issues use SIMPL-EDI format for message definition [4] [5] [6]. In SIMPL-EDI each message consists of several segments and each segment consists of several segments and elements [10]. In the suggested framework, messages are in SIMPL-EDI format. In fact, XML complex elements are used instead of EDI segments and XML simple elements instead of EDI elements. To have different names in different languages for each tag, a unique identifier has been assigned. Hence, users may assign any name in any language to the existing XML elements. In order to perform semantics checking, unique identifiers are used instead of element's name. In the suggested framework, each B2B scenario, message and element has its own unique ID. The compiler embedded within the framework, checks the semantics of messages with regards to these unique IDs. The following is a part of an XML message:

```
< Buyer    id="E8787987" >
    <Code    id="E8787984" > 1234 </Code >
    <Name    id="E8787985" > Intel </Name >
</ Buyer >
```

It is observed that each element of the message has a unique ID. The semantics is checked by the element ID. As mentioned before, most of the XML based technologies use DTD files to explain the structure of messages. In our suggested framework, XSD[3] files are used instead of DTD files to define the structure of messages. XSD files are fully described in section 4-2.

3.2 Defining XML Tags' Name by User

As mentioned in section 2, big companies such as Rosetta Net and ebXML, have defined their own XML tag dictionary and put it in a global repository on Internet. These dictionaries usually specify XML elements and their attributes such as name, goal, position and ID. When a party wants to exchange business data with another party, it has to use the terms defined in repository. These terms often are in English.

To solve the problem, a possible solution is to let the parties to define an alias for each element in the global repository provided if the repository supports aliasing. Here, each party can define its own alias for the elements in its own conversational language. Other parties may find the meaning of the element by referring to its English explanation. Here, the major issue is to keep hundreds of aliases in different languages for each XML element in the global repository. Another problem is the large number of references to the global repository. Each party has to refer to the repository to extract the meaning of any message.

Another solution, as mentioned in section 2, is to send references to the XML elements in the global repository, instead of the tag names. The meaning of messages

---

[3] XML Schema Definition

can be found by referring to the global repository. Here, the problem is the large number of references made by the parties to the repository, to find the meaning of the messages.

Our suggested solution with regards to the elements ID is to keep the elements name defined by each party, in a local repository on the computer used by the party. In this local repository or user's dictionary the ID of each element with its related name is maintained. Each element name is defined by the user. To identify each element in the repository, the compiler uses the elements ID rather than the name. Hence, the name of the element can be anything defined by the users. Using this approach, parties can send and receive messages in their own language. If a received massage is not in the expected language, each element will be first recognized by its ID and then replaced with the name stored in the local repository. Using this approach, not only each party can define its own name for the XML elements in its own language, but also the number of references to the global repository will be highly reduced. The global repository will be referenced only if a new element ID is found. In such situations, the framework will find the semantics of new elements from the global repository through the Internet.

3.3 Scenarios

In B2B conversations, the sequence of interchanged messages is called scenario. One of the major issues concerning the use of traditional EDI is that trading relationship must be understood and defined before EDI starts and two parties can not define new scenarios [16]. In the suggested framework, XSD files are used to control the sequence of messages. These XSD files are kept in a global repository. Therefore, a party can search the global repository for any other party which supports a particular scenario. A party can define its own scenario and store it in the global repository, to be accessed and used by the other parties. For instance a company may define a new insurance service, by using XML elements stored in a global B2B repository. Below, is an example of an XSD file which holds the sequence of messages for exchanging keys in a security protocol:

```
<xs:element name="SenarioForExchangingKey" id="S8787987" …>
    <xs:complexType>
        <xs:sequence>
            <xs:element name ="RequestKey"              id
            ="M8787984" …/>
            <xs:element name ="SendingFirstKey"         id
            ="M8787985" …/>
            <xs:element name ="SendingSecondKey"        id
            ="M8787986"… />
            <xs:element name ="EndingSenario"           id
            ="M8787987"… />
            111
        </xs:sequence>
    </xs:complexType>
</xs:element>
```

The compiler embedded within the suggested framework uses this scenario to check the sequence of messages. Each message is known by its ID and the compiler will check the sequence of the messages with regards to their related scenario.

3.4 Extensibility and Security

One of the main features of our suggested framework is its extensibility such that, new elements or new scenarios can be defined by any party, when required. This feature is necessary in today's B2B transactions; because, the nature of today's business is so changeable and volatile such that every day some new needs are emerged.

Another characteristic of the framework is using encryption to protect business transactions from any malicious and unauthorized access or modifications. Unfortunately XML has no means for encryption by itself [15]. To have an independent security system, within the suggested framework, the Diffie-Hellman key agreement protocol [17] is used to create a symmetric key. The key is then applied along with a hash function to encrypt XML messages. To hash data, SHA-1 [19] or MD5 [18] algorithms can be used. The details of implementation are described in the next section.

4 Implementation

In this section the architecture and some implementation details of the suggested framework is presented. Overall architecture of the framework is illustrated in figure 2. There framework architecture consists of two major parts, called sender and receiver. The sender gets the XML message which is created with sender defined language. This language might be French, Spanish or any language defined by the user. At first, the compiler embedded within the framework checks the syntax of message with regards to XML standard structure. The compiler uses a related XSD scenario file to check the sequence of XML messages. Here, a message is identified by its ID. The compiler also uses XSD files to check the type of data and sequence of the elements appearing in XML messages. After checking the structure, syntax and semantics a key is used to encrypt the XML message. This key can be either symmetric or asymmetric. However, a symmetric key created by Deffie-Hellman Algorithm, is preferred.

On the receiver side, arriving messages are first decrypted, using the symmetric key used for the encryption. Then the compiler performs syntax and semantics checks, using the same procedure as the sender side. The framework looks up the ID of each XML element in its local repository. If the name assigned to an element with a certain ID is different from the name defined in the local repository, it will be replaced in the message. At the end there will be a message in the receiver side language.

4.1 Defining Tags in Any Language

After the framework is installed, the user should initialize it. In this stage the user can determine the name of each XML element used in B2B messages. The user can also use the default element name. After this stage we will have a local repository which consists of the element's ID with the related name defined by the user. Table 1 represents a part of this local repository.

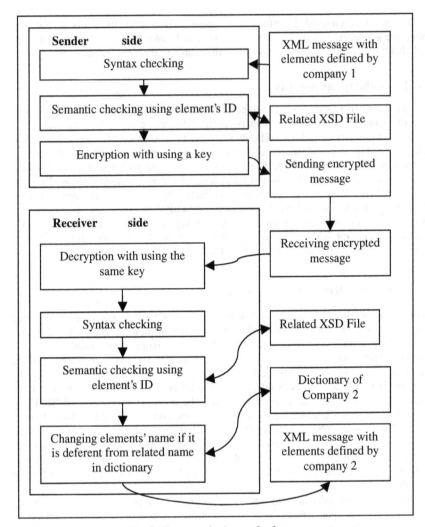

Fig. 2. The general schema of software.

Table 1. A part of local dictionary contains user defined elements.

ID	Name
E8787987	فروشنده
E8787984	کد
...	...

Table 2. A part of local dictionary contains EAN number related to each ware.

EAN	Name
2572315643	Television
2572315676	Radio
...	...

We use Unicode (UTF 8) for representing characters and fortunately XML supports this code, so the framework can support any language. As an example English companies can use <DATE> element, while Spanish companies use <FECHA>.

Within the suggested framework, each product item is numbered according to the EAN[4] standard. Using this numbering system, the framework can easily translate each ware's name, as well as XML tags into the user defined language. The mechanism is the same as translating XML tags, but a table which maintains EAN code of goods and the names defined by the user is used.

4.2 Syntax and Semantics Checking

The main task of the compiler in the suggested framework is checking syntax and semantics of messages. As mentioned before, the compiler uses XSD files for this task. Each XSD file is related to a message and describes that message. In each XSD file the number, sequence and type of the XML elements is defined. The point in syntax and semantics checking is using IDs for identifying elements rather than names. Below is an example of an XSD file:

```
...
<xs:element name="Quantity" id="E100000016" maxOccurs="10">
  <xs:complexType>
    <xs:simpleContent>
      <xs:extension base="TAlphaNumeric">
        <xs:attribute name="SIMPL-EDI-SegmentName"
        type="xs:string" fixed="QTY" use="required" />
        <xs:attribute name="Type" type="xs:string"
        fixed="OrderedQuantity" use="required" />
        <xs:attribute name="Unit" type="xs:string"
        use="optional" />
        <xs:attribute name="eid" type="xs:string"
        fixed="E100000016" use="required" />
      </xs:extension>
    </xs:simpleContent>
  </xs:complexType>
</xs:element>
...
```

Here, each element has a unique ID defined by an attribute, called *eid*. In addition each element has some other attributes which define the element completely. On the other hand, each element with all attributes and some detailed explanation is maintained in a table. A row of this table is shown in table 2.

Table 3. A part of table which describes elements.

ID	Name	Attributes	Position	Occurrence	Type	Children	Description
E100000016	Quantity	eid,unit,...	...	(1,10)	Complex	null	...

---

[4] European Article Numbering

In fact, this table is the same as an XSD file and describes each element. However, this table is simpler for people to understand. In fact this table will be used only by the experts to create B2B XML messages, and help them to know the standards of each message. Experts use these standards and produce messages which have all the attributes defined in table 2. The name of elements can be different from the default name.

The compiler of the framework uses XSD files to check the structure. In fact, the compiler uses two kinds of XSD files to do this task:

- *XSD file of scenarios:* In this kind of XSD files the sequence of messages in a particular scenario is defined.
- *XSD file of messages:* In this kind of XSD files the type, number and sequence of elements in a particular message is defined.

5 Conclusions

The barrier of English language in B2B conversations can be taken by the suggested framework. To facilitate the translation of B2B messages in any conversational language, unique IDs should be assigned to the elements. Also to translate the name of products, EAN code can be employed to uniquely identify the products. Each party should use its own local repository, to name elements in its own language. Also, to provide extensibility, a global repository should be used to keep any new element defined by the parties. To analyze the syntax, semantics and the sequence of XML messages, XSD files are preferred to the DTD.

References

1. "Global Internet Statistics", September 2003, http://global-reach.biz/globstats/index.php3.
2. www.rosettanet.org
3. www.ebxml.org
4. Kari Kellokoski, "XML Repositories", 1999,
   http://mia.ece.uic.edu/~papers/WWW/MultimediaStandards/XML_Repositories.pdf
5. "Proposal for a UN Repository for XML Tags Based on UN/EDIFACT", CEFACT, September 1998, http://www.unece.org/cefact/docum/download/98cp25.pdf.
6. White Paper, "The Basic Semantic Repository" ICARIS Project Documentation, 1999, http://www.icaris.net/icaris/bsr.html
7. D. Kiely., "Xml schema slowly matures", devX, January 2001,
   http://www.fawcette.com/archives/listissue.asp?pubID=2&MagIssueId=429#
8. David L. Woodruff, Optimization Software Class Libraries, Handbook, March 2002. Growley B.,Webber D., "Preliminary Findings and Recommendations on the Representation of X12 Data Elements and Structures in XML", X12C Ad Hoc Task Group on the use of XML with X12 EDI, August 1998,
   http://www.x12./xorg12org/Subcommittees/X12C/C0300_XML_EDI_Rep_V10.pdf.
9. Chris Nelson, "The ABC of EDI", http://www.edi.wales.org/feature4.htm
10. Whittle J., "Simpl-EDI Introduction to Concepts and Principles", ecentre UK, 1999, http://www.ebxml.org/project_teams/core_components/simpl-edi.pdf.
11. Tim Weitzel ,"A Communication Architecture for the Digital Economy 21st century EDI", IEEE, Proceedings of the 33rd Hawaii International Conference on System Sciences, 2000. http://www.computer.org/proceedings/hicss/0493/04936/04936020.pdf.

12. White Paper, Umesh Kumar Rai, "Realizing xml benefits in life insurance",
    http://www.wipro.com/pdf_files/Wipro_XML_in_Insurance.pdf.
13. "Electronic data interchange repositories",
    http://www.dcnicn.com/lamp/cals_97f/task11/html/Fbsr_udef/Repos-03.htm
14. David Webber, Anthony Dutton "Understanding ebXML, UDDI, XML/EDI", October
    2000, http://www.xml.org/xml/feature_articles/2000_1107_miller.shtml.
15. Ernesto Damiani , "Design and Implementation of an Access Control Processor for XML
    Documents", 2003,
    http://www9.org/w9cdrom/419/419.html.
16. Goldfarb F., Prescod P., "The XML Handbook", Prentice Hall, 2000.
17. Jerry Crow, "Prime Numbers in Public Key Cryptography an Introduction", 2003,
    http://www.giac.org/practical/GSEC/Gerald_Crow_GSEC.pdf.
18. RFC 3174
19. RFC 1321

An Analysis of Bidding Activity
in Online Auctions

Vasudeva Akula[1] and Daniel A. Menascé[2]

[1] School of Information Technology and Engineering
George Mason University, Fairfax, VA 22033, USA
vakula@gmu.edu
[2] Department of Computer Science
George Mason University, Fairfax, VA 22033, USA
menasce@cs.gmu.edu

Abstract. Online auctions are rapidly becoming one of the significant
forms of electronic commerce to buy and sell goods and services. This
form of electronic commerce has unique workflows that do not exist in
other forms of e-commerce infrastructures. Bidding activity is one of the
most important transactions in online auction sites and trends within
bidding activity can be used to design business-oriented metrics and
resource management techniques specific to online auction sites. This
paper provides an analysis of bidding activity of online auction sites
including i) popularity of bidders, sellers, and winners, ii) bidding activity
within different auction price ranges, and iii) arrival rate of new bidders
and bidding activity within groups of auctions with the same unique
number of bidders.

1 Introduction

Many traditional auction businesses are moving into the online auctions space
joining winners in this market space, such as eBay and Yahoo! Auctions [13, 14].
English auctions are one of the popular categories of auctions in which bidders
compete by increasing the price of an auction until either the time is over or
no one else competes with a higher bid or a combination of both. Most online
auction sites allow users to place automatic bids, called proxy bids, which allow
a user to specify a maximum amount and automatically place a bid if another
user bids more than the current bid but below the user's maximum bid. Alert
services to indicate creation of a new auction or changes in an existing auction,
and watch lists to monitor the progress of an auction are common among many
online auction sites.

Building websites that can scale well is one of the challenges faced by archi-
tects of e-commerce sites. Benchmarks can be used to compare competing site
architectures. One such available benchmark for e-commerce sites is the TPC-W
benchmark [11], which mirrors the activities of e-tailers such as online book-
stores. An e-commerce site developed for auctioning goods online, such as eBay,
exhibits significantly different characteristics from e-tailers. Thus, TPC-W is not

K. Bauknecht, M. Bichler, and B. Pröll (Eds.): EC-Web 2004, LNCS 3182, pp. 206–217, 2004.

well-suited for auction-related e-commerce sites. A specific benchmark for auction sites, RUBiS, was developed at Rice University [2]. This benchmark is not as thorough as TPC-W and its workload generation process does not reflect the characteristics of a real auction site. The analysis presented in this paper will be used for designing a realistic benchmark for online auction sites. This benchmark and its workload generator will be used in our research on the design and analysis of algorithms and resource allocation policies to increase the revenue throughput (i.e., dollars/sec generated by a site [10]) of auction sites.

Online auction sites have significantly different workloads compared to other forms of e-commerce sites with activity spiking during closing minutes and dropping to zero immediately after closing each auction [6]. Services such as proxy agents, alerts, and watch lists allow users to create various strategies for different auctions, resulting in interesting workloads on auction sites. A good understanding of the workload of auction sites should provide insights about their activities and help in the process of designing business-oriented metrics and designing novel resource management policies based on these metrics, as done in [10]. Our ongoing workload characterization includes detailed analyses of real data, obtained through automated agents, from online auctions to uncover patterns related to their major activities. We also analyzed how the features of the workload change within clusters determined by some specific rules. For example, it is quite likely that the bidding activity will be different for higher priced auctions than for lower priced ones. These results can be used to devise dynamic pricing and promotion models by offering discounts to auctions that are not gaining popularity as opposed to others.

Previous work in workload characterization of e-commerce sites in general was presented in [3, 8, 9] and was discussed in the more specific case of auction sites in [2, 6]. We address in this paper user behavior aspects that were not treated in our previous work on workload characterization [6] in addition to using a significantly larger dataset.

The rest of the paper is organized as follows. Section two describes some basic terms and notation used in the paper and provides the necessary background for this paper. Section three discusses the experimental setup used in data collection. The next section provides the analysis of popularity of winners, sellers and bidders in online auctions. The next section presents the analysis of bidding activity within different price clusters. Sections six and seven present the analysis of unique bidder arrival rates and bidding activity grouped by unique bidders, respectively. Section eight summarizes our findings and presents some concluding remarks.

2   Background

An online auction is a method of selling on the Internet in a public forum through open and competitive bidding. A bid is a prospective buyer's indication or offer of a price he or she will pay to purchase an item at an auction. Proxy bidding is the process of submitting a confidential maximum bid to an auction service.

The auction will automatically increase the bid to maintain the high bid. Proxy bidding stops when the bid has won the auction or reached the limit of the proxy bid.

Figure 1 introduces several terms and notation used in the paper. The lifetime of an auction is the difference $t_c - t_o$ between the time, t_c, at which the auction is scheduled to close and its opening time, t_o. The first bid occurs at time t_f and the last bid of the auction occurs at time t_e. The age, A, of an auction is defined

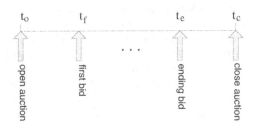

Fig. 1. Auction Times and Prices

as the percentage of time elapsed since the auction's opening time relative to its lifetime. In other words, $A = (t_{\text{current}} - t_o)/(t_c - t_o)$.

The activity on each auction increases as closing time increases [6]. Also, as noted in our earlier study, there are periods of time during the day in which the activity on auction sites is more intensive compared to others. Resource management is of concern for auction sites because failing to properly allocate site resources to auctions closing soon may result in loss of revenue to the site. Users may not tolerate slower response times when the activity on individual auctions is high. These problems can be minimized by using priority-based resource allocation policies. The priorities should take into account different factors including how close is an auction to its closing time and the current price of the auction.

To minimize peak loads on the site, the load on the site can be distributed as much as possible, possibly by offering incentives to the users and by suggesting alternate closing times that balance out the load on the site. Our closing time rescheduling algorithm produced improved response times as a result of rescheduling auction closing times by distributing the predicted load on the site [7]. Improved response times and reduced number of timeouts may result in potentially increasing revenue throughput of the auction site as more users would be able to participate in bidding activity, especially in the last minutes.

3   Experimental Setup

We collected data for auctions created during the month of January 2003 from the Yahoo! auctions site using automated data collection agents. Figure 2 helps to illustrate the process used to collect data for workload characterization purposes. The data collection agent was designed based on the fact that for this particular

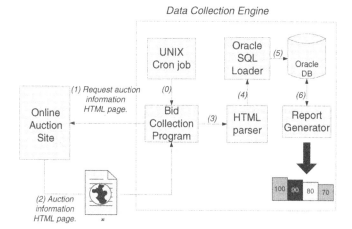

Fig. 2. Data Collection Engine

online auction site, auction information is available online after the close of an auction and can be fetched using a URL that is constant except for a sequential auction ID embedded in the middle of the URL. A Unix `cron` job invokes the data collection agent at programmed regular time intervals. The data collection agent is written in Java and submits HTTP requests to the auction site with a dynamically generated URL that contains the next auction ID to collect. The retrieved auction HTML pages are sent to an `awk` shell script that parses the HTML page to extract the auction and bid information. The output of the parsing program is used as input to the Oracle SQL Loader program, which loads the information into a relational database. After successfully extracting the auction and bid information, the auction item is marked as processed in the database so the process is not repeated for already processed auction items when the program runs next time. The information collected for each auction includes its opening and closing times, price information, the list of all bids placed during the auction (including bidder id), price and time of each bid and an indication of whether the bid was placed manually or by a proxy agent. Several SQL queries were written against the database to identify significant patterns and generate the graphs discussed in the rest of the paper.

3.1   Data Collection

The data collection agent gathered a total of 344,314 auction items created during the month of January 2003, belonging to over two thousand categories. A total of 1.12 million bids were placed on these auctions before their closing time, which varied from the same day of opening to 90 days from the opening date. Summary statistics of the data collected and results of clustering these auctions based on their closing price are presented below.

Table 1. Summary of Data Collected (January 2003)

Total Auctions	344,314
Total Bids	1,125,183
Manual Bids	485,727 (43%)
Bids by Proxy Agents	639,456 (57%)
Auctions with at least 1 bid	140,039 (41%)
Auctions with a winner	133,121 (39%)

Table 2. k-Means Clustering of Auctions on Closing Price

Cluster Num.	Min.	Max.	Average	Count	%Count
1	0.01	48.20	14.62	19673.00	73.74
2	48.50	144.01	82.17	3930.00	14.73
3	144.49	322.50	206.62	1623.00	6.08
4	325.00	657.58	443.35	671.00	2.52
5	660.00	1185.00	874.50	344.00	1.29
6	1190.00	1975.00	1498.66	209.00	0.78
7	1995.00	3200.00	2479.73	94.00	0.35
8	3450.00	6200.00	4396.73	80.00	0.30
9	6500.00	14500.00	8516.57	35.00	0.13
10	15500.00	32000.00	21866.83	19.00	0.07

3.2 Summary Statistics

Table 1 shows some summary statistics for the auctions monitored during the data collection period. The table indicates that proxy agents placed 57% of all bids and bidders placed the remaining 43% bids manually. Forty one percent of the auctions received at least one bid and 39% of the auctions had a winner. Some auctions had a reserve price, which allows the seller to cancel the auction if no bids above the reserve price are placed. Auctions that receive some bids but do not have a winner can be attributed to cancellations due to reserve prices.

3.3 Clustering Auctions on Closing Price

We used the k-means clustering algorithm [4] to divide auctions with at least 10 bids into 10 clusters based on the auction closing prices. The result of the clustering process is shown in Table 2 and indicates that as the size of the cluster decreases, the average closing price increases. A large percentage of auctions have relatively low closing prices and a very small, but non-negligible, number of auctions has very high closing prices. This may be an indication that the closing price distribution is heavy-tailed. These clusters of auctions were analyzed to investigate properties of the auctions within each price cluster and compare these properties to all auctions, as discussed later.

4   Popularity of Winners, Sellers, and Bidders

This section presents an analysis of the popularity (or rank) of winners, sellers, and bidders. The purpose of this analysis is to try to establish an empirical relationship between the relative frequency and rank in each case as discussed below. The basic motivation was to verify a conjecture that this relationship may follow a Zipf's Law [12] given that Zipfian distributions have been observed in many instances related to Web [1] and E-commerce environments [9]. Zipf's Law establishes that the relative frequency f by which an object (or a word in a text) is accessed is inversely proportional to its rank r (also known as the popularity of the object). Thus, $f = K/r$, where K is a normalization constant so all frequencies add to one. According to Zipf's Law, the second most popular object (i.e., rank = 2) receives half the number of accesses of the most popular object (i.e., rank = 1) and the n-th most popular receives $1/n$ of the number of accesses of the most popular. As a result of this, relatively few objects are responsible for the majority of the accesses. This property is very important for system design considerations. For example, caching a relatively small number of objects (i.e., the most popular ones) can result in significant performance improvement [5]. Applying logarithms to both sides of Zipf's law equation yields $\log f = \log K - \log r$. In other words, if Zipf's Law is plotted in a log-log scale, the resulting curve is a straight line with a slope of -1. Zipf's Law is a special case of power-law distributions, i.e., distributions in which the exponent of r is not necessarily 1. Thus, in what follows we are interested in investigating whether the relationship between f and r follows a Zipf or, more generally, a power-law distribution. A straight line with negative slope in the log-log plot of f vs. r is such an indication.

4.1   Winner's Popularity

We first consider the winner's popularity analysis. For that purpose, all the winners are sorted in decreasing order of the number of auctions they won. The relative winning frequency in this case is the percentage of auctions won by the winner. The one with the highest winning frequency is assigned a rank equal to 1, the one with the second highest winning frequency receives a rank equal to 2, and so on. Figure 3(a) shows a log-log plot of the winner frequency versus its rank. The plot shows that the data follows a power law. In practical terms, this means that relatively few bidders are responsible for winning a large percentage of the auctions.

4.2   Seller's Popularity

Consider now the sellers popularity analysis. In this case, all the sellers are sorted in decreasing order of the number of auctions created by a seller. The frequency f in this case is the percentage of all auctions created by the seller. As before, the one with the highest frequency receives a rank equal to one. Figure 3(b) shows a log-log plot of a seller's frequency versus its rank. As with the winner's

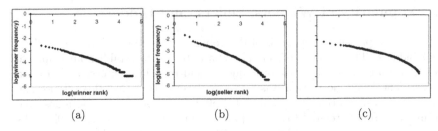

Fig. 3. (a) Log-Log Plot of User's Winning Frequency vs. Rank; (b) Log-Log Plot of Seller's Frequency vs. Rank; (c) Log-Log Plot of User's Bidding Frequency vs. Rank

popularity, the relationship follows a power-law distribution with a slope very close to -1, which indicates a Zipf's distribution. Thus, relatively few sellers are responsible for creating the majority of the auctions.

4.3 Bidder's Popularity

We now turn our attention to bidder popularity. All bidders were sorted in decreasing order of the number of bids placed among all the auctions. The frequency f in this case is the fraction of the total number of bids placed by the bidder. The one with the highest frequency receives a rank of one. Figure 3(c) plots a log-log graph of bidder's frequency versus rank. A power law distribution is apparent in most of the rank range indicating that the majority of bids are placed by a relatively small number of unique bidders.

The results of this section are useful for the design of resource management techniques aimed at optimizing performance and site revenue, which is the goal of our future research.

5   Activity Within Price Clusters

As indicated in section 3.3, auctions were clustered based on their closing price. This section presents the bidding activity within different price clusters in order to examine the influence of the price on the bidding activity of an auction.

For Figure 4(a) we divide the auction age (see definition in Section 2) in 10 intervals. We selected four out of the ten clusters for better readability of the picture. The price ranges of these four clusters cover a large price range, from very cheap items to very expensive ones. The figure indicates the percentage of bids placed in each 10% interval of the auction age for the four clusters. In all price ranges, the bidding activity surges in the last 10% of the auction lifetime as noted in our earlier work [8], which did not consider the effect of price. The graphs of Figure 4(a) indicate that higher priced items attract relatively more bids initially and relatively few bids compared to other groups in the final stages of the auction. This may be explained, as users tend to take more time and place

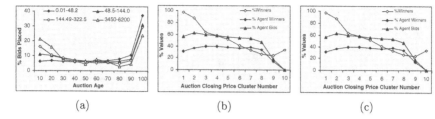

(a)   (b)   (c)

Fig. 4. (a) Percentage of Bids Placed vs. Auction Age Within Price Clusters; (b) Average Bidders, Agents, Number of Days on Auction Within each Cluster; (c) Percentage of Auctions with Winner, Percentage of Winners with Proxy Agent Bid, Percentage of Proxy Agent Bids Within each Cluster

bids cautiously and avoid rushing into the final closing minutes of an auction when purchasing expensive items.

Figure 4(b) indicates the average number of unique bidders per auction, average unique bidders using proxy agents to place automatic bids for them, and the average auction length (in days) for auctions for all 10 price clusters. Remember that as the cluster number increases, the price range also increases. We can see that the higher priced items stay longer in an auction and the average number of unique users using proxy agents drops gradually for higher priced items. This may indicate that bidders may want to exert a closer control when buying expensive items. The number of average unique bidders participating in different price clusters raises initially, stays at similar levels for intermediately priced auctions, and drops for very high priced items. This may reflect a smaller market for very expensive items.

It should be noted that although higher priced items are being auctioned for longer periods, our analysis on the effect of auction length on the closing price did not reveal any particular trend based on price range. This means that many lower priced items are also being auctioned for larger periods of time, which reduces the average closing price of items auctioned for longer periods.

Figure 4(c) indicates the percentage of auctions with a winner, the percentage of auctions with a proxy agent placing the winning bid, and the percentage of total bids placed by proxy agents for each of the 10 price clusters. Note that if an auction does not meet its reserve price, the seller can cancel the auction, leaving the auction without a winner. It is clear from the graphs that higher priced items have lower success rate, a lower number of bids by proxy agents, and a smaller chance of proxy agents winning auctions. As more expensive items require more manual control and thought before bids are placed, these numbers tend to go down in higher priced auctions.

6   Bidder Arrival Time and Bidding Activity

In this section we present the results of our analysis of unique bidder arrival time and bidding activity in auctions with the same number of unique bidders.

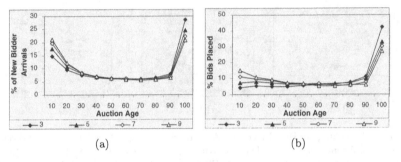

Fig. 5. (a) Percentage of New Bidder Arrivals vs. Auction Age within Auctions with Different Number of Unique Bidders; (b) Percentage of Bids Placed vs. Auction Age with Different Number of Unique Bidders

Note that we used only the number of unique bidders in this analysis, not the number of bids. For example, 5 unique bidders could be placing 50 total bids in a given auction.

Figure 5(a) indicates the percentage of unique bidders entering auctions during each 10% time interval of the auction age. Each unique bidder's entry time is the time at which that user placed his first bid on the auction. Subsequent bids were not counted for this study. There are four curves in Figure 5(a), one for each number of unique bidders: 3, 5, 7, and 9. It is interesting to note that as the number of unique bidders increases per auction, the percentage of bidders participating in the early stages increases. Similarly, the percentage of unique bidders entering the auction during the final stages decreases. For example, for auctions with three unique bidders, about 15% of the unique bidders for all such auctions enter during the first 10% of the auction age and close to 30% enter during the last 10% of the auction age. Consider now auctions with 9 unique bidders. About 21% of the unique bidders for all such auctions enter during the first 10% of the auction age and 22% enter during the final 10% of the auction age.

Figure 5(b) indicates the percentage of bids placed during each 10% time interval of the auction age. Again this graph indicates that the bidding activity surges in the closing minutes of an auction irrespective of the number of unique bidders participating on the auction.

As in Figure 5(a), this graph also shows that the percentage of bids placed increases in the early stages with the number of unique bidders and the percentage of bids placed in the final stages decreases with the number of unique bidders in each auction. We show only four unique bidders in Figures 5(a) and 5(b) for clarity of the graphs.

7   Activity Grouped by Unique Bidders

This section presents an analysis of bidding activity within auctions grouped by the number of unique bidders. Figure 6(a) indicates the average number of bids

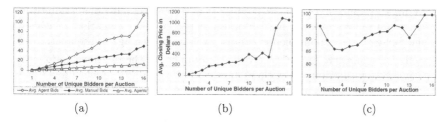

Fig. 6. (a) Average Number of Bids by Proxy Agents, Average Number of Manual Bids and Average Number of Proxy Agents used per Auction vs. Number of Unique Bidders per Auction; (b) Average Closing Price in Dollars vs. Number of Unique Bidders per Auction; (c) Average Percentage of Successful Auctions vs. Number of Unique Bidders per Auction

by proxy agents, the average number of manual bids, and the average number of users using proxy agents within auctions as a function of the number of unique bidders. As the number of unique bidders increases, the number of users using proxy agents also increases. It is clear that the difference between the percentages of bids by proxy agents to manual bids increases with an increasing number of unique bidders. This indicates that as more and more proxy agents compete, the number of overall bids they generate increase very fast resulting in higher closing prices.

Figure 6(b) shows the average closing price of auctions as a function of the number of unique bidders. The graph indicates that higher priced items attract more unique bidders. Note that this holds only up to a few thousand dollars in closing price. Very high priced items such as new and used cars attract few bids from a very small number of unique bidders. Since there are very few of these auctions, the average price of auctions with few unique bidders is still low, given that a large number of auctions have few bidders and a large number of auctions are in the lower price range.

Figure 6(c) indicates the average percentage of successful auctions (i.e., an auction with a winner) as a function of the number of unique bidders participating in the auction. As shown in the graph, with a larger number of unique bidders participating, the success rate increases and after more than 15 unique bidders, the success rate approaches 100%. Note that the success rate in auctions with one bidder is high since there is a large number of items (usually lower priced items) that are won with just one bid. Many of these auctions do not have reserve prices. The same explanation also applies to the large number of items with 2 unique bidders.

8 Concluding Remarks

The main results of our analysis can be summarized as follows:

- Summary statistics: Proxy agents placed 57% of all bids and bidders manually placed the remaining 43% bids. 41% percent of the auctions received at least one bid and 39% had a winner.

- Winner's popularity: Winner's popularity in terms of number of auctions won by a user follows a power law. In practical terms, this means that relatively few bidders are responsible for winning a large percentage of the auctions.
- Seller's popularity: As with the winner's popularity, the relationship follows a power-law distribution with a slope very close to -1, which indicates a Zipf's distribution. Thus, a relatively few sellers are responsible for creating the majority of the auctions.
- Bidder's popularity: A power law distribution is apparent in most of the rank range indicating that the majority of bids are placed by a relatively small number of unique bidders.
- Bidding activity within price clusters: Higher priced items attract relatively more bids initially and relatively few bids in the final stages of the auction compared to less expensive items. Higher priced items stay longer in an auction and the average number of unique users using proxy agents drops gradually for higher priced items. This may indicate that bidders may want to exert a closer control when buying expensive items. The number of average unique bidders participating in different price clusters raises initially, stays at similar levels for intermediately priced auctions, and drops for very high priced items. This may reflect a smaller market for very expensive items.
- Unique bidder analysis: As the number of unique bidders increases per auction, the percentage of bidders participating and bids placed in the early stages of auction increases. Similarly, the percentage of unique bidders entering the auction and bids placed during the final stages decreases. Higher priced items attract more unique bidders. The success rate of auctions increases with an increasing number of unique bidders.
- Proxy agent bidding activity: The difference between the percentages of bids by proxy agents to manual bids increases with an increasing number of unique bidders. This indicates that as more and more proxy agents compete, the number of overall bids they generate increases very fast resulting in higher closing prices. Auctions with an agent placing the final bid to win the auction tend to have a larger number of total bids and unique bidders. These auctions tend to have higher closing prices as agents compete automatically to increase the final price. Therefore, use of agents within auctions results in higher revenue throughput for the auction sites.

The results of our analysis can be used to design innovative algorithms for improving the quality of the service provided to buyers and sellers through optimized resource allocation and for improving revenue throughput [8]. These results will be used to develop workload generators as well as a research testbed for auctions sites. This testbed will be used for the validation of resource management techniques for online auction sites. Auction systems need to prioritize and provide optimal performance during the last minutes of the auction as most of the bids are placed in that period. Our conclusions on popularity of winners, sellers and bidders can play a significant role in designing caching techniques and dynamic resource management techniques for online auction sites.

References

1. V. A. F. Almeida, A. Bestavros, M. Crovella, and A. Oliveira, "Characterizing Reference Locality in the WWW," *Proc. 4th Int. Conf. Parallel and Distributed Information Systems (PDIS)*, IEEE Computer Society, Dec. 1996, Miami Beach, FL, pp. 92–103.
2. C. Amza, E. Cecchet, A. Chanda, A. Cox, S. Elnikety, R. Gil, J. Marguerite, K. Rajamani and W. Zwaenepoel, "Specification and Implementation of Dynamic Web Site Benchmarks," *Proc. IEEE 5th Annual Workshop on Workload Characterization (WWC-5)*, Austin, TX, November 25, 2002.
3. M. Arlitt, D. Krishnamurthy, and J. Rolia, "Characterizing the scalability of a large web-based shopping system," *ACM Tr. Internet Technology (TOIT)*, v.1, n.1, pp. 44–69, Aug. 2001.
4. B. Everitt, *Cluster Analysis*, 4th ed., Oxford University Press, Oxford, 2001.
5. D. A. Menascé, "Scaling Web Sites Through Caching," *IEEE Internet Computing*, July/August 2003, vol. 7, no. 4.
6. D. A. Menascé, Vasudeva Akula, "Towards Workload Characterization of Auction Sites," *Proc. IEEE 6th Annual Workshop on Workload Characterization (WWC-6)*, Austin, TX, October 27, 2003.
7. D. A. Menascé, Vasudeva Akula, "Improving the Performance of Online Auction Sites through Closing Time Rescheduling," *1st International Conference on Quantitative Evaluation of SysTems (QEST-2004)*, Enschede, the Netherlands, September 27-30, 2004.
8. D. A. Menascé, V. Almeida, R. Fonseca, and M. Mendes, "A Methodology for Workload Characterization for E-Commerce Servers," *Proc. ACM Conference in Electronic Commerce*, Denver, CO, Nov. 3-5, pp 119-128, 1999.
9. D. A. Menascé, V. A. F. Almeida, R. Riedi, F. Ribeiro, R. Fonseca, and W. Meira Jr., "In Search of Invariants for E-Business Workloads," *Proc. Second ACM Conference on Electronic Commerce*, Minneapolis, MN, October 17-20, 2000.
10. D. A. Menascé, V. A. F. Almeida, R. Fonseca, and M.A. Mendes, "Business-oriented Resource Management Policies for E-Commerce Servers," *Performance Evaluation*, Vol. 42, Sept. 2000, pp. 223–239.
11. Transaction Processing Council, The TPC-W Benchmark, http://www.tpc.org
12. G. Zipf, *Human Behavior and the Principle of Least Effort*, Addison-Wesley, Cambridge, MA, 1949.
13. eBay - http://www.ebay.com.
14. Yahoo! Auctions - http://auctions.yahoo.com.

Negotiating over Bundles and Prices
Using Aggregate Knowledge

D.J.A. Somefun[1], T.B. Klos[1], and J.A. La Poutré[1,2]

[1] Center for Mathematics and Computer Science (CWI)
P.O. Box 94079, 1090 GB Amsterdam, The Netherlands
[2] Eindhoven University of Technology, School of Technology Management,
P.O. Box 513, 5600 MB Eindhoven, The Netherlands
{koye,tomas,hlp}@cwi.nl

Abstract. Combining two or more items and selling them as one good, a practice called bundling, can be a very effective strategy for reducing the costs of producing, marketing, and selling goods. In this paper, we consider a form of multi-issue negotiation where a shop negotiates both the contents and the price of bundles of goods with his customers. We present some key insights about, as well as a technique for, locating mutually beneficial alternatives to the bundle currently under negotiation. When the current negotiation's progress slows down, the shop may suggest the most promising of those alternatives and, depending on the customer's response, continue negotiating about the alternative bundle, or propose another alternative. Extensive computer simulations show that our approach increases the speed with which deals are reached, as well as the number and quality of the deals reached, as compared to a benchmark, and that these results are robust to variations in the negotiation strategies employed by the customers.

1 Introduction

Combining two or more items and selling them as one good, a practice called bundling, can be a very effective strategy for reducing the costs of producing, marketing, and selling products [1]. In addition, and maybe more importantly, bundling can stimulate demand for (other) goods or services [2–4], by using aggregate knowledge of customer preferences. Traditionally, firms *first* acquire such aggregate knowledge, for example through market research or by mining sales data, and *then* use this knowledge to determine which bundle-price combinations they should offer. Especially for online shops, an appealing alternative approach would be to *negotiate* bundle-price combinations with customers[1]: in that case, aggregate knowledge can be used to facilitate an *interactive* search for the desired bundle and price, interactively adapting the configuration of the bundle to the preferences of the customer. A high degree of bundle customization increases customer satisfaction, which may lead to an increase in the demand for future goods or services.

In this paper, we present a procedure for such an interactive search, using aggregate knowledge about *many* customers, in bilateral negotiations of bundle-price combinations with *individual* customers. Negotiating concerns selecting a subset from a collection of goods or services, viz. the bundle, together with a price for that bundle. In

---

[1] See [5, 6] for other online bundling approaches.

K. Bauknecht, M. Bichler, and B. Pröll (Eds.): EC-Web 2004, LNCS 3182, pp. 218–227, 2004.

theory, this is just an instance of multi-issue negotiation. Like the work of [7–10], our approach tries to benefit from the so-called win-win opportunities offered by multi-issue negotiation, by finding mutually beneficial alternative bundles during negotiations. The novelty of our approach lies in the use of aggregate knowledge of customer preferences. We show that a bundle with the highest 'gains from trade' Pareto-dominates all other bundles within a certain collection of bundles[2,3]. Based on this important insight, we develop a procedure for finding alternative bundles that are likely to lead to the highest Pareto improvements. Computer simulations show how, for various types of customers – with distinct negotiation heuristics – our procedure increases the speed with which deals are reached, as well as the number and the Pareto efficiency of the deals reached.

In the context of bundling, the issue of complementarity of goods is important. In the case of complementary goods, the valuation of a bundle is higher than the sum of the valuations of the individual goods, so that bundling clearly results in higher gains from trade and is therefore mutually beneficial. Firms usually know beforehand which goods do and which do not complement one another (e.g., bicycle and bicycle tier, copier and toner, etc.), and for complementary goods they will make straightforward bundling decisions accordingly. For an important subclass of non-complementary goods – so-called additively separable goods – the bundle valuation is obtained by just adding up the individual valuations. In that case, which is the focus of the current paper, the way in which bundling may be advantageous is less clear: it depends on the shop's and the customer's valuations. The shop may enjoy economies of scale or scope in the production or distribution of goods, while the customer's valuations for different goods may be correlated (see [12] and the references cited therein). Examples of additively separable goods include a cable provider with TV, phone, internet, and pay TV services; the common practice of mobile phone operators in Europe to offer prepaid subscriptions for fixed amounts of SMS, long-distance minutes, international calls, and other services; and an online news provider selling news items in relatively independent categories such as sports, finance, culture, and science.

For many such real world applications, considered in this paper, the number of individual goods to be bundled is relatively small, say $n \leq 10$, which already yields $2^n - 1 = 1023$ distinct bundles; facilitating the search among all those bundles is highly valuable. Obtaining the desired aggregate knowledge, on the other hand, is still manageable, since with additively separable goods this only requires information about customers' valuations for the individual goods, and not for all possible bundles.

The next section provides a high-level overview of the interaction model. In Section 3 we introduce relatively mild conditions on the seller's and his customers' preferences. Based on these conditions, Section 4 develops a procedure for finding the most promising alternative bundles. In order to test the performance of our system, we used it in interactions with simulated customers. Section 5 presents our computer experiments and discusses the results. Conclusions follow in Section 6.

---

[2] The gains from trade for a bundle are equal to the customer's 'valuation' of the bundle minus the shop's valuation, which is his (minimum) price (cf. [11]).

[3] An offer constitutes a Pareto improvement over another offer whenever it makes one bargainer better off without making the other worse off. Bundle b' 'Pareto-dominates' bundle b whenever switching from b to b' results in a Pareto improvement (cf. [11]).

2   Overview

The shop sells a total of $n = 10$ goods, each of which may be either absent or present in a bundle, so that there are $2^n - 1$ distinct bundles containing at least 1 good. A negotiation is conducted in an alternating exchange of offers and counter offers [13], typically initiated by the customer. Our procedure finds mutually beneficial alternatives to the current bundle by searching for Pareto improvements resulting from changing the bundle content. These alternatives are recommended whenever the current negotiation stalls. Information about to the current negotiation process is used to determine *when* an alternative bundle is needed, while aggregate knowledge is used to determine *which* bundle should be recommended.

Figure 1 provides a high-level overview of the interaction between the shop and a customer; the shaded elements form the actual exchange of offers. The customer starts by specifying the initial bundle to negotiate about. After that, they enter into a loop (indicated by the dotted line) which ends only when a deal is made, or with a 1% exogenous probability, that models the chance of bargaining breakdown. In the loop, the customer makes an offer for the current bundle b, indicating the price she wants to pay for it. The shop responds either by accepting the offer, or by considering a recommendation. In any case, conditional upon the 99% continuation probability, the shop also makes an offer, either for the current bundle b or for a newly recommended bundle b' (which then becomes the current bundle b).

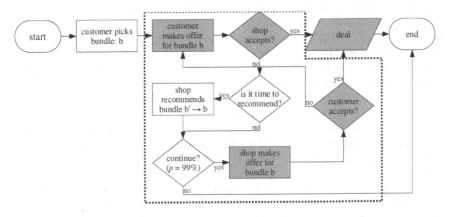

Fig. 1. Integrating recommending in an alternating exchange of (counter) offers.

3   Preference Model

The essence of our model of valuations and preferences lies in the assumption that the shop and his customers order bundles based on their 'net monetary value;' the bundle with the highest net monetary value is the most preferred bundle. A customer's net monetary value of a bundle is equal to the customer's valuation of the bundle (expressed in money) minus the bundle price; the seller's net monetary value is equal to the bundle price minus the seller's bundle valuation (also expressed in money).

Given this assumption and the assumption that a customer wants to buy at most one bundle (within a given time period), it can be shown that any deal involving the bundle with the highest gains from trade is Pareto efficient – see [14] for a formal statement and proof of this proposition. So, faced with the problem of recommending one bundle out of a collection of bundles, the "best" bundle for the shop to recommend is the bundle with the highest expected gains from trade; this bundle Pareto dominates all other bundles.

4   Recommendation Mechanism

4.1   Deciding *When* to Recommend

The mechanism we propose monitors the negotiation process to determine *when* to recommend (Section 4.1) and then generates a recommendation (Section 4.2). The obvious input for the decision of when to recommend is the progress of the current negotiation process, which is a sequence of offers and counteroffers. (An offer O contains a bundle definition and a price: $O = (b, p)$ with $b \in B$ and $p \in P$; B and P denote the collections of all possible bundles and prices, respectively.) So, for every possible sequence of offers and counter offers, we simply need a mapping f onto $\{yes, no\}$, where "yes" means: recommend a new bundle.

We construct a heuristic for f based on the assumption that there is always a probability of not reaching a deal with a customer (e.g., because of a break off, endless repetition, or a deadline): the longer the negotiation is expected to take, the less likely a deal is expected to become. So, as a deal becomes less likely, the incentive for the shop to recommend negotiating about an alternative bundle should increase. Given the shop's bargaining strategy and the pace with which the customer is currently giving in, our heuristic extrapolates the time the current negotiation process will need to reach a deal. More precisely, if we let $O = (b, p)$ and $O' = (b, p')$ denote the customer's current and previous offers for bundle b, then Δt, the predicted remaining number of negotiation rounds needed to reach a deal, is defined as follows:

$$\Delta t = \frac{v_s(b) - p'}{p - p'}, \tag{1}$$

where $v_s(b)$ denotes the seller's monetary value for bundle b. The higher Δt, the higher the probability that the shop makes a recommendation: $p_{rec} = 1 - \exp(-0.25\Delta t)$. The mapping onto $\{yes, no\}$ is obtained by comparing p_{rec} with a draw from a random distribution.

4.2   Deciding *What* to Recommend

Suppose that a customer offers to buy a bundle b at a price p. When a recommendation is needed (see Section 4.1), then – following Section 3 – the idea is to select, from the "neighborhood" of bundle b, the bundle b' that maximizes the expected gains from trade, given that a customer is willing to pay at least the price p for bundle b: $E[v_c(b') - v_s(b')|v_c(b) \geq p]$. Since the shop knows his own monetary value for bundle b', $v_s(b')$, the aim is really to maximize $E[v_c(b')|v_c(b) \geq p] - v_s(b')$. The difficulty here lies in estimating the customer's expected valuation of the bundle:

$$E[v_c(b')|v_c(b) \geq p] = \sum_{i \in P} i \cdot pr(v_c(b') = i|v_c(b) \geq p), \qquad (2)$$

where $pr(v_c(b') = i|v_c(b) \geq p)$ denotes the probability that the customer's valuation for bundle b is equal to i, given that she is willing to pay at least p for bundle b. (To simplify notation we will write $E[v_c(b')|b]$ instead of $E[v_c(b')|v_c(b) \geq p]$.)

Aggregate knowledge can provide an estimation of $E[v_c(b')|b]$. Given that the shop sells n individual goods, there are $2^n - 1$ possible bundles containing at least 1 good. To determine $E[v_c(b')|b]$ for all possible bundle pairs, requires – worst case – an order of $(2^n)^2$ estimations. When the customer's valuation for a bundle is just the sum of her valuations of the individual goods comprising the bundle, however, as assumed in the current paper, this complexity is reduced significantly. Given that a customer's valuation of bundle b, $v_c(b)$, is simply the sum of the valuations of the goods comprising bundle b,

$$E[v_c(b')|b] = \sum_{i \in b'} E[v_c(i)|b]. \qquad (3)$$

This requires at worse "only" $n \cdot 2^n$ estimations of conditional expectations, which is manageable for $n = 10$, as in the current paper.

Generating Recommendations. A customer initiates the negotiation process by proposing an initial bundle $b \in B$ and offering an opening price $p \in P$. The shop stores bundle b as the customer's "interest bundle," in the neighborhood of which he searches for promising alternatives. This neighborhood of bundle b, $Ng(b)$, contains the bundles which, in binary representation, have a Hamming distance to b of 1 [4]. The advantage of advising bundles within the neighborhood of b is that the advice is less likely to appear haphazard.

Having defined a bundle's neighborhood, let the ordered set A denote the so-called "recommendation set," obtained by ordering the neighborhood $Ng(b)$ on the basis of the estimated expected gains from trade of all the bundles b' in bundle b's neighborhood, $\hat{E}[v_c(b')|b] - v_s(b')$, where $\hat{E}$ denotes the estimation of E. Let $\bar{A}$ denote the unordered set of previously proposed bundles.

To recommend a bundle b_k (the kth recommendation, with $k \geq 1$), our mechanism removes the first bundle from A, adds a price to it and proposes it as part of the shop's next offer, and then adds it to $\bar{A}$. Depending on how promising the customer's response to the shop's offer for b_k is, the shop may consider bundle b_k as the customer's *new* interest bundle, in the neighborhood of which the search continues. In order to determine how promising a bundle b_k is in terms of its potential for generating gains from trade, the shop needs to compare the difference in net monetary values of the new bundle

---

[4] Remember that each bundle can be represented as a string containing n bits indicating the presence or absence of each of the shop's n goods in the bundle.

b_k, with the current highest difference among all previously considered bundles. However, because the shop does not know the customer's valuation of a bundle, he simply compares offered and asked prices for bundles.

To specify this in more detail, let O_t^c denote the sequence of offers placed by the customer up until time t, and let $max(O_t^c)$ specify the customer's past offer with the highest difference between the customer's offered and the shop's asked price. Then the shop will determine the impact of recommending bundle b_k by comparing the customer's counter offer for bundle b_k, $O(t+1)$ with that of offer $max(O_t^c)$, from the perspective of his own bid for bundle b_k. For this purpose, the shop uses the function $sign : \mathbb{R} \times \mathbb{R} \mapsto \{0, 1, 2\}$. If we let $max(O_t^c) = (b', p'_c)$, the customer's current offer $O(t+1) = (b, p_c)$, and the shop's corresponding bids for bundles b and b' be $O(b', p'_s)$ and $O(b, p_s)$, then

$$sign_{b,b'}(p, p') = \begin{cases} 2 \text{ if } \frac{p_c - p_s}{p'_c - p'_s} > (1 + \text{threshold}) \\ 1 \text{ if } 1 \le \frac{p_c - p_s}{p'_c - p'_s} \le (1 + \text{threshold}) \\ 0 \text{ otherwise} \end{cases} \qquad (4)$$

If $sign(p, p') = 2$, then the shop's assessment of the customer's interest bundle is updated to be b_k: the customer's response is promising enough to divert the search towards the neighborhood of b_k, and add that neighborhood to A such that the first elements of A all lie in the neighborhood of b_k. That is, the first element of A becomes the bundle $b' \in Ng(b_k)$ with the maximum difference $\hat{E}[v_c(b')|b_k] - v_s(b')$, the second element of A becomes the bundle b'' with the second highest difference $\hat{E}[v_c(b'')|b_k] - v_s(b'')$, and so on. In addition, duplicates are removed from A, as are bundles already present in $\bar{A}$. In case $sign(p, p') = 1$, the customer's response is promising enough to continue negotiating about the current bundle b_k, but not promising enough to change the assessment of the customer's interest bundle, and if $sign(p, p') = 0$, the proposed bundle was not promising at all and the shop will immediately make the next recommendation.

5   Numerical Experiments

In order to test the performance of our proposed mechanism, we implemented it computationally, and tested it against many simulated customers. First we describe how we handled the estimation process and how we implemented negotiations in the simulation, and then we present our experimental design and simulation results.

5.1   Estimating Customer Valuations

In the experiments we abstract away from actually learning $E[v_c(b')|b]$, for example from sales data. Instead we derive these conditional expectations directly from the way we specified the underlying stochastic process.

As explained earlier, we assume additively separable customer preferences. To compute the customer's valuation for a bundle b we simply add up her valuations for the individual goods that constitute the bundle: $v_c(b) = \sum_{i \in b} v_c(i)$. Let N denote the collection of all the individual goods from which bundles are constructed, with $|N| = n$.

We specify the joint probability density function of the customer's valuations for the individual goods, $pr(z_1, \ldots, z_n)$, as an n-variate normal distribution. Let the vector $\mu = (\mu_1, \cdots, \mu_n)$ denote the mean of the distribution and let the matrix $\Sigma = [\sigma_{ij}]$ denote the covariance matrix. Then $pr(z_1, \ldots, z_n) \sim N[\mu, \Sigma]$.

The joint probability mass function of all bundle valuations, $pr(z_1, \ldots, z_{2^n})$, is then simply a linear transformation of $pr(z_1, \ldots, z_n)$. Since a linear transformation of a multivariate normal distribution is also a multivariate normal distribution [15], we have $pr(z_1, \ldots, z_{2^n}) \sim N[\mathbf{T}\mu, \mathbf{T}\Sigma\mathbf{T}']$, where the matrix $\mathbf{T}$ specifies the linear transformation (a row in $\mathbf{T}$ specifies a bundle in binary representation). Given $N[\mathbf{T}\mu, \mathbf{T}\Sigma\mathbf{T}']$ we can derive the value of $E[v_c(b')|b]$ for any bundle pair. Notice that although this approach implies that we hand the shop the distributions underlying customers' valuations, the shop does not know each individual customer's valuations.

5.2 Modeling Negotiations

Besides setting customer preferences it is necessary to specify how the shop and the customer actually negotiate. To allow initiation of the negotiation process by the customer, we assume that the customer starts negotiating about an initial bundle b_{init}. In order to give the shop some room for improvement, we initialize the customer's initial bundle as the bundle containing all the goods for which her valuation is lower than her average valuation across all goods. Although this seems to make it very easy for the shop to make an improvement, bear in mind that performance refers to gains from trade, which depends on both the customer's and the shop's valuations. Besides, we measure performance relative to this starting point in our experiments.

Time-Dependent Strategy. For the customer (shop), the time-dependent bidding strategy is monotonically increasing (decreasing) in both the number of bidding rounds (t) and her (his) valuation. In particular, a bidding strategy is characterized by the gap the customer leaves between her initial offer and her valuation, and by the speed with which she closes this gap. The gap is specified as a fraction of the bundle valuation and it decreases over time as $gap(t) = gap_{init} \cdot \exp(-\delta t)$. This strategy is therefore called "time-dependent-fraction" (TDF)[5]. The initial gap, gap_{init}, and δ are drawn randomly from a uniform distribution between $[0, 0.5]$ and $[0.1, 0.4]$, respectively. Almost the same holds for the shop's bidding strategy, *mutatis mutandis*. Since δ already fluctuates for the customer's strategy we do, however, set $\delta = 0.1$ for the shop, in order to reduce the number of jointly fluctuating parameters somewhat.

Tit-for-Tat Strategy. The time-dependent strategy described above generates bids irrespective of what the opponent does. As an example of a strategy that responds to the opponent, we implemented a variant of tit-for-tat (TFT) [16]. The initial 'move' is already specified by gap_{init} like in the TDF-strategy. If in subsequent moves the utility level of the opponent offer improves, then a fraction δ of that amount is conceded by the

---

[5] We originally implemented a time-dependent strategy that decreases an *absolute* gap over time, but the results were qualitatively similar to the fraction strategy's results, so we describe only the latter as it is more intuitive.

bargainer. Note that it is the increment in the utility level as perceived by the bargainer. Furthermore, this perceived utility improvement can also be negative, but to make the bidding behavior less chaotic, no negative concessions are made. That is, we used a so-called monotone version called tit-for-tat-monotone-fraction (TFTMF) which can never generate a bid with a worse utility than the previous bid.

5.3   Results

A Benchmark. In order to assess the relative performance of the system we conducted the same series of experiments (see below) with a benchmark procedure, which randomly recommends a bundle from the current bundle's neighborhood. That is, the benchmark does not base the order in which it advises the next bundle on the estimated expected gains from trade like our system does.

In our experiments there are 10 individual goods. We generate the means of the underlying probability density function $pr(z_1, \ldots, z_{10})$ by randomly sampling numbers between 40 and 250 without repetition. To test the robustness of our procedure to quantitative changes in the underlying distributions we conducted a series of experiments with 100 different distributions. For each distribution we tested the influence on the system's performance of changes in the ease with which the shop updates his estimation of the customer's "interest" (see the discussion of the *sign* function in Section 4.2). The "threshold" used in the *sign* function captures this sensitivity; we experimented with 11 values between 0 and 0.5, with stepsize 0.05. For each of these settings we simulated negotiations between the shop, with randomly drawn valuations, which were kept constant across negotiations with 100 customers, each with her valuations drawn randomly from the particular distribution used. The values in the graphs are averages across 100 customers per distribution, and across 100 different distributions.

The shop's bundle valuations are not additively separable, due to the following non-linear pricing strategy. Bundles with a higher than average expected customer valuation – compared to a bundle containing the same number of individual goods – are relatively expensive. That is, for expensive bundle it is less likely that customers are actually willing to buy the offered good. Similarly, bundles with a lower than expected valuation are relatively inexpensive (compared to bundles of the same size).

Figure 2 reports the results of three series of experiments (see the caption) where we vary the bargaining strategy of the customers. For low thresholds, our system generates roughly 70% of the maximum gains from trade ('pct.') and roughly 60% of the gains from trade attainable given the initial bundle ('rel. pct.')[6]. Its performance in both cases is roughly 20% better than the benchmark. Additionally, more deals are reached ('deals') and it requires less time to reach these deals than the benchmark ('rounds'). The effect of the threshold is that, as it increases, the interest bundle is updated less

---

[6] Given the shop's and the customer's valuations, certain maximum and minimum gains from trade are attainable. The graph for 'perc' shows the gains from trade of the final bundle, as a percentage of the difference between the maximum and minimum gains from trade, and 'relP' shows the gains from trade of the final bundle, relative to the difference between the maximum gains from trade and the gains from trade of the initial bundle (the starting point of the negotiation).

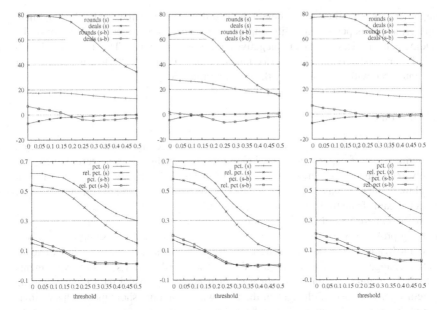

Fig. 2. Results for our system ('s'), when the shop uses the TDF strategy with $\delta = 0.1$, and the customers use either the TDF strategy with random δ (on the left), or the TFTMF strategy with random δ (in the middle) or with $\delta = 1$ (on the right), as described in section 5.2. The difference with the benchmark is indicated by the '$(s - b)$'-graphs.

easily, thereby preventing the search in regions in the neighborhood of promising bundles. Also, the difference with the benchmark, which searches randomly and therefore takes longer to zoom in on promising regions of the search space – often not even finding them before the negotiation ends – decreases as the threshold increases and our system's diminishing performance becomes equal to the benchmark's.

6 Conclusions and Future Work

We consider the problem of negotiating over both bundle contents and price, which permits a high degree of personalization of bundles to the preferences of customers. We develop a procedure for a seller to search for Pareto improvements in bundle contents, while negotiating about the price of bundles. Computer experiments show how this procedure increases both the speed with which agreements are reached, as well as the number and quality of agreements reached.

In the current paper, we have only considered additively separable consumer preferences. The most important issue currently under investigation is the extension of our procedure to cases involving non-linear preferences.

Another issue concerns the distribution of valuations we used. The distribution generates customers' preferences, based on which customers decide to buy the shop's (bundles of) goods. Data about such sales, in turn, enable the shop to estimate the distribution underlying his customers' preferences. In the current paper we provided the shop with the aggregate knowledge required for our procedure directly. Even without modeling this process explicitly, we are interested in providing the shop with only an estimate of the real distribution and in testing the robustness of our procedure to variations in the accuracy of the estimate.

References

1. Baumol, W., Willig, R., Panzar, J.: Contestable Markets and the Theory of Industry Structure. Dryden Press (1987)
2. Stigler, G.J.: United states v. Loew's inc.: A note on block-booking. Supreme Court Review (1963) 152–157
3. Schamlensee, R.L.: Gaussian demand and commodity bundling. Journal of Business **57** (1984) S211–S230
4. Bakos, Y., Brynjolfsson, E.: Bundling information goods: Pricing, profits and efficiency. Management Science **45** (1999)
5. Kephart, J.O., Fay, S.A.: Competitive bundling of categorized information goods. In: Proceedings of ACM EC'00. (2000)
6. Somefun, D.J.A., La Poutré, J.A.: Bundling and pricing for information brokerage: Customer satisfaction as a means to profit optimization. In: Proceedings of Web Intelligence 2003 (WI2003), IEEE Computer Society (2003) 182–189
7. Klein, M., Faratin, P., Sayama, H., Bar-Yam, Y.: Negotiating complex contracts. Group Decision and Negotiation **12** (2003) 111–125
8. Faratin, P., Sierra, C., Jennings, N.R.: Using similarity criteria to make issue trade-offs. Journal of Artificial Intelligence **142** (2003) 205–237
9. Ehtamo, H., Hämäläinen, R.: Interactive multiple-criteria methods for reaching pareto optimal agreements in negotiation. Group Decision and Negotiation **10** (2001) 475–491
10. Somefun, D.J.A., Gerding, E., Bohte, S., La Poutré, J.A.: Automated negotiation and bundling of information goods. In: Proceedings of Agent-Mediated Electronic Commerce V (AMEC'03). (2003)
11. Mas-Collel, A., Whinston, M.D., Green, J.R.: Mircoeconomic Theory. Oxford University Press (1995)
12. Mankila, M.: Price bundling applied to retail banking. FE Rapport 367, Göteborg University, School of Economics and Commercial Law (1999) online available at "http://swoba.hhs.se/gunwba/".
13. Rubinstein, A.: Perfect equilibrium in a bargaining model. Econometrica **50** (1982) 97–109
14. Somefun, D.J.A., Klos, T.B., La Poutré, J.A.: Negotiating over bundles and prices using aggregate knowledge. Technical Report SEN-E0405, CWI, Amsterdam (2004)
15. Green, W.H.: Econometric Analysis. Prentice Hall, New Jersey (1993)
16. Axelrod, R.: The Evolution of Cooperation. Basic Books, New York (1984)

A Model for Multi-party Negotiations with Majority Rule[*]

Sheng Zhang[1], Fillia Makedon[1], James Ford[1], and Lin Ai[2]

[1] Department of Computer Science
Dartmouth College
Hanover, NH 03755, USA
{clap,makedon,jford}@cs.dartmouth.edu
[2] erin_ai@hotmail.com

Abstract. Our model of multi-party negotiations is a many parties, many issues model. The whole multi-party negotiation consists of a set of mutually influencing bilateral negotiations that are focused on different bilateral issues. We propose to use majority rule to help parties reach group agreements. When a party is not satisfied with another party's negotiation progress, he can send a primitive *oppose* to the other. Those negotiation parties who get a sufficient number of *oppose* primitives from others or those negotiation parties who lack support in opposing others will be warned to make satisfactory concessions in the following negotiation round. So the will of majority affects each party's negotiation behavior and leads to the final group agreement.

1 Introduction

Suppose there are a group of participants (which are referred to as players) in the model, each pair of them has a bilateral negotiation issue. The final group agreement is based on a set of bilateral agreements. In other words, every two players conduct a bilateral negotiation to reach an agreement on their own bilateral issue, then all these bilateral agreements are merged to form a multilateral agreement. All the bilateral negotiations are conducted synchronously. A player will be involved in the final group agreement only if he has bilateral agreements with all the other players in the group. One difficulty in reaching a group agreement is that parties in each bilateral negotiation may make slower progress or even reach a stalemate due to a disagreement. To solve this problem, we propose to use majority rule by taking into account opinions from all the players. More intuitively, when two players have a disagreement, the player who gets more support from the other players should have an advantage over the player who has less support. For example, in a three players game, if both player A and player B are opposing player C in their respective bilateral negotiations with player C (assuming the negotiation between player A and B goes well), then player C should be warned to make concessions. Using majority rule also seems to bring

---

[*] This work was supported in part by NSF ITR 0312629.

K. Bauknecht, M. Bichler, and B. Pröll (Eds.): EC-Web 2004, LNCS 3182, pp. 228–237, 2004.

players more fairness. We can imagine that in traditional bilateral negotiations, if player C is a hard-bargaining player, player A and player B may be required to make unnecessary or larger concessions in their respective bilateral negotiations to reach agreements with player C.

The rest of this paper is organized as follows. Section 2 analyzes the related work on multi-party negotiations. Section 3 presents our negotiation model. The first part describes the negotiation objective, negotiation primitives, negotiation protocols, and players negotiation behaviors. In the second part, two approaches are introduced to resolve disagreements in negotiations according to majority rule. Finally, Section 4 concludes the paper.

2   Related Work

Kraus [1] presents a strategic negotiation model which is based on Rubinstein's model of alternating offers [2]. In the strategic model there are N agents, and they need to reach an agreement on a given issue. In each period t of the negotiation, if the negotiation has not terminated earlier, an agent whose turn it is to make an offer and each of the other agents choose to either accept of offer (choose *Yes*), reject it (choose *No*), or opt out of the negotiation (choose *Opt*). If an offer is accepted by all the agents, then the negotiation ends with an agreement. If at least one of the agents opts out of the negotiation, then the negotiation ends and a conflictual outcome results. If no agent has chosen *Opt* but at least one of the agents has rejected the offer, the negotiation proceeds to period $t+1$. Sycara [4] presents a model that combines case-based reasoning and optimization of multi-attribute utilities. The model uses persuasive argumentation as a means of guiding the negotiation process to a settlement. Sierra et al. [3] present a model for autonomous agents to reach agreements about the provision of service by one agent to another in multi-agent environments.

Our work presents a model of multi-party negotiations with multiple bilateral issues, in which the group agreement is based on a set of bilateral agreements. The main contribution of our work is that we introduce a new negotiation primitive, *oppose*, that allows the negotiation process to take into account opinions from all parties. In this approach, we use majority rule to resolve the possible disagreement in each bilateral negotiation.

3   Negotiation Model

This section describes all aspects of the proposed negotiation model.

3.1   Negotiation Objectives

The group agreement involves a number of acceding players, in which every pair has a bilateral agreement. There are two kinds of final group agreements after the whole negotiation process ends. The first kind is a *global group agreement* in which all players in the game accede. The second kind is a *local group agreement*. This agreement is a group consensus of a set of players, where this set is the subset of all the players in the game. The objective of our model is to reach a global group agreement. In cases where a global group agreement is not reached, it is possible that multiple local group agreements may have been agreed to, and that a single player may be involved in more than one local group agreement. If no global group agreement is reached, the objective of the model becomes twofold reaching more local group agreements and involving as many players as possible in each local group agreement.

3.2   Notations

P_i ith player (N players in total)
N_i^n number of players still negotiating with P_i in the nth round
O_i^n number of *oppose* primitives P_i receives in the nth round
UL_i^n upper limit for P_i in the nth round
LL_i^n lower limit for P_i in the nth round
T time limit
$Pr(w)$ probability of a player getting a warning
$Pr(w_1)$ probability of a player getting a warning because of the case 1 (see 3.3)
$Pr(w_2)$ probability of a player getting a warning because of the case 2 (see 3.3)
λ probability of a player opposing another player in a round

3.3   Negotiation Primitives

This section describes six negotiation primitives used in the proposed model. The first four primitives are widely used in bilateral negotiations and the last two primitives are newly introduced to help us achieve group agreements using majority rule in multi-party negotiations.

- *Call-For-Proposal (CFP)*: At the start of negotiations, each player sends one initial proposal to each of the other players, or $N - 1$ proposals in total. The CFP helps each player form conjectures about what the others would like to commit and what they would like to require in the final agreement.
- *Proposal*: After players get CFPs from the other players, they begin formal negotiations by sending proposals or counterproposals to each other.
- *Accept*: P_i accepts the proposal sent by P_j when he is satisfied, which means that P_i and P_j have finished the negotiation successfully with a bilateral agreement. However, P_i and P_j may still have ongoing negotiations with other players.
- *Reject*: When P_i rejects continuing the negotiation with P_j, P_i sends *reject* to P_j to end their negotiation. Moreover, this rejection also announces that P_i has quit the final group agreement, and thus all bilateral negotiations that P_i is conducting are also aborted. However, P_j can still continue those negotiations that he is conducting with other players. Therefore, a player should never rashly use *reject*. To let P_i register dissatisfaction with proposals from P_j while still keeping himself in the negotiation process, P_i can use the primitive *Oppose*.

- *Oppose*: *Oppose* gives P_i an opportunity to oppose or give notice to P_j if P_i thinks that P_j has not made satisfactory progress in their negotiation. However, *oppose* will not terminate the ongoing negotiation.
- *Warn*: This primitive is used by either the system or a chairman in a multi-party negotiation. It will be sent to P_i in the nth round only in one of the following two cases:
  1. *Warning Case* 1: In all of the last T (*time limit*) rounds, the number of *oppose* primitives that P_i receives has always exceeded P_i's *upper limit*;
  2. *Warning Case* 2: If P_i currently gives an *oppose* to P_j, and in the past T rounds (including the current round) P_i gave *oppose* primitives to P_j, the number of *oppose* primitives that P_j receives has never exceeded P_j's *lower limit*.

When receiving a warning, P_i is also notified of the case for which he gets this warning. If P_i receives a warning for the same case in two consecutive rounds, he will be driven out of the negotiation automatically (all those negotiations that P_i is currently conducting will be aborted), and he cannot join any final group agreement although he might have some bilateral agreements with other players already. So after receiving a warning, P_i needs to take action immediately. If he was warned because of the second case, then sending a new proposal instead of using *oppose* will (by definition) ensure P_i that he will not get another warning for the second case in the next round. However, if P_i was warned because of the first case, then even if he were to make concessions immediately, other players may still give him *oppose* primitives. For example, they might not be satisfied with his negotiation performance from the view of a whole process. Different players in different rounds may have different upper limits and lower limits. We will discuss how to compute them in subsection 3.7.

3.4   Negotiation Behaviors

In the following, we describe the main negotiation behaviors of a certain player P_i in his bilateral negotiation with another player P_j. (We do not list all possible cases as that would be too complicated.)

The negotiation starts in State 1 (see Figure 1). After P_i and P_j get CFPs from each other, they start a formal negotiation (State 2) and continuously send proposals and counterproposals to each other. If either P_i or P_j accepts the proposal given by the other, the negotiation between them is finished successfully (State 3).

If P_i sends *oppose* to P_j in State 2, then P_i moves to the state (State 4) of opposing the other. If P_j makes a satisfactory concession, then the parties will go back to the ongoing negotiation state (State 2). However, if P_j does not make an effective concession and P_i chooses to abort the negotiation, the negotiation will fail in state 7. If P_i chooses not to terminate the negotiation in this case, then if P_i is the only or one of a small number of players currently opposing P_j, P_i will get a warning (State 6) later to urge him to make a concession (*i.e.*, to give a new proposal instead of merely opposing P_j). If P_i fails to do so, he will

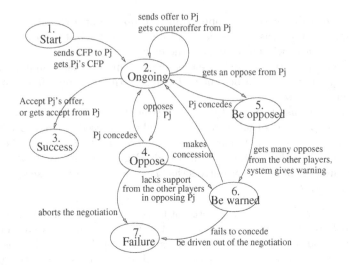

Fig. 1. The main behaviors of P_i in his negotiation with P_j

be driven out of the negotiation, so the negotiation between P_i and P_j also fails (State 7).

In State 2, P_i may also get an *oppose* from P_j and would then move to the state of being opposed (State 5). If P_i then produces a new proposal or counterproposal, they will return to State 2. Otherwise, if P_i also receives many *oppose* primitives in the other negotiations he is joining, then he will be warned to make concessions in these negotiations (State 6). Failing to do so will lead to State 7.

3.5   Negotiation Protocols

As all the bilateral negotiations are synchronized, only one player is allowed to send proposals (or other primitives) out at any time. So we need to coordinate all the players to ensure proposals are sent serially, one at a time. This can be done by using a ring structure like that of the strategic negotiation model [1]. Take each player as a node in the ring, and pick a node as the start node, which is the first node to send primitives to all the other nodes in the ring. Then, the next node (either clockwise or counter-clockwise) sends his primitives, and so on. When there is a player who aborts the negotiations or is driven out of the negotiations, or finishes negotiations successfully with all the other nodes in the ring, his corresponding node is removed and two neighbor nodes are connected.

A *round* for P_i is the duration from the last turn of P_i to the current turn of P_i. According to the protocol, P_i has received all the primitives sent to him from the other nodes in each round. Thus, in P_i's turn, he can apply his negotiation strategy (whatever it is) to produce counterproposals for all ongoing bilateral negotiations. P_i may also need to coordinate those counterproposals if there is a dependence constraint among two or more negotiations.

Moreover in P_i's turn, the system or chairman will compute the current upper limit and lower limit for P_i and check whether the conditions for any of the warning cases are satisfied. If the conditions for warning case 1 are satisfied, P_i will get a warning immediately. If the conditions for warning case 2 are satisfied, other corresponding players will get warnings in their next turns.

3.6   Abusing Oppose

The *oppose* primitive helps to resolve a disagreement between two players in their bilateral negotiation. In other words, a player can consider those *oppose* primitives going to the other party as support. Although this support is not direct (because other players do not know about negotiations that they don't join), it still represents important feedback summarizing the opinions of a player's negotiation partners. Practically speaking, a player who gets less support is more likely to get a warning later. However, regulating the use of *oppose* requires some care. Having only an upper limit would be problematic because a player could abuse *oppose* without ever triggering any negative effects on himself. Therefore we also set a lower limit, which is used to control this kind of abuse. Since a player only knows those primitives that he sends out or receives (he does not know how many *oppose* primitives another player receives currently), it is not possible for a player to predict whether his use of oppose can trigger a Case 1 warning for another player, and it always runs the risk of triggering a Case 2 warning for himself.

3.7   Setting Warning Limits

We have introduced three kinds of limits: a lower limit for player i in the nth round (LL_i^n), an upper limit for player i in the nth round (UL_i^n) and the time limit (T) described in the primitive *warn*. Adjusting these limits directly affects the probabilities of players getting warnings. If the lower limit is too low, we cannot prevent players from abusing *oppose* because they will probably not get warnings. On the other hand, if the lower limit is too high, we may inadvertently punish innocent players. Likewise for the upper limit, settings that too high (so that neither player in a negotiation gets a warning) or too low (so that both players get warnings) will not help in resolving disagreements. A similar tradeoff also applies to the time limit: a higher time limit may make the whole multi-party negotiation last longer, but a lower time limit may cause warnings to become increasingly arbitrary. Here, we assume that the time limit is set already and discuss how to set lower limits and upper limits based on this assumption.

We assume that the probabilities of a player opposing another player (λ) in different rounds are independent (which is based on the assumption that a player will make a positive response after getting an *oppose*), so λ is always the same during the whole negotiation process. We assume that in the nth round, the number of *oppose* primitives that player i gets in the nth round (O_i^n)

is binomially distributed. So the expected number is λN_i^n and the standard deviation is $\sqrt{N_i^n \lambda(1-\lambda)}$.

The probabilities of a certain player getting a warning ($Pr(w)$), getting a warning for Case 1 ($Pr(w_1)$), and for Case 2 ($Pr(w_2)$) satisfy $(1 - Pr(w_1)) \times (1 - Pr(w_2)) = 1 - Pr(w)$. If we hope $Pr(w_1) = Pr(w_2)$, and $Pr(w) \leq \epsilon$, we need to satisfy:

$$Pr(w_1) = Pr(w_2) \leq 1 - \sqrt{1 - \epsilon}.$$

P_i will get a warning in the kth round because of warning Case 1 if $\forall n: k - T + 1 \leq n \leq k$, we have $O_i^n \geq UL_i^n$, so

$$Pr(w_1) \geq \prod_{n=k-T+1}^{k} Pr(O_i^n \geq UL_i^n).$$

A player other than P_i who intends to abuse the primitive *oppose* to P_i will get a warning if $\forall n$: nth round is one of those past T rounds (including the current round) in which he sends an *oppose* to P_i, we have $O_i^n \leq LL_i^n$. Therefore, $Pr(w_2)$ is larger than or equal to the probability that this player gets a warning in this case. So we have:

$$Pr(w_2) \geq \prod_{n\text{th round} \in \text{those T rounds}} Pr(O_i^n \leq LL_i^n).$$

To simplify the computation, we just let

$$Pr(O_i^n \geq UL_i^n) \leq \sqrt[T]{Pr(w_1)} \leq \sqrt[T]{1 - \sqrt{1 - \epsilon}},$$

$$Pr(O_i^n \leq LL_i^n) \leq \sqrt[T]{Pr(w_2)} \leq \sqrt[T]{1 - \sqrt{1 - \epsilon}}.$$

Using Chebyshev's Inequality, we can get:

$$UL_i^n \geq \lambda N_i^n + \frac{\sqrt{N_i^n \lambda(1-\lambda)}}{\sqrt[2T]{1 - \sqrt{1 - \epsilon}}},$$

$$LL_i^n \leq \lambda N_i^n - \frac{\sqrt{N_i^n \lambda(1-\lambda)}}{\sqrt[2T]{1 - \sqrt{1 - \epsilon}}}.$$

So UL_i^n and LL_i^n are decided by N_i^n, ϵ, λ, and T. Of these four terms, N_i^n can be computed directly, ϵ and T can be decided from previous experience, and λ can be computed from past multi-party negotiations.

We introduced upper limits to resolve disagreements in bilateral negotiations. However, whatever upper limits are set to, we can always meet a problem like the following that we cannot handle by our current approach. Consider two players opposing to each other in a bilateral negotiation, who meanwhile both get a number of *oppose* primitives (more than or equal to their respective upper limits). If this situation is maintained, they will both ultimately get warnings. This is probably not fair to one of them. We propose to solve this problem by introducing another approach which also uses the idea of majority rule.

3.8   Potential Value

In the following, we will use a simple example which is based on coalitions to present this approach. In our example (see Figure 2(a)), five players are conducting a multi-party negotiation. After several rounds of negotiation that resolve the competition in each coalition, P_1, P_2, and P_3 form one coalition while P_4 and P_5 form another. Suppose each bilateral negotiation between two players in the same coalition has succeeded. However, suppose that in those bilateral negotiations across coalitions, players give *oppose* to each other. Because to each P_i, $O_i^n = N_i^n$ (assuming all players just finished the nth round), all players will get warnings soon.

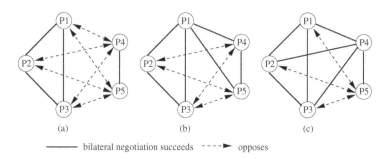

Fig. 2. An example of Potential Value. (a) is the original situation. (b) is the situation when P_1 finishes all negotiations successfully with those players currently opposing him. (c) is the situation when P_4 finishes all negotiations successfully with those players currently opposing him

If each player is considered as a vertex in an undirected graph and an edge is added between P_i and P_j if the negotiation between them has succeeded, then each connected component in the graph exactly represents a local group agreement. For any connected component c in this graph, we define $Value(c)$ (the value of component c) as the number of edges in this component. Furthermore, we define $Value(P_i)$ (the value of a player P_i) as the sum of values of those connected components that include P_i. In other words,

$$Value(P_i) = \sum_{\forall c, P_i \in c} Value(c).$$

In our example (see Figure 2(a)), the connected component including P_1 is $\{(P_1, P_2, P_3)\}$, so the current value of player P_1 is 3. Similarly, the connected component including P_4 is $\{(P_4, P_5)\}$, so the current value of P_4 is 1.

The potential value of a player P_i (defined as $PV(P_i)$) is the difference between the future value of P_i (when all the players who currently *oppose* P_i finally finish negotiations successfully with P_i) and the current value of P_i. When all the players who currently *oppose* P_1 (*i.e.*, P_4 and P_5) finally finish negotiations successfully with P_1, the case is like Figure 2(b). In that situation, connected components including P_1 are $\{(P_1, P_2, P_3), (P_1, P_4, P_5)\}$, so the future contribution of P_1 is $3 + 3 = 6$. Therefore, $PV(P_1) = 6 - 3 = 3$. Similarly in figure 2(a), if all the players who currently *oppose* P_4 (*i.e.*, P_1, P_2 and P_3) finish negotiations successfully with P_4, then the situation is like Figure 2(c). So the future value of P_4 is $6 + 1 = 7$, and $PV(P_4) = 7 - 1 = 6$.

Those players who have larger potential values have the potential to contribute to more and larger connected components (more and larger local group agreements) when getting warnings compared with those players having smaller potential values. Idea is therefore that if two players *oppose* each other and meanwhile both of them receive *oppose* primitives in excess of their upper limits, we will do the following modification: we remove the *oppose* that is sent from the player having a higher potential value to the player having a lower potential value. Algorithm 1 is used to compute the updated number of *oppose* ($O_i'^n$) after this modification. This value replaces the original value O_i^n in checking warning Case 1 for P_i in the nth round. (O_i^n is still used in checking warning Case 2.) This algorithm ensures that as long as those players who will possibly be warned do not have the same potential value, there is at least one player who will be warned so that the whole multi-party negotiation will not become a stalemate.

Algorithm 1: Computation of $O_i'^n$ in checking warning Case 1

(1)   compute O_i^n and $PV(P_i)$
(2) $O_i'^n \leftarrow O_i^n$
(3)   **if** $O_i^n \geq UL_i^n$
(4)   **foreach** P_j currently sending *oppose* to P_i
(5)   **if** P_i is also currently sending *oppose* to P_j and ($O_j^n \geq UL_j^n$ or $O_j^{n-1} \geq UL_j^{n-1}$ if O_j^n is not computed yet)
(6)   **if** $PV(P_i) < PV(P_j)$
(7) $O_i'^n \leftarrow O_i'^n - 1$

In our example, the original computation of O_i^n in warning Case 1 gives us the Figure 3(a). After applying Algorithm 1, we have Figure 3(b), in which $O_1'^n$ is now equal to 0 because $PV(P_1) < PV(P_4)$ and $PV(P_1) < PV(P_5)$. Similarly, $O_2'^n = 0$, $O_3'^n = 0$, $O_4'^n = 3$ and $O_5'^n = 3$. If this situation continues for a series of rounds, P_4 and P_5 will eventually be warned to make concessions. From another point of view, we can see that a larger coalition (*i.e.*, $\{P_1, P_2, P_3\}$) will eventually dominate over a smaller coalition (*i.e.*, $\{P_4, P_5\}$).

However, it is still possible that disagreements cannot be resolved when all the players who receive more *oppose* primitives than their upper limits have the same potential value. If at that time players continue to *oppose* each other in all ongoing bilateral negotiations, which means there is no real progress in any bilateral negotiation, then the system can terminate the whole multi-party negotiation. It is also necessary to terminate the whole multi-party negotiation when it has undergone a longer time than a predetermined limit. This limit can be decided by all the players to prevent negotiations going to an infinite loop.

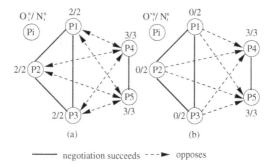

Fig. 3. (a) is the original computation of O_i^n. (b) is the computation of $O_i'^n$ after using potential values. Those *oppose* primitives from players having higher potential values to player having lower potential values are removed in (b)

Thus, in this approach several resolutions are possible. The multi-party negotiation ends (either finishes naturally or is terminated by the system) as one of the following three cases: 1) all the remaining players reach a local group agreement; 2) those players not finishing all their negotiations have a same potential value; 3) the multi-party negotiation lasts too long. In cases 2) and 3), all local group agreements in the ending moment can still be considered valid.

4   Conclusion

We present a model of multi-party negotiations where group agreements are constructed using multiple bilateral agreements. The whole negotiation process is based on a set of synchronous bilateral negotiations. Two approaches using majority rule are presented to resolve possible disagreements in these bilateral negotiations to help all parties reach a final group agreement. One uses the statistical method to set upper limits and lower limits and the other uses potential values. Future work includes conducting more accurate analysis on the statistical method, and designing other approaches or incentives to induce players to reach a group agreement.

References

1. S. Kraus. Automated negotiation and decision making in multiagent environments. volume 2086 of *Lecture Notes in Computer Science*, pages 150–172, 2001.
2. A. Rubinstein. Perfect equilibrium in a bargaining model. *Econometrica*, 1982.
3. C. Sierra, P. Faratin, and N. Jennings. A service-oriented negotiation model between autonomous agents. In *Proceedings of the 8th European Workshop on Modeling Autonomous Agents in a Multi-Agent World (MAAMAW-97)*, pages 17–35, Ronneby, Sweden, 1997.
4. K. Sycara. Persuasive argumentation in negotiation. *Theory and Decision*, 28(3): 203–242, May 1990.

Analysis of Mobile Business Processes
for the Design of Mobile Information Systems

André Köhler and Volker Gruhn

University of Leipzig
Chair of Applied Telematics / e-Business
Klostergasse 3
04109 Leipzig, Germany
{koehler,gruhn}@ebus.informatik.uni-leipzig.de

Abstract. The adoption of mobile technologies into companies frequently follows a technology-driven approach without precise knowledge about the potential benefits that may be realised. Especially in larger organisations with complex business processes, a systematic procedure is required if a verifiable economic benefit is to be created by the use of mobile technologies. Therefore, the term "mobile business process", as well as requirements for information systems applied in such processes, are defined in this paper. Subsequently, we introduce a procedure for the systematical analysis of the distributed structure of a business process model in order to identify mobile sub-processes. For that purpose, the method Mobile Process Landscaping is used to decompose a process model into different levels of detail. The method aims to manage the complexity and limit the process analysis to the potentially mobile sub-processes from the beginning. The result of the analysis can be used on the one hand as a foundation for the redesign of the business processes and on the other hand for the requirements engineering of mobile information systems. An application of this method is shown by the example of business processes in the insurance industry.

1 Motivation and Related Work

1.1 Motivation

The orientation towards business processes and their optimisation has been an important issue for some years [1]. The identification of opportunities for cost reduction, as well as integrated IT-support for processes are increasingly coming to the fore, with technologies supporting mobility making an important contribution. Particular potential benefits lie in the seamless, company-comprehensive integration of all partners participating in the business process, especially when this process is distributed [2]. Thus, each process-step on the value chain can be connected directly to the operational information processing, so the goal-oriented control of the whole business process becomes feasible [3].

To exploit these advantages effectively, specialized information systems, supporting not only the business process but handling the mobility of the process-executing person if necessary, are required. In order to develop such systems we propose the method Mobile Process Landscaping. This method allows the goal-oriented analysis of a process model and its distribution structure to explore mobilisation opportunities.

K. Bauknecht, M. Bichler, and B. Pröll (Eds.): EC-Web 2004, LNCS 3182, pp. 238–247, 2004.

1.2 Related Work

A number of recent publications showed that certain activities can be improved regarding efficiency and effectiveness through the use of mobile technologies (see e.g. [4], [5]).The mentioned examples are case studies describing successfully released solutions in certain companies, however, how these companies choose the described business processes and activities for the use of mobile technologies remains open questions.

Frequently, a technology-driven approach can be observed for realising potential benefits, which adjusts processes corresponding to the available features of certain mobile devices. But often, a large number of complex processes with many involved people prevails, e.g. in large companies and corporate groups. Such an approach may then lead to wrong decisions, especially in the long term. In our opinion, the process of decision-making about the use and the design of a mobile information system needs to be systematic and comprehensible.

For this purpose, section 2 deals with basic characteristics of mobility in connection with business processes and information systems. Section 2.1 defines the term "mobile business process" and illustrates our understanding of mobility from an application-oriented point of view. Hence, requirements for the development of mobile information systems can be deduced, as illustrated in section 2.2. Subsequently, the Mobile Process Landscaping method is explained by an example from the insurance industry (section 3). The need for further research is pointed out in section 4.

2   Mobility Within Business Processes and Information Systems

2.1 Mobility in Business Processes

The term "business process" was defined by numerous authors (i.e. [6], [7], [1]). Below, we follow the commonly used definition of Davenport [7] according to which a business process can be understood as "a specific ordering of work activities across time and place, with a beginning, an end, and clearly identified inputs and outputs: a structure for action." A business process can be decomposed in different levels into process partitions. Thus, a business process can be understood as an abstract description of workflows in a company. The actual occurrence of such a business process in reality is called a business process instance.

In the following, only business processes with a specific distribution structure and thus a certain mobility of the process-executing persons are considered. We propose that mobility is given when for at least one process partition:

a) there is an "uncertainty of location",
b) this "uncertainty of location" is externally determined, and
c) a cooperation with external resources (from the process-point of view) is needed in the execution of the process .

The assumption a) is based on the concept of "location uncertainty" by Valiente and van der Heijden [8], according to which the place of the execution of an activity can be different in different instances of the business process or the places can change during the execution of an activity. Thus, we deal with a mobile process partition within a business process. Because multiple mobile process partitions are conceivable, and a mobile process partition often affects the whole business process, the complete business process is called "mobile business process".

Further on, assumption b) presumes that the location uncertainty is caused by external factors and that the process-executing person has therefore no freedom of choice regarding the place of the process execution. Assumption c) restricts the term "mobile business process" to the necessity of cooperation with external resources within the considered process partition, for instance caused by the need for communication or coordination with other persons or interaction with other objects.

For example, at the moment of the customer inquiry the place where the field staff will meet a customer for sales conversation is unknown (location uncertainty). During the sales conversation, the field staff interacts with the customer and possibly simultaneously with the information system of the company (cooperation with external resources). Thus, the business process is a mobile one. In contrast, an employee working on office duty, moving his wireless LAN-connected notebook to the conference room for a short time, does not conduct a mobile business process because there is no compulsory location uncertainty, i.e. his movement is not externally triggered.

The above definition of mobility is deduced from the characteristics of the task the process-executing persons need to perform in the mobile process partition. The definition of mobile business processes does not imply the existence of any automatic information processing in any way. In fact, the following section will show, how the need for an information system to support mobile business processes can be identified.

2.2 Mobile Information Systems in Mobile Business Processes

An information system can be defined as "a set of interrelated components that collect (or retrieve), process, store, and distribute information to support decision making, coordination, and control in an organisation", as proposed in [9]. Because of the mentioned specifics of mobile business processes the information system must be adapted to deal with the location uncertainty within activities. An information system that is adapted to location uncertainty will be called "mobile information system" in the following. Its outstanding characteristic is the ability to provide coordination, control and decision support within the business process under the restriction of spatial limitations [8].

Thus, a mobile information system can on the one hand support mobile business processes by the improvement of efficiency during their execution and on the other hand create premises for turning so far not mobile business processes into mobile ones. In the following, we assume that an information system can be transformed into a mobile information system by adding a mobile element to it. To enable this transformation, the mobile element of an information system needs to allow its use for a mobile activity just as well as if the activity was not mobile.

A number of recent publications showed in case studies how mobile technologies can be used to improve workflows and single activities in terms of efficiency and duration. Unfortunately, it often remains unexplained how the concerned companies chose the corresponding business processes and activities for bringing mobile technologies into operation. If there are manageable processes with just a few people involved, the impacts caused by the use of mobile technologies, as well as the effects of the process changes can probably be estimated roughly.

In [5], the mobile equipment of taxi drivers in Stockholm is described, that was introduced with the aim to improve the dispatching process. "Based on a number of requirements the company identified an opportunity to ameliorate the dispatching process by the use of improved mobile technology based on GPS, radio communication, and information system technology." The exciting question how these requirements and opportunities were acquired, remains open, unfortunately.

In the shown example, business processes are adjusted to the possibilities offered of mobile technology, starting from available mobile devices and mobile networks. In doing so, they follow a technology-driven approach to realise potential benefits. As soon as we are dealing with a large amount of complex processes, in which numerous persons are involved (as it is typical for large companies and corporate groups), such a procedure could lead to wrong decisions, especially in the long term. The decision about the use and the design of a mobile element for existing information systems has to be made systematically and traceably in our opinion.

Thus, we see the necessity of representing the workflow in a company by a specialised process model in order to identify potential process improvements on the basis of the definition of mobile business processes. Subsequently, the requirements for the creation of the mobile element of the existing information system need to be defined in order to be able to examine whether the mobile technology and devices meet the demands. For this procedure, we propose the following steps [10]:

(1) Analysis of the process model and identification of mobile business processes.
(2) Redesign of the identified process partitions (under the assumption of the producibility of a mobile element for the information system).
(3) Specification of the mobile element as required by the new business processes.
(4) Validation of the profitability of the change (valuation of the relationship between estimated costs and forecast benefit).
(5) Implementation of the change (actual redesign of the processes and development of the mobile element).

In the following, we will describe how the analysis of existing processes and the identification of mobile potentials in step (1) can be conducted by the use of the Mobile Process Landscaping method. Steps (2) to (4) are beyond the scope of this paper, and (5) is rather a point for further research, as outlined in the conclusion.

3   Identification of Mobile Business Processes Through Mobile Process Landscaping

3.1   Specialisation of Process Landscaping

With Mobile Process Landscaping, we propose a systematical approach for identifying and analysing mobile business processes. It is a specialisation of the "Process Landscaping" method [11]. The idea of the method is to split the modelling of processes into different tiers, starting with a coarse and simplified form of the process description and then increasing the level of detail with each tier. Other approaches for the modelling of (mobile) processes (see e.g. [12], [8], [13]) neglect the question of the level of detail. We believe that in practice, this will lead to difficulties in the description and analysis caused by different understandings of processes [11].

The aim of the proposed procedure is twofold: on one hand, it should help to handle the complexity of processes. On the other hand, it should help to recognise the distribution structure very early. Thus, the method can only be applied to distributed process structures. At an early stage, process partitions with mobile potentials can be located. The process analysis should just at these points be continued in order to minimise the analysis effort. For the presentation of the different levels of detail, we propose four different tiers, that are determined by the global company structure.

The first level of detail represents the coarse company structure, i.e. the main elements of the value chain. The processes identified on this level are called "core processes" in the process model. A result of this description could be *"There is a sales process."* On the second level, the processes are described on the basis of the tasks and functions within the core processes on the first level. These processes are called "sub-processes" in the process model. A core process can be composed of multiple sub-processes. On this level, we could answer the question *"What is the field staff doing in the sales process?"* The third level describes the activities in the processes identified on the second level. In the process model, those processes are called "activities." A sub-process can consist of multiple activities. On this level, it should be possible to answer the question *"How is the field staff doing it?"* On the fourth level, workflows for the above defined activities are described. If an information system is used, this level could describe dialog structures and data flows. These objects are called "information objects" in the model. At this point one could ask: *"How is the workflow organized?"*

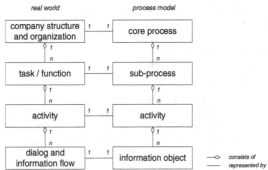

Fig. 1. Correlation between the levels of detail in the process model and the real world.

Figure 1 shows the correlation between the levels of detail in the process model and the real world according to [14]. Applying this procedure in a top-down-approach to process modelling, we identify the process partitions which need to be redesigned in order to be supported by a mobile information system. Our aim is the identification of mobile potentials on each level of detail. A refinement of the process model on the next level of detail is just needed for identified partitions. This way, the complexity can be reduced and the effort for the analysis can be minimised.

3.2 Notation of the Process Model

Process models can be described by different notations. Established approaches are e.g. (high-level) petri-nets [15], UML Activity Diagrams [16], Event-Driven Process

Chain Markup Language [17], Business Process Modeling Notation [18] and the Business Process Modeling Language [19], of which [20] provides an apt overview. These approaches are widely spread and tested by practical experience, so we do not want to add a new one. In order to identify mobile process partitions, for the creation of a process landscape it is necessary to describe both the spatial distribution and the cooperation with external resources, as demanded by the definition in section 2.2. In the approaches given above, this is not the case or realised very differently. In the following we abstract from these approaches and choose a simplified notation fulfilling the given aspects of process modelling completely.

Organisational units whose subjects (single persons or groups of persons) are not spatially separated from each other are symbolized by a grey rectangle with rounded corners. Processes inside organisational units are represented by a white rectangle. Relations between processes inside an organisational unit are symbolized by a solid line (internal interaction). A dashed line indicates a relation between processes in different organisational units (external interactions).

Fig. 2. Symbols for the process model.

On the first level of detail, the relations between the processes are undefined in terms of their order (unsigned edges). Only the existence of a relationship is shown. Starting from the second level of detail, signed edges are used to show the logical and temporal order of the processes. The aim of this kind of description is to identify mobile potentials within the considered processes which, according to our definition, is induced by an externally determined location uncertainty as well as a cooperation with external resources.

An externally determined location uncertainty is present in processes that cannot be allocated clearly to a single organisational unit. This means, multiple, spatially separated persons or groups of persons are involved in their execution. This is a necessary, but not sufficient condition for a mobile business process. If such a partition is identified in the process model, we assume a potential mobility that can be approved or disproved by a stepwise refinement of the process partition. The potential mobile process partition is indicated in the graphical representation by different processes lying on top of each other. The cooperation with external resources is shown by a dashed line, indicating an exchange of information between different process partitions across organisational units. This is also a necessary, but not sufficient condition for a mobile business process. Again, the potential mobility can be approved or disproved by a stepwise refinement of the process partition.

3.3 Mobile Process Landscaping Exemplified in the Insurance Industry

In the following, the application of Mobile Process Landscaping, is shown using examples from the insurance industry. We assume that during the preparation of the process analysis four spatially separated organisational units could be identified: the company itself, the field staff, customers and partners (Figure 3).

Fig. 3. Spatially separated organisational units.

In the first step of the analysis the core processes of the company are identified on the basis of the company structure and assigned to the organisational units. Figure 4 shows the results of this step, completing the analysis on the first level of detail.

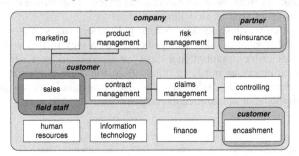

Fig. 4. Core processes in an insurance company.

It is noticeable that there are relationships between some core processes of the company. Furthermore, it is obvious that in some processes (sales, contract management, reinsurance, encashment) different, spatially separated organisational units (company, field staff, customer, partner) are involved. By definition, those core processes are potential mobile processes. A refinement of the process model should therefore only be conducted at these specific core processes. For the further process analysis, we limit the examination to the core process "sales" here. Within this process, tasks, functions and their relationships need to be defined, as shown in Figure 5.

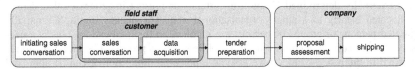

Fig. 5. Sub-processes for the core process "sales".

The field staff initiates a sales conversation and calls the customer. Both participate in the sales conversation as well as in the ensuing data acquisition, so the corresponding sub-processes are potentially mobile. In the following, the field staff returns to the agency for preparing the tender and sends it via mail to the company (cooperation with external resources). This is a potentially mobile business process as well. The company examines the tender before it is shipped to the customer. Within the process "tender preparation", classified as potentially mobile, the third level of detail is now refined (Figure 6). The field staff submits the customer data to the company. There, the valuation of risk is performed in order to calculate the rate and generate the tender. During the submission of the customer data, the boundary between the organisational units "field staff" and "company" is crossed. Thus, this activity is potentially mobile.

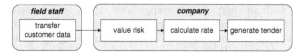

Fig. 6. Activities for sub-process "tender preparation".

Finally, we consider the fourth and last level of detail (Figure 7). The field staff prints a data sheet for submitting the customer data and sends it to the company via mail. There, the data is again acquired and saved. Among the information objects "send mail" and "acquire data", an information exchange across the boundaries of spatially separated organisational units takes place, so both information objects are potentially mobile.

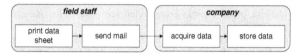

Fig. 7. Information objects for activity "transfer customer data".

Furthermore it is noticeable, that the organisational boundary between "transfer customer data" and "value risk" (Figure 6) has moved more into the activity "transfer customer data". This is a result of the task decomposition. This way, the last level of detail of the analysis is reached. The information objects "send mail" and "acquire data" highlight a process partition which renders the activity "transfer customer data", the sub process "tender preparation" and the core process "sales" potentially mobile.

At this point, a redesign of the process can be applied in order to develop a mobile information system, as proposed in step (2) of our procedure in section 2.2. All processes identified as potentially mobile as well as their preliminary and subsequent elements, come into question for a redesign. In our example, displayed in figure 7, those processes are "send mail" and "acquire data", as well as the preliminary process "print data sheet" and the subsequent process "store data". In this case, the whole process partition is affected. It should be considered that preliminary and subsequent elements on a superior level of detail could be affected, too. Concerning those, an analysis up to the fourth level of detail needs to be conducted in order to identify the specific preliminary and subsequent information objects.

4   Conclusion

This paper focused on business processes in the field of m-business, called mobile business processes due to their special characteristics of a location uncertainty and cooperation with external resources from the process' point of view. The according definition of mobility is task-oriented, abstracting completely from potentially existing information systems. At this point, we see a need for research because in our experience, no comprehensive definition of mobility that includes the different aspects like logical, technical, or application-related mobility exists. Furthermore, it was shown that the application of mobile technology is usually technology-driven. The economic benefit of such a solution is often not exactly quantifiable in advance. Especially in large organisations with various business-critical processes and numerous involved persons such an approach is not applicable. Thus, we proposed a procedure to systematically analyse mobile potentials in business processes. The first step of this procedure was conducted using the Mobile Process Landscaping method and illustrated using a simple example from the insurance industry. At this point, we see a need for further research in order to integrate the shown procedure into the established approaches for modeling business processes. Finally, the drafted procedure aims to support the development of mobile information systems whose characteristics are not defined by mobile technology, but are rather deduced from the requirements of newly designed mobile business processes.

References

1. Scheer, A.: Business process engineering: reference models for industrial enterprises. Springer, Tokyo (1998)
2. Gruhn, V., Wellen, U.: Software Support for Distributed Business Processes. Proceedings of the Sixth Asia Pacific Software Engineering Conference. IEEE Computer Society Press, (1999) 200-206
3. Craighead, C. W., Shaw, N. G.: E-commerce value creation and destruction: a resource-based, supply chain perspective. ACM SIGMIS Database 2 (2003) 39-49
4. Dustdar, S., Gall, H.: Architectural concerns in distributed and mobile collaborative systems. Journal of Systems Architecture 49 (2003) 457-473
5. van der Heijden, H., Valiente, P.: Mobile Business Processes: Cases from Sweden and the Netherlands. Stockholm School of Economics, SSE/EFI Working Paper Series in Business Administration, 14 (2002)
6. Hammer, M., Champy, J.: Reengineering the corporation: a manifesto for business revolution. Brealey, London (1993)
7. Davenport, T. H.: Process innovation: reengineering work through information technology. Harvard Business School Press, Boston, Mass. (1993)
8. Valiente, P., van der Heijden, H.: A method to identify opportunities for mobile business processes. Stockholm School of Economics, SSE/EFI Working Paper Series in Business Administration, 10 (2002)
9. Laudon, K. C., Laudon, J. P.: Management Information Systems: managing the digital firm. Prentice Hall, Upper Saddle River, NJ (2002)
10. Köhler, A., Gruhn, V.: Mobile Process Landscaping am Beispiel von Vertriebsprozessen in der Assekuranz. In: Pousttchi, K., Turowski, K. (eds.): Mobile Economy - Transaktionen, Prozesse, Anwendungen und Dienste. GI-Lecture Notes in Informatics, P-25. Köllen Druck + Verlag GmbH, Bonn, (2003) 12-24
11. Gruhn, V., Wellen, U.: Process Landscaping: Modeling Distributed Processes and Proving Properties of Distributed Process Models. Lecture Notes in Computer Science, 2128. Springer, (2001) 103-125
12. Noor, N. M. M., Papamichail, K. N., Warboys, B.: Process Modeling for Online Communications in Tendering Processes. Proceedings of the 29th EUROMICRO Conference 'New Waves in System Architecture'. IEEE Computer Society, (2003) 17-24
13. Ritz, T., Stender, M.: Modeling of B2B Mobile Commerce Processes. 17th International Conference on Production Research ICPR-17. Virginia Tech, Blacksburg, (2003)
14. Gruhn, V., Wellen, U.: Structuring Complex Software Processes by 'Process Landscaping'. EWSPT European Workshop on Software Process Technology, Kaprun, Austria. Lecture Notes in Computer Science, 1780. Springer, (2000) 138-149
15. Aalst, W. v. d., Hee, K. M. v.: Workflow management: models, methods, and systems. MIT Press, Cambridge, Mass. (2002)
16. OMG: Unified Modeling Language Specification. http://www.omg.org (2001)

17. Scheer, A., Nüttgens, M.: ARIS Architecture and Reference Models for Business Process Management. In: van der Aalst, W., Desel, J., Oberweis, A. (eds.): Business Process Management - Models, Techniques,and Empirical Studies. LNCS 1806, Berlin et al., (2000) 366-379
18. White, S. A.: Business Process Modeling Notation. Business Process Management Initiative, BPMI.org (2003)
19. Arkin, A.: Business Process Modeling Language. Business Process Management Initiative, BPMI.org (2002)
20. http://xml.coverpages.org/bpm.html.

Enriching Conceptual Modeling
of XML-Aware Adaptive Web Systems
with Object-Oriented Constructs and UML Diagrams

Alfredo Cuzzocrea[1] and Carlo Mastroianni[2]

[1] Department of Electronics, Computer Science, and Systems
University of Calabria, 87036 Rende, Cosenza, Italy
cuzzocrea@si.deis.unical.it
[2] High Performance Computing and Networks Institute of the
Italian National Council of the Researches, 87036 Rende, Cosenza, Italy
mastroianni@icar.cnr.it

Abstract. This work presents a model for Adaptive Web Systems designed with a two-layer architecture. For the description of the high-level structure of the application domain we propose an object-oriented model based on the class diagram of the Unified Modeling Language, extended with (*i*) a graph-based formalism for capturing navigational properties of the hypermedia and (*ii*) a logic-based formalism for expressing further semantic properties of the domain. The model makes use of XML for the description of metadata about "neutral" pages that have to be adapted to user characteristics. Moreover, we propose a three-dimensional approach to model different aspects of the adaptation model, based on different user characteristics: an adaptive hypermedia is modeled with respect to such dimensions, and a view over it corresponds to each potential position of the user in the "adaptation space". In particular, a rule-based method is used to determine the generation and deliver process that best fits technological constraints.

1 Introduction

In hypertext-based multimedia systems, the personalization of presentation and content, i.e. their adaptation to user requirements and goals, is becoming a major requirement. Application fields where content personalization is useful are manifold: they comprise on-line advertising, direct web-marketing, electronic commerce, on-line learning and teaching, etc. Users are more and more heterogeneous due to different interests and goals, world-wide deployment of information and services, etc. Furthermore, nowadays hypermedia systems must be delivered to different kinds of terminals and networks.

To face these problems, in the last years the concepts of user-based adaptive systems and hypermedia user interfaces converged in the *Adaptive Web Systems* (AWS) research theme [1,4,6]. The basic components of adaptive Web systems are (*i*) the *Application Domain Model*, used to describe hypermedia basic contents and their

K. Bauknecht, M. Bichler, and B. Pröll (Eds.): EC-Web 2004, LNCS 3182, pp. 248–258, 2004.

organization to depict more abstract concepts, (*ii*) the *User Model*, which describes user characteristics and expectations, and (*iii*) the *Adaptation Model* that describes how to adapt content, i.e. how to the manipulate basic *information fragments* and links. More recently, the capability to deliver information to different kind of terminals, i.e. the support of multi-channel accessible Web systems, is becoming an important requirement. To efficiently allow the realization of user-adaptable content and presentation, a modular and scalable approach to describe and support the adaptation process must be adopted. A number of interesting models, architectures and methodologies have been developed in the last years for describing and supporting adaptive Web systems [2,3,8,10].

In particular, WebML [5] is a conceptual Web modeling language that uses the entity-relationship (ER) model for describing data structures and an original, high-level notation for representing Web content composition and navigation in hypertext form. In [9], a component-based architecture and an implementation framework for building complex Web applications is presented. Web applications are managed as views on Object Models; this allows for decoupling the design decisions related with the domain model from those related with the navigation and interface architecture.

In this paper we present a model for Adaptive Web Systems. Our work is specifically concerned with a complete and flexible *data-centric* support of adaptation. We focus on (*i*) the description of the structure and content of an Adaptive Web System; (*ii*) a representation of the adaptation process, distinguishing between adaptation driven by user needs and adaptation driven by technological constraints.

Adaptive Web Systems are composed of two layers: the *Description Layer* and the *Profile Layer*. The Desciption Layer defines the content of XML pages, their structure (defined through an object-oriented model), and the navigational features of the hypermedia (described with a directed graph). The Profile Layer describes the structure of the hypermedia as a set of views associated to *stereotype profiles* (i.e. groups of users) and the semantic relationships among those profiles.

2 Adaptive Web Systems Modeling

In our approach to the modeling of adaptive hypermedia we chose to adopt XML as the basic formalism due to its flexibility and data-centric orientation. XML permits an abstract description of information, allowing for the use of pre-existing multimedia basic data (e.g. stored in relational databases and/or file systems) and for the description of the content in a terminal-independent way.

We model the heterogeneous data sources by means of XML meta-descriptions (Sec. 2.2). Basic information fragments are extracted from data sources and used to compose descriptions of pages which are "neutral" with respect to user characteristics and preferences; such pages are called *Presentation Descriptions* (PD). In the Description Layer, the PDs are organized in an object-oriented structure to describe their structural properties (Sec. 2.3). Semantics related to the PDs is managed by the *Profile Layer* through the definition of knowledge-related concepts (*topics*), which are associated to PDs and user profiles (Sec 2.4).

The adaptation process is based on a multidimensional approach. The characteristics of a user are described through three *adaptivity dimensions*: (*i*) user behavior, (*ii*) external environment, and (*iii*) technology. The transformation from an abstract PD to the delivered final page is carried out on the basis of the position of the user in the *adaptation space* (Sec. 2.1). This process is performed in two phases: in the first phase a PD is instantiated with respect to the user behavior and external environment dimensions, and a "technological independent" PD is generated. In the second phase (described in Sec. 2.5) a PD is instantiated with respect to the technology dimension.

2.1 Adaptation Space

As mentioned above, the application domain is modeled along three orthogonal adaptivity dimensions:

1. User behavior (browsing activity, preferences, etc.);
2. External environment (time-spatial location, language, socio-political issues, etc.);
3. Technology (type of terminal, client/server processing power, network, etc).

The position of a user in the *adaptation space* can be denoted by a tuple having the form [*B,E,T*]. The *B* value captures the user's profile; *E* and *T* values respectively identify the external environment and the used technology.

Variables *B* and *E* mainly drive the generation of content and links, whereas the technology dimension drives the page layout adaptation and the page generation process. For example, an e-commerce web site could offer a class of products that fits the needs of a user (deducted from his/her behavior), formats data with respect to the kind of terminal, and sizes data on the basis of the measured network bandwidth.

2.2 Information Fragments

Information fragments are the atomic elements used to build hypermedia contents; fragments are extracted from data sources that, in the proposed model, are described by XML meta-descriptions. A fragment can be associated to a different portion of the multidimensional adaptation space. By means of meta-descriptions, data fragments can be managed at a high level, regardless of their actual sources: in the construction of pages the author can use metadata, thus avoiding a low-level access to fragments.

A number of XML meta-descriptions have been designed by using specific *XML Schemas* [12]. These schemas allows for the description of text, data extracted from relational and object-relational databases, queries versus such data, queries versus XML data (expressed in *XQuery* [13]), video sequences, images, XML documents and HTML documents.

2.3 The Description Layer

In the description layer the application domain is modeled as a directed graph, where nodes correspond to presentation descriptions and arcs represent navigational requirements. Furthermore, we apply the object-oriented paradigm to capture the structural relationships among the PDs.

A presentation description is composed of four sections:

1. The *OOStructureInfo* section includes information concerning the object-oriented organization of the domain. The interface of each class of PDs is composed of a set of ingoing and outgoing links, which represent relations among PDs with respect to the object-oriented modeling (e.g., grouping, inheritance, generalization, etc.). A *type* is associated to each link, and is used to define the compatibility among outgoing and ingoing links of different classes. With regard to inheritance, a subclass inherits the information fragments and the links of the parent classes. The *OOStructureInfo* section is edited by means of a tool based on the *Unified Modeling Language* (UML) [11] (specifically, on the class diagram), that allows the author to design the overall PD hierarchy of the application domain.

2. The *ContentLayout* section contains references to the information fragments that compose the PD. Such references are modelled as XML Schema elements and the information fragments are accessed by using a SQL-like querying language running on their metadata. As the *OOStructureInfo* section, the *ContentLayout* section is edited by means of a UML class diagram tool that also allows to automatically map UML diagrams into XML Schema documents.

3. The *AdapDimensionsInfo* section contains information about the instantiation of the PD with respect to the adaptivity dimensions; this information describes how to extract fragments on the basis of the user position in the adaptation space, and which XSL stylesheets should be applied to transform the PD into the final page delivered to the client.

4. The *AuxInfo* section contains auxiliary information (e.g. data islands), which is not to be processed by the system, but can be used by the client (for example, it can contain embedded code for client applications), or by network lower layers.

In the following, we show the XML Schema structure of the *OOStructureInfo* section. It includes the name of the PD class (*entityName* element), a set of parent classes (*superEntityName* elements) and a set of links that define the PD interface with respect to the object-oriented model (*link* elements, each with an associated name and type).

```
<xs:element name = "entityName" type = "xs:string"/>
<xs:element name = "superEntityName" type =
 "xs:string"/>
<xs:element name = "linkName" type = "xs:string"/>
<xs:element name = "linkType" type = "xs:string"/>
<xs:attribute name = "direction" use = "required">
  <xs:simpleType>
    <xs:restriction base = "xs:string">
      <xs:enumeration value = "in"/>
      <xs:enumeration value = "out"/>
    </xs:restriction>
  </xs:simpleType>
</xs:attribute>
<xs:element name = "link">
  <xs:complexType>
    <xs:sequence>
      <xs:element ref = "linkName"/>
      <xs:element ref = "linkType"/>
    </xs:sequence>
    <xs:attribute ref = "direction"/>
  </xs:complexType>
```

```
    </xs:element>
    <xs:element name = "OOStructureInfo">
      <xs:complexType>
        <xs:sequence>
          <xs:element ref = "entityName"/>
          <xs:element ref = "superEntityName" minOccurs =
          "0" maxOccurs = "unbounded"/>
          <xs:element ref = "link" minOccurs = "1"
          maxOccurs = "unbounded"/>
        </xs:sequence>
      </xs:complexType>
    </xs:element>
```

As an example of a PD's content design, in the following (see Fig. 1) we show an UML class diagram that describes the application domain for an *e*-tourism Web system:

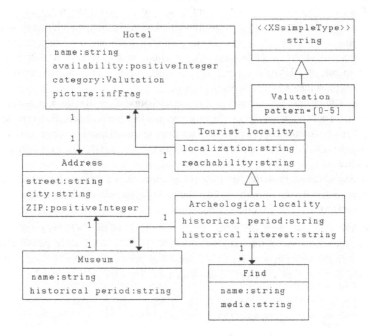

Fig. 1. UML Class Diagram for an *e*-Tourism Web System.

The corresponding XML Schema-based description, i.e. the *ContentLayout* section of the generated PD, is the following:

```
<xs:simpleType name = "Valutation">
  <xs:restriction base = "xs:string"/>
    <xs:length value = "1"/>
    <xs:pattern value = "[0-5]"/>
  </xs:restriction>
</xs:simpleType>
<xs:element name = "Address">
  <xs:complexType>
    <xs:sequence>
      <xs:element name = "street" type = "xs:string"/>
      <xs:element name = "city" type = "xs:string"/>
      <xs:element name = "ZIP" type = "xs:positiveInteger"/>
```

```
      </xs:sequence>
    </xs:complexType>
  </xs:element>
  <xs:element name = "Find">
    <xs:complexType>
      <xs:sequence>
        <xs:element name = "name" type = "xs:string"/>
        <xs:element name = "media" type = "xs:string"/>
      </xs:sequence>
    </xs:complexType>
  </xs:element>
  <xs:element name = "Hotel">
    <xs:complexType>
      <xs:sequence>
        <xs:element name = "name" type = "xs:string"/>
        <xs:element name = "availability" type = "xs:positiveInteger"/>
        <xs:element name = "category" type = "Valutazione"/>
        <xs:element name = "picture" type = "infFrag"
                    class = "images" extension = "jpg">
                    SELECT FileAbsPath
                    FROM IFMetaDataRepository
                    WHERE Profile="Standard"
        </xs:element>
        <xs:element ref = "Address" minOccours = "1" maxOccours = "1"/>
      </xs:sequence>
    </xs:complexType>
  </xs:element>
  <xs:element name = "Museum">
    <xs:complexType>
      <xs:sequence>
        <xs:element name = "name" type = "xs:string"/>
        <xs:element name = "historical period" type = "xs:string"/>
        <xs:element ref = "Address" minOccours = "1" maxOccours = "1"/>
      </xs:sequence>
    </xs:complexType>
  </xs:element>
  <xs:element name = "Tourist locality">
    <xs:complexType>
      <xs:sequence>
        <xs:element name = "localization" type = "xs:string"/>
        <xs:element name = "reachability" type = "xs:string"/>
        <xs:element ref = "Hotel" minOccours = "1" maxOccours =
          "unbounded"/>
      </xs:sequence>
    </xs:complexType>
  </xs:element>
  <xs:element name = "Archeological locality">
    <xs:complexContent>
      <xs:extension base = "Tourist locality">
        <xs:sequence>
          <xs:element name = "historical period" type = "xs:string"/>
          <xs:element name = "historical interest" type = "xs:string"/>
          <xs:element ref = "Find" minOccours = "1" maxOccours =
            "unbounded"/>
        </xs:sequence>
      </xs:extension>
    </xs:complexContent>
  </xs:element>
```

We highlight that the XML Schema document allows for the inclusion of an information fragment (i.e., an image) inside the PD. Such an inclusion is made by means of an element having type *infFrag*, a primitive type of the namespace defined by the PD XML Schema model. Moreover, an SQL statement needed to retrieve the information fragment is edited by the author. In the case shown above, the selected picture is valid for the standard user profile. At run-time, the system loads the information fragment by executing the SQL statement against the database that stores the metadata about the information fragments.

2.4 The Profile Layer

The goal of the Profile Layer is to model the domain adaptivity with respect to stereotype user profiles. A set of *Profile Views* (PV) are individuated, where each PV is a view of the overall hyperspace domain associated to a user profile. The PV associated to the profile p includes all the PDs accessible by users belonging to profile p, therefore it represents the hypermedia domain and the navigational space for that profile.

The design of this layer is made in two phases. In the first phase, the author designs the overall structure of the application domain by defining the interconnections among the PDs according to the traditional link structure of a Web system. In the second phase, the author identifies the user profiles and, on the basis of his/her domain knowledge, designs the PVs associated to each profile (see Fig. 2). The design of a PV can be carried out incrementally: for each PD, the author determines the user profiles that can access it. At the end of the process, each PV is composed of all the PDs that have been associated to the corresponding user profile.

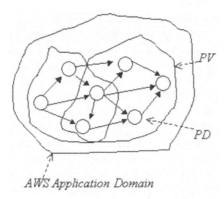

AWS Application Domain

Fig. 2. Profile Design as Editing of Views over the Application Domain.

Each PV (and consequently each associated profile) corresponds to a set of topics that represent the knowledge contained in the PV (*knowledge description*). This correspondence can be formally defined through a function $k(\cdot)$, that can be applied to a single PD, or to a user profile, and returns the corresponding set of topics:

- $k(\cdot)$, applied to the presentation description PD_i, returns the set of topics captured by PD_i;
- $k(\cdot)$, applied to the user profile p, returns the knowledge domain of p: $k(p) = \cup_i k(PD_i) \mid PD_i \in PV_p$, where PV_p is the profile view associated to p.

The instantiation of a particular PD with respect to a given profile and a given position along the external environment dimension can be seen as the application of a function δ that transforms a given PD into a technology-independent XML page, called PD^n ("neutral" PD), which will be given as input to the multichannel module (Sec. 2.5):

$$\delta(PD,B,E) \rightarrow PD^n$$

Furthermore, we improve the logical description of the hypermedia structure by means of a *Semantic Precedence Operator*, $\Leftarrow$, which is used to define constraints about profile changes. If applied to two knowledge domains, e.g. $k(p_2) \Leftarrow k(p_1)$, the operator indicates that a user cannot access topics related to the profile p_2 until he/she accesses some topics included in the knowledge domain of p_1 (i.e. until he accesses the PDs that capture those topics). This constraint can be better specified by means of a *semantic precedence matrix*. This matrix has as many rows as the topics of $k(p_2)$ and as many columns as the topics of $k(p_1)$. Each element (i, j) of the matrix can assume a boolean value; *true* means that the user must visit a PD containing the topic j of the domain $k(p_1)$ before his/her profile can change form p_1 to p_2 and the topic i of the domain $k(p_2)$ can be accessed. Therefore each row specifies which topic of $k(p_1)$ a user belonging to the profile p_1 must know to change his profile to p_2 by entering a particular topic of $k(p_2)$. For example, a semantic precedence matrix with all values equal to *true* means that, whatever is the entry point to the profile p_2, the user must have visited all the topics of $k(p_1)$. An entry point of a profile p_2 is defined as a node (PD) that, when accessed through a hyperlink, allows the user to change his profile to p_2. The semantic precedence operator can be used in general logic rules; e.g. $k(p_1) \Leftarrow k(p_2) \wedge (k(p_3) \vee k(p_4))$ is a rule that expresses a more complex relationship among the involved profiles.

2.5 Adaptation Model for the Technological Dimension

The technology dimension drives the adaptation of the page layout to the client device (PC, handheld computer, WAP device, etc.), and the page generation method. The technology adaptation is performed by means of a *Multichannel Module*. In the following we will describe (*i*) the alternative page generation methods, (*ii*) the technological variables, and (*iii*) the multichannel module.

Page Generation Methods. A final page displayed on the client device (written in HTML, WML, etc.) is dynamically generated by transforming the corresponding PD^n with a XSL document/program. Several XSL stylesheets can be used to transform a PD^n, depending on the client device features. Moreover, three different page generation methods can be exploited:

a. The page generation takes place entirely on the server. It picks out the *Information Fragments*, applies the transformation using the appropriate XSL document, and then sends the page (HTML, WML, etc.) to the client. The main drawback of this method is that the client cannot access the XML content. As an example, if the client is an application, e.g. a workflow or a distributed computing application, it could need to access and process XML data.

b. Similar to method **a**, but the server sends to the client HTML (WML) pages that contain XML data islands. Data islands are not processed by the server XSL processor, and are not displayed on the client device, but can be accessed by client programs.
c. The page generation is performed entirely on the client: the server sends to the client both the XML document and the XSL document that the client device will use to carry out the transformation.

The Technological Variables. The technological variables are used by the multichannel module to adapt the presentation and the generation process to the client device. On our system we use five groups of technological variables:

1. Variables related to the XML and XSL support on the client device.
2. Variables addressing the client device processing power (client-side XSL formatting may take place only if the device can manage such a complex and time-consuming operation).
3. Variables describing the display features of the client device (resolution, dimensions, etc.).
4. Variables concerning the kind of client data usage (e.g., it is useful to know whether or not clients need to access and process "pure" XML data).
5. Variables related to the server processing workload.

The variables belonging to the first three groups are extracted from the *device knowledge repository* (shown in the next Sec.), while data usage variables are associated to the client (e.g. they can be associated to the user profile), and the last group of variables is determined by the server.

The Multichannel Module. The main components of the multichannel module are the *Device Knowledge Repository* (DKB) and the *Presentation Rules Executor* (PRE).

The device repository is composed of a set of entries, each describing the features of a specific client device. For each client request, the client device is determined according to the data contained in the *User Agent* field of the request, and the corresponding device entry is selected. Each entry is composed of variable-value pairs, where variables correspond to the technology variables belonging to the first three groups.

The presentation rules executor determines the presentation layout and the page generation method based on a set of rules that check the values assumed by the technological variables. Rules are defined in an ad hoc XML syntax, and are modeled according to the well known *Event-Condition-Action* (ECA) paradigm. The following XML fragment shows a typical presentation rule.

```xml
<rule id="1">
  <conditions>
    <technological-variable group="1" xml-
    support="yes"/>
    <technological-variable group="2" processing-
    power="high"/>
    <technological-variable group="3" display-
    area="small" res-value="medium"/>
    <technological-variable group="4" xmldata-
    need="no"/>
  </conditions>
```

```
<action>
  <xsl-formatting value="clientside" method="c"
   stylesheet="AdHocStylesheet.xsl"/>
</action>
</rule>
```

The rule states that if the client does not need to elaborate the XML data content (the variable xmldata-need belongs to group 4), the client device fully supports XSL transformation (group 1 and 2 variables), and display features are appropriate (group 3 variables), the PRE chooses the page generation method c (client-side XSL formatting), and the XSL stylesheet *AdHocStylesheet.xsl*.

In general, events of the ECA paradigm are implicitly managed by the adaptive system and correspond to the user choice of a given PD. Conditions correspond to checks on the technological variable values. Actions are performed when a logical expression (a *presentation rule*), composed of atomic conditions, is evaluated. Actions mainly consist of the choice of the page generation method and the choice of the most suitable XSL stylesheet that will drive the XSL formatting.

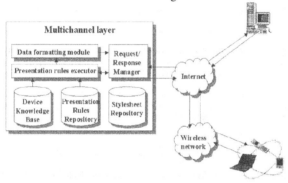

Fig. 3. The Multichannel Module.

Fig. 3 shows the multichannel module architecture. The request/response manager processes client requests (coming from either a wired or a wireless device) and drives the PD instantiation process, i.e. the selection of the information fragments and the transformation of the PDs into the set of corresponding PD^n, according to the user position along the user behavior and the environmental dimensions. The instantiation process is fully described in [7]. The request/response manager passes the PD^n and the client requests to the PRE. The PRE checks the data in the user agent request field, identifies the client devices, and accesses the DKR to evaluate the technological variables. Then the PRE executes the presentation rules contained in the presentation rules repository, according to the ECA paradigm, and chooses the page generation method and the XSL stylesheet (picking it out from the stylesheet repository).

In the case of client-side formatting (page generation method c), the PRE passes both the XML data (the PD^n) and the selected stylesheet to the Request/Response manager, which in turn sends them to the client. In the case of server-side formatting (page generation methods a or b), the PRE activates the XSL processor, which converts the XML data according to the XSL directives, and then passes the formatted data to the *Request/Response Manager*, which in turn sends it to the client.

3 Conclusions

In this paper we proposed a data-centric model for adaptive hypermedia systems using the object-oriented paradigm and XML. In addition, we presented a modular architecture for the run-time support of the adaptation process.

In our model, an adaptive hypermedia is described considering a three-dimensional adaptation space, including user behavior, technology, and external environment dimensions. The adaptation process is performed evaluating the proper position of the user in the adaptation space, and transforming "neutral" XML pages according to that position. The main contribution of the model is a new approach to the description of adaptive hypermedia specifically concerned with a flexible and effective support of the adaptation process; the model integrates a graph-based description of navigational properties and an object-oriented description of the hypermedia, and uses a logical formalism to model knowledge-related aspects.

References

1. "Adaptive Hypertext and Hypermedia Home Page", http://wwwis.win.tue.nl/ah.
2. De Bra, P., Houben, G.J., and Wu, H., "AHAM - A Dexter-based Reference Model for Adaptive Hypermedia", Proc. of the ACM Int. Conf. on Hypertext and Hypermedia, pp. 147-156, 1999.
3. Mecca, G., Atzeni, P., Masci, A., Merialdo, P., and Sindoni, G., "The Araneus Web-based Management System", Proc. of the ACM Int. Conf. on Management of Data, pp.544-546, 1998.
4. Brusilovsky, P., "Adaptive Hypermedia, User Modeling and User Adapted Interaction", Kluwer Academic Publishers, Vol. 11, pp. 87-110, 2001.
5. Ceri, S., Fraternali, P., and Matera, M., "Conceptual Modeling of Data-Intensive Web Applications", IEEE Internet Computing, Vol. 6(4), pp. 20-30, 2002.
6. De Bra, P., Brusilovsky, P., and Conejo, R., (eds.) "Adaptive Hypermedia and Adaptive Web-based Systems", LNCS 2347, Springer-Verlag, 2002.
7. Cannataro, M., Cuzzocrea, A., and Pugliese, A., "A Multidimensional Approach for Modelling and Supporting Adaptive Hypermedia Systems", Proc. of the Int. Conf. on Electronic Commerce and Web Technologies, LNCS 2115, Springer-Verlag, pp. 132-141, 2001.
8. Bordegoni, M., Faconti, G., Feiner, S., Maybury, M.T., Rist, T., Ruggieri, S., Trahanias, P., and Wilson, M., "A Standard Reference Model for Intelligent Multimedia Presentation Systems", Computer Standards and Interfaces, Vol. 18, pp.477-496, 1997.
9. Jacyntho, M.D., Schwabe, D., and Rossi, G., "A Software Architecture for Structuring Complex Web Applications", Journal of Web Engineering, Vol. 1(1), pp. 37-60, 2002.
10. Fernandez, M.F., Florescu, D., Levy, A.Y., and Suciu, D., "Catching the Boat with Strudel: Experiences with a Web-Site Management System", in Proc. of ACM Int. Conf. on Management of Data, pp.414-425, 1998.
11. "The Object Management Group, Unified Modeling Language", http://www.uml.org.
12. "The World Wide Web Consortium, XML Schema", http://www.w3.org/XML/Schema.
13. "The World Wide Web Consortium, XML Query", http://www.w3.org/XML/Query.

Modelling Content Aggregation
for Developing e-Commerce Web Sites

Pedro Valderas, Joan Fons, and Vicente Pelechano

Department of Information Systems and Computation
Polytechnic University of Valencia
Camí de Vera s/n
46022 Valencia, Spain
{pvalderas,jjfons,pele}@dsic.upv.es

Abstract. Currently, e-commerce web sites are integrators of heterogeneous information and services that are oriented to providing content aggregation. From a Model-Driven perspective, e-commerce applications need conceptual mechanisms that make it easy to describe, manage and reuse contents and services in order to deal with content aggregation at a higher level of abstraction. Our work presents conceptual modeling techniques that extend the OOWS navigational modeling by refining the navigational context definition and introducing the concept of information abstraction unit to specify the contents of web applications of this kind. These new abstractions provide powerful reuse mechanisms that produce considerable benefits because both development time and effort can be reduced. Finally, the paper presents some ideas to implement content aggregation taking these enhanced navigational models as input.

1 Introduction

Web sites like Fnac (www.fnac.com), Ebay (www.ebay.com) or Amazon (www.amazon.com) allow the user to buy different kinds of products such as books, DVD's, software, etc. This kind of aplications provides the user with web pages made up of several sections. In this way, web pages are built from the aggregation of diverse contents or information blocks. Each content defines a conceptual view that provides the user with a specific perspective of the product catalogue. Figure 1 shows the welcome page of the Amazon web site. This page provides the user with: (1) the latest product releases, (2) a list of future releases and (3) a list of news books releases.

From a methodological point of view, the most outstanding approaches (OOHDM [3], WebML [6], OOH [2], WSDM [1], UWE [7], etc.) focus their efforts on defining web applications from conceptual models that allow them to systematically obtain implementations. These approaches provide abstraction mechanisms that make it easy to conceptualize and develop the web applications allowing the analyst to specify hypermedial and functional requirements. The mechanisms for hypermedia modeling allow the analyst (1) to define web pages as conceptual schema views and (2) to interconnect these views to define the navigational structure of the web application. However, considering a web page only as a view of the conceptual schema makes difficult to specify aggregation of contents, where web pages are built as a composite of several conceptual schema views (see each numbered area in Figure 1). In this way, although some of the approaches mentioned above provide support in the design and/or implementation steps, none of them explicitly supports the specification of web applications with aggregation of contents in the conceptual modeling step.

K. Bauknecht, M. Bichler, and B. Pröll (Eds.): EC-Web 2004, LNCS 3182, pp. 259–267, 2004.

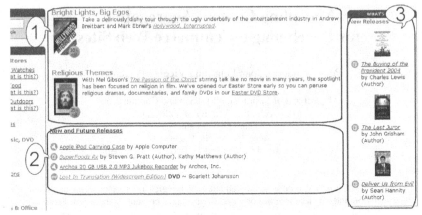

Fig. 1. Amazon Welcome Page.

In this work, we present conceptual modeling techniques that extend the OOWS (Object-Oriented Web Solution) [4] navigational modeling by refining the navigational context definition and introducing the concept of information abstraction unit (IAU) in order to specify the contents for web applications of this kind. This new expressive capacity makes it easy to describe at a higher level of abstraction web applications with content aggregation. It also provides powerful reuse mechanisms that can reduce development time and effort. Following a Model-Driven Development (MDD [8]) approach, the paper presents some ideas to implement web applications that support content aggregation by taking these enhanced navigational models as input.

This paper is organized in the following way: section 2 introduces an overview of the OOWS method. Section 3 presents the concept of IAU to support content aggregation. In section 4 the different kinds of IAUs are presented. Section 5 introduces mechanisms to reuse IAUs. Finally, conclusions and future works are commented on in section 6. The Amazon web site has been taken as a case study to clearly map the new concepts and abstraction mechanisms and their implementation in a real web environment.

2 OOWS Overview

OOWS (Object-Oriented Web Solutions) [4] is the extension of an object-oriented software production method (OO -Method [5]) that introduces the required expressivity to capture the navigational requirements of web applications. In order to do this, OOWS introduces the **Navigational Model** that allows for capturing the navigation semantics in two steps: the "Authoring-in-the-large" (global view) and the "Authoring-in-the-small" detailed view).

The *Authoring-in-the-large* step refers to the specification and design of global and structural aspects of the web application. These requirements are specified in a *Navigational Map* that provides a specific kind of user with its system view. It is represented using a directed graph whose nodes denote navigational contexts and whose arcs denote navigational links or valid navigational paths. Figure 2 shows a piece of the navigational map for the Amazon web site related to an anonymous *Internet User*.

Navigational contexts (graphically represented as UML packages stereotyped with the *«context»* keyword) represent the user interaction units that provide a set of cohesive data and operations. In order to define the context reachability, we provide two types of contexts:

- *Exploration navigational contexts* (represented by an "E" label) represent reachable nodes from any node (see Figure 2, *Welcome, Books, Electronics, Toys and Games* and *Home and Garden* navigational contexts).
- *Sequence navigational contexts* (represented by the "S" label) can only be accessed via a predefined navigational path by selecting a sequence link. For instance, in Figure 2 we can see the *Book Description* context, which can only be accessed from *Books* or *Welcome* navigational contexts following the solid arrows defined among navigational contexts.

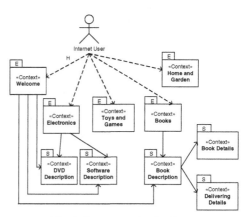

Fig. 2. Amazon navigational map.

The *navigational links* (navigational map arcs) represent context accessibility or *"navigational paths"*. There are two types of navigational links:

- *Sequence links* or *"contextual links"* (represented by solid arrows) which define a *semantic* navigation between contexts. Selecting a sequence link implies carrying contextual information to the target context (e.g. the object that has been selected, the source navigational context, etc.).
- *Exploration links* or *"non contextual links"* (represented by dashed arrows) which represent an intentional change of task by the user. They are implicitly defined from the root of the navigational map (depicted as a user) and terminate in an exploration context. When an exploration link is activated, no contextual information is carried to the target context. One of these links can be defined as *default* or *home* (graphically represented by an *"H"* label). When this occurs, the user automatically navigates to the exploration contexts when the user connects to the system (see Figure 2 *Welcome* context).

Following the specification in Figure 2, when an anonymous *Internet User* connects to the Amazon web site, he automatically navigates to the *Welcome* navigational context. From this context, the user can reach the exploration contexts (*Books, Electronics, Toys and Games* and *Home and Garden*) through the exploration links. Also, the user can navigate to the *Book Description,* the *DVD Description* or the *Software Description* navigational contexts by means of the sequence links (contextual links) that carry a selected object to get additional information about it.

The *"Authoring-in-the-small"* step refers to the detailed specification of the contents of the navigational contexts. The following section presents how these contexts must be defined in order to achieve content aggregation.

3   Navigational Contexts with Content Aggregation

In order to support content aggregation, navigational contexts should be considered as user interaction units which provide access to several information abstraction units. An *information abstraction unit* (IAU), stereotyped with the «iau» keyword, represents a specific view on the class diagram. Each IAU is made up of a set of navigational classes that represent class views (including attributes and operations). These classes are stereotyped with the «view» keyword. Figure 3 shows the navigational context corresponding to the welcome page of the Amazon site: the *Welcome* navigational context. It is defined using three IAUs: *Latest Releases* (corresponding to area 1 in Figure1), *Future Releases* (corresponding to area 2) and *New Books Releases* (corresponding to area 3). Figure 3 also shows the *Latest Releases* IAU definition (that provides information about the latest product releases) and the *New Book Releases* IAU definition (that provides information about the new books). *Future Releases* IAU definition has been omited due to space problems.

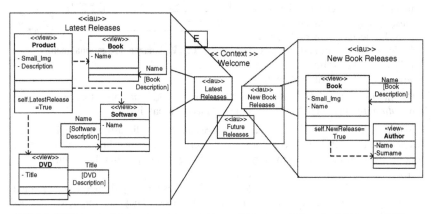

Fig. 3. *Welcome* navigational context and *Latest Releases* and *New Book Releases* IAUs.

Each IAU has one mandatory navigational class, called *manager class* (see Figure 3, *Product* class in the *Latest Releases* IAU and *Book* class in the *New Book Releases* IAU) and optional navigational classes that provide complementary information to the manager class. These classes are called complementary classes (see Figure 3, *Book*, *Software* and *DVD* classes in *Latest Releases* IAU and *Author* class in *New Book Releases* IAU). Moreover, selection filters (expressions that allow us to select specific objects) can be defined in OCL upon an object population which has been retrieved by a navigational class (see Figure 3, lower side of both IAUs manager class, "self.latestRelease=True" in *Latest Releases* IAU and "self.newRelease=True" in *New Book Releases* IAU).

Navigational classes must be related by unidirectional binary relationships, called navigational relationships. They are defined over existing aggregation/association/composition or specialization/generalization relationships. There are two kind of navigational relationships:

(1) A context dependency relationship (graphically represented by dashed arrows) which represents a basic information recovery by selecting a structural relationship between two classes. When a context dependency relationship is defined, all the instances related to the source class are retrieved. Relationships of this kind do not define any navigation capability. Figure 3 shows four context dependency relationship: Product-Book, Product-DVD and Product-Software relationships in Latest Releases IAU (defined over specialization relationships), and Book-Author relationship in New Book Releases IAU (defined over an asociation relationships).

(2) A context relationship (graphically represented by solid arrows) which represents the same information recovery as a context dependency relationship plus a navigation capability to a target navigational context, creating a sequence link in the navigational map. Figure 3 shows four context relationships: Book-Book, DVD-DVD and Software-Software relationships in Latest Releases IAU and Book-Book relationship in New Book Releases IAU. In these cases, no complementary information is retrieved but these contextual relationships create links to the target contexts (Book Description, DVD Description, Software Description (Latest Releases IAU) and Book Description (New Book Releases IAU)) that provide more detailed information about products.

Implementation Issues. *Welcome* context implementation has been presented in Figure 1. According to the *Latest Releases* IAU definition (see Figure 3, *Welcome* context specification), the web page must specify each product providing its description, a small image of it and, its name (if the product is a book or some software) or its title (if the product is a DVD) (see area 1 in Figure 1). In addition, when a user clicks on a product (a book, a software product or a DVD), *Book Description*, *Software Description* or *DVD Description* contexts will be accessed (by means of the context relationship). These navigational contexts provides more information about the particular product selected by the user.

According to the *New Books Releases* IAU definition, the web page must specify each book providing its name, a small image of it and (due to the context dependency relationship) its author's name and surname (see area 3 in Figure 1). In a similar way, when a user clicks on a book, *Product Description* context will be accessed (by means of the context relationship). This navigational context provides more information about the particular book selected by the user.

4   Categorizing IAUs

It is necessary to distinguish between IAUs that give support to contextual navigation and those that do not. Contextual navigation carries the information of a selected object (from the source context) to a target context. This contextual information must be captured by an IAU in order to show specific information concerning the selected object. In this way, there exist two kind of IAUs:

– *Contextual IAUs* (represented by the "C" label) are IAUs that instantiate the manager class[1] to the object that is received as contextual information through a contextual navigation. One contextual IAU is required in all sequence navigational contexts.

---

[1] The manager class of this IAU must be the same as the received object class.

– *Non-contextual IAUs* (unlabeled): are IAUs that does not depend on the contextual information received by the navigational context. They provide the information for all the objects belonging to the manager class population. Non contextual IAUs can be defined in any navigational context.

IAUs presented in the *Welcome* navigational context (see Figure 3) are both non contextual IAUs. Figure 4 shows the *Book Description* navigational context. This context is made up of two contextual IAUs: *Book* and *Best Value*. When a user selects a book from the *Welcome* context (from *Latest Releases* or *New Book Releases* IAUs, see Figure 3), the user navigates (see sequence link in Figure 2) to the *Book Description* navigational context (see Figure 4) and the selected book is taken along. This book is instantiated in the manager class of the *Book* and the *Best Value* IAUs (represented as contextual IAUs) showing specific information about it. In the *Book* IAU the *Small_Img*, *Name*, the *List Price*, the *Price*, the *Availability* attributes, the *Author*'s *Name* and *Surname* and the *Delivering* and the *Payment Description* are shown. On the other hand, the *Best Value* IAU shows information about special promotions that allow the user to save some money if he/she buys this book and other one together.

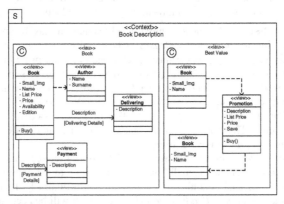

Fig. 4. *Book Description* navigational context.

Implementation Issues for IAU Categorization. Figure 5 shows the Web page corresponding to the *Book Description* context implementation. This page is provided to the user when he selects a *book* from the *Welcome* page (see Figure 1).

Area 1 shows the specific information retrieved by the *Book* contextual IAU (see Figure 4). This information relates to the book information specified by means of the class atrributes of the *Book* IAU definition. In addition, access to on-line buying is also provided (*Buy()* service) through a button. The layout and graphical representation of the information and services are implemented following specific presentation pattern specification defined in our Presentation Model [4].

Area 2 presents the implementation of the contextual *Best Value* IAU (see Figure 4). In such a case, the information about a special sale promotion of the received book is showed.

During the building process of a Web application with content aggregation, some of these contents can be reused to specify and implement several pages. For instance, due to a marketing strategy, information about the new books is shown on several pages of the Amazon web site. In order to support these marketing requirements, we can (1) define this information in each navigational context or (2) reuse the *New Book Releases* IAU that provides this information. Abstract mechanisms to reuse IAU are presented in the following section.

Fig. 5. *Book Description* context implementation.

5 Reuse Mechanisms

Introducing IAUs into the OOWS navigational model allows us to provide some mechanisms to reuse contents at a high level of abstraction. These mechanisms allow us (1) to specify new navigational contexts and/or (2) to specify new IAUs taking a predefined IAU as an input.

1. *Specifying New Navigational Contexts:* an IAU specified in a navigational context can be used to define other new contexts. In this way, a new navigational context can be made up of: (1) new IAUs (mandatory option for the navigational context which is specified first) or (2) IAUs specified in other navigational contexts.

2. *Specifying New IAUs Through Specialization:* new IAUs can be defined taking an already defined one as a basis. We do this by extending the IAU definition by means of specialization mechanisms: the specialized IAU inherits a parent IAU definition. It can be refined to adapt the retrieved information, services and navigation capabilities to the needs of a particular navigational context. IAU specialization is performed by means of some kind of **is_a** operator and using the following operations:

   - Adding/Removing information (navigational class attributes)
   - Adding/Removing functionality access (navigational class services)
   - Adding/Removing/Redefining population selection filters (navigational class filters)
   - Adding/Removing navigational complementary classes
   - Adding/Removing context dependency relationships
   - Adding/Removing context relationships

In Figure 6, we can observe *Books* navigational context. In order to define this context, *New Book Releases* IAU, which is specified in *Welcome* context (see Figure 3), has been reused including a reference to it (depicted as a box with the «iau» stereotype and the name of the IAU). In this way, we are giving support to marketing requirements which suggest showing information about the new book realeses in this navigational context. Figure 7 shows the *Books* context implementation. In this figure we can see that the

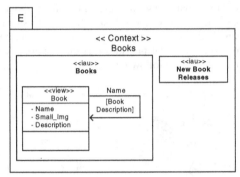

Fig. 6. IAU Reuse in *Books* context.

information in area 2 is the same as the information that appear in area 3 of the Figure 1 (new books releases information that corresponds to the *New Book Releases* IAU). Area 1 shows the name, the small image and the description of some other books of the Amazon catalogue. This information corresponds to *Books* IAU definition.

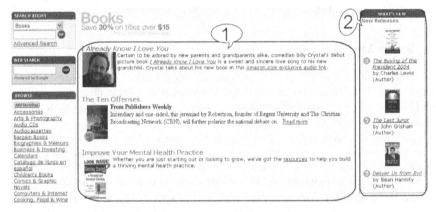

Fig. 7. *Books* context implementation.

6 Conclusions

Currently, marketing policies have made that web sites become applications that provide the user with web pages made up of diferent views of the same information (contets). Due to the interest in specifying and developing appropriate web applications with content aggregation, we have proposed a solution from the conceptual modeling perspective in order to give methodological support for the construction of applications of this kind.

This solution refines the navigational context definition presented by the OOWS approach by introducing the concept of information abstraction unit (IAUs) in order to allow for the representation at the conceptual modeling step, of different and heterogeneous contents that can define a whole web page. This approach redefines the navigational context as a conceptual abstraction that can be built using multiple IAUs. Also, the IAU allows us to carry out content reuse mechanisms, making it easier to give support to marketing requirements.

We have applied these extensions to a real case study (the Amazon web site, www.amazon.com) where it is necessary to provide the user with different views of its product catalogue (news products releases, products on sale, the most sold products, etc) in single web pages. We have built the navigational model of the web site (using the OOWS approach), including the extensions for both the aggregation of contents and the reusing mechanisms. Furthermore, we have introduced intuitive mapping mechanisms to give support to the implementation of the primitives introduced at a conceptual level.

As future work, it would be necessary both to extend the presentation patterns that OOWS Presentation Model provides to attach them to the IAUs and to detect presentation relationships and dependencies between different IAUs in the same navigational context.

References

1. De Troyer O. and Leune C. WSDM: A user-centered design method for Web sites. In Proc. of the 7th International World Wide Web Conference, 1998.
2. Gómez J., Cachero C., and Pastor O. Extending a Conceptual Modeling Approach to Web Application Design. Proc. Conference on Advanced Information Systems Engineering (CAiSE'00), Springer- Verlag, LNCS 1789, pp. 79-93, 2000.
3. Schwabe D., Rossi G., "An Object Oriented Approach to Web-Based Application Design", Theory and Practice of Object Systems 4(4), 1998. Wiley and Sons, New York, ISSN 1074-3224).)
4. Joan Fons, Vicente Pelechano, Manoli Albert y Oscar Pastor. Development of Web Applications from Web Enhanced Conceptual Schemas. Springer-Verlag, Lecture Notes in Computer Science. Proc. Of the International Conference on Conceptual Modelling, 22nd Edition, ER'03, pp 232-245. Chicago, EE.UU, 13 - 16 October 2003.
5. Pastor O., Pelechano V., Insfrán E,. and Gómez J. From Object Oriented Conceptual Modeling to Automated Programming in Java. 17th International Conference on Conceptual Modeling (ER'98). Springer-Verlag, LNCS 1507, pp. 183-196. Singapore, November, 1998.
6. Ceri S., Fraternali P., Bongio A. Web Modeling Language (WebML): a Modeling Language for Designing Web Sites. In WWW9, Vol. 33 (1-6), pp 137-157. Computer Networks, 2000.
7. Koch, N., Wirsing, M.: Software Engineering for Adaptive Hypermedia Applications. In: 3rd Workshop on Adaptive Hypertext and Hypermedia. (2001).
8. Mellor, S.J.; Clark, A.N.; Futagami, T. "Model-driven development" – Guest editor's introduction. IEEE Software, p. 14-18, Sept.-Oct. 2003.

On the Use of Bipolar Scales
in Preference–Based Recommender Systems

Miguel-Ángel Sicilia and Elena García

Computer Science Department. Polytechnic School.
University of Alcalá. Ctra. Barcelona km. 33.6
28871 – Alcalá de Henares, Madrid, Spain
{msicilia,elena.garciab}@uah.es

Abstract. Recommendations in e–commerce collaborative filtering are
based on predicting the preference of a user for a given item according to
historical records of other user's preferences. This entails that the interpretation of user ratings are embodied in the prediction of preferences,
so that such interpretation should be carefully studied. In this paper,
the use of bipolar scales and aggregation procedures are experimentally
compared to their unipolar counterparts, evaluating the adequacy of both
techniques with regards to the human interpretation of rating scales. Results point out that bipolarity is closer to the human interpretation of
opinions, which impacts the selection of recommended items.

Keywords: Collaborative filtering, e–commerce recommendations, bipolar aggregation.

1 Introduction

Recommender systems in e–commerce are aimed at helping customers by suggesting them products that could be of their interest, according to some algorithm the operates on navigation or purchase history or any other kind of data
regarding products and customers. More specifically, *collaborative filtering* (CF)
techniques [8, 10, 5] analyze preference data for the purpose of producing useful
recommendations to customers. CF systems proceed by first matching the target user against the user database to discover *neighbors* – i.e. users that have
historically had similar preferences –, and then recommending products that
neighbors like, since it is assumed that the target user will "probably" also like
them [9]. Other recommendation approaches are content–based, i.e. they use
some kind of semantic representation of the product descriptions and use them
as a source of similarities for the task of selecting recommendations. Content–
based and preference–based techniques are complementary, as demonstrated in
existing recommender systems, e.g. [7].

The rationale behind collaborative filtering algorithms has been said to be
the automation of the process of "word-of-mouth", by which people recommend
products or services to others with similar taste [10], so that preferences (either
explicitly or implicitly collected) are the main source for recommendations. But

K. Bauknecht, M. Bichler, and B. Pröll (Eds.): EC-Web 2004, LNCS 3182, pp. 268–276, 2004.

in most current e–commerce systems, customers are not informed about the identity of their *neighbors*, so that "reputation" in trusting recommendations is not exploited, and in fact, it would be almost impossible to use in practice, due to the large population of users and the generalized unwillingness to reveal oneself's identity. In consequence, the mathematical models used to predict user preferences only deal with past recorded preferences, which are in most cases expressed in numerical scales, e.g. $\{1,5\}$ or $[1,5]$. If we look at the problem from the perspective of modeling human trust processes, it can be hypothesized that the *interpretation* of such scales and the volume of neighbors that are taken into account for each given recommendation – among other aspects – influence the trust of customers with regards to the "quality" of the recommendation. The latter aspect has been somewhat addressed in the diverse techniques designed to overcome the so–called *latency problem* – i.e. the problem of how CF system should behave when they have low volumes of historical data –, but the former one remains largely neglected.

In this paper, the polarity in the *interpretation* of numerical preference scales is studied from the perspective of its influence in the degree of trustworthiness of preference predictions, provided that explanation details for them (like those described in [3]) are showed to customers. The main objective of such inquiry is to come up with some evidence to devise CF algorithms that behave more closely to humans in the process of inferring preferences from the judgements of anonymous peers, eventually resulting in more "commonsensical" approaches to generate and explain recommendations. At the best of our knowledge, this is the first study regarding polarity in e–commerce ratings used for recommendation. The consideration of polarity in ratings may eventually result in more "conservative" recommendations, that tend to penalize the recommendation of an item that has received ratings in the "negative" part of the scale, thus avoiding compensation. This points out to the necessity of combining bipolar interpretations with a notion of 'democracy' as the one used in `RACOFI` [1].

The rest of this paper is structured as follows. Section 2 details the overall motivation for the present research, and Section 3 describes a concrete experimental study that provides evidence of the influence of polarity in the human judgement of preference predictions. Finally, conclusions and future research directions are sketched in Section 4.

2   Bipolar Aggregation Versus Unipolar Preference Predictors

The goal of a CF algorithm is that of predicting the degree of preference of a given item or product for an specific user based on the user's previous likings and the opinion of other like–minded users. A typical CF setting consists on a set of users $\mathcal{U} = \{u_1, \ldots u_m\}$, a collection of items $\mathcal{I} = \{i_1, \ldots i_n\}$, and a collection of ratings that can be modeled as a relation $\mathcal{R}$ as defined in expression (1), where $\mathcal{S}$ denotes the rating scale used.

$$\mathcal{R} : \mathcal{U} \times \mathcal{I} \to \mathcal{S} \tag{1}$$

Typical scales are integer or real intervals, so that they can be normalized to other intervals without loosing information (this is used in this paper only for notational convenience). The relation $\mathcal{R}$ is usually incomplete, so that many ratings for pairs $(user, item)$ are actually missing (simply because users normally rate explicitly only a small portion of the item database). This leads to implementing prediction of ratings, in which $\mathcal{R}$ is considered to produce as output the explicit rating of a user (if available) **or** an estimation (prediction) based in the collection of explicit ratings, so that the relation can be defined in terms of a rating matrix $\mathcal{M}$ storing the explicit ratings, and resorting to a prediction algorithm for missing values – see expression (2).

$$\mathcal{R}(u,i) = \left\{ \begin{array}{l} \mathcal{M}[u,i] \;\; if\,\mathcal{M}[u,i] \neq null \\ pred(\mathcal{M}), \;\; otherwise \end{array} \right\} \tag{2}$$

Score prediction processes in collaborative filtering (i.e. *pred* functions) – like the classical Pearson correlation–based one described in [8] – can be considered as complex aggregation processes that take as input the history of ratings and produce the "expected" rating for a concrete item of a specific user, which serves as a basis for recommendation decisions. In fact, lightweight approaches like the one described in [1] are also based on historical records.

Bipolar aggregation operators [6] act on the interval [-1,1] instead of the unipolar unit interval, dealing with positive, supporting information as well as negative, excluding one. This difference may influence significantly rating predictions due to the consideration of negative ratings as inhibitors of preference matching, in what can be considered as *conservative* strategies to prediction. This has lead us to study the influence of bipolarity in CF settings. More concretely, the first two research questions addressed are described in what follows.

Hypothesis 1 *Users of e–commerce sites interpret rating scales as bipolar ones, with negatives acting as inhibitors of recommendation.*

Hypothesis 2 *The use of negative weights according to bipolar scales is interpreted by users as more adequate than unipolar interpretations.*

The first hypothesis is directly connected with the human interpretation of rating scales in e–commerce, and the second one complements it by suggesting that the bipolar interpretation positively influences prediction "appropriateness" as seen by users.

Previous work have raised research questions about the provision of explanations for CF recommendations [3] showing users the rationale for the prediction process, but always operating on a unipolar interpretation. Our current focus introduces a new variation in existing models that could affect the whole prediction process.

3   Experimental Study

In this section, the results of an experimental study aimed at gathering evidence about hypotheses 1 and 2 are described. The study used the large *MovieLens*[1] rating database that contains more than a million ratings from approximately 3.900 movies made by 6.040 users.

3.1   Experimental Design

Hypothesis 1 states that the interpretation of the rating scales is bipolar (at least in a significant proportion). This is to say that the scale is interpreted as having a "neutral" element that distinguishes between two opposite notions, as in "good/bad", rather than being interpreted in unipolar, comparative terms as in "more satisfactory than". Bipolarity has been studied in attitude measurement, and the the mid–point on bipolar scales is considered to "represent the neutral point in attitude"[11], so that we will follow a similar initial assumption for ratings.

The experimental design for this first question was based on asking participants to assess rating exemplars. Concretely, there were obtained five significant ratings for each participant, extracted from the *MovieLens* database (using the prediction procedure described in [5]), and distributed over the rating interval to prevent biases related to the distribution of predictions.

Users were asked to assess two related aspects about each of the examplars:

– To classify them as "good" or "'bad" films according to their (aggregated) rating, allowing for any arbitrary linguistic hedge to be added to the rating.
– To answer wether a "negative" (i.e. lower than the midpoint) rating should influence negatively her decision to recommend the item to other users, below the averaging of the ratings.

These questions provided a measure of the bipolar interpretation of the ratings, along with its intensity of influence in consuming decisions. To avoid biases, it was required that the users had neither watched the movies nor have heard previous comments about them. An example set of ratings for question 1 could be (1.05, 1.99, 3.07, 4.0, 4.98), which are (approximately) distributed over the rating interval.

The second question was investigated through a comparison between two lists of ratings that yield the same average rating, but with one of them having greater variance (due to some negative ratings, compensated with positive ones).

Hypothesis 2 is aimed at measuring the comparative "rationality" of predictions for two standard *pred* functions that differ in the consideration of bipolarity. In this case, experimental design requires the presentation of concrete prediction cases to users, describing the history of ratings for each concrete situation, and asking them for which prediction is seen as more acceptable. In addition,

---

[1] Available at http://www.cs.umn.edu/Research/GroupLens/

the number of ratings used for each prediction is fixed to a specific constant, to isolate the study from the influence of the size of the ratings database. In order to make the procedure feasible and non–biased, the details of the computation procedure are not disclosed to participants. The mathematical models used for the comparison are based in the classical *GroupLens* heuristic described in the seminal paper [5]. Expression (3) shows the model for predicting the rating to item l by user u, where correlation coefficients (between each pair of users a and b) are in the form described in (4), being $v_{x,y}$ the explicit rating element $\mathcal{M}[x, y]$ and $\overline{v_x}$ is the average rating of user x.

$$p_{u,l} = \overline{v_u} + \frac{\sum_{i \in \mathcal{U}} (v_{i,l} - \overline{v_i}) w(u, i)}{\sum_{i \in \mathcal{U}} |w(u, i)|} \tag{3}$$

$$w(a, b) = \frac{\sum_{j \in \mathcal{I}} (v_{a,j} - \overline{v_a})(v_{b,j} - \overline{v_b})}{\sqrt{\sum_{j \in \mathcal{I}} (v_{a,j} - \overline{v_a})^2 \sum_{j \in \mathcal{I}} (v_{b,j} - \overline{v_b})^2}} \tag{4}$$

Bipolarity in expressions (3) and (4) can be introduced by changing the one to five scale to [-1,1] by the simple transformation $y = \frac{x}{2} - 1.5$, but this by itself do not change the interpretation of ratings under zero as negative. An additional transformation is required to differentiate the influence of negative ratings in the overall prediction. We have chosen not to change the correlation coefficient in (4) to avoid changing its robust interpretation of matching profiles, so that it is expression (3) which becomes modified. Expression (5) shows the simple change introduced, i.e.

$$p'_{u,l} = \overline{v_u} + \frac{\sum_{i \in \mathcal{U}} (\Phi(v_{i,l}) - \overline{v_i}) w(u, i)}{\sum_{i \in \mathcal{U}} |w(u, i)|} \qquad \Phi(v_{i,l}) = \left\{ \begin{array}{ll} v_{i,l}, , & v_{i,l} \geq 0 \\ \frac{v_{i,l}}{k}, , & v_{i,l} < 0 \end{array} \right\} \tag{5}$$

The k value in (5) acts as a parameter of the influence of negative ratings in the overall prediction[2]. Values in the [1,5] interval can be used to produce reasonable conservative variants of different intensity in large rating databases like *MovieLens*. For example, the predicted ratings for two specific user and item pairs are provided in Table 1.

Table 1. Example bipolar predictions for concrete user and item pairs with diverse values of the k parameter

user, item	k=1 (unipolar)	k=1.25	k=1.5	k=1.75	k=2	k=5
4, 1	3.28	3.18	3.08	2.98	2.88	2.48
7, 13	2.6	2.4	2.16	1.99	1.7	0.98

As illustrated in Table 1, the bipolar correction provides a slight modification for cases with a low proportion of negative ratings (row one), so that a significant

---

[2] k could be also used to decrease the rating proportionally to its negative intensity, but we will not deal with this here.

amount of negative ratings is required to make a difference with the standard approach(row two). In consequence, the problem of finding an "ideal value" for k is dependant on the profile of negative ratings in the database, and on the perception of users about the effect bipolarity should have in the final ratings. The second part of this study is intended to gather some initial evidence about this issue.

3.2   Results and Discussion

The profile of the users that participated in the study was that of students of Computer Science aged 20–35, and considered regular e–commerce buyers with around six to twenty purchases per year through the Web. Most often consumed product were books, music, video–games and movies. The experiment took place at one of the University laboratories. In what follows, the results and main findings are briefly described.

Hypothesis 1. Considering that a majority of e–commerce users can be properly represented by a 80% (this decision may seem controversial, but clearly represents a concept of 'majority' for the purposes of this study), the null hypothesis can be formulated in terms of the proportion of individuals that provided a (consistent) bipolar interpretation to samples.

Thus, we have $H_0^1 : bipolar \geq 0.8$ and $H_1^1 : bipolar < 0.8$. With a significance level $\alpha = 0.05$ and using a z–test we have that $z = \frac{p - \pi_0}{\sqrt{\pi_0(1-\pi_0)/n}} = \frac{0.77-0.8}{\sqrt{0.8 \cdot 0.2/123}} =$ -0.766 which does not entails the rejection of H_0^1. In addition, if we count as successes users that do not adhere to bipolarity having the value 3 as midpoint, but at a higher or lower value, the proportion of bipolar interpretations grows to 0.91 which is consistent with even stronger null hypotheses.

Several linguistic hedges were used by more than one user. Table 2 details the frequencies of the most employed ones (translated from the original Spanish expressions). The significant but not completely consistent frequency (i.e. the use of the same height for different numerical ratings depending on the user) of use of a number of linguistic hedges suggests that the intensity of positive and negative polarities have not clear boundaries.

Table 2. Most frequently used hedges

hedge	frequency
very	62
rather	53
extremely (translated from the slang "super")	32
not very	12
spanish superlative	9

The second question was used to study the relation between bipolar interpretations and recommendation decisions. A simple χ^2 test between two variables, called $X = bipolar$ and $Y = negative$ respectively – with Y being the users that think that below–midpoint values should influence (negatively) the final recommendation of the item – can be used to assess such relationship, with $H_0^{1'} : \chi^2 = 0$ and $H_1^{1'} : \chi^2 > 0$. Given $\alpha = 0.05$, $\chi^2 = 10.258$, which has a significance level below 0.005 for $df = 1$, so that we can consider to have some degree of interaction between the criteria.

Results for Hypothesis 1 point out that a significant proportion of users do interpret common one–to–five rating scales (like the one used in $amazon^3$) as bipolar. Results for question 2 of hypothesis one points that bipolarity is interpreted as "negative" information influencing recommendations below average–based compensation. Both results can be considered as evidence in favor of devising bipolar approaches to recommendations, as the straightforward one studied in Hypothesis 2.

Hypothesis 2. A sample of 25 predictions from *MovieLens* were used for this part of the study, reasonably covering the domain of resulting ratings. Then, the results of the original unipolar prediction algorithm (in which $k = 1$) were put together with te results of a number of parameterized bipolar versions with $k \in \{1.25, 1.5, 1.75, 2, 5\}$. The examples were presented to the users, providing the frequencies of ratings for each value in the one to five point scale that were used to compute the predictions.

Table 3 provides the results of the study in terms of frequencies of first and second–option selection of each prediction version.

Table 3. Frequencies of preference for each of the prediction versions

	k=1 (unipolar)	k=1.25	k=1.5	k=1.75	k=2	k=5
Preferred option frequencies (o_1)	16	27	39	26	15	0
Second–best option frequencies (o_2)	19	23	28	29	22	2

Table 3 can be interpreted as a tentative degree of acceptability of bipolar interpretation intensity. Such acceptability is showed in Figure 1, in which the results from both a least–square (LS) and a fuzzy regression method [4] are depicted. The LS regression obtained the expression $a = -164.2 + 282.3 \cdot k - 93.71 \cdot k^2$, where a represents the values of $o_1 \cdot \frac{o_2}{2}$, which here is intended to represent "strength of preference" for a value of k. A fuzzy variant has been used just to try with an alternate method in which an explicit modeling of input imprecision can be used, but no significant divergences have been found. Such degree can be considered as an elicited parameter from users of the rating database, but further testing is required to assess its generality.

In any case, results evidence that negative interpretations are often considered as more appropriate than unipolar ones to a large extent, although the intensity of such interpretation is still subject to empirical adjustment.

---

^{3} http://www.amazon.com

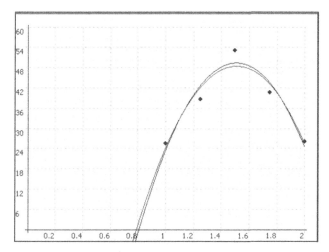

Fig. 1. Regression curves for approximate preferences on the degree of bipolarity k, where $k = 1$ represents unipolarity

4   Conclusions and Future Work

A bipolar interpretation of rating scales in the context of e–commerce entails slightly modified collaborative–filtering recommendation algorithms that are more conservative in the presence of negative ratings. A concrete study has been described in order to explore this issue and gather some initial evidence regarding the bipolar interpretation of rating scales and their perceived influence in final recommendations. Results point out that bipolarity may lead to recommendation strategies that are more consistent with the human interpretation of other's ratings. It is commonly acknowledged that the most important errors to avoid in e–commerce recommendations are *false positives* – as pointed out in [9] –, since they may lead to "angry customers". In consequence, bipolar approaches may eventually be more appropriate to reduce false positives, due to its consideration of negative ratings as inhibitors of the recommendation process.

Further studies are required to obtain a more general insight on bipolar–rating recommendations, extending both the user population and experimental setting and also covering other, more recent collaborative recommendation procedures [9]. In addition, future work should address the measure of accuracy called "*AllBut1* Mean Average Error" [1] for different values of k in existing rating databases.

Future work should also study the effect of considering bipolarity in the resulting amount of false positives generated by the recommender system, and in the concrete form of bipolar aggregation that best captures the human interpretation of positive and negative item assessment in concrete item categories and rating contexts. In the case of content–based approaches, bipolar decision operators [2] can be used to model complex situations.

References

1. Anderson, M., Ball, M., Boley, H., Greene, S., Howse, N., Lemire, D., McGrath, S. RACOFI: A Rule-Applying Collaborative Filtering System, In *Proc. IEEE/WIC COLA'03*, Halifax, Canada, October (2003).
2. Grabisch, M. and Lebreuche, C. Bi–capacities for decision making on bipolar scales. In: Proceedings of EUROFUSE Workshop on Information Systems, 185–190 (2002)
3. Herlocker, J., Konstan, J., and Riedl, J.: Explaining Collaborative Filtering Recommendations. In: Proceedings of ACM 2000 Conference on Computer Supported Cooperative Work 241–250 (2000)
4. Izyumov, B., Kalinina, E., Wagenknecht, M., Software tools for regression analysis of fuzzy data. Proceedings of 9th Zittau Fuzzy Colloquium, Zittau, Germany (2001), pp. 221-229.
5. Konstan, J., Miller, B., Maltz, D., Herlocker, J., Gordon, L., and Riedl, J.: GroupLens: Applying Collaborative Filtering to Usenet News. Communications of the ACM 40(3): 77–87 (1997)
6. Mesiarová, A., Lázaro, J. and Calvo, T.: Bipolar Aggregation Operators. In: Proceedings of the International Summer School on Aggregation Operators and their Applications, 119–122 (2003)
7. Paulson, P. and Tzanavari, A.: Combining Collaborative and Content–Based Filtering Using Conceptual Graphs. In: J.Lawry, J.G.Shanahan and A.Ralescu (eds.): Modeling with Words: Learning, Fusion, and Reasoning within a Formal Linguistic Representation Framework, LNAI 2873, Springer–Verlag Berlin Heidelberg 168–185 (2003)
8. Resnick, P., Iacovou, N., Suchak, M., Bergstrom, P. and Riedl J.: GroupLens: An open architecture for collaborative filtering of netnews. In: Proceedings of ACM 1994 Conference on Computer Supported Cooperative Work, Chapel Hill, NC: ACM, 175–186 (1994)
9. Sarwar, B. M., Karypis, G., Konstan, J. A., and Riedl, J.: Analysis of Recommender Algorithms for E-Commerce. In: Proceedings of the ACM e–Commerce 2000 Conference. 158–167 (2000)
10. Shardanand U. and Maes, P.: Social information filtering: Algorithms for automating "word of mouth". In: Proceedings of CHI'95 – Human Factors in Computing Systems, 210–217 (1995)
11. Mehling, R. A Simple Test for Measuring Intensity of Attitudes. Public Opinion Quarterly, 23, 576–578(1959)

Applying Text Mining on Electronic Messages for Competitive Intelligence*

José Palazzo M. de Oliveira[1], Stanley Loh[2], Leandro Krug Wives[3],
Rui Gureghian Scarinci[1], Daniela Musa[1], Lydia Silva[1], and Christian Zambenedetti[4]

[1] Federal University of Rio Grande do Sul – Instituto de Informática (II/UFRGS)
{palazzo,rgs,musa,lydia}@inf.ufrgs.br
[2] Catholic University of Pelotas (UCPEL) and Lutheran University of Brasil (ULBRA)
sloh@terra.com.br
[3] Centro Universitário Feevale – Instituto de Ciências Exatas e Tecnológicas (ICET/Feevale)
wives@feevale.br
[4] University of Caxias do Sul (UCS)
czambene@ucs.tche.br

Abstract. This paper presents an application of text mining to support Competitive Intelligence (CI). A case study was built using the ETO System, which enables trade-related bodies to exchange information by e-mail. As this information is available in textual formats, we used text-mining tools to support the CI process. The strategy uses domain knowledge to extract concepts from the texts. A mining tool searches for patterns in concept distributions and correlations, aiding the identification of strategic information. The main contribution of the paper is the use of an inexpensive strategy to allow a competitive advantage to Small and Medium Enterprises with minimal cost.

1 Introduction

The Internet is becoming the basic infrastructure for communication among people and companies. The Web and the e-mail system offer a large and growing collection of texts containing a huge volume of useful information. The mainstream is to take advantage of this information source to discover new and useful knowledge. Organizations can find information to infer whether a market is saturated or whether there is a niche for acting. Changes in the information along the time, for example, may indicate companies' strategies, new products being offered or old products being discontinued.

An outstanding trade data source is the Electronic Trading Opportunities (ETO) System [1]. The United Nations Trade Point Development Centre (UNTPDC) developed this system as a compensatory mechanism to the globalization processes. The ETO system provides assistance to Small and Medium Enterprises (SME), offering the same benefits that were previously only enjoyed by large organizations, enabling trade-related bodies to exchange information on a global basis, using semi-structured texts sent by e-mail. The ETO System connects many trade related bodies in more than 140 countries and generates more than 130,000 records monthly.

* This work was partially supported by CAPES, CNPq, and by research funding from the Brazilian National Program in Informatics (Decree-aw number 3800/01).

K. Bauknecht, M. Bichler, and B. Pröll (Eds.): EC-Web 2004, LNCS 3182, pp. 277–286, 2004.
© Springer-Verlag Berlin Heidelberg 2004

The use of this amount of information in an efficient way is the scope of Competitive Intelligence (CI). CI is a business activity whose goal is to provide strategic information about markets for management activities. Strategic information includes the company position in the market, its relation to other competitors and its status according to the customers' opinion and a well developed knowledge on products and services offers and demands [2]. In the current perspective of high competition among enterprises, information is the main resource for acquiring competitive advantage. CI observes who is acting (competing companies), what they are doing (products, services and strategies) and what are the opinions and feelings of the customers about these actions. This approach needs software tools to minimize the information overload.

In this paper we experimentally demonstrate the feasibility of analyzing the ETO messages using text-mining tools. The strategy is based on concepts instead of words, thus minimizing the vocabulary problem. In addition, the paper presents a mining strategy specially suited for CI processes.

2   Text Mining

Text Mining or Knowledge Discovery in Texts [3] is an emerging area for dealing with textual information. Its goal is to find unexpected and interesting patterns in textual collections. Text mining techniques can help in CI processes. The approaches of Feldman et al. [4] and Lin et al. [5], for example, uses text-mining tools for analyzing statistical distribution of terms in a textual collection of economic news. In this case, names of countries frequently appearing together in documents may indicate commercial associations between them. Similarly, Moscarola et al. [6] analyses keyword distributions in patent registries to discover strategies of competing companies. Then, most frequent words can lead to saturate markets and rare words can reveal special activities. Words that appear frequently together raise the hypothesis of special associations between themes, areas, products or companies. Watts and Porter [7] make technological forecasting through bibliometric measures. Statistics about texts are used to understand the life cycle of certain technologies. Names indicate organizations acting in a specific field and citations lead to important people or organizations (authorities in a field).

However, these techniques and tools are based on words, that is, statistical techniques are applied over terms resulting of a lexical analysis. When words are analyzed independently, the context is lost. This leads to the vocabulary problem, a problem considered for a long time. Furnas et al [9], for example, identified the vocabulary problem in vocabulary-driven interactions. As discussed in [10; 11], the language may cause semantic mistakes due to synonymy (different words for the same meaning), polysemy (the same word with many meanings), lemmas (words with the same radical) and quasi-synonyms (words related to the same subject, object or event, like "bomb" and "terrorist attack").

The strategy proposed in this paper uses a concept-based technique for discovering knowledge in texts of e-mail messages, allowing qualitative and quantitative analyses over the content of a textual collection.

Concepts belong to the extra-linguistic knowledge about the world and can be expressed by a language, and are determined by the environment, activities, and culture of the people who speak that language [12]. So, the use of concepts depends on who is doing that, for what purpose and in what context. A concept, in a short definition, may be characterized as a mental model associated to a real world entity. There are many and different approaches to express mental models. However, we are interested in a simple structure that allows us to represent real world objects, trends, events, thoughts, intentions, opinions and ideas easily and with a certain degree of quality for the discovery process. They help the user to explore, examine and understand the contents of talks, documents etc. Chen, for example, uses concepts to identify the content of comments in a brainstorming discussion [13].

We use the vector space model [10; 14] to represent concepts. So each concept is stored as a set or vector of terms. We have decided to use a non-ordered vector, assuming that all terms inside a concept description are related to each other in a same degree. The decision for this structure is to simplify classification and categorization tasks.

The approach presented here combines a categorization task with a mining task. Categorization identifies concepts in texts and mining discovers patterns by analyzing and relating concepts distributions in a collection, creating association rules. In the next section, the strategy for CI processes is presented in details.

3 A Text Mining Strategy for Competitive Intelligence

The fundament of the "light" strategy is to use a concept-based text mining approach over the ETO's messages. The main decision was to use an approach accessible to small and medium-sized enterprises in developing countries, without the need to buy expensive information retrieval software. The approach allows qualitative and quantitative analyses on the content of a textual collection. Qualitative analysis identifies concepts present in the texts and quantitative analysis extracts patterns in concepts distributions through statistical techniques. Then, comparisons help to identify different characteristics that can be used as competitive advantages. The strategy is segmented in the following steps: *pre-processing (text retrieval and data normalization), concept extraction, pattern mining, definition and execution of rules to extract relevant data for each concept,* and *evaluation and analysis of the results for CI.*

3.1 Pre-processing

This step combines data retrieval and data cleansing sub-processes. The first is used to collect (retrieve) the texts that will be used in the next steps, according to their source and type. If the quantity of documents is very large, it is possible to select only a sample of them, using statistical sampling techniques. After the documents are collected it is necessary to clean them, to exclude unnecessary information like prepositions, articles, conjunctions, adverbs and other frequently used words, plus ETO domain specific and structural words. These words are named *stop words* and they are excluded in the *stop word removal process.*

3.2 Concept Extraction

The purpose of this step is to identify concepts present in texts. However, documents do not have concepts explicitly stated, but instead they are composed of words that represent the concepts. As concepts are expressed by language structures (words and grammars), it is possible to identify concepts in texts analyzing phrases [12].

Considering that many concepts can be found in a document and that the user has specific needs, the first thing to do is to define the concepts that are relevant to him. The user must express which words and expressions indicate the presence or absence of each concept he is interested to extract from the System. To help the user in this process, it is necessary to analyze some ETO that belong to the context of the user's business and look for the most frequent words of a document or a set of documents.

Combining this analysis with clustering techniques [15], which are able to identify clusters of co-related documents, it is possible to identify the most relevant words to define a concept. The idea is that documents belonging to the same cluster have the maximum probability of having the same concept(s). Thus, their words have also a high probability of belonging to the same concept(s). A cluster concept can be identified by analyzing the most frequent words in the cluster centroid (a set of the most frequent words belonging to all documents in the cluster). The other words in the centroid can be used as concept descriptors.

After the concepts are identified they can be expressed and modeled by rules. Rules combine positive and negative words that indicate the presence or the absence of concepts in individual phrases. If the concept is present more than once in a text, the total counting is used to define an associative degree between the text and the concept, indicating how much a concept is referred by a text.

3.3 Pattern Mining

The goal of this step is to find interesting patterns in concepts distributions inside a collection or sub-collection. A used technique is the concept distribution listing, which analyses concept distributions in a group of texts. A software tool counts the number of texts where each concept is present, generating a vector (the centroid) of concepts and their frequencies inside the group. This technique allows finding what dominant themes exist in a group of texts. Also we can compare one centroid to another to find common concepts in different groups or to find variations in distributions of a certain concept from one group to another. Other possible usage is to find differences between groups, that is, concepts present in only one group (exclusive concepts).

Another used technique is association, which discovers associations between concepts and expresses these findings as rules in the format $X \rightarrow Y$ (X may be a set of concepts or a unique one, and Y is a unique concept). The rule means "if X is present in a text, then Y is present with a certain confidence and a certain support". Following the definitions of [5] and [8], confidence is the proportion of texts that have X AND Y compared to the number of texts that have only X, and support is the proportion of texts that have X AND Y compared to all texts in the collection. Confidence is similar to the conditional probability (if X is present, so there is a certain probability of Y being present too). This allows predicting the presence of a concept according to the presence of another one.

3.4 Rules to Extract Relevant Data Associated with Concepts

Each message belonging to the concept(s) selected by the user may contain much relevant information. In this case, the user must specify which information he wants or needs for each concept chosen. So, each concept may have specific information to be extracted. Let's consider an example: imagine the user needs to know the "price" and the "battery" type of all offers related to "notebook computers". This necessity of information is specific to this particular concept. When this concept is identified in a message this information should be extracted. The user may have different needs of information for different concepts. For another concept like "Manufacturer", for example, the need would be "Address", (maybe) "Product" and "Phone". More details on this approach may be found in [16].

The creation of rules for extracting different types of information for each concept is the central point to the success of the extraction process. The rules must be defined and constructed by the user with the aid of an expert in the field of his business (probably himself). After the identification of association of words is performed, the user must examine the results looking for words or concepts associated to the concept he is interested in. If he is interested in "laptops", for example, he should look for associations like: *Laptop → price (35%)* and *Laptop → weight (100%)*.

The idea behind this method is that associations that have high support indicate that almost all documents within the concept chosen have the associated information and this information may be important. Of course this is only a technique used to aid the rules construction process. The expert must do the final decision and refinement.

It is important to state clearly that these rules, beyond retrieving the most important and relevant information to the user, according to the context of the message (its concepts), allow the user to read only the subset of messages considered to be related to the concepts of interest. This is extremely interesting in case the number of messages is very high. In this case, only the most important information of each message is extracted and the user obtains a summary or a report of the information received [17].

3.5 Analysis of the Results for CI

In the competitive intelligence arena the concept analysis allows identifying players within a market, products, services, their characteristics, benefits, and events of the real world, vendors' strategies, opinions of people and media companies. The associative technique is useful to find strong correlations between themes, for example: "people complaining about certain product always refer to a special problem".

A textual collection can be divided in many sub-collections according to various conditions. For example, groups of texts can be composed according to *different time periods, the presence of specific words* or *the presence of specific concepts*.

This segmentation helps to compare strategies looking for common themes or differences (saturated markets, niches of market, most popular products, and new services). Analyzing sub-collections composed by companies Web sites allows understanding how themes are being dealt by each company, which themes are more important for each one, how different is this degree of importance, which themes are common to many companies, and which ones are exclusive of only one company. If sub-collections represent time slices, variations in a concept distribution can lead to changes in strategic plans or goals (new companies or products, themes losing importance, discontinuing services, changes in the competitors' marketing strategy).

4 Case Study

The evaluation protocol was conceived taking into account the methodology stated in the previous sections. Its objective was to validate the proposed methods and approaches. In this section we detail how each step described above was conducted with data acquired from the ETO System.

4.1 Pre-processing

In this experiment we retrieved 2101 e-mail messages sent by the ETO System. The collection was composed basically of business opportunities containing offers (product's information and sales catalogs). Each message has a unique content. All stop words and numbers where removed.

4.2 Concept Extraction

Some of the messages retrieved from the ETO System have been processed to discover the most frequent subjects. Such processing was executed both manually (checking each message subject field) and automatically with the aid of automated clustering algorithms for evaluation purposes. Both approaches identified "computer" as the area of the majority of the ETO. This concept (area) was selected, so we could test our approach. Then, after the methodology efficiency was evaluated, other least frequent subjects were analyzed.

The next step consisted of the identification and definition of relevant concepts and terms associated with the most frequently subjects discovered in the previous steps. As previously stated a concept is defined by a set of terms. In this step, we checked the messages looking for the frequency of terms in all documents where the term "computer" appeared (91 from the set of 2101 documents). Then the most frequent words were used to compose the "computer" concept. Table 1 shows some of the terms found.

Table 1. Selection of the list of terms present within documents containing the word "computer".

Term (Word)	Weight
Computer	1.0
Laptop	1.0
Notebook	1.0
Celeron	0.5
Celleron	0.2
MHZ	0.5
Pentium	0.8
MMX	0.5
PII	0.5
PIII	0.5
CPU	0.8

The table content produces the following rule:

```
Computer ← +computer (1), +laptop (1), +notebook (1),
        +celeron(0.5), +celleron (0.2), +Mhz (0.5),
        +Pentium(0.8), +PII(0.5), +PIII (0.5), +CPU (0.8)
```

It is possible to see in this list that any misspelling errors can be taken into account (e.g. celleron). If the expert identifies that a significant amount of documents contains this error. The expert must aggregate the misspelling errors to reach a correct frequency evaluation.

After the procedure explained in section two, the messages associated with the "computer" concept were retrieved. The processing of the whole set of words allows the analyst to reach a better knowledge about the concept. Perhaps new visions will be discovered by this inspection. The next paragraph contains an excerpt of the list of words used in the messages associated with the "computer" concept. This list was constructed using the methodology described in section two (proposed by [18]).

```
Computer ← +notebook (1), +laptop (1), +computer (1),
    +VGA (1), +MMX (1), +PCE (1), +CD-ROM (1), +CD-RW
    (1), +DVD-ROM (0.5), +LCD (1), +monitor (1),
    +memory (1), +intel (1), +celeron (1), +MHZ
    (0.5), +KB (0.5), +L2 (0.5), +PPGA (0.5), +CPU
    (1), +MB (1), +syncdram (1), +PCI (1)...
```

In the concept above there is a value associated to each term. This value is the weight of the term in the concept. The weight is the probability of the concept to be identified just by the presence of this term (weights are rated from 0 to 1). We performed a clustering technique in the result set in order to understand the "computer" concept.

The clustering process, a variation of the Stars algorithm described by [19], identified 25 clusters. Each cluster displayed significant words related to the ones already present in the concept. For example, one group contained messages related to the term "notebook", and some of the words present in its centroid appeared relevant to this context (e.g. notebook, laptop, IBM, Dell, and Compaq). This technique could be used to create new sub-concepts associated to the "computer" concept (e.g. "notebooks", "desktops", "hardware", "software", "processors", "storage" etc).

Through association analysis of concepts some hints of the most relevant information of each concept could be discovered and many associations were found. Among them we have selected only the ones related to the words that appeared in the concept definition. Table 2 shows some of the associations found.

Table 2. Identified Associations.

Computer	Laptop	Notebook
computer → SDRAM (287)	Laptop → MB (239)	Notebook → SDRAM (334)
computer → MB (263)	Laptop → Computer (55)	Notebook → MB (247)
computer → PC (256)	Laptop → notebook (36)	Notebook → PC (234)
computer → software (100)	Laptop → equipment (42)	Notebook → card (60)
computer → keyboard (79)	Laptop → monitor (35)	Notebook → MHZ (49)
computer → Pentium (74)	Laptop → IBM (24)	
computer → laptop (69)	Laptop → parts (19)	
computer → desktop (63)	Laptop → price (18)	
computer → notebook (62)		

Analyzing the association rules, it is possible to discover which words are correlated to other words. The numbers between brackets indicate the number of co-occurrences in the full collection. The Table shows that in the "computer" concept the most relevant information to be extracted is the configuration of the computer (amount of memory and the speed of the computer) as the high co-occurrence indicates.

4.3 Rules to Extract Relevant Data Associated with Each Concept

Based on the association rules found in the previous step, it is possible to identify the most relevant information to be extracted on each concept. In supplement, the expertise and interest of the decision maker will adjust the rules. A support toll, named SES [20], was developed to help the rules definition.

The extraction tool uses a set of rules with the following syntax:

```
If <condition> then <action> else <action> end
```

Each word of each input file is tested against the set of defined rules. If a rule is held then the action it contains is executed and part of the file is extracted. The condition of a rule is expressed in terms of searching conditions and verification conditions. When a searching condition is true, then its verification conditions are tested. The body of a searching condition consists of specified values of some parameters (i.e. Term, Format, Begin, End, and Type).

The first rules to be modeled are the ones relative to the producer of the message: the origin, the name, his intentions and ways of contact. To extract this information the rules incorporate conditions on the mandatory e-mail header fields. For example, the rule *if searchString(From,FmFree,1,5) and verifyChar(:, FmFree,1,1,Word,Aft) then Copy(1,Line,Aft,Nalt,FROM)*, states that if the pattern "From:" occurs in any of the first 5 lines of the text, then all the line where it is found must be extracted. Some other rules like that were modeled to search for other "hint terms" which could indicate the presence of relevant information.

4.4 Evaluation and Analysis of the Results

The patterns discovered in the mining step enable users to discover the dominant themes (most frequent) and those that receive less attention (least frequent). The statistical distribution analysis leads to many conclusions about trends in the market, like how important certain topics are, how active a market is and which companies are acting in a specific segment.

The case and the experiments presented in this paper help to demonstrate how the strategy can help the CI process. However, some cautions should be taken when using the strategy. The textual collection must be a representative sample of the application domain. Since analysis is made on the selected texts, the information available in the collection is supposed to be complete and true.

5 Concluding Remarks

This paper presented a text mining strategy for supporting CI processes. The strategy analyses textual information available in e-mail messages of the ETO and discovers concepts present. As concepts represent real world entities and events, it is possible to infer how companies within a market are acting. The identification of concepts in the textual collection needs the work of an expert with support of software tools to perform this activity. Attention is required in order not to leave out important concepts. The same attention is necessary in defining the rules extraction. Other text mining tools, such as a lexical analyzer, are important for identifying false hits and missing concepts. A good point is that some concepts appear in different applications with the same extraction rules, allowing part of them to be reused.

The main advantage of the proposed strategy is to allow the analysis of huge volumes of semi-structured texts, where manual analysis is impossible or difficult due to the data volume and time limitations. With the proposed strategy, people can get a summary of the main themes presented in huge volume of electronic textual data without having to read all the texts. The strategy takes advantage of textual information publicly available on the Internet. As more and more information is being freely published on the Internet and Web as unstructured texts, companies can perform CI processes with less cost and reduced efforts.

References

1. UNTPDC. Electronic Trading Opportunities (ETO) System, United Nations Trade Point Development Center, UNTPDC. http://www.wtpfed.org. Last Access Date: Sep, 2002.
2. Zanasi, A. Competitive Intelligence through data mining public sources. Competitive Intelligence Review, v.9, n.1, 1998.
3. Tan, Ah-Hwee. Text mining: the state of the art and the challenges. Pacific-Asia Workshop on Knowledge Discovery from Advanced Databases, Beijing, 1999.
4. Feldman, R. et al. Text mining at the term level. The 2nd European Symposium on Principles of Data Mining and Knowledge Discovery. Lecture Notes in Computer Science Vol. 1510, Springer-Verlag, 1998.
5. Lin, Shian-Hua et al. Extracting classification knowledge of Internet documents with mining term associations: a semantic approach. ACM-SIGIR Conference on Research and Development in Information Retrieval, Melbourne, 1998.
6. Moscarola, J. et al. Technology watch via textual data analysis. Note de Recherche n° 98-14, Université de Savoie. July 1998.
7. Watts, R. J.; Porter, A. L. Innovation forecasting. Technological Forecasting and Social Change, v.56, 1997.
8. Garofalakis, M. N. et al. Data mining and the web: past, present and future. ACM Workshop on Web Information and Data Management, Kansas City, 1999.
9. Furnas, G. W. et al. The Vocabulary Problem in Human-System Communication. Communications of the ACM, v. 30, n. 11, p. 964-971.
10. Chen, H. et al. (1994). Automatic concept classification of text from electronic meetings. Communications of the ACM, v.37, n.10, 1994.
11. Chen, H. et al. A concept space approach to addressing the vocabulary problem in scientific information retrieval: an experiment on the worm community system. Journal of the American Society for Information Science, v.48, n.1, January 1997.
12. Sowa, J. F. Knowledge representation: logical, philosophical, and computational foundations. Brooks/Cole Publishing Co., Pacific Grove, CA, 2000.
13. Chen, H. The vocabulary problem in collaboration. IEEE Computer, v.27, n.5, 1994.
14. Salton, G.; McGill, M. J. Introduction to modern information retrieval. McGraw-Hill, 1983.
15. Aldenderver, M. S.; Blashfield, R. K. Cluster Analysis. Sage Publications Inc: London, 1984.
16. Loh, S. et al., Concept-based knowledge discovery in texts extracted from the web, ACM SIGKDD Explorations, v.2, n.1, pp.29-39, June 2000.
17. Loh, S; Oliveira, J. P. M. de; Gameiro, M. A. Knowledge Discovery in Texts for Constructing Decision Support Systems. Applied Intelligence, New York, NY, USA, v. 18, n. 3, p. 357-366, 2003.

18. Loh, S.; Oliveira, J. P. M. de; Gastal, F. L. Knowledge Discovery in Textual Documentation: qualitative and quantitative analysis. Journal of Documentation, London, v. 57, n. 5, p. 577-590, 2001.
19. Korfhage, R. R.; Information Retrieval and Storage. John Wiley & Sons. 1997.
20. Zambenedetti, C. Extraction of Information on text databases. Master thesis, PPGC UFRGS, 2002. (in Portuguese).

Web Page Ranking Based on Events

Ajay Gupta, Manish Bhide, and Mukesh Mohania

IBM India Research Laboratory,
Block-1 IIT Delhi, Hauz Khas, New Delhi-110016
{agupta,abmanish,mkmukesh}@in.ibm.com

Abstract. Search results of web search engines are displayed according to their ranking function, which is a function of the in-links and the out-links of the web page. Users are generally overwhelmed by the thousands of results retrieved by the search engine, few of which are useful. Most of the search engine users are interested in the latest information about the searched keywords. Such pages containing the latest information about an event (or incident) are not always ranked high by the search engines due to the lack of sufficient in-links pointing to these web pages. For example, if a search query "DaWaK" is given to Google, the users are generally interested in the latest information i.e., the home page of DaWaK 2004 conference, which is not ranked in the top 10 results returned by Google. In this paper we address the problem of ranking the web pages based on events (or incidents) related to the searched keywords. We provide a method for finding patterns that constitute events in the search results returned by a conventional search engine and then rank the web pages based on these event patterns. We also describe a mechanism whereby our technique can be used inside the ranking function of a conventional search engine such as Google. We provide experimental results that validate the efficiency and use of our technique in capturing the user intentions.

1 Introduction

Many a times when a user is searching for information about events that are repeatable in nature, the user is interested in information about the latest events. Search engines today, cannot capture these user intentions and the results returned by the search engine are oblivious of this requirement of the user. The main reason for this is that the ranking functions of the search engines depends on the in-links and out-links of the web pages and the web page that has the latest information is generally not pointed to by many other web pages. Further, the ranking function of the search engines does not consider the semantic similarity between web pages and the user query while ranking. Hence there is a need to identify the users' intentions while ranking the web pages and displaying them to the user. In the paper, we outline a technique that is able to capture such user intentions, when the user is interested in searching information about recurring events. Our technique ranks the web pages based on the events related to the searched keywords. We make use of the search results of a conventional search engine (like Google) and discover patterns that constitute a periodic event in these search result. We then re-rank these results, based on discovered patterns and their relevance to the searched keywords.

K. Bauknecht, M. Bichler, and B. Pröll (Eds.): EC-Web 2004, LNCS 3182, pp. 287–295, 2004.
© Springer-Verlag Berlin Heidelberg 2004

1.1 Related Work

There has been lot of work in improving the web search results. A meta-search agent based methodology has been proposed in [3] that captures the semantics of a user's search intent, transforms the semantic query into target queries for existing search engines, and ranks resulting page hits according to a user-specified weighted-rating scheme. In [2], the authors have described a meta-search architecture that allows users to provide preferences in the form of an information need category. This extra information is used to direct the search process, providing more valuable results than by considering only the query. The difference in these approaches and the one proposed in this paper is that the former approaches improve the search results based on some extra user-specified information, where as our approach does not require any extra information from the user. [4,5,6] organize the search results into hierarchical categories whereas [7,8] organize search results into clusters. However all of these approaches do not have a concept of events and recentness of information.

1.2 Contributions

In this paper, we focus on displaying the search results in accordance with the users' intentions, when the user is interested in information about recurring events. We address the following important problems:
1) How to find the user intentions when the user is searching for information related to a recurring event?
2) How to find the web pages that contain information about recurring events?
3) How to rank the web-pages based on their relevance to the recurring event and based on the semantic similarity of web-pages to the searched keywords?

We have laid out the rest of the paper as follows. In the next section, we give an overview of our technique when it is implemented outside a conventional search engine. Section 3 gives an outline of our algorithm that can be implemented inside a search engine, thereby making the process faster. The performance of our technique is shown in section 4 and we conclude the paper in section 4.

2 Architecture of the System

Our technique can be implemented both inside as well as outside a conventional search engine. This section gives a brief overview of the tool when it is implemented outside a conventional search engine. At a high level, our technique tries to identify web pages that constitute a *pattern* related to the searched keywords. For e.g., if the user query is "DaWaK" then there will be a set of pages that will have "DaWaK 2002", "DaWaK 2003", "DaWaK 2004" etc. in the title of the web page. We identify such web pages and rank them higher as the user is generally interested in latest information which will be part of such a pattern. Figure 1 shows the architecture of our system when it is implemented outside a conventional search engine. The details of the architecture are given below:
1) The input to the system is the user query (i.e. keywords). In this technique we re-rank the search results based on the user intentions. To get the relevant web-pages related to the searched keywords, the user query is sent to a conventional search engine like Google. The results (URL's) returned by the search engine along with their snippet are sent to the Query Characterizer.

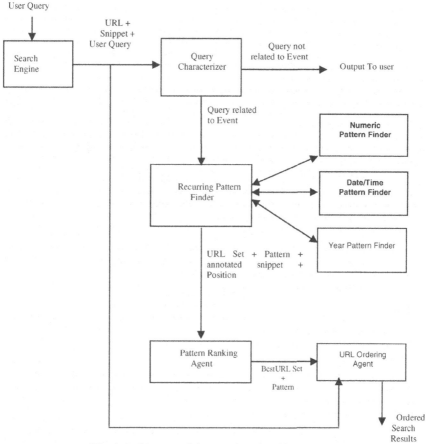

Fig. 1. Architecture of the event based ranking system.

2) The Query Characterizer is used to avoid invoking the event based ranking system when the user is not interested in information about a recurring event. For example when the user searches for the keywords "DaWaK 2004", there is no need to find any patterns, as the user is interested in a specific event. Based on the user query, the query characterizer characterizes the query into one of the following two categories: Query related to the recurring events and query that does not have a recurring event associated with it i.e., a point query. In order to identify a point query, the query characterizer can check for presence of keywords in the user query, which can be a part of a pattern. For e.g. in the above case, the year 2004 appeared in the searched keywords. 2004 can be a part of a year pattern (for e.g. DaWaK 2003, DaWaK 2004…). If any such keywords that can be a part of a pattern are present in the searched keywords then the system learns that the user is interested in a point query and the results returned by the search engine are directly returned to the user.

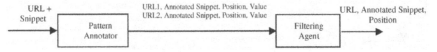

Fig. 2. Architecture of Pattern Finder.

3) If the Query Characterizer identifies that the user query is not a point query, then the URL along with their snippets are sent to the recurring pattern finder. The recurring pattern finder is responsible for finding those set of web pages (from the input set of web-pages), which contain information about the recurring event. Different kinds of pattern finders such as numeric pattern finders, alphanumeric pattern finders, Data/Time pattern finders etc., can be plugged into this component. The recurring pattern finder sends the URL's along with the snippet to each of the registered pattern finders. The pattern finders return those sets of URL that satisfy the pattern along with the information about the pattern. Generally only one set of pattern will be present in a search result. However if multiple sets of patterns are present in the result, then these patterns along with the member URL's are sent to the Pattern Ranking agent. There can be multiple ways in which the pattern finders can be implemented. One approach to find a pattern is to find the text preceding or following the searched key words in the web pages. If the searched key words are related to a recurring pattern then the pattern is generally present in the words immediately preceding or following the searched keywords in the web pages.

The architecture of a generic pattern finder is shown in Figure 2. The input to the pattern finder is the output given by the search engine i.e. the URL and the snippet. The first component is the pattern annotator, which can be of different types such as date annotator, number annotator etc [9]. Depending on the type of the annotator, the annotator annotates the dates, number etc. present in the snippet and outputs only those URL's that have an annotation. The annotator also outputs the position at which the annotation is found in each page i.e. either the snippet or the title. This information is given to the filtering agent. Based on the annotated text, its position and the user search keywords, the filtering agent identifies if there is a pattern such as DaWaK 2001, DaWaK 2002 etc. in the set of URL's returned by the pattern annotater. If the annotator returns no URL, then the pattern is not present in the search results. If a pattern appears in the title of the web page then it has much higher weight than a pattern that is found in the snippet. Consider an example where the user is searching for "DaWaK". The user is interested in the web pages of DaWaK conferences, which will have the keyword DaWaK in the title of the page. However in this case, a date pattern finder will also return pages that have DaWaK in the body of the web page. This set of web pages might include web pages of people who have published papers in DaWaK. The user intention generally is not in viewing such web pages. Hence if there is a set of web pages, which have a pattern (such as DaWaK 2001, DaWaK 2002 etc.) in the title, then such a pattern has much higher value than the other patterns. However if the number of web pages having a pattern in the title is very small as compared to the web pages that have a pattern in the body, then the set of web pages that have a pattern in the body is the right pattern. To find the correct pattern a weight is assigned to the patterns. Let the number of web pages having a pattern in the title be M, and those having a pattern in the body be N. A heuristic to find the right pattern is to compare $(k*M)$ and N, where k is the weight assigned to the pattern occurring in the title. If (k*M) > N, then the pattern is formed in M web pages, else in the N web pages. The set of URL's that form the pattern along with the position of the pattern is the output by the filtering agent.

4) As mentioned earlier, the output of the Recurring pattern finder is given to the Pattern Ranking Agent. Given a set of patterns, the Pattern Ranker is responsible for finding the best pattern that captures the users' intentions. The search results might contain some noise patterns and the pattern-ranking agent filters out these noise patterns and finds the best pattern. Based on the characteristics of the pattern such as the position of the recurring information in the web page etc., the Pattern ranking agent assigns a rank to the pattern. For example if the pattern 5th, 6th etc is appearing closely (either immediately preceding or following) the searched key word, then this pattern will have a higher rank than a pattern 2003, 2005 which might be appearing in the body of the web page.

5) The final component of the system is the URL ordering agent. This component is responsible for sorting the results in the correct order based on the presence or absence of the recurring pattern and displaying it to the user. The Pattern ranking agent gives those URL that satisfy the pattern with the highest rank i.e., if multiple patterns are found, then the Pattern ranking agent ranks these patterns and returns those URL's that constitute the highest ranked pattern. This URL set is not the complete set returned by the search engine. Hence the URL ordering agent merges this set with the rest of the URL's that don't satisfy any pattern. The agent obtains the remaining set of URL's directly from the search engine. Using the URL as a key, the agent identifies those web pages that are not present in the pattern and merges the two sets. Based on the pattern that is identified in the search results, the agent orders the URL's, with the web site that has information about the latest event being ranked the highest. There are various options for ranking of these web pages. For example, one possible ordering mechanism could be that the web pages that are part of the pattern being ranked the highest (with the web page having the latest information being the first in the list) and the rest of the URL's (that are not a part of the pattern) being displayed after the web pages that form the pattern. Another ordering mechanism could be that the URL's satisfying the patterns being moved to the position at which the first event of the pattern was ranked by the conventional search engine. The re-ranked web-pages are returned to the user.

Thus in this technique, we identify the pattern (related to year, numbers etc.) present in the search results of a conventional search engine and then re-rank the web-pages based on the pattern.

3 Alternative Architecture

Our technique can also be implemented inside a conventional search engine. In this mechanism the ranking function of the search engine will incorporate functionality to capture the similarity between web pages (i.e. to identify if the web pages contain different events or versions of the same information) and rank them accordingly. We outline below how the architecture of Google search engine can be enhanced to make use of our technique to rank the web pages.

For ranking the web-pages, Google maintains a hitlist, which includes position, font, and capitalization information for every word in the document. Additionally, they also factor in hits from anchor text and the PageRank of the document while ranking the document. Combining all of this information into a rank is difficult. Google's ranking function is designed such that no particular factor can have too much influence. In order to rank a document with a single word query, Google looks at that document's hit list for that word. Google considers each hit to be one of several different types (title, anchor, URL, plain text large font, plain text small font, ...), each of which has its own type-weight. The type-weights make up a vector indexed by type. Google counts the number of hits of each type in the hit list. Then every count is converted into a count-weight. Count-weights increase linearly with counts at first but quickly taper off so that more than a certain count will not help. Google then takes the dot product of the vector of count-weights with the vector of type-weights to compute an IR score for the document. Finally, the IR score is combined with PageRank to give a final rank to the document.

For a multi-word search, the situation is more complicated. In this case multiple hit lists must be scanned through at once so that hits occurring close together in a document are weighted higher than hits occurring far apart. The hits from the multiple hit lists are matched up so that nearby hits are matched together. For every matched set of hits, a proximity is computed. The proximity is based on how far apart the hits are in the document (or anchor) but is classified into 10 different value "bins" ranging from a phrase match to "not even close". Counts are computed not only for every type of hit but for every type and proximity. Every type and proximity pair has a type-prox-weight. The counts are converted into count-weights and we take the dot product of the count-weights and the type-prox-weights to compute an IR score. For the details of this algorithm consult [1].

3.1 Changes to the Ranking System

In order to incorporate the information about recurring events, the pages wont be ranked as in [1]. Instead of ranking the web page, the web pages that have all the searched keywords are collected. This set of web pages is then given to the recurring pattern finder module. Based on the pattern that is found, the ranking of the page is changed. While ranking the web pages we consider an additional kind of hit, which will be a hit for the keyword along with information about recurring event. The type weight associated with such a kind of hit (i.e., a hit which has information about recurring event) will be much larger than the type weights for the rest of the types. The count weight of such a type won't be large as the pattern will not be present many times in the web page. Hence if this type is to make an impact in the overall rank, then the value of the count weight should be large enough. Hence in case of this recurring event type, the count weight is proportional to the time of occurrence of the event. If the event is the latest then the count weight associated with the type will be very large and at the same time if the event is not recent then the count weight will be small. We will also have to consider the proximity of the pattern with the search keywords while ranking. The proximity will be factored into the type weight of the recurring pattern. Using this technique the overall rank of the page is computed using the ranking algorithm. This kind of ranking will take into consideration the semantic information about the web pages and it will rank those web pages that have information about the recent events much higher than the ranking of a conventional search engine.

Fig. 3. Search Results returned by Google.

4 Performance

We implemented a prototype of out technique that uses the search results returned by Google. The prototype identifies the recurring events related web pages based on the presence of any form of date or year occurring in the title or the snippet of the search results. The prototype makes use of a date pattern annotator that annotates any form of date appearing in the snippet or the title of the web page. We have built our own custom annotator that identifies any form of date appearing in the input text. Once all the web pages that have any form of dates have been tagged, the filtering agent tries to identify a symmetric pattern in the occurrence of these dates. The filtering agent uses the annotations that are present within a fixed threshold of the searched keywords in the search results. For e.g., if the user query is DaWaK, then the filtering agent will only use those annotations (of years, dates etc.) that are appearing within a fixed distance of 10 words from the word DaWaK in the snippets returned by Google. We give more preference to the pattern appearing in the title of the web page. The architecture of our date pattern finder is as shown in figure 2. The pattern finder uses the first 100 search results returned by Google to search for web pages that formed the pattern. The prototype uses the snippet and the title returned by Google to find the patterns.

The results returned by our prototype are shown in the Figure 4. Figure 3 shows the search results returned by Google. The important point to note in this search result is that the web page having information about the latest event[1] (i.e. DAWAK 2003) is

---

[1] This snapshot was taken in 2003 when the web page of DaWaK 2004 was not present.

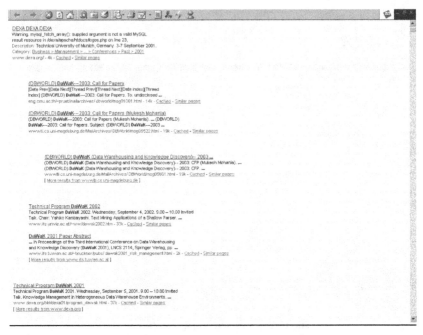

Fig. 4. Results returned by our prototype[1].

appearing at position 14. Generally this will be present on the second page of search results of Google and the user will have to evaluate the first 10 results and then ask for more results. On the other hand, as is evident from Figure 4, the web page having the latest information is second in the search results returned by our prototype. Our prototype was able to identify the pattern in the search results returned by Google and it ranked the results based on the order of occurrence of the event. The example given about clearly outlines the efficiency of our technique. As mentioned earlier, the ordering mechanism in our prototype was that the web pages forming a pattern were moved to the first position given by Google to the any web page that belongs to the pattern. In this example the second web page is part of the pattern. Hence the entire pattern was moved to the second location.

The time taken by the prototype is about 2 seconds for the entire process (of annotation, sorting etc.) when it evaluates 100 search results. This overhead can be further reduced if the system is implemented inside a conventional search engine. The system is able to discern the correct patterns related to conferences, recurring events such as DaWaK, VLDB, world cup, Olympics etc, which were ranked very low by Google.

5   Conclusion and Future Work

Capturing the user intention in a search engine is a difficult task. In this paper we have presented a technique wherein the user intention can be captured when the user is searching for information related to a recurring event. We have outlined two techniques which can be used either inside the ranking function of a search engine, or can be used to re-rank the web pages returned by a conventional search engine. We have introduced the notion of a new type weight (while ranking) which accounts for the web page having information about the recurring event. We have also outlined an architecture which can re-rank the web page based on the presence of information related to the recurring event. Our experimental results show that the technique is successful in capturing the user intention and displaying the search results in the right order. Implementing the technique inside a conventional search engine is left as future work.

References

1. S Brin and L Page, *The Anatomy of a search Engine*, http://www-db.stanford.edu/~backrub/google.html
2. E. J. Glover, S. Lowrence, M.D. Gordon, W. P. Birmingham, and C. L. Giles, *Web Search – Your Way,* Communications of the ACM, 44(12): 97-102, December 2001.
3. L. Kerschberg, W. Kim, and A. Scime, *Intelligent Web Search via Personalizable Meta-Search Agents,* International Conference on Ontologies, Databases and Applications of Semantics (ODBASE), 1345-1358, 2002.
4. H. Chen and S. Dumais, *Bringing Order to the Web: Automatically Categorizing Search Results*, CHI 2000 conference on Human factors in computing systems, Hague Netherlands, 2000.
5. Allen, R.B., *Two digital library interfaces that exploit hierarchical structure*, DAG95: Electronic Publishing and Information Superhighway, 1995.
6. Pratt, W., *Dynamic organization of search results using the UMLS*, American Medical Association Fall Symposium, 1997.
7. Zamir, O, and Etzioni, O, *Grouper: A dynamic clustering interface to web search results*. WWW8 Toronto, Canada, May 1999.
8. Zamir, O, and Etzioni, O, *Web Document Clustering: A feasibility Demonstration*. 19th International ACM SIGIR conference on Research and Development in Information Retrieval, 1998.
9. D. Gruhl, L. Chavet, D. Gibson, J. Meyer, P. Pattanayak, A. Tomkins, and J. Zien, "How to build a WebFountain: An architecture for very large scale text analytics" in IBM Systems Journal, Volume 43.

A Personalized Offer Presentation Scheme
for Retail In-Store Applications

Yew-Huey Liu, Jih-Shyr Yih, and Trieu C. Chieu

IBM T. J. Watson Research Center,
P.O.Box 704,
Hawthorne, NY 10532
{yhliu,jyih,tchieu}@us.ibm.com

Abstract. Retailers are constantly seeking new innovations to improve people's shopping experience in order to deliver greater consumer and business values. One key objective is to keep the shoppers internet-connected for seamless and informed shopping, and be offered with timely and relevant shopping ideas. Complementing the existing Point-Of-Sale (POS) system, a new retail in-store server supporting personal mobile devices or kiosks is emerging in the retail chains towards the objective. This paper introduces such an in-store server and its role in the overall retail architecture, with the main focus placed on the in-store offer presentation scheme for personalizable service. A lightweight keyword-based rule engine is proposed for selecting offers. A detailed rule processing flow and an efficient implementation for the engine are described. For the ease of reviewing presented offers on a limited display space of a wireless shopping device, an offers layout method which organizes presented offers with individual items is also suggested. The in-store server can lead to seamless multi-channel collaborative shopping.

1 Introduction

Since 1995, we have seen the explosion of B2C electronic commerce. For an enduring web store, exemplified and excelled by Amazon, it goes beyond the usual catalog browsing and order entry, and generates "stickiness" of the site by adding rich information such as latest sales, personalized promotions and consumer tips. However, despite the innovations, the percentage of retail GDP contributed by web-hosted e-commerce is still projected to be in the lower single digits for this decade. The majority of the retail commerce still takes place inside the "brick-and-mortar" branches, where there are plenty of opportunities in innovating as the in-store channel and in collaborating with other channels.

It is a common practice among retailers to use loyalty schemes to encourage purchases by offering points or cash rewards. Retailers also get to collect individual purchase history via such loyalty schemes. However, shoppers are usually anonymous in the store until they reach the checkout counter, where they identify themselves as loyalty customer, and then were offered coupons for future use. Statistics show that a low percentage of such coupons issued in this way are ever redeemed, reflecting the inconvenience of collecting and carrying paper coupons and the low degree of relevance to many shoppers. Additionally, there is no chance to influence or assist the customers' in-store shopping in real-time, other than with generic point-of-promotion displays, which are non-personalized and will be irrelevant to most shoppers.

K. Bauknecht, M. Bichler, and B. Pröll (Eds.): EC-Web 2004, LNCS 3182, pp. 296–304, 2004.

To catch up with shopper expectation, a small subset of retailers are actively engaging in testing a variety of advanced in-store techniques with a new type of in-store commerce server [1]. Figure 1 shows an example of such server introduced by IBM. This in-store commerce server complements the existing POS system and supports a variety of wireless personal mobile devices and kiosks. The in-store server is also used as an integration platform to synchronize information with other channels and enterprise applications, for the delivery of real-time product information, personalized promotions and consistent shopping experience to shoppers at every touch point. The new server investment is supposed to be offset by shoppers' additional purchases through the personalized promotions.

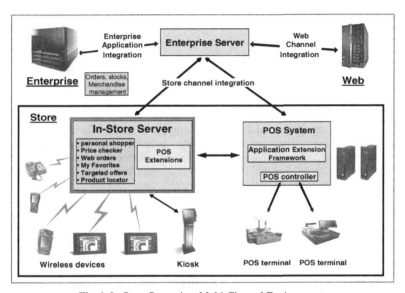

Fig. 1. In-Store Server in a Multi-Channel Environment

Delivery of personalized promotions to shoppers is not a new concept. *Recommender* systems [2] utilizing predicate-based rules, derived from historical or demographic information corresponding to shopper groups, have been deployed in enterprise web sites. There are a number of special considerations that a retailer needs to consider in constructing a recommender system for in-store offer presentation. For examples: 1) A store branch does not have a dedicated IT department for server operations and database maintenance, and can only afford a low-end, personal-computer based in-store server, which has to handle about 200 concurrent shopping sessions. The in-store offer presentation engine needs to be light weight and in small footprint, to meet the CPU and memory usage requirements. 2) There are unique in-store only characteristics such as shopper location and movement within the store. 3) The anticipated limited display size of wireless shopping devices also requires special design considerations for offer layout scheme. 4) Finally, there are always ease-of-use challenges to the programming of offer presentation rules by the retail operators, who don't want to deal with over complex languages.

To address these issues, this paper describes a practical implementation of an intelligent in-store server with an efficient keyword-based offer presentation engine to provide personalized offers to shoppers via personal mobile devices. We will illustrate how the new services are designed to enhance in-store shopping experience with personalized real-time shopping information and ideas, and touch on how the experience can be continued across other channels.

This paper is organized as follows: Section 2 presents an offer presentation engine design. We will identify various shopper behaviors as system input; describe a set of keyword-based rules and the construction of the offer presentation engine. A novel layout scheme for organizing offers with respect to shopping cart contents is presented in Section 3. Finally, Section 4 concludes the paper with the scenarios of seamless multi-channel collaborative shopping.

2   In-Store Personalized Offer Presentation

In-Store offer personalization requires implicitly or explicitly collecting shopper information and leveraging that knowledge to decide what information to present to shoppers and how to present it. Since late 1990s, the world-wide web and the emergence of e-commerce have led to the development of personalization system and recommender systems. There are two main approaches that are used in delivery of personalized information: rule based approaches and collaboration filtering [3].

Rule-base personalization involved extensive domain knowledge setup, which can be difficult to manage, and is particularly so with a large product catalog [4,5]. *Collaborative filtering*, also sometimes known as *data mining*, has emerged as an approach to help remedy this. Collaboration filtering involves gathering user preference and behavior, and then uses that data to algorithmically produce personalized information for shoppers [6,7,8]. The disadvantage of collaborative filtering is that it needs a large body of data in order to produce reasonable personalization information.

The paper reports an *offer presentation scheme* with a keyword-driven rule engine, which analyzes and classifies shopper behavior in order to personalize the offer presentation. The key elements in the offer presentation engine are discussed in the following subsections.

2.1   Rule Engine Input Information

The input information is analyzed and classified by the engine to select offers. New offers are chosen, each time when there is a new input event. The following list summarizes several types of input information:

- Items and item quantities in the shopping cart
  The act of placing an item into the shopping cart triggers the computation of a new set of offers associated with every item in the shopping cart. Item quantity is also considered as an input.
- Price check and item removal
  Action of a shopper scanning an item to check for item price can be an indicator of interest in the item. Shopper removing an item from the cart can trigger offering of some alternative items.

- Shopper's in-store location
  Location specific offers are generated using shopper's in-store location with respect to the store layout.
- Shopper profile
  Typical examples which constitute a shopper profile are: 1) shopper preferences, which are supplied by the registered shopper from time to time, 2) shopper categorizations, which are given to the shopper based on the demographic information, such as age, income, education, occupation, marital status and home address, and 3) shopper's past shopping history.
- Shopper's current shopping list
  Shopper's current shopping list can be composed on the enterprise web site or in-store. The list can also be edited in-store when browsing through the weekly specials using the in-store wireless device.

2.2 Rules for Offer Presentation

To fit into an inexpensive PC-based server, our in-store rule engine employs a small number of rule types and utilizes only keywords to categorize shopper's preference and behavior. We will discuss these keywords and rules in the following subsections.

2.2.1 Keywords

Our rule engine uses keywords to describe and classify each shopper behavior in a shopping session. A keyword may activate rules to introduce more keywords. There are two main types of keywords: *global* keyword and *local* keyword, being used by the offer rules. *Global* keyword affects the offer rule throughout the entire shopping session. *Local* keyword only affects the current purchased item and has no impact on the offers for any previous purchased items. Both keywords are further classified in the following ways.

1. *Item keyword:* An item keyword is a global keyword that defines a primary event. It can be the item's UPC code or a set of keywords that best describe the particular item. For example: For an item with UPC Code = 02550080262, Item Description = *"Folgers Coffee, Classic Roast, Automatic Drip"*, its global keywords can be "02550080262", "Coffee", and "Ground". For an item with UPC Code = "02550000034", Item Description=*"Folgers Instant Coffee, Aroma Roasted"*, its global keywords can be "02550000034", "Coffee" and "Instant".

2. *Category Keyword:* A category keyword is a local keyword, derived from a set of item keywords and is used to categorize multiple items into the same category. For example: For the two items in the previous example, their category keywords are both "Beverage".

3. *Relationship Keyword:* A relationship keyword is a local keyword, used to introduce other category keywords that have a predefined cross relationship with the original category. For example: "Beverage" and "Coffee" can result in a relationship keyword of "Dairy Cream".

4. *Scenario Keyword:* A scenario keyword is a global keyword, and is used to categorize one's shopping purpose. It is derived from a set of keywords and the count of each of the keyword. A count can be the number of appearances of a particular keyword. For example: multiple occurrences of "plastic" and "utensil" could introduce a scenario keyword of "party". Similarly, multiple instances of "hot dogs" and "pork chop" could result in a scenario keyword of "barbecue".

5. *Profile Keyword:* A profile keyword is a global keyword, and is used to identify a shopper. Profile keywords of a shopper can be self-described preferences, or be assigned according to the enterprise analytical results.

2.2.2 Rules

There are two types of rules used by the offer engine, *classification keyword rules* and *offer matching rules (personalization rules)*. Figure. 2 illustrates the relationship between these rules. A *classification keyword rule* is used to expand the keyword set that is used to classify an item. While an *offer matching rule* is used to associate a set of keywords with an offer. The detailed definitions of these rules are given below.

1. *Item keyword rules:* This rule defines the global keywords for an item being scanned.

   Item UPC code $\rightarrow$ (keyword$_1$, keyword$_2$, ...)

2. *Category keyword rules:* This rule defines the category keywords based on a set of global and local keywords. The set of global keywords includes the newly added item's global keywords and previously added items' global keywords.

   keyword$_1$+keyword$_2$+... $\rightarrow$ (CategoryKeyword$_1$, CategoryKeyword$_2$, ...)

3. *Relationship keyword rules:* This rule defines the relationship keywords. Item quantity is also an element in this rule. Item quantity can be from zero to any positive value. When the quantity is zero, the rule is also known as replacement rule. A replacement rule is typically used to suggest an alternative item when shopper removed an item from cart.

   CategoryKeywords+ItemQuantity $\rightarrow$ (RelationshipKeyword$_1$, ...)

4. *Scenario keyword rules:* This rule defines the scenario keywords

   (keyword$_1$,quantity$_1$)+(keyword$_2$,quantity$_2$)+... $\rightarrow$ (ScenarioKeyword$_1$, ...)

5. *Offer matching rules:* Once no more new keyword can be introduced, the offer engine decides on what offers are selected for presentation using *offer matching rules*. A typical offer rule has the format of

   keyword$_1$+keyword$_2$+... $\rightarrow$ (Offer$_1$, Offer$_2$, ...)

   An additional *dynamic rule* can be added either by the enterprise or by the store manager to promote an over-stocked item. A dynamic rule has the following format:
   keywords+ItemInventory $\rightarrow$ (Offer$_1$, Offer$_2$, ...)

2.3 Offer Engine

In this section, we will discuss the design and implementation of the offer engine. We will first explain the offer rules processing flow to help readers understand the relationship between the keyword rules and offer matching rules.

2.3.1 Offer Rules Processing Flow

It is important to understand the flow of how these rules are executed and the purpose of the category keyword pool and the domain keyword pool. The detailed processing flow, as illustrated in Figure 2, is discussed in steps.

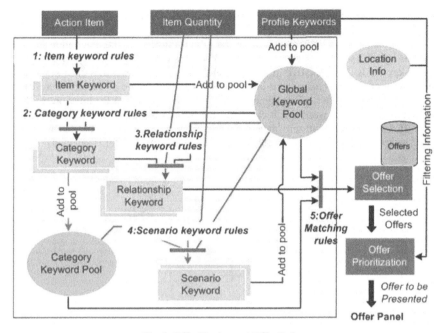

Fig. 2. Offer Engine and Offer Rules

Step 1 shows when an item is added into the shopping cart, a list of global keywords is derived using *item keyword rules*. Using this new list of global keywords and the keywords saved in the domain keyword pool, a list of category keywords is derived using *category keyword rules* as shown in Step 2. Depending on the item quantity, *relationship keyword rules* are applied to see if any relationship keyword can be added (Step 3). Combining item quantity, a list of category keywords and keywords from category keyword, *scenario keyword rules* are applied to see if any scenario keyword can be added.

For each of these steps, if a new keyword is introduced by a rule, earlier rules are re-executed to determine if any new keyword can be added. At this point, the rule engine will use the *offer matching rules* to see if any of the offer rules can be applied. There can be many offers eligible to be presented by the different combination of keywords.

Any newly acquired category keywords are added to the category keyword pool to be used later. The newly acquired item keyword and the scenario keyword are also added to the domain keyword pool to be used later as well. The domain keyword pool contains keywords that affect the entire shopping session, while the category keyword pool is used only to determine the scenario keyword.

2.3.2 Offer Engine Design and Implementation
Some of the key requirements of the offer engine are simplicity and efficiency. If an offer cannot be generated in real-time, the offer information might not be useful to a shopper, who may be walking away from the items to be promoted. To achieve this

goal, we developed an incremental rule scoring method to efficiently monitor if any offer rule can be fired.

Figure 3 shows the implementation of the proposed offer engine. Each item in the cart has an offer score list associated with it. Each score is initialized to the total number of keywords to be satisfied in an offer rule. Offer engine examines each keyword in the item classification keyword list and decrements the score of an offer that contains this keyword. After offer engine repeats the steps for each of the keyword in the item classification keyword list, it checks to see if any offer now has a score of zero. The offer with a score of zero means the lists of keyword that are needed for this offer, as specified by an offer rule, have all been found and this offer is selected.

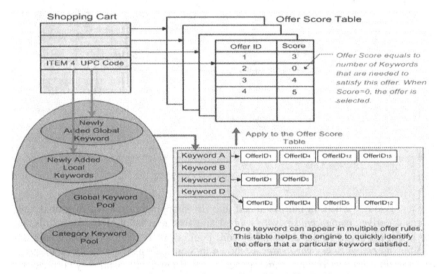

Fig. 3. Design and Implementation of the Offer Engine

Any newly added global keyword is also rechecked against other in-cart items' offer score lists. Any offer that has a score of zero after applying a global keyword is added as a new offer for that item. The objective is to ensure that a later added item's global keywords affect the offers of an earlier item in cart.

3 Offers Layout for Ease of Use

We have implemented a novel offer presentation method to display a set of promotion offers to shoppers in a personal shopping device environment. The method allows an efficient use of limited display area in a personal device. Item's offers are organized and displayed as a group for an item in the shopping cart. A highlight icon, such as a light bulb, is used to visually signal the shopper of the existence of a new (unread) collection of offers associated with an item. The collection of available offers is structured in such a way that allows a shopper to expand or collapse its views similar to Microsoft Windows file system tree-like structure using different icons (+ or – icons). Deleted items are first marked as delete, and then can be permanently removed by activating a delete (x) icon. In Figure 4, we illustrate several scenarios of how a set of offers is displayed when using these icons.

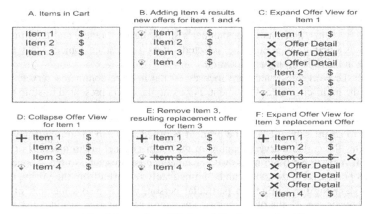

Fig. 4. Examples of Various Offer Presentation View

Due to the limited display space on a wireless shopping device, it may be undesirable to use the tree-like view to display offers that can occupy entire shopping cart area. Alternatively, multiple views of a separate offer panel may be used to allow shopper to switch views between a collection of offers associate with a selected item or with the shopper's location. Figure 5 shows a screen capture of such an implementation in a personal shopping device.

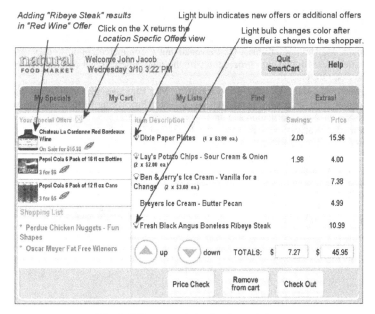

Fig. 5. Offer presentation implementation

4 Concluding Remarks

In this paper, we have presented an offer presentation engine for the in-store commerce server. It changes the way a retailer presents offers, from product push to consumer pull. By better understanding shopper's shopping preference, and tailoring to the specific shopping intentions, the selected offers suggest customers what they likely want, in the right timing and location.

Although the work presented here focuses on the in-store commerce server, it is relevant in the multi-channel environment. For example, offers presented in-store may not be limited to in-store items. An offer presented in-store can also be viewed and added into the future-shopping list which can be manipulated from the web channel. In addition to seamlessly ordering the product between web and in-store channels, it can also offer the collaborative shopping in the multi-channel environment. For example, a gift registry list build in the web channel can be presented to the shopper in store. Items purchased in the store can be immediately removed from the gift registry list. When shopping for a gift for a particular person, who is also a member of the store, the shopper can ask the offer engine to present a personalized gift idea list. Any member can choose to share a subset of his past purchase or his profile to the offer engine for offer presentation purpose only.

References

1. Smart Store: Enhancing the retail customer's shopping experience, IBM Executive Technology Report. IBM Business Consulting Services (2003)
2. Konstan, J. A. and Riedl, J. T.: Recommender systems in e-commerce, Proceeding of the 1st ACM conference on Electronic commerce, 1999 (158-166)
3. Sarwar, B., Karypis, G., Konstan, J., Riedl, J.: Analysis of recommendation algorithms for e-commerce , Proceedings of the 2nd ACM Conference on Electronic Commerce (2000)
4. Anupam, V., Hull, R,. Kumar, B.: Personalizing E-commerce applications with on-line heuristic decision making, Proceedings of the tenth international conference on World Wide Web (2001)
5. Mobasher, B., Dai, H., Luo, T., Nakagawa, M.: Effective personalization based on association rule discovery from web usage data, Proceeding of the third international workshop on Web information and data management (2001)
6. Sarwar, B., Karypis, G., Konstan, J., Reidl, J.: Item-based collaborative filtering recommendation algorithms,   Proceedings of the tenth international conference on World Wide Web, (2001)
7. Herlocker, J., Konstan, J. A., Terveen, L. G., Riedl, J. T.: Evaluating collaborative filtering recommender systems , ACM Transactions on Information Systems (TOIS), volume 22, Issue 1, (5-53)
8. Deshpande, M., Karypis, G.: Item-based Top-N recommendation algorithms, ACM Transactions on Information Systems (TOIS), Volume 22 Issue 1. (2004)

Combining Usage, Content, and Structure Data to Improve Web Site Recommendation*

Jia Li and Osmar R. Zaïane

Department of Computing Science, University of Alberta
Edmonton AB, Canada
{jial,zaiane}@cs.ualberta.ca

Abstract. Web recommender systems anticipate the needs of web users and provide them with recommendations to personalize their navigation. Such systems had been expected to have a bright future, especially in e-commerce and e-learning environments. However, although they have been intensively explored in the Web Mining and Machine Learning fields, and there have been some commercialized systems, the quality of the recommendation and the user satisfaction of such systems are still not optimal. In this paper, we investigate a novel web recommender system, which combines usage data, content data, and structure data in a web site to generate user navigational models. These models are then fed back into the system to recommend users shortcuts or page resources. We also propose an evaluation mechanism to measure the quality of recommender systems. Preliminary experiments show that our system can significantly improve the quality of web site recommendation.

1 Introduction

A web recommender system is a web-based interactive software agent. A WRS attempts to predict user preferences from user data and/or user access data for the purpose of facilitating and personalizing users' experience on-line by providing them with recommendation lists of suggested items. The recommended items could be products, such as books, movies, and music CDs, or on-line resources, such as web pages or on-line activities (*Path Prediction*) [JFM97]. Generally speaking, a web recommender system is composed of two modules: an off-line module and an on-line module. The off-line module pre-processes data to generate user models, while the on-line module uses and updates the models on-the-fly to recognize user goals and predict a recommendation list.

In this paper, we investigate the design of a web recommender system to recommend on-line resources using content, structure, as well as the usage of web pages for a web site to model users and user needs. Our preliminary goals are to recommend on-line learning activities in an e-learning web site, or recommend shortcuts to users in a given web site after predicting their information needs.

One of the earliest and widely used technologies for building recommender systems is *Collaborative Filtering* (CF) [SM95] [JLH99]. CF-based recommender

---

* Research funded in part by the Alberta Ingenuity Funds and NSERC Canada.

K. Bauknecht, M. Bichler, and B. Pröll (Eds.): EC-Web 2004, LNCS 3182, pp. 305–315, 2004.
© Springer-Verlag Berlin Heidelberg 2004

systems aggregate explicit user ratings or product preferences in order to generate user profiles, which recognize users' interests. A product is recommended to the current user if it is highly rated by other users who have similar interests. The CF-based techniques suffer from several problems [SKKR00]. They rely heavily on explicit user input (e.g., previous customers' rating/ranking of products), which is either unavailable or considered intrusive. With sparsity of such user input, the recommendation precision and quality drop significantly. The second challenge is related to the system scalability and efficiency. Indeed, user profile matching has to be performed as an on-line process. For very large datasets, this may lead to unacceptable latency for providing recommendations.

In recent years there has been increasing interest in applying *web usage mining* techniques to build web recommender systems. Web usage recommender systems take web server logs as input, and make use of data mining techniques such as association rules and clustering to extract navigational patterns, which are then used to provide recommendations. Web server logs record user browsing history, which contains much hidden information regarding users and their navigation. They could, therefore, be a good alternative to the explicit user rating or feedback in deriving user models. In web usage recommender systems, navigational patterns are generally derived as an off-line process. The most commonly used approach for web usage recommender systems is using association rules to associate page hits [SCDT00] [FBH00] [LAR00] [YHW01]. We will test our approach againt this general technique.

However, a web usage recommender system which focuses solely on web server logs has its own problems:

- Incomplete or Limited Information Problem: A number of heuristic assumptions are typically made before applying any data mining algorithm; as a result, some patterns generated may not be proper or even correct.
- Incorrect Information Problem: When a web site visitor is lost, the clicks made by this visitor are recorded in the log, and may mislead future recommendations. This becomes more problematic when a web site is badly designed and more people end up visiting unsolicited pages, making them seem popular.
- Persistence Problem: When new pages are added to a web site, because they have not been visited yet, the recommender system may not recommend them, even though they could be relevant. Moreover, the more a page is recommended, the more it may be visited, thus making it look popular and boost its candidacy for future recommendation.

To address these problems, we propose an improved web usage recommender system. Our system attempts to use web server logs to model user navigational behaviour, as other web usage recommender systems do. However, our approach differs from other such systems in that we also combine textual content and connectivity information of web pages, which also do not require user input. We demonstrate that this approach improves the quality of web site recommendation. The page textual content is used to pre-process log data to model content coherent visit sub-sessions, which are then used to generate more accurate users' navigational patterns. Structure data, i.e., links between pages, are used to expand navigational patterns with a rich relevant content. The connectivity information is also used to compute the importance of pages for the purpose of ranking recommendations.

A few hybrid web recommender systems have been proposed in the literature [MDL+00] [NM03]. [MDL+00] adopts a clustering technique to obtain both site usage and site content profiles in the off-line phase. In the on-line phase, a recommendation set is generated by matching the current active session and all usage profiles. Similarly, another recommendation set is generated by matching the current active session and all content profiles. Finally, a set of pages with the maximum recommendation value across the two recommendation sets is presented as recommendation. This is called a weighted hybridization method [Bur02]. In [NM03], the authors use association rule mining, sequential pattern mining, and contiguous sequential mining to generate three kinds of navigational patterns in the off-line phase. In the on-line phase, recommendation sets are selected from the different navigational models, based on a localized degree of hyperlink connectivity with respect to a user's current location within the site. This is called a switching hybridization method [Bur02]. Whether using the weighted method or the switching method, the combination in these systems happens only in the on-line phase. Our approach combines usage data and content data in the off-line phase to generate content coherent navigational models, which could be a better model for users' information needs. Still in the off-line phase, we further combine structure data to improve the models. Also in the off-line process, we use hyperlinks to attach a rating to web resources. This rating is used during the on-line phase for ranking recommendations.

The contributions of this paper are as follows: First, we propose a novel web recommender system, which combines and makes full use of all three available channels: usage, content, and structure data. This combination is done off-line to improve efficiency, i.e, low latency. Second, we propose a novel users' navigational model. Rather than representing the information need as a sequence of visitation clicks in a visit, our model assumes different information needs in the same visit; third, we address all three problems mentioned above by combing all available information channels.

This paper is organized as follows: Section 2 presents the off-line module of our system, which pre-processes available usage and web site data, as well as our on-line module, which generates the recommendation list. Section 3 presents experimental results assessing the performance of our system.

2   Architecture of a Hybrid Recommender System

As most web usage recommender systems, our system is composed of two modules: an off-line component, which pre-processes data to generate users' navigational models, and an on-line component which is a real-time recommendation engine. Figure 1 depicts the general architecture of our system. Entries in a web server log are used to identify users and visit sessions, while web pages or

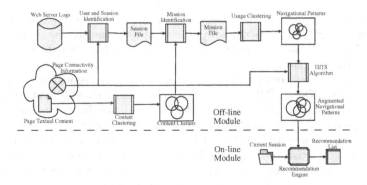

Fig. 1. System Architecture

resources in the site are clustered based on their content. These clusters are used to scrutinize the discovered web sessions in order to identify what we call *missions*. A *mission* is a sub-session with a consistent goal. These *missions* are in turn clustered to generate navigational patterns, and augmented with their linked neighbourhood and ranked based on resource connectivity, using the *hub* and *authority* idea [Kle99]. These new clusters (i.e., augmented navigational patterns) are provided to the recommendation engine. When a visitor starts a new session, the session is matched with these clusters to generate a recommendation list. The details of the whole process are given below.

2.1   User and Visit Session Identification

A web log is a text file which records information regarding users' requests to a web server. A typical web log entry contains a client address, the requested date address, a timestamp, and other related information. We use similar pre-processing techniques as in [CMS99] to identify individual users and sessions. For sessionizing, we chose an idle time of 30 minutes.

2.2   Visit Mission Identification

The last data pre-processing step proposed in [CMS99] is transaction identification, which divides individual visit sessions into transactions. In [CMS99], two transaction identification approaches are proposed: *Reference Length* approach and *Maximal Forward Reference* approach, both of which have been widely applied in web mining techniques. Rather than dividing sessions into arbitrary transactions, we identify sub-sessions with coherent information needs. We call these sub-sessions *missions*. We assume that a visitor may have different information needs to fulfill during a visit, but we make no assumption on the sequence in which these needs are fulfilled. In the case of transactions in [CMS99] it is assumed that one information need is fulfilled after the other. A *mission* would model a sub-session related to one of these information needs, and would allow overlap between missions, which would represent a concurrent search in the site. While in the transaction-based model, pages are labeled as *content* pages and *auxiliary* pages, and a transaction is simply a sequence of auxiliary pages that ends with a content page, in our mission-based model, the identified sequence is based on the real content of pages. Indeed, a content page in the transaction-based model is identified simply based on the time spent on that page, or on backtracking in the visitor's navigation. We argue that missions could better model users' navigational behavior than transaction. In the model we propose, users visit a web site with concurrent goals, i.e., different information needs. For example, a user could fulfill two goals in a visit session: a, b, c, d, in which pages a and c contribute to one goal, while pages b and d contribute to the other. Since pages related to a given goal in a visit session are supposed to be content coherent, whether they are neighbouring each other or not, we use page content to identify missions within a visit session.

All web site pages are clustered based on their content, and these clusters are used to identify content coherent clicks in a session. Let us give an example to illustrate this point. Suppose the text clustering algorithm groups web pages a, b, c, and e, web pages a, b, c, and f, and web pages a, c and d into three different content clusters (please note that our text clustering algorithm is a soft clustering one, which allows a web page to be clustered into several clusters). Then for a visit session: a, b, c, d, e, f, our system identifies three missions as follows: mission 1: (a, b, c, e) ; mission 2: (a, b, c, f); and mission 3: (a, c, d). As seen in this example, mission identification in our system is different from transaction identification in that we can group web pages into one mission even if they are not sequential in a visit session. We can see that our mission-based model generates the transaction-based model, since missions could become transactions if visitors fulfill their information needs sequentially.

To cluster web pages based on their content, we use a modified version of the DC-tree algorithm [WF00]. Originally, the DC-tree algorithm was a hard clustering approach, prohibiting overlap of clusters. We modified the algorithm to allow web pages to belong to different clusters. Indeed, some web pages could cover different topics at the same time. In the algorithm, each web page is represented as a keyword vector, and organized in a tree structure called the DC-tree. The algorithm does not require the number of clusters to discover as a constraint, but allows the definition of cluster sizes. This was the appealing property which made us select the algorithm. Indeed, we do not want either too large or too small content cluster sizes. Very large clusters cannot help capture missions from sessions, while very small clusters may break potentially useful relations between pages in sessions.

2.3   Content Coherent Navigational Pattern Discovery

Navigational patterns are sets of web pages that are frequently visited together and that have related content. These patterns are used by the recommender system to recommend web pages, if they were not already visited. To discover these navigational patterns, we simply group the missions we uncovered from the web server logs into clusters of sub-sessions having commonly visited pages. Each of the resulting clusters could be viewed as a user's navigation pattern. Note that the patterns discovered from missions possess two characteristics: usage cohesive and content coherent. Usage cohesiveness means the pages in a cluster tend to be visited together, while content coherence means pages in a cluster tend to be related to a topic or concept. This is because missions are grouped according to content information. Since each cluster is related to a topic, and each page is represented in a keyword vector, we are able to easily compute the topic vector of each cluster, in which the value of a keyword is the average of the corresponding values of all pages in the cluster. The cluster topic is widely used in our system, in both the off-line and on-line phases (see below for details). The clustering algorithm we adopted for grouping missions is *PageGather* [PE98]. This algorithm is a soft clustering approach allowing overlap of clusters. Instead of attempting to partition the entire space of items, it attempts to identify a small number of high quality clusters based on the *clique* clustering technique.

2.4   Navigational Pattern Improved with Connectivity

The missions we extracted and clustered to generate navigational patterns are primarily based on the sessions from the web server logs. These sessions exclusively represent web pages or resources that were visited. It is conceivable that there are other resources not yet visited, even though they are relevant and could be interesting to have in the recommendation list. Such resources could be, for instance, newly added web pages or pages that have links to them not evidently presented due to bad design. Thus, these pages or resources are never presented in the missions previously discovered. Since the navigational patterns, represented by the clusters of pages in the missions, are used by the recommendation engine, we need to provide an opportunity for these rarely visited or newly added pages to be included in the clusters. Otherwise, they would never be recommended. To alleviate this problem, we expand our clusters to include the connected neighbourhood of every page in a mission cluster. The neighbourhood of a page p is the set of all the pages directly linked from p and all the pages that directly link to p. Figure 3(B) illustrates the concept of neighbourhood expansion. This approach of expanding the neighbourhood is performed as follows: we consider each previously discovered navigational pattern as a set of seeds. Each seed is supplemented with pages it links to and pages from the web site that link to it. The result is what is called a connectivity graph which now represents our augmented navigational pattern. This process of obtaining the connectivity graph is similar to the process used by the HITS algorithm [Kle99] to find the *authority* and *hub* pages for a given topic. The difference is that we do not consider a given topic, but start from a mission cluster as our set of seeds. We also consider only internal links, i.e., links within the same web site. After expanding the clusters representing the navigational patterns, we also augment the keyword vectors that label the clusters. The new keyword vectors that represent the augmented navigational patterns have also the terms extracted from the content of augmented pages.

We take advantage of the built connectivity graph by cluster to apply the HITS algorithm in order to identify the *authority* and *hub* pages within a given cluster. These measures of *authority* and *hub* allow us to rank the pages within the cluster. This is important because at real time during the recommendation, it is crucial to rank recommendations, especially when the recommendation list is long. *Authority* and *hub* are mutually reinforcing [Kle99] concepts. Indeed, a good *authority* is a page pointed to by many good *hub* pages, and a good *hub* is a page that points to many good *authority* pages. Since we would like to be able to recommend pages newly added to the site, in our framework, we consider only the *hub* measure. This is because a newly added page would be unlikely to be a good authoritative page, since not many pages are linked to it. However, a good new page would probably link to many *authority* pages; it would, therefore, have the chance to be a good *hub* page. Consequently, we use the *hub* value to rank the candidate recommendation pages in the on-line module.

2.5   The Recommendation Engine

The previously described process consists of pre-processing done exclusively off-line. When a visitor starts a new session in the web site, we identify the navigation pattern after a few clicks and try to match on-the-fly with already captured navigational patterns. If they were matched, we recommend the most relevant pages in the matched cluster. Identifying the navigational pattern of the current visitor consists of recognizing the current focused topic of interest to the user. A study in [CDG+98] shows that looking on either side of an anchor (i.e., text encapsulated in a *href* tag) for a window of 50 bytes would capture the topic of the linked pages. Based on this study, we consider the anchor clicked by the current user and its neighbourhood on either side as the contextual topic of interest. The captured topics are also represented by a keyword vector which is matched with the keyword vectors of the clusters representing the augmented navigational patterns. From the best match, we get the pages with the best *hub* value and provide them in a recommendation list, ranked by the *hub* values. To avoid supplying a very large list of recommendations, the number of recommendations is adjusted according to the number of links in the current page: we simply make this number proportional to the number of links in the current page. Our goal is to have a different recommendation strategy for different pages based on how many links the page already contains. Our general strategy is to give $\sqrt{n}$ best recommendations (n is the number of links), with a maximum of 10. The limit of 10 is to prevent adding noise and providing too many options. The relevance and importance of recommendations is measured with the *hub* value already computed off-line.

3   Experimental Evaluation

To evaluate our recommendation framework, we tested the approach on a generic web site. We report herein results with the web server log and web site of the

Computing Science Department of the University of Alberta, Canada. Data was collected for 8 months (Sept. 2002 – Apr. 2003), and partitioned the data into months. On average, each monthly partition contains more than 40,000 pages, resulting in on average 150,000 links between them. The log of each month averaged more than 200,000 visit sessions, which generated an average of 800,000 missions per month. The modified DC-tree content clustering algorithm generated about 1500 content clusters, which we used to identify the missions per month.

3.1 Methodology

Given the data partitioned per month as described above, we adopt the following empirical evaluation: one or more months data is used for building our models (i. e., training the recommender system), and the following month or months for evaluation. The idea is that given a session s from a month m, if the recommender system, based on data from month $m - 1$ and some prefix of the session s, can recommend a set of pages p_i that contain some of the pages in the suffix of s, then the recommendation is considered accurate. Moreover, the distance in the number of clicks between the suffix of s and the recommended page p_i is considered a gain (i.e., a shortcut). More precisely, we measure the *Recommendation Accuracy* and the *Shortcut Gain* as described below.

   Recommendation Accuracy is the ratio of correct recommendations among all recommendations, and the correct recommendation is the one that appears in the suffix of a session from which the prefix triggers the recommendation. As an example, consider that we have S visit sessions in the test log. For each visit session s, we take each page p and generate a recommendation list $R(p)$. $R(p)$ is then compared with the remaining portion of s (i.e., the suffix of s). We denote this portion $T(p)$ (T stands for Tail). The recommendation accuracy for a given session would be how often $T(p)$ and $R(p)$ intersect. The general formula for *recommendation accuracy* is defined as:

$$RecommendationAccuracy = \frac{\sum_s \frac{\left| \bigcup_p (T(p) \bigcap R(p)) \right|}{\left| \bigcup_p R(p) \right|}}{S}$$

   The *Shortcut Gain* measures how many clicks the recommendation allows users to save if the recommendation is followed. Suppose we have a session a, b, c, d, e, and at page b, the system recommends page e; then if we follow this advice, we would save two hops (i.e., pages c and d). There is an issue in measuring this shortcut gain when the recommendation list contains more than one page in the suffix of the session. Should we consider the shortest gain or the longest gain? To solve this problem, we opted to distinguish between *key* pages and *auxiliary* pages. A *key* page is a page that may contain relevant information and in which a user may spend some time. An *auxiliary* page is an intermediary page used for linkage and in which a user would spend a relatively short time. In our experiment, we use a threshold of 30 seconds as this distinction. Given these two types of pages, a shortcut gain is measured as being the smallest jump gain towards a *key* page that has been recommended. If no *key* page is recommended, then it is the longest jump towards an *auxiliary* page. The set of pages in the session we go through with the assistance of the recommender system is called the shortened session *s'*. For the total S visit sessions in the test log, *Shortcut Gain* can be computed as:

$$ShortcutGain = \frac{\sum_s \frac{|s| - |s'|}{|s|}}{S}$$

In addition, we would like to compute the *Coverage* of a recommender system, which measure the ability of a system to produce all pages that are likely to be visited by users. The concept is similar to what is called *recall* in information retrieval. *Coverage* is defined as:

$$RecommendationCoverage = \frac{\sum_s \frac{\left| \bigcup_p (T(p) \bigcap R(p)) \right|}{\left| \bigcup_p T(p) \right|}}{S}$$

3.2 Results

Our first experiment varies the *Coverage* to see the tendency of the *Recommendation Accuracy*, as depicted in Figure 2(A). For the purpose of comparison, we also implement an Association Rule Recommender System, the most commonly used approach for web mining based recommender systems, and record its performance in the same figure. As expected, the accuracy decreases when the we increase coverage. However, our system was consistently superior to the *Association Rule* system by at least 30%.

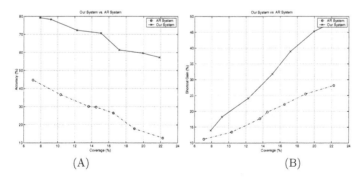

(A)   (B)

Fig. 2. Performance Comparison: our system vs. *Association Rule* Recommender System. (A): *Recommendation Accuracy* (B): *Shortcut Gain*

We next varied the *coverage* to test the *Shortcut Gain*, both with our system and with the *Association Rule* System, as illustrated in Figure 2(B).

From Figure 2(B), we can see that in the low boundary where the *Coverage* is lower than 8%, the *Shortcut Gain* of our system is close to that of the *AR* system. With the increase of the *Coverage*, however, our system can achieve an increasingly superior *Shortcut Gain* than the latter, although the performance of both systems continues to improve.

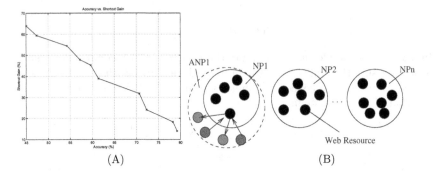

(A)   (B)

Fig. 3. (A) *Accuracy* vs. *Shortcut Gain.* (B) Navigational Patterns(NPs) and Augmented Navigational Patterns(ANPs)

Figure 3(A) depicts the relationship of *Recommendation Accuracy* and *Shortcut Gain* in our system. It shows that *Recommendation Accuracy* is inversely proportional to the *Shortcut Gain*. Our study draws the same conclusion from the *Association Rule* recommender system. We argue this is an important property of a usage-based web recommender system, and therefore, how to adjust and balance between the *Accuracy* and *Shortcut Gain* for a web recommender system to achieve the maximum benefit is a question that should be investigated. Some web sites, e.g., those with high link density, may favour a recommender system with high *Accuracy*, while some others may favor a system with high *Shortcut Gain*.

4   Conclusion

In this paper, we present a framework for a combined web recommender system, in which users' navigational patterns are automatically learned from web usage data and content data. These navigational patterns are then used to generate recommendations based on a user's current status. The items in a recommendation list are ranked according to their importance, which is in turn computed based on web structure information. Our preliminary experiments show that the combination of usage, content, and structure of data in a web recommender system has the potential to improve the quality of the system, as well as to keep the recommendation up-to-date. However, there are various ways to combine these different channels. Our future work in this area will include investigating different methods of combination.

References

[Bur02]   Robin Burke. Hybrid recommender systems: Survey and experiments. In *User Modeling and User-Adapted Interaction*, 2002.

[CDG⁺98]   S. Chakrabarti, B. Dom, D. Gibson, J. Kleinberg, P. Raghavan, and S. Rajagopalan. Automatic resource list compilation by analyzing hyperlink structure and associated text. In *Proceedings of the 7th International World Wide Web Conference*, 1998.

[CMS99]   Robert Cooley, Bamshad Mobasher, and Jaideep Srivastava. Data preparation for mining world wide web browsing patterns. *Knowledge and Information Systems*, 1(1):5–32, 1999.

[FBH00]   Xiaobin Fu, Jay Budzik, and Kristian J. Hammond. Mining navigation history for recommendation. In *Intelligent User Interfaces*, pages 106–112, 2000.

[JFM97]   Thorsten Joachims, Dayne Freitag, and Tom M. Mitchell. Web watcher: A tour guide for the world wide web. In *IJCAI (1)*, pages 770–777, 1997.

[JLH99]   Al Borchers John Riedl Jonathan L. Herlocker, Joseph A. Konstan. An algorithmic framework for performing collaborative filtering. In *Proceedings of the 22nd annual international ACM SIGIR conference on Research and development in information retrieval*, pages 230 – 237, 1999.

[Kle99]   Jon M. Kleinberg. Authoritative sources in a hyperlinked environment. *Journal of the ACM*, 46(5):604–632, 1999.

[LAR00]   C. Lin, S. Alvarez, and C. Ruiz. Collaborative recommendation via adaptive association rule mining, 2000.

[MDL⁺00]   Bamshad Mobasher, Honghua Dai, Tao Luo, Yuqing Sun, and Jiang Zhu. Integrating web usage and content mining for more effective personalization. In *EC-Web*, pages 165–176, 2000.

[NM03]   Miki Nakagawa and Bamshad Mobasher. A hybrid web personalization model based on site connectivity. In *Fifth WebKDD Workshop*, pages 59–70, 2003.

[PE98]   Mike Perkowitz and Oren Etzioni. Adaptive web sites: Automatically synthesizing web pages. In *AAAI/IAAI*, pages 727–732, 1998.

[SCDT00]   Jaideep Srivastava, Robert Cooley, Mukund Deshpande, and Pang-Ning Tan. Web usage mining: Discovery and applications of usage patterns from web data. *SIGKDD Explorations*, 1(2):12–23, 2000.

[SKKR00]   Badrul M. Sarwar, George Karypis, Joseph A. Konstan, and John Riedl. Analysis of recommendation algorithms for e-commerce. In *ACM Conference on Electronic Commerce*, pages 158–167, 2000.

[SM95]   Upendra Shardanand and Patti Maes. Social information filtering: Algorithms for automating "word of mouth". In *Proceedings of ACM CHI'95 Conference on Human Factors in Computing Systems*, volume 1, pages 210–217, 1995.

[WF00]   W. Wong and A. Fu. Incremental document clustering for web page classification, 2000.

[YHW01]   Arbee L.P. Chen Yi-Hung Wu, Yong-Chuan Chen. Enabling personalized recommendation on the web based on user interests and behaviors. In *11th International Workshop on research Issues in Data Engineering*, 2001.

Towards a Multidimensional Model
for Web-Based Applications Quality Assessment

Ghazwa Malak[1], Linda Badri[2], Mourad Badri[2], and Houari Sahraoui[1]

[1] Department of Computer Science and Operational Research
University of Montreal, Montreal, Qc, Canada, H3T 1J4
{rifighaz,sahraouh}@iro.umontreal.ca
[2] Department of Mathematics and Computer Science
University of Quebec at Trois-Rivières
Trois-Rivières, Qc, Canada, G9A 5H7
{linda_badri,mourad_badri}@uqtr.ca

Abstract. Several approaches for quantitative evaluation of Web-based applications have proposed test-benches, checklists and tools. In this paper, we propose an evaluation approach that integrates and extends the various approaches proposed in this field. We have developed a list of over than 300 criteria and sub-criteria, which we classified using the ISO/IEC 9126 standard as a guide. These criteria represent a first basis for the development of a hierarchical quality model specific to Web-Based Applications. In order to refine our quality model, we followed a systematic approach using the GQM paradigm. A tool supporting our assessment approach has been developed. With this tool, we conducted an experience on several Web systems. The obtained results were rather encouraging. However, they have shown that more dimensions have to be considered to increase the reliability of our model. As a next step, we introduce a three-dimensional model where the initial model is one dimension. The two others represent respectively the life cycle processes and the Web applications domains.

1 Introduction

Web-Based Applications (WebApps) development has experienced, during these last years, a tremendous growth and an unusual evolution with new devices and new services. Achieving high quality WebApps become a big challenge because of the multiple technologies, the multiple architectures and the dynamic changes of the Web. In this field, technology evolves very quickly and developed systems have a very fast lifecycle. This can be explained by the market pressure and the lack of distribution barriers [4]. Web pages are created by software on user request and the control of user interface varies depending on many factors [21]. Web sites are now interactive and highly functional systems, implemented in many languages and paradigms, interact with users, other systems and databases. In the same time, we know very little about how to measure or ensure their quality attributes [25].

As mentioned in [5, 9], the majority of Web sites are poorly conceived and miss navigability as well as functionality and traceability. Several studies from industry suggest that this lack of quality leads to huge losses in productivity and revenue [19, 21].

K. Bauknecht, M. Bichler, and B. Pröll (Eds.): EC-Web 2004, LNCS 3182, pp. 316–327, 2004.

To circumvent these weaknesses, many evaluation approaches have been proposed in the literature. The majority of the work done so far concentrates specifically on the various aspects of usability, though the fact that the other quality characteristics are of equal importance. Nevertheless, there is still no standard, nor consensus between these initiatives. Beside the consensus that we need principles, methods and tools, which are specific to WebApps development, it is important to have the same specificity for quality assurance.

The main objectives of our work are: (1) to better specify the problems related to WebApps quality, while proposing an evaluation, an integration and an extension of the various approaches proposed in the literature; (2) to propose a first basis for a hierarchical quality model specific to WebApps and (3) to extend this model by considering the life cycle and the application domain dimensions.

The rest of the paper is organized as follows. Section 2 presents a brief summary on related work. Section 3 presents the main phases of the proposed hierarchical model setting process. The use of the GQM paradigm in our process is presented in section 4. A synthesis of the main steps of the proposed assessment methodology is presented in section 5. Section 6 presents some experiment results obtained using the prototype that we developed. Finally, following the several evaluations that we have realized, a three-dimensional model for WebApps quality assessment is introduced in section 7. A conclusion and future work directions are given in section 8.

2   Related Work

Due to the lack of engineering standard specific to Web applications, several studies on Web quality evaluation are based on the description of the quality characteristics suggested by the ISO/IEC 9126 standard [10]. Some specific work proposes guidelines, checklists, models and tools that allow an objective assessment of web sites or pages quality.

In fact, many studies have been made towards building usable Web sites. For instance, a collection of recommendations and guidelines that addresses a broad range of Web site features [18] and a checklist on usability assessment, which is rather user-oriented than developer-oriented [13]. A more general approach, considering several quality characteristics, the QEM (Quality Evaluation Method), proposed by [22], for the evaluation and the comparison of web sites quality, and a three dimensional model for web quality assessment is presented in [23, 24].

Previous works, not based on the ISO standard, developed workbench to support web sites development and maintenance [7] and are more focused on the evolution aspects of web sites [3]. While subsequent ones, discuss some of the technical challenges in building today's complex web software applications, their unique quality requirements, and how to achieve them besides new problems encountered because of the rapid evolution of Internet [25]. On the other hand, many tools were developed to automate, at least partially, the evaluation process. For illustration we mention the design tool that incorporate a quality-checker [12], and "WebQEM_Tool" related to the QEM proposed by [1].

By observing the very fast development of Web software and technologies, and the evolution of the research in this field, we notice the absence of common vision on the quality and the lack of a solid foundation on which this research can evolve. As presented in a previous work [16,17], we recognize that, in general, there is no common standard followed by the authors, and the quality criteria do not totally comply with the ISO/IEC 9126 standard. Recently, [25] proposes some other characteristics and [19] suggests several sub characteristics for usability which are different from those defined in the ISO 9126 standard and more relevant for WebApps.

3   Quality Model Definition Process

Starting from the above-mentioned work, we attempted to collect the criteria proposed by the different authors, along with the suggested directions and recommendations [15]. Moreover, we extended this list by considering additional criteria that, in our opinion, are interesting in the evaluation process of the different aspects, such as functionality, reliability, maintainability, etc. These phases are described below.

3.1   Integration Phase

During this stage, each of the criteria was studied in the corresponding author's proposed framework and compared to the quality characteristics and subcharacteristics definitions according to the ISO/IEC 9126 standard. We tried first to release the common points, according to a given quality characteristic. For instance, given the fact that according to all the authors, "Site Map" or "Style" is a usability criterion, it is grafted as is in the model, and so are the other criteria. Thereafter, we have examined the remaining criteria attached to each of the considered characteristics, to determine whether the criterion characterizes specifically the characteristic to which it is related, but not the others. For instance, "On-line Feedback" are displayed in certain studies in order to evaluate functionality, while in others to assess usability [4, 18, 22], and finally, to determine maintainability [7]. Indeed, the "On-line Feedback" may characterize functionality, usability and maintainability as well. The other criteria were examined accordingly.

3.2   Extension Phase

We classified, during this step, some criteria. For instance, "Titles" characterizes functionality in [22], and usability in [3, 4, 13, 18]. While examining the various points of views of the authors, and on the basis of the characteristics and subcharacteristics definitions according to the ISO 9126 standard [10], it seems to us that considering "Titles" as usability criterion is more suitable. The others criteria have been considered in the same way.

Moreover, we have taken into account some of the proposed directives [7, 18, 21], in order to represent them by criteria, which may be connected either to one or more characteristics. For example, [21] highlighted the importance of the site availability. It seems indeed that web customer expect the web site to be operational every second of the year. This would facilitate the use of the site, and hence, site availability may be considered as a usability criterion. Designing and building web sites that can be easily scaled help the site to remain reliable. So, scalability could be considered as a reliability criterion. In the same respects, many usability and maintainability criteria have been drawn from other recommendations [7, 18], such as Credibility, Dates, Authority, Trade marks, Documentation, Readability, etc. Besides, some subcharacteristics of usability were somewhat modified in order to make them more easily applicable to web sites e.g. "finding information" or "attractiveness" [15].

3.3   Criteria Fractionation Process

Following a top-down process, we tried to figure out a kind of sub-criteria that would be likely to characterize the retained criteria, and allow a better evaluation of the latter as well. For example, it is much more accurate to estimate "Titles" quality by examining the information that may influence the process, or could provide information as to the criterion itself, such as: descriptiveness, explicitness, etc. Further, in order to study the "URLs" criterion, to provide with appreciation annotation, it is of importance to have precise reference marks, which allow objective estimation of the value of the mentioned criterion. Thus, with more specific requests: significant and concise, using current words, no spaces, relatives (if local to site), including a final slash, etc. We could define over than 300 different criteria and sub-criteria. The criteria that we propose take into account the point of view of users, developers and managers. A portion of the developed hierarchical quality model is presented in Fig. 1.

Site organisation	Orthography is correct
Name of the site on each page	Grammar is correct
Logo of the site on each page	Hypertext links
Presence of a plan or list of contents	To structure the contents
Accessibility to the plan of the site	Towards the interior of the site
Home page organisation	Towards the same page
Can be seen on a screen	Towards relevant information
Index included	All the pages of the site related to Home
Glossary included	Relevance of links towards the pages
Small paragraphs	Relevance of links towards other sites
Short pages	Number of links per page (<10)
Information organization	Return button every 295 pixels
Important information is quickly accessible	Distinction between internal / external links
Based on the course expected of the user	Etc.

Fig. 1. Portion of the model representing some criteria and sub-criteria of "Finding the Information" (Usability).

4   Application of the GQM Paradigm

The GQM (Goals, Questions, Metrics) paradigm supports a top-down approach for defining the goals behind measuring software processes and products and using these

320   Ghazwa Malak et al.

goals to decide precisely what to measure (choosing metrics). It additionally supports a bottom-up approach for interpreting data based on the previously defined goals and questions. The GQM paradigm is based on the idea that measurement should be goal-oriented. All data collection should be based on a rationale that is explicitly documented as stated in [8]. This approach allowed us to better structure, validate and extend our quality model. The result of the application of this paradigm is the specification of a measurement system targeting a particular set of issues and rules for the interpretation of the measurement data [2]. Thereafter, it will allow us to determine metrics for the retained criteria.

Finding information (Usability) : Effort to perform by the user to find required information				
Goal : Analyse a Web site with an aim of evaluating the facility to find the information from the point of view of the users and the developers within the framework of a research project.				
Object Web Site	**Purpose** Evaluation	**Focus** Finding information	**Viewpoint** User, Developer	**Environment** Research project

Quality Focus - Accessibility - On-line Help - Site Organisation - User Support - User-Oriented Tasks - Etc.	**Variation Factors** Domain of the site Size of the site

Baseline Hypotheses
 	
- We must easily find required information
in a Web site (just one click is needed to leave a site)
	Impact on Baseline Hypotheses
	- according to the site domain, the
	  information retrieval is more or less
	  easy
	- the facility can decrease with the size

3.2 Finding the Information **3.2.1 Accessibility to Information** 3.2.1.1 Information Identification 3.2.1.1.1 Presence of research mechanism 3.2.1.1.2 Presence of a site map 3.2.1.1.2.1 Access facility to the site map 3.2.1.2 Index included 3.2.1.3 New Information indicated 3.2.1.4 Site Depth (number of clicks) 3.2.1.5 Acronyms rate 3.2.1.6 Titles 3.2.1.6.1 Significant or Descriptive 3.2.1.6.2 Explicit 3.2.1.6.3 Unique 3.2.1.6.4 Short (< 25 characters) 3.2.1.6.5 Each page has a title 3.2.1.6.6 number of levels (2 or 3) **3.2.4 On-line Help** ... **3.2.5 User Support**	**3.2.3 Site organisation** 3.2.3.1 Site Identification 3.2.3.1.1 Name of the site on each page 3.2.3.1.2 Logo of the site on each page 3.2.3.1.3 All pages have the same style 3.2.3.2 Home page can be seen on a screen 3.2.3.3 Short pages 3.2.3.4 Hypertext links 3.2.3.4.1 To structure the contents 3.2.3.4.2 Towards the interior of the site 3.2.3.4.3 Towards the same page 3.2.3.4.4 Towards relevant information 3.2.3.4.5 All the pages of the site related to Home 3.2.3.4.6 Number of links per page (<10) 3.2.3.4.7 Distinction between int. / ext. links **3.2.3 User-Oriented Tasks** 3.2.3.1 Based on the course expected by the user 3.2.3.2 The title represent a major task 3.2.3.3 The topic order represent the subtask order Etc.

Fig. 2. Portion of the hierarchical quality model (list of criteria) after using the GQM paradigm.

An example of the application of this paradigm to one of the usability subcharacteristics (illustrated in Fig. 1) is illustrated in Fig. 2 (partial results). By comparing Figures 1 and 2, we notice that the selected criteria characterize better the sub-characteristic "Finding the Information": some criteria found their place under another sub-characteristic (e.g. orthography, grammar), others were better structured (e.g. site map), and several others were added (e.g. presence of a research mechanism, etc.).

On the basis of ISO/IEC 9126 and QUINT2 model [20], we tried to identify, organise, and define precisely the characteristics, sub-characteristics, criteria and sub-criteria for WebApps. Actually, this is done only for Usability and Functionality characteristics.

3- **Usability**: Capability of a site to be understood, to present relevant information, easy to operate and attractive for the user, when it is used under specified conditions [10]

    3.1- **Understandability**: Capability of a site to enable the user to understand whether it suitable, and how to recognize the logical concept and its applicability [10]

        3.1.1- **Contextualization**: capability of a site to allow the user to understand the context of use in a given field [14]

        3.1.1.1- **Standardization**: capability of a site to allow the user to understand the common elements between the pages [14]

            3.1.1.1.1- Rate of standard menus used: number of standard menus used compared to the total number of menus in site

            3.1.1.1.2- Rate of standard icons used: a number of standard icons used compared to the total number of icons in site

            3.1.1.1.3- Rate of standard pictograms used: number of standard pictograms used compared to the total number of pictograms in the site

Fig. 3. Portion of the hierarchical quality model with some definitions (for Understandability sub characteristics).

5 Quality Assessment Methodology

The methodology that we propose in this paper for WebApps quality assessment is structured in several phases:

1. Data collection using a questionnaire,
2. Data exploitation to characterize the selected criteria,
3. Attributing weight to criteria,
4. Metrics development for criteria assessment.

At this stage of our work, only the two first phases of the methodology are developed. The objective of the third phase is balancing the criteria. In fact, a criterion can be balanced differently according to pre-established objectives' and Web site domain (academic, commercial, etc). Thus, we do believe that determining weight or power for criteria and sub-criteria is necessary in view to improve accuracy evaluation. This is the matter of our current research.

5.1   Data Collection

Starting from the developed list of criteria, we established a questionnaire. Each criterion was defined. This will reduce the ambiguity during the evaluation process. Thereafter, we tried to identify the different quantifiable aspects, and hence release simple questions to which one can answer either YES, NO or NA (non applicable). For instance, to the question "Does the site have a table of content?" it is easy to check the site and answer YES or NO. As to the "Standards Compliance", we do use sub-criteria to evaluate the criterion itself, such as: Code is standard, Colors are standard, Link colors are standard, Menus are standard, Icons are standard, Metaphors are standard, Font is standard, etc. On the basis of former studies [13, 18], quantitative values have been culled out, so that they can be used in the questionnaire, in order to assess certain criteria. For instance: Maximum of 4 different fonts/page, Maximum of 6 different colors/page, Maximum of 10 hyperlinks/page, Home page displays within 10 s, Graphics are under 25K in size, Text font size between 10 and 12, Titles with less than 25 characters, etc.

Moreover, some criteria require the development of metrics, for a better and a more accurate quantification, such as "Number of links in the page", or "Scalability", whereas others are very subjective, such as for example, "Attractiveness" or "Links Relevancy". These criteria depend indeed on the evaluator's personal estimation and require a thorough investigation to get evaluated.

5.2   Data Exploitation

Every criterion is directly evaluated on the basis of its own sub-criteria. On considering the Site Update's example, we may evaluate, for instance, sub-criteria:

– The site is updated every week?	Yes
– The site is automatically updated?	No
– The last update date is present?	Yes
– Old pages are removed?	NA
– Obsolete content is removed?	Yes

We can answer to each criterion either Yes, No or NA. Thereafter, the criterion mark is calculated as follows: Mark = number of YES / (Number of sub-criteria – number of NA). The mark = 3 / (5 - 1) = 3/4 = 0.75, and so on, this calculation is made for each criterion. At this point, it is noteworthy that criteria and sub-criteria are not always of the same importance, whereas they are site type pending (academic, commercial, etc); "Updated Content" is crucial in informational site, but it's less important, for example, for a museum site. Thus, we do believe that determining weight or power for criteria and sub-criteria is necessary in view to improve accuracy evaluation. This is the main objective in the forthcoming phase. Nowadays, the objective is to experiment the developed questionnaire using the prototype that we developed [15], and see whether the questions targeted criteria allow a good characterization of the characteristics to which they are connected.

6   EQAW: Towards a WebApps Quality Assessment Tool

An environment composed of several tools supports the proposed methodology. The environment supports the assessment of the retained quality criteria. The actual version allows quality assessment of a given web site according to a chosen characteristic, some selected sub-characteristics, numerous or all of the retained quality characteristics. Indeed, a user can choose to evaluate the site understandability only (Usability sub-characteristics), or its functionality, reliability and maintainability, or even its global quality according to the retained characteristics. The results are displayed in the form of ranges of values, allowing a fast evaluation of the site. In the current state of our work, the prototype supports the first two phases of the suggested methodology. The choice of the established questions is based on their simplicity, their precision and also on their relevance for a characteristic or a given sub-characteristic.

The main goal at this stage is to validate the questionnaire and especially to make sure that the questions are clear and precise. On this subject, we plan to add help for assisting the evaluators as well as possible. The prototype allows, thus, giving us an outline of the quality of the selected sites and a preliminary evaluation of the proposed approach.

Sites / Factors	F	U
	90 %	93 %
Winner of *Webby* *Awards*	86 %	93 %
	80 %	93 %
	82 %	90 %
	83 %	90 %
Academic sites	65 %	54 %
	73 %	80 %
Amateur sites	64 %	64 %
	43 %	38 %
The *Worst of the* *Web*	39 %	33 %
	20 %	11 %

(a)

Sites / Factors	1 Fame	2 Gold	3 Silver	4 Bronze
Functionality	**88 %**	**96 %**	**77 %**	**77 %**
Suitability	84 %	95 %	81 %	76 %
Compliance	100 %	100 %	66 %	80 %
Usability	**80 %**	**90 %**	**71 %**	**79 %**
Understandability	89 %	97 %	90 %	89 %
Find information	83 %	90 %	73 %	74 %
Operability	75 %	94 %	72 %	85 %
Attractiveness	100 %	100 %	80 %	80 %
Others	60 %	68 %	31 %	58 %
Total	**84 %**	**93 %**	**74 %**	**78 %**

(b)

Fig. 4. Preliminary results of the prototype experimentation for several sites.

As a first experimentation of our approach, we have selected some web sites recognized for their good quality (for example starting from *Top 100 of Webby Awards or the PC Magazine*). Other web sites of average and poor quality were also evaluated for better refining the range of suggested values. The previous table (Fig. 4a) provides the obtained results. The margin of error (in the present version of the prototype) for this evaluation is about 7%. The preliminary results obtained after the experimentation of the prototype are rather promising. We obtained a very good score for the site recognized among the *Webby Awards*. An average score for an academic site (the second in the table) considered as unpleasant by its users. Finally, sites from The *Worst of the Web* achieve a very low score. In addition, for the web sites chosen among the *World*

Best Web sites *Awards*, an evaluation of some subcharacteristics of functionality and usability characteristics were measured.

Table 4b summarizes a part of the obtained results. We note that some criteria of less importance can penalize the sites (silver vs. bronze). This illustrates the importance of weighting the criteria for a more precise quality evaluation of these sites. A thorough study of these results makes it possible to note that:

- The results of the evaluations are very significant (the good sites have a very good score, and conversely for the bad sites), which show that the selected and evaluated criteria seem to be relevant.
- For a more precise evaluation, it will be necessary to balance the criteria and to develop metrics, which is already envisaged in our methodology.
- It will be necessary to make improvements to the prototype to make it more functional and more easily usable. The prototype must make it possible to dynamically generate a specific questionnaire for a web site to be evaluated by taking into account several aspects such as it's domain, nature, purpose, etc.

7   Multidimensional Quality Model

In order to evaluate WebApps, in [23] the authors define a cube structure in which they consider three basic aspects when testing a Web site. Following this idea, [24] proposed another "cube" which can be considered orthogonal, in which the three dimensions represent those aspects that must be covered in the quality evaluation of a Web site:

- Quality aspects using the QUINT2 model [20], which is based on the ISO 9126 standard [10].
- Life cycle processes using the ISO 12207-1 standard [11].
- Features: functions, contents, infrastructure and environment.

Recently, in [5] authors refined the Web features dimensions to the three "classic" Web aspects: Content, Presentation and Navigation. Although the two first dimensions are very suitable for Web sites quality assessment, we believe that the third dimension (Features) is somehow redundant. Indeed, its components are generally covered by some quality characteristics contained in the first dimension.

In addition, we noticed during our work, in particular through the evaluation of several sites, that according to the application domain, some criteria are more or less significant. Consequently, to evaluate a given Web site, we believe that these criteria will be attributed different weight depending on the nature of the application domain. If we consider, for example, the criterion "language", it is of primary importance for an information site or educational one, whereas it has much less importance for a page of "Stock Exchange". In the same way, "downloading time" takes more importance when considering for example a museum site presenting several pictures by comparison to Web sites presenting only textual information. We can also note the importance of "safety" for bank or e-commerce sites versus an amateur site where the problems of safety do not have much importance.

Moreover, several application domains have their own specific criteria. Some authors presented, initially, for each application domain its specific quality tree. Then in

[22], they propose a quality tree in which the criteria related to the application domain characterise the functionality. The application domain has also been proposed as a quality characteristic for Web sites in [3].

Thus, we consider that it would be relevant to adopt the model in three dimensions suggested in [23, 24], and to consider the variation of the "Application domain" as the third dimension replacing the "Features" dimension as illustrated in Figure 5. The application domain of Web sites can be subdivided in several categories: ecommerce, e-learning, e-gouv., e-edu., etc., as many different fields, where weighting criteria will be very different. Moreover, this model will have the advantage of being extensible. It will be able to support any new kind of Web sites in the future. We can also suggest the same possibility of extension for the "Quality Characteristics" dimension, considering that some work propose other quality characteristics or sub-characteristics than those proposed by ISO 9126 and which are more specific to the Web. For instance, in [21], authors suggest security, availability and scalability instead of functionality and portability. In the same idea, in [19], five quality sub-characteristics are proposed for the usability: learnability, efficiency, memorability, errors and user satisfaction.

The fields of Web applications quality attract many researchers and each year many interesting contributions are proposed. With this respect, an evaluation model must be flexible and extensible. With the suggested model, the evaluation of a given criterion will depend on the quality factor that it characterises. Its importance will be probably different according to the considered Life Cycle step, but will depend on the application domain of the site. In this way, the evaluation of a given criterion will be much more significant taking into account all the aspects that may affect this criterion. Our reasoning may be also extended to metrics, which will be used to evaluate a given criterion. We are conscious that the new model that we propose is very preliminary and more investigation for its complete application will be necessary.

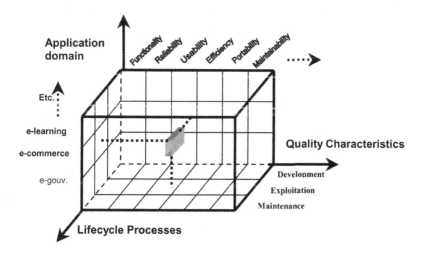

Fig. 5. A three-dimensional quality model.

8   Conclusion and Future Work

In this paper, the approach that we propose defines a global quality model taking into account various aspects, which currently affect the world of the web. Starting from several studies realized by researchers specialized in this field, we gathered the proposed criteria for WebApps quality assessment, defined other criteria which we considered relevant and then integrated the whole in a hierarchical model. Thus, we obtained a list with over than 300 criteria and sub-criteria, which we classified as quality characteristics and sub-characteristics according to the ISO/IEC 9126 standard. This list was restructured, extended and validated using the GQM paradigm. From the retained criteria, we have developed a questionnaire (first version) and a tool supporting its evaluation. As a first stage of the validation of our approach, we experimented the prototype on several Web sites (some of them are well-known). The preliminary results are rather encouraging.

Moreover, we noticed during our research, particularly through the evaluation of several Web sites, the relevance of the application domain of a Web site and its impact on the selection and the weighting of the majority of the criteria. Knowing that the majority of the authors in this field do not agree on the way of taking into account this very significant aspect in the web sites evaluation, we defined a threedimensional WebApps Quality Model including the developed hierarchical model, the life cycle processes and the WebApps domain. This constitutes, in our opinion, a unified framework for the WebApps quality assessment taking into account their several characteristics.

We believe that the present work constitutes an interesting starting point in this field and represents an improvement of WebApps evaluation. However, more conclusive results are waited after the association of metrics with the selected criteria according to the GQM paradigm. As future work, we plan to: (1) improve the developed prototype particularly by generating dynamically a specific questionnaire for a given application domain, (2) extend our methodology, especially, by pondering criteria and using existing web metrics, and (3) validate the multidimensional model proposed in this paper.

References

1. Abrahao, S., Olsina, L., Pastor, O.: A Methodology for Evaluation Quality and Functional Size of Operative WebApps. Proceedings of 2nd International Workshop on Web Oriented Software Technology, ECOOP'02 Workshops. Malaga, Spain. (2002)
2. Basili, V.R.: Software Modeling and Measurement: The Goal Question Metric Paradigm. Computer Science Technical Report Series, CS-TR-2956 (UMIACSTR-92-96). University of Maryland, College Park, MD. (1992)
3. Boldyreff, C., Gaskell, C., Marshall, A., Warren, P.: WEB-SEM Project: Establishing Effective Web Site Evaluation Metrics. Proceedings of 2nd International Workshop on Web Site Evolution WSE'2000, Zurich, Switzerland. (2000)
4. Brajnik, G. Automatic Web Usability Evaluation: Where is the Limit?. Proceedings of the 6th Conference on Human Factors & the web. Austin TX. (2000)
5. Calero, C., Ruiz, J., Piattini, M.: A Web Metrics Survey Using WQM. Proceedings of the International Conference on Web Engineering (ICWE'04). (2004)
6. Cutter Consortium: Poor Project Management – Problem of E-Projects. (2000) www.cutter.com/press/001019.html

7. Dalton, S.: A Workbench to Support Development and Maintenance of World-Wide Web Documents. MSc Thesis, Supervisor: Dr. C. Boldyreff, Department of Computer Science, University of Durham. (1996)
8. Differding, C., Hoisl, B., Lott, C.M.:Technology Package for the Goal Question Metric Paradigm. Internal Report 281/96. (1996) wwwagse.informatik.uni-kl.de/publications/paper/gqm-96.pdf
9. Fleming, J.: WEB Navigation: Designing the User Experience. O'Reilly. (1998)
10. ISO/IEC 9126.: Software Product Evaluation - Quality characteristics and Guidelines for their use. (2001)
11. ISO/IEC 12207. *Information Technology*. Software Life Cycle Processes. (1995)
12. Ivory, M., Hearst, M.: Towards Quality Checkers For Web Site Designs. IEEE Internet Computing. (2002)
13. Keevil, B.: Scaling the Heights: The Future of Information Technology. SIGDOC98 Conference. Quebec City, QC. (1998)
14. Lycett, M.: Understanding Variation in Component-based Development: Case Finding from Practice. Information and Software Technology Journal, 43. (2001) 203-213
15. Malak, G.: Évaluation de la Qualité des Applications Web. Mémoire de maîtrise. Département d'informatique, Université Laval, Québec, Canada. (2002)
16. Malak, G., Belkhiter, N., Badri, L., Badri, M.: Evaluation de la Qualité des Applications Web: État de l'Art. INFORSID'02 Conference. Nantes, France. (2002)
17. Malak, G., Badri, L., Badri, M., Belkhiter, N.: Web-Based Applications Quality: Evaluation and Perspectives. Proceedings of the International Conference on Internet Computing IC'02. Las Vegas, USA. (2002) 939-946
18. Nielsen, J.: Designing Web Usability: The Practice of Simplicity. New Riders Publishing. (2000)
19. Nielsen, J.: 1996-2003, The Alertbox. Available on-line at www.useit.com/alertbox/
20. Niessink, F.: Software Requirements: Functional & Non-functional Software Requirements. (2002) www.cs.uu.nl/docs/vakken/swa/20012002/Slides/SA-2-Requirements.pdf
21. Offutt, J.: Web Software Applications Quality Attributes. Quality Engineering in Software Technology (CONQUEST 2002). Nuremberg, Germany. (2002) 187-198
22. Olsina, L. Rossi, G.: Measuring Web Application Quality with WebQEM. IEEE MultiMedia, Vol. 9, No. 4. (2002)
23. Ramler, R., Weippl, E., Winterer, M., Shwinger, W., Altmann, J.: A Quality-Driven Approach to Web Testing. Iberoamerican Conference on Web Engineering, ICWE'02. Argentina. Vol. 1. (2002) 81-95
24. Ruiz, J., Calero, C., Piattini, M.: A three Dimensional Web Quality Model. Proceedings of the International Conference on Web Engineering (ICWE'03), LNCS 2722. (2003) 384-385
25. Wu, Y., Offutt, J.: Modeling and Testing Web-based Applications. GMU ISE Technical ISE-TR-02-08. (2002)

Structuring Web Sites Using Linear Programming*

Wookey Lee[1], Seung Kim[2], and Sukho Kang[2]

[1] Dept. of Computer Engineering, Sungkyul Univ., Anyang-8-dong, Manan-gu, Anyang, Korea
wook@sungkyul.edu
[2] Dept. of Industrial Engineering, Seoul National Univ., San 56-1, Sillim-dong, Gwanak-gu,
Seoul, Korea
{seung2@netopia,shkang@cybernet}.snu.ac.kr

Abstract. World Wide Web is nearly ubiquitous and the tremendous growing number of Web information strongly requires a structuring framework by which an overview visualization of Web sites has provided as a visual surrogate for the users. We have a viewpoint that the Web site is a directed graph with nodes and arcs where the nodes correspond to Web pages and the arcs correspond to hypertext links between the Web pages. In dealing with the WWW, the goal in this paper is not to derive a naïve shortest path or a fast access method, but to generate an optimal structure based on the context centric weight. We modeled a Web site formally so that a linear programming model can be formulated. Even if changes such as modification of the query terms, the optimized Web site structure can be maintained in terms of sensitivity.

1 Introduction

The World Wide Web is now almost ubiquitous. Web browsers allow users to access on the order of 8 billion Web documents [1]. Because of a vast amount of Web information (pages), as a browser session progresses, the users sometimes feel "being lost in hyperspace" [2, 3]. So, users of Web information, accessible over the global Internet, require assistance by appropriate visualization methods.

The WWW can be viewed as a digraph consisting a bag of Web sites. The Web site is a directed graph with Web nodes and arcs, where the Web nodes correspond to HTML files having page contents and the arcs correspond to hypertext links interconnected with the Web pages. A Web site can be viewed as a specific directed graph that consists of an initial node (called homepage) and other nodes connected to it. There is a natural mapping approach of a Web onto a directed graph where the nodes correspond to Web pages and the arcs to URIs (Uniform Resource Identifiers) [4, 5]. A hierarchical structuring such as Web catalogues or super books [6, 7, 8] is one of the typical examples of web site structuring. But complex and static Web abstractions do little to help a Web designer who wants to get modeled within a Web site and often cause navigation problems of their own. The problem of finding a tree structure of a Web site from a directed graph is exponential or NP-hard [9]. What is needed is a virtual Web site structure based on the current query or interest of a user.

---

* This work was supported by Korea Science and Engineering Foundation(KOSEF) through Advanced Information Technology Research Center (AITrc).

K. Bauknecht, M. Bichler, and B. Pröll (Eds.): EC-Web 2004, LNCS 3182, pp. 328–337, 2004.
© Springer-Verlag Berlin Heidelberg 2004

This paper is organized as follows. In section 2, we present the data model of Web sites, the Web schema and conventional approaches. In section 3, we treat keyword-based weight measure endowed to Web node. We developed a linear programming model and treat sensitivity analysis of proposed LP model in section 4. Then, the example of our model and the comparison of LP method between some relative methodologies are presented in section 5. Finally, we conclude the paper.

2   Web Data Model

2.1   Web Nodes

We assume that the data model of the World Wide Web consists of a hierarchy of Web objects. The WWW is viewed as a bag of Web sites. The Web schema contains the Meta information that represents a bag of Web pages in a Web site. The Web site is a directed graph with Web nodes and arcs, where the Web nodes correspond to HTML files having page contents and the arcs correspond to hypertext links interconnected with the Web pages. The Web node (W_i) is defined as follows:

$$W_i = [Webpage\text{-}Id, \{URI\}, \; weight] \tag{1}$$

Where the W_i represents a node corresponding to an HTML file (without loss of generality we set a node identifier i). Where the homepage is defined as a default page (for example, index.html or default.asp or index.php3, etc.) predetermined by the Web server. The {URI} is the bag of Web nodes having the hypertext links within which the Web page indicates. The *weight* represents the values specified by the measure of keywords (it will be discussed later in more detail). The Web page contents can be described as the attributes of the Web page such as title, Meta, format, size, modified date, text, figures, and multimedia files etc. In this paper, for convenience's sake, the Web page weight is generated by the method described in the following section 3.

2.2   Web Arcs

A Web site can be viewed as a directed graph that consists of an initial node (called the homepage) and the other nodes inter-connected among them. Complex Web representations do little to help the user orientation within the site and usually tolerate navigation problems themselves. A hierarchical abstraction is useful in organizing information and reducing the number of alternatives that must be considered at any one-time [10]. If the Web site can be represented as a hierarchical structure, those problems such as the multiple paths, the recursive cycle, the multi-path cycle, and multiple parents would be resolved. The problem is treated more specifically in [11, 12].

In this paper, the URI's are specified two types: interior arcs and exterior arcs. The interior arcs are the URI's that indicate the HTML files somewhere within the Web site, but the exterior arcs out of the Website. We are interested in the interior arcs only, for the structure of a Web site is generated in this paper. After preprocessing the URI's of a Web site, then standard (full length) IP addresses of every Web page are derived.

The exterior arcs are, however, discarded in the Preprocessing phase, for they have a different server IP address, i.e., a different site.

It can be noted that in some references [12, 13] the interior arcs are additionally classified two types such as interior and local. But it is needless to differentiate the internal arc in more detail. Because once a Web page is transferred from the Web server, there is no need to access the same Web page physically again. Actually in some web sites, there is only a Frame in the default page (ex, index.html). In that case, we give the URI's of the Web pages that the default frame includes.

2.3 Conventional Approaches

Depth first approach (DFA) is easy to adopt to cope with this kind of graphs, and from a cognitive science point of view, it seems similar with the behaviors of human snoopers. But the DFA seems not applicable in Web environment. Since usual Web pages are complicatedly inter-connected with other Web pages, it may bring about a long series of Web pages. The long series of Web pages may imply long time consumption to access a specific page.

On the other hand, there are several strengths in applying the breadth first algorithm (BFA) to Web site graphs. With the BFA an important Web page can easily be accessed. It is done by clicking relatively fewer steps from its homepage rather than by the DFA. It is easy to resolve a graph to a hierarchical tree and to minimize the depths to visit in a Web page. It can also be said that the access time can be minimized.

Wookey and Geller [14] suggested a weighted tree by a topological ordering algorithm that the tree is unbiased and minimize an average access from the root node. It also consider semantic relevance (*tf-idf*) between nodes in the same depth. But, when the Web page's weight is changed or the link structure is altered, total tree structure should be wholly reorganized.

3 Semantic Representation

3.1 Overview Visualization of a Web Sites

If an overview visualization of a Web site is additionally suggested to a user, it will be helpful to find a way where the user is. The tree structure applied by the breadth first algorithm is simple and easy to implement. But it is no use finding a significant page in a Web site or clustering pages with semantics. Thus we introduce an attribute called the weight to evaluate the significance of Web pages. Some experimental researches said that graphical representations support better navigation because this type of representation more precisely matches a user's mental model of the system [15, 16, 17]. Textual tools, however, suggest further advantages by allowing users to rapidly calibrate the extent of the site and to search visually in an efficient manner for particular information [18]. In this paper, we use the keyword-based measure as follows.

3.2 Evaluating the Weight Values

One common way to compute a Web page (or document) W is the *tf-idf* that is first to obtain an unnormalized vector $W' = \langle w'_1, \ldots, w'_m \rangle^T$, where each $w'_i (i = 1$ to m,

m is number of query terms) is the product of a word frequency (tf) factor and an inverse document frequency (idf) factor. The tf factor is equal (or proportional) to the frequency of the ith word within the document. The idf factor corresponds to the content discriminating power of the ith word: a word that appears rarely in documents has a high idf, while a word that occurs in a large number of documents has a low idf. Typically, idf is computed by $\log_2[N/df(qi)]$, where N is the total number of documents, and $df(q_i)$ is number of documents containing the ith word. (If a word appears in every document, its discriminating power is 0. If a word appears in a single document, its discriminating power is as large as possible.) Once W' is computed, the normalized vector W is typically obtained by dividing each w'_i term by $\sqrt{\sum_{i=1}^{m}(w'_i)^2}$. The weight can be specified in this paper indicating the importance of the Web page.

3.3   Semantic Representation

If we can measure the weight of Web nodes corresponding to their significance, then the structure of the nodes can be manipulated by the weight. We introduce the tf-idf as the weight measure and it can be used to determine the topological ordering of Web sites. Then simply by comparing the numerical differences of the tf-idf, it can be said that a node is closer to a specific node. As previously described before, the tf-idf measure is applied as a weight of the Web node. The weight of Web node W_i corresponding to query vector Q composed of each query term $q_i (i = 1$ to $m)$ is defined as a scalar derived as the inner product of the query vector Q with the Web page vector W_i:

$$weight(W_i) = Q \bullet W' = [q_i] \bullet tf_i \cdot \log_2[N/df(q_i)]]^T$$
$$= \sum_i q_i \cdot (tf_i \cdot \log_2[N/df(q_i)]) \qquad (2)$$

The prototype system called AnchorWoman (ver. 1.4.0) [14] has been implemented to search for which the link structure of the site. The processes to extract the weight of keywords and the abstraction of Web sites are achieved by following (refer to the figures Fig. 1(a) and Fig. 1(b)). If we select four search terms 'site, graph, structure, visualization', then the weights are calculated as in Fig. 1(a). The word 'site', for example, appears 5 times in the homepage W_0 (the page number in the system appears as page 1), and in turn 2, 1, 5, 2, 6, and 2 times in W1.html to W7.html, respectively.

Finally, we get the normalized vectors as follows: $W0 = \langle 0, 0.37, 0.32, 0.09 \rangle$, $W1 = \langle 0, 0.55, 0.16, 0.18 \rangle$, ..., $W7 = \langle 0, 0.18, 0, 0 \rangle$ (Fig. 1(b)). As a similar process, we can obtain the weight vector W for the query word 'web' (of the Web test site). $W = \langle 9.49, 3.45, 6.21, 7.59, 9.66, 12.42 \rangle$.

4   LP Modeling and Sensitivity Analysis

4.1   LP Modeling

LP(Linear Programming) can be used to convert a digraph to a tree. First, a tree possesses its own property to which an LP's constraints can be derived.

site	graph	structure	visualizat
1	5	2	2	1
2	2	3	1	2
3	1	0	0	1
4	5	0	1	4
5	2	0	0	0
6	6	4	2	2
7	2	1	0	0
N	7	7	7	7
DF	7	4	4	5
IDF	0	0,24	0,24	0,15

Word	W'						
site	0,00	0,00	0,00	0,00	0,00	0,00	0,00
graph	0,37	0,55	0,00	0,00	0,00	0,73	0,18
structure	0,32	0,16	0,00	0,16	0,00	0,32	0,00
visualizat	0,09	0,18	0,09	0,35	0,00	0,18	0,00

(a) Term Frequency and *tf-idf* Values   (b) Normalized Weight Vector Generator

Fig. 1. Weight Production Module of the System

- The objective function is to maximize the summation of the weight of nodes.
- Node's indegree should be 1. (Except for the root node)
- A cycle should be removed.
- A self-cycle within a node should be removed.
- Duplicated paths between adjacent two nodes should be removed.

So, considering to above constraints, LP formulation is as followed.

$$Max \sum_{i,j \in N} w_{ij} x_{ij} \tag{3-(1)}$$

$$s.t. \sum_{i,j \in N} x_{ij} \begin{cases} = 0 & j = 0 \\ \le 1 & j \ne 0 \end{cases} \quad \forall i \tag{3-(2)}$$

$$x_{ij_1} + \sum_{k=1}^{m-1} x_{j_k j_{k+1}} + x_{j_m i} \le m \quad \text{for} \quad m \ge 2 \tag{3-(3)}$$

$$x_{ii} = 0 \quad \forall i \in N \tag{3-(4)}$$

$$x_{ij} = 0 \quad \forall i, j \notin N \tag{3-(5)}$$

$$x_{ij} = 0 \quad \text{or} \quad 1. \tag{3-(6)}$$

A directed Web graph G(N, A) consists of a Web node N and a Web link between Web nodes, where a Web node (called node) corresponds to a Web page and a Web link (called link) a hypertext link. A Web site is defined as a directed graph G (**W**, **E**) consisting of a finite Web node bag **W** and a finite Web arc bag **E** of ordered pairs of Web nodes. **W** and **E** are represented as a bag of Web node elements W_i and a bag of Web arc elements (W_i, W_j) respectively, where $i, j \in \psi = \{0, 1, 2, 3, \dots, n-1\}, n$ represents cardinality of web pages $= |\mathbf{W}|$, and ψ a Web node set. Then the variable x_{ij} is 0 (when a Web link from node i to node j does not exist) or 1 (link from node i to node j exists). The parameter w_{ij} represents an average weight from node i to node j. There are several alternatives to derive the weight of a node and to generate a geometric distance to the link, including the number of inward or outward links [19]. Of course, it is not restricted to the method to generate a distance between the Web nodes. In this paper, we get a weight by *tf-idf* to each node, and generate a Euclidian distance w_{ij} from node i to node j.

The objective function 3-(1) means maximization of tree path's total sum of average mean weight. The constraint 3-(2) means each tree node's *indegree* should be 1 (except for the root node). The constraints 3-(3) and 3-(4) are to remove a cycle and a self-cycle respectively. The constraint 3-(6) represents the LP problem is a sort of IP(Integer Programming). That is to say, there is a link or not. According to the constraint 3-(6), the variable x_{ij} can be 0 or 1, i.e. it can be used to remove multiple paths. Additionally, a virtual path from all nodes to all nodes without physical links should be nullified in constraint 3-(5). Finally, by using the above LP, the path that owns a high weight in the digraph survived in the result tree.

The cycle detection algorithm plays a role to detect cycle in digraph, and make topological order in digraph. Note that not limited a specific cycle detection algorithm, but refer to [21] for further consideration. It is used in making *equation 3-(3)*.

4.2 Sensitivity Analysis

When the query terms are altered, *tf-idf* measures of the Web Node are also altered. In this case, sensitivity analysis can be used in determining whether whole problem should be reformulated and recalculated or not. The standard LP problem form separated basic variable between nonbasic variable likes follows 4-(1), 4-(2), we can get equation $c_{BV}x_{BV} + c_{BV}B^{-1}Nx_{NBV} = c_{BV}B^{-1}b$ by multiplying $c_{BV}B^{-1}$ to constraint 4-(2).

$$z - c_{BV}x_{BV} - c_{NBV}x_{NBV} = 0 \qquad (4\text{-}(1))$$
$$st \quad Bx_{BV} + Nx_{NBV} = b \qquad (4\text{-}(2))$$
$$x_{BV}, x_{NBV} \geq 0$$

Now, we can get the equation $c_{BV}x_{BV} = c_{BV}B^{-1}b - c_{BV}B^{-1}Nx_{NBV}$. And substitute this equation for $c_{BV}x_{BV}$ term in 4-(1). Then,

$$z - (c_{BV}B^{-1}b - c_{BV}B^{-1}Nx_{NBV}) - c_{NBV}x_{NBV} = 0 \qquad (5\text{-}(1))$$
$$z + (c_{BV}B^{-1}N - c_{NBV})x_{NBV} = c_{BV}B^{-1}b \qquad (5\text{-}(2))$$

The criteria of optimality in simplex algorithm is that an objective *function*'s coefficient of nonbasic variable, i.e., $\bar{c}_j = C_{BV}B^{-1}a_j - c_j$ is non negative. Also, the feasibility condition of the current basis solution is that equation $(x_{BV} + B^{-1}Nx_{NBV} = B^{-1}b)$ which obtained by multiply equation 4-(2) by B^{-1})'s RHS is nonnegative. In other words, sufficient and necessary condition of current solution's optimality is as follows [21][1].

- $\bar{c}_j = C_{BV}B^{-1}a_j - c_j \geq 0$ (dual feasible, optimality condition)
- $B^{-1}b \geq 0$ (primal feasible)

When the weight of the Web node is changed, if these change does not influence the above two conditions (i.e., the optimality and feasibility condition) current basis is conserved. Details are explained in chapter 5.

---

[1] Besides above two conditions, complementary lackness condition should be added. But, the Gaussian elimination in t Si plex Algorithm always keeps comple entary slackness.

5   Motivating Examples and Comparison

5.1   Motivating Example

Fig. 2 (a) represents a digraph consist of 7 Web pages from Web page W_0 to Web page W_6. The weight of a arc is the mean average value(*tf-idf*) of two terminal nodes of the arc. By using the LP problem consists of equations from (3)-1 to (3)-6, we can get the solution in Fig. 2 (b).

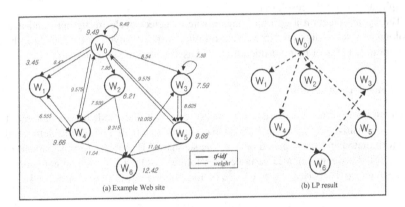

(a) Example Web site   (b) LP result

Fig. 2. An example Web site and its hierarchical abstraction using LP

5.1.1 The alteration of the Web page's *tf-idf*. If Web page's *tf-idf* value is changed, corresponding objective function's coefficients of the variables are also changed. But, it don't break primal feasibility condition. So, if all nonbasic variable's $\bar{c}_j = C_{BV}B^{-1}$ $a_j - c_j$ is nonnegative, i.e. if optimality condition is conserved, current basis does not change.

5.1.2 The insertion of the new link. Consider the case of node W_4 and W_3 is connected (from W_4 to W_3). In matrix N, coefficient of variable x_{43}, i.e., a_{43}'s value is changed from 1 to 0. In this case, x_{43} is a nonbasic variable, so nonbasic matrix N's change does not hurt feasibility($\mathbf{B}^{-1}\mathbf{b}\geq0$) and optimality($\bar{c}_j = C_{BV}B^{-1}a_j - c_j \geq 0$) condition. Hence, the only coefficient that may change from positive to negative, i.e., $\bar{c}_{43}$'s sign confirmation is sufficient for determining basis alteration.

5.1.3 The deletion of the link. In case of link deletion, the constraint that forms as $x_{ij} = 0\ \forall i,j \notin N$ is inserted into LP formulation. Now, if current solution does satisfy the new constraint, current basis is maintained. In other case, dual simplex algorithm can be used. Consider the case where two links between node W_1 and W_4 are disconnected. Then it should be included the two constraints($x_{14} = 0$ and $x_{41} = 0$) into previous LP formulation. Because the current solution satisfies the inserted constraints, current basis is maintained.

5.1.4 The insertion of the new Web page. In this case, the objective *function* coefficient, the element of **N** matrix for new inserted variable, and all constraint type(3-(1)–3-(4), except nonnegative constraint 3-(5)) can be included in LP formulation. So, this case's current basis does not conserved.

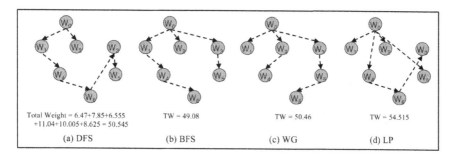

Fig. 3. The solution comparison to LP and others

5.2   The Comparison to the Other Methodologies

Fig. 3 represents trees constructed by an LP and other methodologies. First, the tree that is constructed by DFS(Depth First Search) and BFS(Breath First Search) can easily be constructed by only traversing the digraph's link structure. But, DFS produces a left(or right) biased tree because it uses only the digraph's link structure and its depth first search strategy. In this case, it ignores Web page's semantic priority or a relationship between the nodes so that it may lead to user's wrong web traversing. In BFS, it makes a tree that minimizes an average access step from the root node to each node. But, it also ignores Web page's semantic priority, so the result tree can be semantically irrelevant.

The tree that is constructed by Wookey and Geller [14] is unbiased and minimize an average access from the root node to each nodes like BFS. It also considers semantic relevance(*tf-idf*) between nodes in the same depth. But, when the Web page's weight is changed or the link structure is altered, total tree structure should be wholly reorganized. Especially, because its own tie-breaking scheme, when Web page's *tf-idf* value is infinitesimally altered and previously, tie is occurred including that page, the tree structure should be changed though variation is infinitesimal.

Unlike other methods, because it considers semantic relevance among Web pages in the digraph, the tree constructed by LP can lead user's right web traversing. In Fig. 3, W_3's depth is 1 so that it can be accessed from the root node directly in the digraph. But, semantic relevance between W_3 and W_6 is higher rather than that of distance between W_1 and W_3, so W_3 is connected through W_6 instead of the root node in the result tree. Also, it is self-evident that the tree is constructed by LP maximize total tree weight (In this example, total weight of LP tree is 54.515. See Table 1). In respect of the tree depth or the number of span, the LP tree also represents superior result than the others. In DFS, due to the DFS strategy, maximum depth of the result tree mostly be larger than that of original web site. In case of BFS and WG[14], maximum depth of the

Table 1. The result table of each methodology

		DFS	BFS	WG	LP
Total weight		50.545	49.08	50.46	54.515*
Depth		3	2	2	1.67*
Avg.		5	3*	3*	3*
	Max.	1*	1*	1*	1*
	Min.				
Span		2	3	3	4
Max.					

result tree may be less than or equal to that of original web site structure. The method, however, can be inferior to that of the LP in the average depth measure because the result tree of LP is reconstructed based on *tf-idf* criteria and the number of span can be more reduced than these two methods. Finally, because LP methodology facilitates incremental tree construction from the current basis, it is useful to apply to homepage that changes frequently.

6   Conclusions

In this paper, we proposed the method that makes a virtual hierarchical tree structure of a given Web site in dynamic manner. By using further visual information like this, users can access web sites effectively and assess the whole web site range fast. Also, linear programming that we adopt can make website structure optimally. When Web site structure is changed frequently by applying sensitivity analysis, web site structure can keep stability.

References

1. Barabasi A., Albert R., and Jeong H.: Scale-free characteristics of random networks: the topology of the world-wide web. Physica A 281 (2000) 69-77
2. Conclin, J.: Hypertext, an introduction and survey. IEEE Computer 20(9) (1987) 17-41
3. Lau, T., Etzione, O., and Weld D. S.: Privacy interfaces for information management. Communications of the ACM 42(10) (1999) 89-94
4. Chi, E. H.: Improving Web Usability Through Visualization. IEEE Internet Computing 6(2) (2002) 64-71
5. Korfhage, R.: Information Storage and Retrieval. Wiley Computer Publishing (1997)
6. Thomas K. Landauer, Dennis E. Egan, Joel R. Remde, Michael Lesk, Carol C. Lochbaum, and Daniel Ketchum.: Enhancing the usability of text through computer delivery and formative evaluation: the SuperBook project. Hypertext: A Psychological Perspective. Ellis Horwood (1993) 71-136
7. Dennis E. Egan, Joel R. Remde, Louis M. Gomez, Thomas K. Landauer, Jennifer Eberhardt, and Carol C. Lochbaum.: Formative design evaluation of SuperBook. Transaction on Information Systems 7(1) (1989) 30-57
8. Dennis E. Egan, Joel R. Gemde, Thomas K. Landauer, Carol C. Lochbaum, and Louis M. Gomez.: Behavioral evaluation and analysis of a hypertext browser. In Proc of the ACM SIGCHI Conference on Human Factors in Computing Systems. May (1989) 205-210

9. Pandurangan, G., Raghavan, P. and Upfal, E.: Using Page Rank to Characterize Web Structure. Proc. Int'l Conference on COCOON (2002) 330-339
10. Pilgrim, C. J. and Leung, Y. K.: Designing WWW Site Map Systems, Proc. 10th Int'l Workshop on DEXA (1999) 253-258
11. Huang, M., Eades, P., Wang, J. and Doyle, B.: Dynamic Web Navigation with Information Filtering and Animated Visual Display. Proc. Int'l Conference on APWeb98 (1998) 63-71
12. Mendelzon, A. O. and Milo, T.: Formal model of web queries, Proc. ACM PODS (1997) 134-143
13. Ng, W. K., Lim, E. P., Huang, C. T., Bhowmick, S., and Qin, F. Q.: Web warehousing: An algebra for web information. Proc. of the IEEE ADL (1998) 228-237
14. L. Wookey, J. Geller: Semantic Hierarchical Abstraction of Web Site Structures for Web Searchers. Journal of Research and Practice in Information Technology, Vol. 36, No. 1, Feb. (2004) 71-82
15. Hasan, M. Z., Mendelzon, A. O. and Vista, D.: Applying database visualization to the world wide web. ACM SIGMOD RECORD 25(4) (1996) 45-49
16. Zwol, R. and Apers P.: The webspace method: On the integration of database technology with multimedia retrieval. Proc. CIKM International Conference on Information and Knowledge Management, McLean, VA, USA, ACM Press (2000) 438-445
17. Risse, T., Leissler, M., Hemmje, M., Aberer, K. and Klement, T.: Supporting dynamic information visualization with VRML and databases. Proc. Workshop on New paradigms in information visualization and manipulation (1998) 69-72
18. Glover, E. J., Tsioutsiouliklis, K., Lawrence, S., Pennock, D. M., and Flake G.: Using web structure for classifying and describing web pages. Proc. WWW (2002) 562-569
19. Jingyu Hou and Yanchun Zhang.: Effective Finding Relevant Web Pages from Linkage Information. IEEE Trans. Knowledge and Data Engineering 15(4) (2003) 940-951
20. Subramani, K. and Kovalchick L.: Contraction versus Relaxation: A Comparison of Two Approaches for the Negative Cost Cycle Detection Problem. Proc. Computational Science (2003) 377-387
21. Katta G. Murty: Linear Programming. Wiley, New York. (1983)

Use of Semantic Tools for a Digital Rights Dictionary[*]

Jaime Delgado, Isabel Gallego, and Roberto García

Universitat Pompeu Fabra (UPF), Departament de Tecnologia,
Pg. Circumval·lació 8, E-08003 Barcelona, Spain
{jaime.delgado,isabel.gallego,roberto.garcia}@upf.edu

Abstract. RDDOnto is an ontology that translates the MPEG-21 RDD (Rights Data Dictionary) specification into a hierarchical set of definitions with semantic content included. In the event that this set of definitions is used, the RDDOnto must provide well-defined semantics to determine which rights apply to data at all points within the hierarchy. RDDOnto translates the RDD specification into a machine-readable semantic engine that enables automatic handling of rights expressions. The Terms defined in the RDD Specification are what is going to be modelled using OWL (Web Ontology Language). For each Term, its description is composed by a set of descriptive attributes. With OWL, all the RDD relations between a term and other terms that capture its semantics have been mapped to RDDOnto. The specification of MPEG-21 RDD using OWL has also allowed to verify the consistency of the dictionary.

1 Introduction

One of the main problems of the electronic commercialisation of multimedia resources in Internet is the management of its associated digital rights. New solutions are required for the access, delivery, management and protection processes of different content types in an integrated and harmonised way, to be implemented in a manner that is entirely transparent to the many different users of multimedia services.

MPEG-21 Part 6, Rights Data Dictionary (RDD), comprises a set of clear, consistent, structured, integrated and uniquely identified Terms to support the MPEG-21 Rights Expression Language. In turn, MPEG-21 Part 5, Rights Expression Language (REL), defines a language that enables to declare rights and permissions using the terms as defined in the Rights Data Dictionary.

The objective of this work is to translate the RDD terms descriptions from its current textual representation in the RDD specification document [1] to a machine processessable representation. Translating these descriptions to a machine-aware form would facilitate the integration of the RDD with the other parts of MPEG-21, specially REL, and the implementation of MPEG-21 compliant software tools.

In order to achieve these objectives, the target has been a knowledge representation framework with a wide range of utilities available. Our approach has been to use the Semantic Web paradigm. The web-orientation of this approach would also facilitate the integration of MPEG-21 implementations in the World Wide Web scenario.

---

[*] This work has been partly supported by the Spanish Ministry of Science and Technology under the AgentWeb project (TIC2002-01336).

K. Bauknecht, M. Bichler, and B. Pröll (Eds.): EC-Web 2004, LNCS 3182, pp. 338–347, 2004.

The Semantic Web paradigm is an attempt to leverage the Web from a distributed information repository to a distributed knowledge one. The Semantic Web basic tools are the Resource Description Framework (RDF) [2] and RDF Schema [3]. A more advanced tool is the Web Ontology Language (OWL) [4]. Using these tools and starting from our previous experience in developing a general ontology for Digital Rights Management [5], we have developed this ontology for the MPEG-21 RDD, IPROnto.

2 MPEG-21 Rights Data Dictionary (RDD)

The aim of MPEG-21 [6] is to define a multimedia framework to enable transparent and augmented use of multimedia resources across a wide range of networks and devices used by different communities. MPEG-21 is organized into several parts already developed or currently under development, see Table 1.

Table 1. MPEG-21 stantdard parts.

Part 1: Vision, Technologies and Strategy	Part 8: Reference Software
Part 2: Digital Item Declaration (DID)	Part 9: File Format
Part 3: Digital Item Identification (DII)	Part 10: Digital Item Processing
Part 4: Intellectual Property Management and Protection (IPMP)	Part 11: Evaluation Methods for Persistent Association Technologies
Part 5: Rights Expression Language (REL)	Part 12: Test Bed for MPEG-21 Resource Delivery
Part 6: Rights Data Dictionary (RDD)	
Part 7: Digital Item Adaptation (DIA)	Part 13: Scalable Video Coding
	Part 14: Conformance Testing

The sixth part of MPEG-21 specifies a Rights Data Dictionary for use within the MPEG-21 Framework. This Rights Data Dictionary forms the basis of all expressions of rights and permissions as defined by the MPEG-21 Rights Expression Language. MPEG-21 sees a Rights Data Dictionary as a dictionary of key terms which are required to describe rights of all users, which can be unambiguously expressed using a standard syntactic convention, and which can be applied across all domains in which rights need to be expressed. A Rights Expression Language is seen as a machine-readable language that can declare rights and permissions using the terms as defined in the Rights Data Dictionary.

The RDD System comprises the RDD Dictionary (Terms and their TermAttributes) and the RDD Database (the tool containing the RDD Dictionary). The Rights Data Dictionary consists in a set of clear, consistent, structured, integrated and uniquely identified Terms to support the MPEG-21 Rights Expression Language. The StandardizedTerms are specifically defined to support the REL and provide the foundation of the RDD Dictionary. New Terms, developed specifically to support REL requirements, independently or from mappings from other schemes, can be added to the RDD Dictionary through the registration of such Terms with the Registration Authority. The process to create such a Registration Authority to administer the RDD is under way.

As a closed ontology, all RDD terms are defined with reference to other Terms in the dictionary. This has two main consequences for the understanding of a term when it is used in an REL license. The first is that no assumptions should be made about the meaning of a term based on the coincidence that it bears the same name as something in an application domain. The second consequence concerns the inheritance of meaning. As the rights data dictionary is a hierarchical ontology, most of the meaning of a term is inherited from its parent(s) (in RDD terminology, its *Archetypes*). This RDD standard contains all the RDD StandardizedTerms listed in alphabetic order, each term is shown with its TermAttributes and all of its immediate Types and Allowed-Values.

The Dictionary has the characteristics of a structured ontology, in which meaning, once it has been defined, can be passed on from one term to another by logical rules of association such as inheritance and opposition.

The fourteen *ActTypes* which provide basic functionality for the REL are: *Adapt, Delete, Diminish, Embed, Enhance, Enlarge, Execute, Install, Modify, Move, Play, Print, Reduce* and *Uninstall*. They are employed within a rights expression.These Multimedia Extension Rights are capable of being used to create licenses required by Rights Holders. The fourteen *ActTypes* have been defined in response to requirements identified in the process of developing the REL and RDD Standards, particularly focused on common processes in the use and adaptation of Digital Resources. However, it is recognised that in future further *ActTypes* will have to be introduced into the RDD Dictionary in response to new requirements from REL users.

3   Semantic Web Concepts

In this section, RDF, RDFS and OWL are presented. RDF and RDFS are referred together as RDF/S. RDF is used to associate metadata to resources in order to make information about them explicit. Resources are named using URIs, i.e. URLs or URNs. The RDF modelling primitive is the graph. It is composed by a set of arcs used to assert property values about resources and to relate resources between them. Arcs are also called triples in RDF terminology. Each graph arc is composed by a subject URI (the resource about which the statement is made), a property URI and a value (literal) or an object URI (the resource to which the subject is related by the property).

An RDF description is composed by a set of arcs describing some resources. The set of arcs constitutes a graph that can be navigated in order to retrieve the desired metadata. There is an example in Fig. 1.

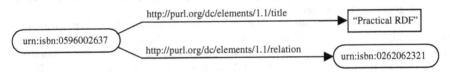

Fig. 1. RDF Graph constituted by three triples.

As it has been seen until now, RDF provides a framework to model metadata. The basic primitive is the graph. This can be compared with the XML context, where the modelling tool is the tree. However, as an XML tree, an RDF graph is on its own basically unrestricted. Therefore, in order to capture the semantics of a particular domain, some primitives to build concrete "how things are connected" restrictions are necessary.

The tool that provides these restriction-building primitives is RDF Schema. It can be compared to XML Schema or DTDs, which provide building blocks to define restrictions about how XML elements and attributes are related. The primitives are some restricted URN names defined in the RDF and RDFS namespaces.

RDFS provides Object Orientation-like primitives. With these primitives, class hierarchies can be defined. Resources are declared members of some of these classes and inherit their associated restrictions. The RDF/S classes are summarised in Section 6.1 of the RDF Schema specification [7]. Moreover, there is a special kind of class: Property. It contains all the resources used to relate subject and object in triples. Property hierarchies can also be defined, and domain (origin) and range (destination) of the RDF graph arcs can be restricted to specific classes. They are summarised in Section 6.2 of the RDF Schema specification [8].

The Web Ontology Language is a more advanced ontology building toolkit. It provides more fine-grained primitives that allow additional restrictions. OWL will allow mapping almost all the relations in Genealogy to RDDOnto. Many of the RDD relations in Genealogy are not mappable using only RDF/S constructs, more details about that are presented in the next section.

OWL is superset of RDF/S, i.e. in an OWL ontology all the primitives of RDF/S can be used. Therefore, when we refer to OWL primitives, all the primitives from RDF/S will be also considered. The primitives are summarised in Appendix A of the OWL Web Ontology Language Reference [9].

4   RDDOnto: An Ontology for Rights Data Dictionary

The set of all predefined classes and properties are the building blocks provided by the OWL and RDF/S frameworks. These building blocks are used to construct Semantic Web ontologies, i.e. sets of restrictions to the basic RDF elements. These restrictions can be automatically validated in order to test that a particular RDF description conforms to the semantics of the particular domain captured by the ontology.

In the next subsection, we will detail how first RDF/S and afterwards OWL frameworks can be used to capture the definition of RDD terms and a great part of their semantics. RDF/S is capable of modelling only a fraction of the RDD semantics. This fraction is augmented when the constructs introduced by OWL are also used. Therefore, two versions of the ontology can be produced. The simpler one uses RDF/S and the more complex uses OWL.

4.1   RDD Specification Analysis

The RDD Specification defines a set of terms. Terms are what is going to be modelled using RDF/S. For each term, its description is composed by a set of descriptive attributes:

- *Headword*: The term name. It must appear in the term description.
- *Synonym*: Some alternative names. It is not mandatory.
- *Definition*: A short text that defines the term.
- *MeaningType*: From a set of predefined types: *Original*, *PartlyDerived* and *Derived*.
- *Comments*: Extended textual information about the term. It is not mandatory.

– *Relationships*: Relations, from a set of predefined ones, between these terms an other terms that capture its semantics. The relations are classified in these categories:
   • *Genealogy*: The relations in this category will be the focus of RDDOnto. They are: *IsTypeOf, IsA, Is, IsEquivalentTo, IsOpposedTo, IsPartOf, IsAllowedValueOf, HasDomain, HasRange* and *IsReciprocalOf.*
   • *Types, Family, ContextView* and *Membership of Sets:* These categories will be analysed in future versions of RDDOnto. They are primarily concerned with the generative semantics of the RDD terms and they are less relevant during final ontology use.

These are the target attributes of RDDOnto. Their values will be mapped to OWL representation tools, which include also RDF/S ones, in order to capture the greatest part of their implicit semantics.

4.2 RDD to RDF/S Mapping

From the RDD Specification analysis two kinds of attributes can be detected. The first group is composed by those attributes with unstructured values, i.e. textual values. They can be easily mapped to predefined or new RDF properties with textual (literal) values. The first option is to try to find predefined RDF properties that have the same meaning that the RDD term attributes that are being mapped. When this is not possible, the RDFS constructs will be used to define new RDF properties to which the corresponding attributes will be mapped.

The mappings of this kind are shown in Table 2. Note that the Dublin Core [10] RDF Schema is also reused in RDDOnto. The Dublin Core (DC) metadata element set is a standard for cross-domain information resource description. The DC RDF Schema implements the Dublin Core standard.

Table 2. RDF mappings for the RDD attributes with textual value.

RDD Attribute	RDF Property	Kind of RDF property
Headword	rdf:ID	Predefined in RDF
Synonym	rddo:synonym	New property defined in RDDOnto
Definition	dc:description	Predefined in Dublin Core RDF Schema
MeaningType	rddo:meaningType	New property defined in RDDOnto
Comments	rdfs:comment	Predefined in RDFS Schema

The other kind of attribute is the Relationships one. Its value is not textual. Firstly, it is categorised in five groups: *Genealogy, Types, Family, ContextView* and *Membership of Sets*. Each of these groups is composed by a set of relation that can be used to describe a term related to other terms of the RDD Specification.

As has been justified in the previous section, only the Genealogy group is considered. The relations in this group are presented in the upper part of Table 3 together with a short description and the equivalent RDF property used to map them in RDDOnto. Only the RDD relations with an equivalent property in RDF/S are mapped at this level, i.e. *IsTypeOf, IsA, HasDomain* and *HasRange*. The other relations have associated semantics that do not have an equivalence in RDF/S.

Therefore, if the mapping is restricted to the possibilities provided by RDF/S, then we get an uncomplete ontology, i.e. it does not capture all the available semantics of RDD. However, on top of RDF/S, more advanced restriction building tools, like OWL, have been developed. In the next sections the improvements that can be done using OWL are presented.

4.3 RDD to OWL Mapping

Using OWL ontology building blocks, some of the previously unmapped RDD relations can be mapped to the RDD ontology. In bottom part of Table 3 they are presented together with a short description and the equivalent OWL property used to map them in RDDOnto. With OWL all the RDD relations that have been considered relevant have been mapped to RDDOnto, i.e. except those from *Relationships* that are not the *Genealogy* group.

Table 3. RDF and OWL mappings for the RDD relations in the Genealogy group.

RDD relation	Short description	RDF
IsTypeOf	Builds the hierarchy of term types	rdfs:subClassOf rdfs:subPropertyOf
IsA	Relates an instance term to its type	rdf:type
HasDomain	For relation terms defines the source term type of the relation	rdf:domain
HasRange	For relation terms defines the target term type of the relation	rdf:range

RDD relation	Short description	OWL
Is	Relates QualifiedResources to AscribedQualities	rddo:hasQuality
IsEquivalentTo	Relates two equivalent terms	owl:equivalentClass owl:equivalentProperty owl:sameIndividualAs
IsOpposedTo	Relates two opposite terms	owl:disjointWith (owl:complementOf)
IsPartOf	Relates a terms that is part of another term	rddo:isPartOf
IsAllowedValueOf	Relates an instance terms that is allowed value of a type term	Inverse of owl:oneOf
IsReciprocalOf	For relation terms defines the relation terms that captures the inverse relation	owl:inverseOf

4.4 Implementation

The RDD to RDF/S and OWL mappings that have been established in Table 2, Table 3 and Table 4 have been implemented in the RDDOntoParser. It is a Java implementation of these mapping using regular expressions [11]. Regular expressions are used to define patterns that detect the RDD part of the mappings. When patterns match, the corresponding RDF is generated in order to build RDDOnto.

The input of the RDDOntoParser is a plain text version of the Table 3 – Standardized Terms of the RDD Specification [1]. The output constitutes the RDDOnto Web ontology [12]. Fig. 2 shows a drawing of the Act hierarchy generated automatically from RDDOnto using the Protégé [13] ontology editor with the OntoViz visualisation plug-in.

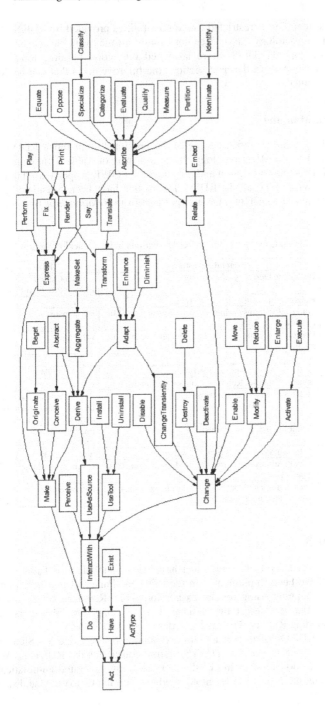

Fig. 2. ActType hierarchy diagram.

During the mapping process, some inconsistencies in the RDD specification have been found. One group are inconsistencies between RDD terms definitions and their graphical representations. Another group are references to terms not defined in the specification.

5 Using RDDOnto

Once the RDD ontology is ready, the Semantic Web tools that are available can be used to develop MPEG-21 RDD implementations. Some of these tools are presented in [14] and in [15]. In the next subsection, our experience with one of these tools is presented.

5.1 Using RDDOnto with Sesame

Sesame [16] is an RDF tool. Concretely, it is an RDF repository. It is used to store both RDF Schemas and metadata. In other words, it can store together web ontologies (Classes and Properties definitions) and instances of them that constitute resource descriptions. The stored schemas and metadata can be queried using three different query languages, navigated or serialised to RDF.

A Sesame RDF repository containing RDDOnto can be accessed at [17]. Sesame repositories can be easily created installing the Sesame software over a Java servlet container (e.g. Tomcat) and then configuring a metadata repository using a relational database (MySQL, Postgres or Oracle).

Once the Sesame repository is ready, the Sesame tool can be accessed using a web browser. From this interface, RDDOnto can be interactively uploaded and queried. For a programming interface, the RDDOntoAPI has been implemented. Some details are presented in the next section.

5.2 Using RDDOnto from Java

An RDDOntoAPI has been developed with Java in order to interact with RDDOnto, once it has been loaded into Sesame. This API is used to integrate RDDOnto with other tools, such as our REL (MPEG-21 Rights Expresssion Language) License Interpreter [18].

In order to facilitate API integration, RDDOntoAPI is also available from a web service interface. Web services are specified using the Web Services Description Language (WSDL) [19]. The RDDOntoAPI WSDL specification is available from [20]. Table 5 shows and example of use of the web service interface.

Table 4. Instancing the client service proxy to invoke getRDDSuperTypes operation.

```
import org.systinet.wasp.webservice.Registry;
import edu.upf.dmag.mpegontos.iface.RDDOntoAPI;
...
String wsdlURI = http://hayek.upf.es:8080/wasp/MPEGOntosAPI";
RDDOntoAPI service =
 (RDDOntoAPI)Registry.lookup(wsdlURI, RDDOntoAPI.class);
String[] superTypes = service.getRDDSuperTypes("Play");
```

The getRDDSuperTypes operation is used to retrieve from the RDD ontology (RDDOnto) all the parents of the given type, from the RDD point of view. For instance, if the RDD term is an act type like *Play*, all the parent act types will be returned: *Transform, Render, Perform, UseAsSource, Make, InteractWith, Expres,…*

This operation is used during license checking. If it fails for the required right, the parents of the right are retrieved and checked as, from the semantics of the acts hierarchy, it is derived that they include the rights appearing as subtypes.

It is implemented as a query submitted to the Sesame repository using one of the Sesame's query languages, RQL [21]. It is an augmented version of SQL that allows exploiting the greater expressive power of RDF, compared to relational databases.

6   Conclusions and Future Work

We have presented RDDOnto, an ontology for the MPEG-21 Rights Data Dictionary (RDD). Its added value over other initiatives to implement rights data dictionaries is that it is based on applying an ontological approach. This is done by modelling the RDD standard using ontologies. Ontologies allow that a greater part of the standard is formalised and thus more easily available for implementation, verification, consistency checking, etc.

RDDOnto demonstrates the benefits of capturing the RDD semantics in a computer-aware formalisation. It can be seen that it is easier to integrate RDD in order to develop MPEG-21 tools.

MPEG-21 tool implementers can use the API in order to facilitate access to many characteristics of this standard that are quite inaccessible from the resources directly provided, i.e. informal terms specifications. Indeed, this has been proven during the development of the REL License Interpreter [18].

Future plans are focused on applying also the ontological approach to another part of the MPEG-21 specification: the Rights Expression Language (REL). REL is specified in MPEG-21 using a different approach: XML Schemas.

Our intention is to automate the XML schema mapping to OWL ontology step. Then, once the REL ontology is available, it would be easier to integrate it with RDD as both will be formalised using the same language, OWL.

References

1. ISO/IEC FDIS 21000-6, MPEG-21 Rights Data Dictionary (RDD). N5842, July 2003
2. Lassila, O. and Swick, R.R. (eds.): "Resource Description Framework (RDF), Syntax Specification". W3C Recommendation, 2004, http://www.w3.org/TR/rdf-syntax-grammar
3. Brickley, D. and Guha, R.V. (eds.): "RDF Vocabulary Description Language 1.0: RDF Schema". W3C Recommendation, 2004, http://www.w3.org/TR/rdf-schema
4. Dean, M. and Schreiber, G. (eds.): "OWL Web Ontology Language Reference". W3C Recommendation, 2004, http://www.w3.org/TR/owl-ref
5. Delgado, J, Gallego I., Llorente, S., García R.: Regulatory Ontologies: An Intellectual Property Rights Approach. LNCS, Vol. 2889. Springer-Verlag, 2003. 621-634
6. Moving Picture Experts Group (MPEG) ISO/IEC/ JTC1 SC29/WG11, http://www.chiariglione.org/mpeg/index.htm

7. RDFSchema Summary: Classes,
   http://www.w3.org/TR/2004/REC-rdf-schema-20040210/#ch_sumclasses
8. RDFSchema Summary: Classes,
   http://www.w3.org/TR/2004/REC-rdf-schema-20040210/#ch_sumproperties
9. OWL Web Ontology Language Reference: Appendix A. Index of all language elements,
   http://www.w3.org/TR/2004/REC-owl-ref-20040210/#appA
10. Dublin Core Metadata Element Set, Version 1.1: Reference Description,
    http://dublincore.org/documents/dces/
11. Java 2 Platform Std. Ed. v1.4.2, Package java.util.regex,
    http://java.sun.com/j2se/1.4.2/docs/api/java/util/regex/package-summary.html
12. RDDOnto (RDD Ontology), http://dmag.upf.edu/ontologies/2003/11/rddonto.owl
13. Protégé Project, http://protege.stanford.edu
14. Dave Beckett's Resource Description Framework (RDF) Resource Guide
    http://www.ilrt.bris.ac.uk/discovery/rdf/resources/#sec-tools
15. DAML Tools, http://www.daml.org/tools
16. Sesame RDF Repository, http://sesame.aidministrator.nl
17. DMAG Sesame Repository, http://hayek.upf.es/sesame
18. Rodríguez, E.; Delgado, J. and Llorente, S.: "DMAG REL license interpretation using
    RDD term genealogy". ISO/IECJTC1/SC29/WG11/M10287. December 2003
19. Web Service Definition Language (WSDL), www.w3.org/TR/wsdl
20. MPEGOntosAPI Web Service Description Language (WSDL) specification,
    http://hayek.upf.es:8080/wasp/MPEGOntosAPI
21. RQL (Rdf Query Language) Tutorial, http://www.openrdf.org/doc/rql-tutorial.html

The Role of Electronic Commerce in Determining Desirable Customer Relationship Outcomes

Seongcheol Kim

School of IT Business, Information and Communications University
119 Munjiro, Yuseong-gu, Daejeon 305-714, Korea
hiddentree@icu.ac.kr

Abstract. In recognizing the significance of linking the power of electronic commerce to relationship marketing in continuously provided service context, this study investigates the role of electronic commerce in determining desirable customer relationship outcomes. In particular, this paper proposes the positive associations between customers' use of electronic commerce in stock trading and four customer relationship outcomes such as perceived service quality, overall satisfaction, attitudinal loyalty, and actual retention. Empirical data were collected from an intercept field survey of 170 customers of two major Korean stock trading brokers. Our main findings from a path analysis indicate that use of electronic commerce in stock trading is strongly associated with high levels of service quality and actual retention. Service quality turns out to play a significant mediating role in predicting the impacts of use of electronic commerce on overall satisfaction and customers' actual retention. Despite several limitations, including cross-sectional design conducted only in Korea, this study advances the understanding of the powerful role of electronic commerce in creating some desirable customer relationship outcomes.

1 Introduction

Recently, use of electronic commerce as a means of enacting transactions and relationships with customers is increasing exponentially [1][2]. Since inherent opportunities of electronic commerce for conducting business online are driving the development of a new customer relationship paradigm, development of new products and pursuit of low cost 'self-service' strategies [3][4], most organizations, large and small, are making major electronic commerce-related investments [5].

For example, in spite of the short history of electronic stock trading in Korea, most local brokers offer electronic stock trading services. The electronic trading value of stocks surged to nearly 60.3% of total trading value in December 2003 [6]. This is remarkable when compared to the online brokerage penetration ratio of other countries.

In recognizing the significance of electronic commerce, a lot of previous studies have concentrated mainly on the adoption of this new technological innovation in the context of business-to-business transactions or one-time business-to-consumer interaction. However, little academic research has investigated electronic commerce in the context of continuously provided service where the customer typically enters into a

K. Bauknecht, M. Bichler, and B. Pröll (Eds.): EC-Web 2004, LNCS 3182, pp. 348–356, 2004.

formal relationship with the service provider and, subsequently, consumes or uses the service (continuously or intermittently) for an extended time period. The goal of this paper is to examine the role of electronic commerce in determining desirable customer relationship outcomes in Korean stock trading industry where the development of electronic stock trading has been faster-than-expected. In particular, this paper would examine the effects of customers' use of electronic commerce in stock trading service context on key customer relationship outcomes such as perceived service quality, overall satisfaction, attitudinal loyalty and actual retention.

This paper is organized into five sections. The second section develops the research hypotheses based on the literature reviews. The third section describes the methods and procedures of this study. The following section presents the results of this study. The final section presents the summary and conclusions with the limitations and implications of this study.

2 Literature Review and Research Hypotheses

2.1 Impacts of Use of Electronic Commerce

The relevant stream of research in marketing has examined the impact of specific marketing efforts on perceptual dependent variables such as perceived service quality, overall satisfaction, attitudinal loyalty and actual retention [7]. These customer relationship outcomes have been the focus of relationship marketing theory and practice since delivering high quality service and having satisfied and loyal customers are viewed as indispensable for gaining a sustainable advantage [8].

Recently, as electronic commerce proliferates, all organizations, large and small, are making major electronic commerce-related investment decisions to stay in business and be competitive [5]. Electronic commerce investments are expected to improve the execution of business transactions over various electronic networks. These improvements may result in greater economic efficiency such as lower costs, and more rapid exchange [9]. In the meantime, according to Coulter and Ligas [10], new technological improvements such as electronic commerce can play important roles in how customers view service relationship. Thus electronic commerce investments are also expected to result in enhanced service quality and customer satisfaction but, ultimately, these two success factors are likely to lead to customer loyalty [11][12].

Given the importance of customer relationship outcomes to service businesses and the recent development of electronic commerce, a critical research agenda that requires attention is whether there is a significant link between electronic commerce-related investments and customer relationship outcomes [11]. A better understanding of the relationship between electronic commerce and customer relationship outcomes may provide service firms with information to decide the future of electronic commerce arrangements.

This research assesses the importance of electronic commerce as a strategic driver of customer relationship outcomes for a continuously provided service firm, in particular stock brokerage firm. We assume that the underlying processes through which customers' use of electronic commerce in stock trading leads to improvements in service quality and higher levels of overall satisfaction, and ultimately to such desired outcomes as attitudinal loyalty and actual behavioral retention

Hypothesis1 (H1): Customers' use of electronic commerce in stock trading is positively associated with their perceived service quality.

Hypothesis 2 (H2): Customers' use of electronic commerce in stock trading is positively associated with their perceived overall satisfaction with their stock brokerage firm.

Hypothesis 3 (H3): Customers' use of electronic commerce in stock trading is positively associated with their attitudinal loyalty.

Hypothesis 4 (H4): Customers' use of electronic commerce in stock trading is positively associated with their actual behavioral retention

2.2 Indirect Impacts of Use of Electronic Commerce

The dynamic relationships among service quality, customer satisfaction and customer behavior (loyalty, switching or repurchasing) constitutes the research area of particular interest [13]. The cumulative insights from previous studies support the general notion that service quality enhances customer satisfaction, which, in turn, contributes to customer loyalty [14]. The quality-satisfaction-loyalty linkage is also consistent with Heskett, Sasser, and Schlesinger's work [15] on the service-profit chain. In terms of retaining customers, previous research shows that service quality and overall service satisfaction can improve customers' intentions to stay with a firm [16].

We assume that use of electronic commerce in stock trading will have a positive effect on each of four key relationship outcomes such as perceived service quality, overall satisfaction, attitudinal loyalty and actual retention. In the meantime, the literature review on the dynamic relationships among those outcomes suggest that service quality can be a more central constructs which mediates the effect of use of electronic commerce in stock trading on overall satisfaction, attitudinal loyalty and actual retention. This leads to the following hypotheses:

Hypothesis 5 (H5): The effect of use of electronic commerce in stock trading on overall satisfaction is mediated by service quality.

Hypothesis 6 (H6): The effect of use of electronic commerce in stock trading on attitudinal loyalty is mediated by service quality.

Hypothesis 7 (H7): The effect of use of electronic commerce in stock trading on actual behavioral retention is mediated by service quality.

As was discussed earlier, if use of electronic trading is the sole exogenous variable, its effect on customer loyalty outcomes can be mediated by the link between service quality and overall satisfaction. This leads to the following hypotheses:

Hypothesis 8 (H8): The effect of use of electronic commerce in stock trading on attitudinal loyalty is mediated by service quality and overall satisfaction.

Hypothesis 9 (H9): The effect of use of electronic commerce in stock trading on actual behavioral retention is mediated by service quality and overall satisfaction.

3 Methods

3.1 Operational Measures

Measurement of most constructed variables in this study was executed by having respondents evaluate numerically a series of survey questions intended for the construction of multi-item composite measures. The validity of individual items was first examined using principal components factor analyses. Items that loaded as expected were included in creating multi-items indices. According to the method of average ratings, scores on items written to measure the same construct are summed and then averaged to create composite measures. All multi-item composite measures were subjected to reliability analyses.

Use of Electronic Trading: In order to measure actual use of electronic commerce in stock trading, the survey asked about the extent or degree to which stock transactions was made through electronic trading during last six months. This is a composite index with two items, including: 1) portion of total number of orders that was made through electronic trading during last six months; and 2) portion of total $value of orders that was made through electronic trading during last six months. The portion was estimated by the percentage, which was stated on a five-point scale ranging from 1 to 5: 1) 1% to 20%; 2) 21% to 40%; 3) 41% to 60%; 4) 61% to 80%; and 5) 81% to 100%. It was because raw percentages needed to be collapsed into more managerial and interpretable number of scale categories. In addition, 0 was assigned to the cases that never used electronic trading.

Service Quality: The items measuring service quality includes 1) consistency and dependability; 2) timeliness; 3) reliability and accuracy; 4) accessibility; 5) responsiveness and 6) personalization and customization.

Overall Satisfaction: The index consists of three statements including 1) I feel that this broker manages my account in a good way; 2) I am delighted with my overall relationship with this broker; and 3) I wish more of my suppliers were like this broker.

Attitudinal Loyalty: To measure the respondent's attitudinal loyalty, a seven-item composite index, representing all of three sub-dimensions such as relationship commitment, willingness to recommend and willingness for one-stop shopping, was operationalized based on previous marketing literature.

Actual Behavioral Retention: In order to measure the actual behavioral loyalty, the survey asked about the extent to which stock transactions was made through the respondent's primary broker during last six months. This is a composite index with two items, including: 1) portion of total number of orders that was made through the respondent's primary broker during last six months; and 2) portion of total $value of orders that was made through the respondent's primary broker during last six months. The portion was estimated by the percentage, which was stated on a five-point scale ranging from1 (1% to 20%) to 5 (81% to 100%).

3.2 Sampling and Data Collection

The individual customers (retail investors) of two major Korean stock trading brokers, that sponsored this empirical study, were selected for the sample population for this study. However, it was impossible to get a complete list of customers from these firms because of the strict regulation and concerns on privacy issues. Since the sampling frame for telephone or mail survey was not available, a field survey at the branches was selected for the alternative way of collecting empirical data for hypotheses testing. This method is often used and justified in marketing research, in particular in service marketing studies [17][18][19]. In spite of the possibility of missing the investors conducting electronic trading from their office or home, we assumed that significant portion of them use the cyber branches near their office or home during lunch or other break time. It is because that they may not be allowed to do electronic trading at work or they may prefer high-speed access to the Internet and better IT (information technology) environment available at the cyber branches to plain dial-up connection at home. In addition, even the investors conducting electronic trading from their office or home need to be supplemented by some periodic or irregular visits to offline branches, where they can monitor real market atmosphere, discuss investment strategy with other investors or catch up informal information.

Sampling of branches for the field survey was conducted based on the type (traditional physical branch versus cyber branch) and geographical dispersion to avoid local bias and to better represent the population. A total of 10 branches including 4 cyber branches were selected for a field survey.

Considering our observation and the suggestions of branch managers, the time zone around the lunch hour (between 11:00 a.m. to 2:00 p.m.) was selected as a convenient time to intercept the investors. It was because that most investors were busy around the market opening or closing time and many employed investors or homemakers seemed to visit the brokers' branches near their office or home during lunch break. Under the help and cooperation of branch managers, respondents were intercepted randomly at the selected branches. Of 220 contacted respondents, 33 refused to participate and 17 respondents did not finish the survey. One of the provided reasons for refusal to participate was their unhappiness with the portfolio performance. The main reason for incompletion was their tight schedule. Upon termination of data collection, a total of 170 retail investors were surveyed successfully, representing a response rate of 77%. Regarding sample characteristics, about half of respondents were in the age between 30 and 39 and more than 80% of respondents were male investors. In addition, about 60% of them turned out to graduate four-year college and have full-time jobs. This is consistent with the common sense that typical individual investors in Korea are normally male investors who are in the age of 30's, hold bachelor's degree, and are fully employed.

4 Results

As Figure 1 indicates, in the path model (structural equation model) use of electronic trading is specified as an exogenous variable, and service quality, overall satisfaction, attitudinal loyalty, and actual retention are specified as endogenous variables. Figure 1 contains the overall goodness of fit indices and the standardized parameter estimates for the hypothesized model (H1 to H9). This model was tested using the LISREL 8.2, which is a program for structural equation modeling.

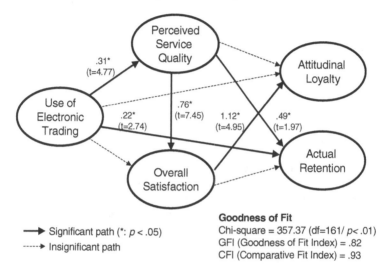

Fig. 1. The Result of Path Model.

The overall goodness of fit indices suggests a suitable and acceptable fit of the model to the data. The value of Chi-square statistic of 357.37 with 161 degrees of freedom indicated that the LISREL model would not be rejected by a test. This Chi-square statistic is statistically significant because our sample size (N = 170) is within the range recommended (100 < N < 200) for this statistic [20]. The goodness of fit index (GFI) value turned out to be .82. Though it is a little smaller than the general cutoff value of .90, this may be acceptable fit value because the sample size of this study is smaller than 250 [21]. The comparative fit index (CFI) value appeared to be .93, which is greater than the cutoff value of .90. This acceptable value of the CFI suggests that the hypothesized path model represented an adequate fit to the data [22].

As shown in Figure 1, five of nine standardized path coefficients are positive and statistically significant at the alpha level of .05 (t value is greater than 1.96). The five supports are found for relationships between use of electronic trading and service quality ($\gamma = .31$, p < .05), between service quality and overall satisfaction ($\beta = .76$, p < .05), between overall satisfaction and attitudinal loyalty ($\beta = 1.12$, p < .05), between use of electronic trading and actual retention ($\gamma = .22$, p < .05), and finally between service quality and actual retention ($\beta = .49$, p < .05). Thus hypotheses H1 and H4 were supported. However, the relationships between use of electronic trading and overall satisfaction (H2) and between use of electronic trading and attitudinal loyalty (H3) were not confirmed here.

Instead of a direct effect, use of electronic trading appeared to have an indirect effect through service quality on overall satisfaction. Thus hypothesis H5 was supported. However, use of electronic trading appeared not to have an indirect effect through service quality on attitudinal loyalty. Thus hypothesis H6 was rejected. In the meantime, use of electronic trading appeared to have not only a direct effect but also an indirect effect through service quality on actual retention. Thus hypothesis H7 was also supported.

In addition, according to Figure 1, use of electronic trading turned out to have an indirect effect through overall satisfaction as well as service quality on customers' attitudinal loyalty. Thus H8 was also supported. However, hypothesis H9 was not supported.

5 Conclusions

This study contributes to the literature on electronic commerce and service relationship marketing by empirically examining the impacts of customers' use of electronic commerce in stock trading on customer relationship outcomes in the context of Korean stock trading industry, where electronic trading has already taken off.

It was the goal of this study to identify the dynamic relationships among use of electronic commerce and four relationship outcomes. The results of a structural equation analysis confirm two of four direct associations between use of electronic commerce and relationship outcomes: 1) use of electronic commerce and service quality, and 2) use of electronic commerce and actual retention. Service quality turns out to play a significant mediating role in predicting the impacts of use of electronic commerce on overall satisfaction and customers' actual retention. Overall satisfaction also appears to play a mediating role with service quality in predicting the impacts of use of electronic commerce on customers' attitudinal loyalty.

While it has successfully addressed the proposed hypotheses, as with most research efforts, this study is not without limitations. One limitation relates to the sampling procedure. This study adopted a customer intercept field survey at the selected branch offices because it was impossible to get a complete customer list for random sampling. Though the sample of this study may not represent the targeted population well, regulation on customer privacy information necessitated and justified the use of this method as an alternative way of sampling and data collection. Moreover, considering the relatively large number of research variables, the sample size of this study may be a little small and need to be increased. Another limitation is regarding the cross-sectional design of this study. Since the data was collected at a single point of time, it is only possible to make conclusions regarding the associations among the research variables. Causal linkages and implications could be strengthened with multiple years of measurement of the research variables. This longitudinal approach may be adequate to capture changes in some variables or establish a direction. For example, the strengths of the findings will be enhanced by the use of longitudinal data in trying to predict actual behavioral retention.

Several managerial implications emerge from this study. For managers, it is evident that the time has arrived where no brokerage firm can ignore the benefits that a sound electronic commerce system can provide. Thus, it is essential that managers should recognize that electronic commerce strategies lie at the heart of the capability for survival. In addition, before they commit adequate resources, managers should make sure that electronic commerce strategies produce the desirable outcomes to justify their required investments. They should assess the potential of electronic commerce in producing favorable outcomes when they implement and operate an electronic commerce system.

For further studies, it would be interesting to examine the possible reverse association between use of electronic commerce and customer relationship outcomes. It is because increased relationship outcomes may encourage more use of electronic commerce. Moreover, this possible causal linkage should be studied by a longitudinal approach.

References

1. Hoffman, D.L., Novak, T.P.: How to acquire customers on the web. Harvard Business Review. 78(3) (2000, May-June) 179-188
2. Davis, R., Buchanan-Oliver, M., Brodie, R.: Relationship marketing in electronic commerce environments. Journal of Information Technology. 14 (1999) 319-331
3. Costello, G.I., Tuchen, J.H.: A comparative study of business to consumer electronic commerce within the Australian insurance sector. Journal of Information Technology. 13 (1998) 153-167
4. Dunn, J.R., Varano, M.W.: Leveraging Web-based information systems. Information Systems Management. (1999, Fall) 60-69
5. Berthon, P., Hulbert, J.M., Pitt, L.F.: To serve or create? Strategic orientations toward customers and innovation. California Management Review. 42(1) (1999) 37-58
6. Korean Securities Dealers Association: A report on online stock trading. (2004).
7. Zeithaml, V.A.: Service quality, profitability, and the economic worth of customers: What we know and what we need to learn. Journal of the Academy of Marketing Science. 28(1) (2000) 67-85
8. Shemwell, D.J., Yavas, U., Bilgin, Z.: Customer-service provider relationships: An empirical test of a model of service quality, satisfaction and relationship-oriented outcomes. International Journal of Service Industry Management. 9(2) (1998). 155-168
9. Kalakota, R., Whinston, A.B.: Electronic commerce: A manager's guide. Reading, MA: Addison Wesley (1997)
10. Coulter, R.A., Ligas, M.: The long good-bye: The dissolution of customer-service provider relationships. Psychology & Marketing. 17(8) (2000) 669-695
11. Appiah-Adu, K.: Marketing effectiveness and customer retention in the service sector. The Service Industries Journal. 19(3) (1999) 26-41
12. Krishnan, M.S., Ramaswamy, V., Meyer, M.C., Damien, P.: Customer satisfaction for financial services: The role of products, services, and information technology. Management Science. 45(9) (1999) 1194-1209
13. Athanassopoulos, A.D.: Customer satisfaction cues to support market segmentation and explain switching behavior. Journal of Business Research. 47 (2000) 191-207

14. Parasuraman, A., Grewal, D.: The impact of technology on the quality-value-loyalty chain: A research agenda. Journal of the Academy of Marketing Science. 28(1) (2000) 168-174

15. Heskett, J.L., Sasser, W.E., Jr., Schlesinger, L.A.: The Service Profit Chain, New York: Free Press (1997)

16. Keaveney, S. M.: Customer switching behavior in service industries: An exploratory study. Journal of Marketing. 59(2) (1995) 71-82

17. Gwinner, K.P., Gremler, D. D., Bitner, M. J.: Relational benefits in services industries: The customer's perspective. Journal of the Academy of Marketing Sciences. 26(2) (1998) 101-114

18. Ruyter, K., Wetzels, M., Bloemer, J.: On the relationship between perceived service quality, service loyalty and switching costs. International Journal of Service Industry Management. 9(5) (1998). 436-453

19. Pritchard, M.P., Havitz, M.E., Howard, D.R.: Analyzing the commitment-loyalty link in service contexts. Journal of the Academy of Marketing Science. 27(3) (1999) 333-348

20. Szymanski, D.M., Hise, R.T.: e-Satisfaction: An initial examination. Journal of Retailing. 76(3) (2000) 309-322

21. Hu, L., Bentler, P.M.: Evaluating model fit. In R.H. Hoyle (eds.): Structural equation modeling: Concepts, issues, and applications. Thousand Oak, CA: Sage (1995)

22. Byrne, B.M.: Structural equation modeling with EQS and EQS/Windows: Basic concepts, applications, and programming. Thousand, CA: Sage (1994)

Value Based Management
and Strategic Planning in e-Business

Chien-Chih Yu

National ChengChi University
Taipei, Taiwan, ROC 11623
ccyu@mis.nccu.edu.tw

Abstract. Value creation has been considered as a central strategic task in e-business management while strategic planning has been noted as a critical step in e-business development. This paper aims at providing a conceptual approach for developing e-business models, identifying e-business values, and then directing subsequent value based strategic planning process according to the integrated e-business model framework. Value-related dimensions identified in this paper include market, supply chain, enterprise, product and service, and customer. Accordingly, value based e-business strategies to be planned include market strategy, supply chain/value chain strategy, organization strategy, product and service strategy, and customer strategy. Also discussed are value management functions and process.

1 Introduction

For the past few years, the issues of value proposition, creation, and management in e-business (EB) have received considerable attention [5,7,9,10,15,19,20,21,22,25]. In a special issue of Industrial Marketing Management on Customer Value in Business Markets [20], value is addressed from three different perspectives: value creation for the customer, value creation for the supplier, and joint buyer-seller value creation. Three domains for future customer value research brought up in this issue include theory development, measurement techniques, and marketing strategy development and implementation. The measurement of business value has also been described using different point of views. Some see it as economic profits involving costs and revenues, others view it as non-monetary benefits such as competitive gains, social relationships, and management capabilities [5,9]. Actual assessment of business values is hard due to the complexity of identifying and measuring both the quantitative and qualitative benefits. Although value creation has been considered as a central strategic task in EB development and management, most of the previous research works focus simply on a specific type and dimension of values such as customer value, supplier value, product value, process value, or value of supply chain, information technology (IT), and information system (IS) etc [1,4,12,13,14,20,21]. A strategic framework for identifying and evaluating business values from an integrated perspective is still not yet explored in the literature.

K. Bauknecht, M. Bichler, and B. Pröll (Eds.): EC-Web 2004, LNCS 3182, pp. 357–367, 2004.
© Springer-Verlag Berlin Heidelberg 2004

Among previous research works, Grey et al. [9] argue that a critical part of business value creation is identifying the business processes to transform and selecting the right initiatives to enable the transformation. They present a methodology involving a value chain modeling tool to quantify the relationship in EB investments and business value. The IT infrastructure, the applications, and the business processes are all identified as a critical role in creating business value. Moller and Torronen [13] address the issue of evaluating business suppliers' value creation potential and propose a framework for connecting specific supplier capabilities to different types of value production. Supplier-value dimensions are classified according to efficiency, effectiveness, and network functions. They reorganize the direct and indirect value functions in a buyer-supplier relationship identified by Walter et al. [22] to include profit, volume, and safeguard functions in the efficiency dimension, innovative function in the effectiveness dimension, as well as resource-access, scout, and market-signaling functions in the network dimension. Ulaga [21] identifies eight dimensions of value creation in manufacturer-supplier relationships from in-depth interviews with purchasing managers. These relationship value drivers are product quality, service support, delivery, supplier know-how, time-to-market, personal interaction, direct product costs (price), and process costs. Zott et al. [25] investigate strategies for value creation in e-commerce (EC) companies. Based on a survey of 30 European companies, two main strategies identified are enhancing transaction efficiency of the business model and creating stickiness to facilitate repeat transactions. Osterwalder and Pigneur [15] describe value proposition as the definition of how items of value and complementary value-added services are packaged and offered to fulfill customer needs. They argue that the value proposition is at the center of strategic tasks and tend to be complex and hard to communicate, and for handling the task well, a framework and a formal method for conceptualizing and modeling value proposition must be developed and applied. They see value proposition as a business model element that can be further decomposed into a set of elementary value propositions, and their framework focuses mainly on the product element. The elementary value proposition is characterized by attributes including description, reasoning, life cycle, value level, and price level. Value can then be created by either matching product attributes with customer needs or by reducing the customer's risks and efforts. Both the value level and price level are measured using qualitative scales. Favaro [5] considers Value Based Management (VBM) as an integrated strategic and financial approach to the general management of businesses. Principles of VBM introduced for IT and software businesses in particular indicate that economic value maximization drives IT investment strategies and strategy drives selection of IT investments. He also points out that due to the multitude of unknowns in predicting economic benefits, a high-level strategy framework linking entire strategies to value creation at the level of the business is needed to make profitability parameters explicit. Two primary determinants of business value creation including market economics and competitive position are identified while a financial metric for measuring economic value creation is also presented. The main idea is to formulate the economic profit as the amount of the investment multiplied by the difference of the return on investment (ROI) and the opportunity cost of capital.

Summarizing the concepts and opinions from the literature regarding EB value creation and strategic planning issues, we may conclude that (1) value creation is a major strategic but complex task in EB, (2) an integrated framework for conceptualizing value creation as well as for linking entire strategies to value creation are needed, (3) a value based metric is required to measure the business value and the effectiveness of business strategies, (4) business value is treated as an element of the business model that guides the process of strategic planning, (5) emerging dimensions and metrics of business values vary considerably among various research works and do not provide guidelines for understanding and performing overall value assessment, and (6) previous research related to integrated framework of value and strategy and associated measurement metrics are still very rare, if not totally missing. It is noted that to be profitable and sustainable in EB, an e-company must develop at the first place a suitable e-business model in which value creation is an integral part, and then conduct the value based strategic planning process based on the EB model framework. Therefore, to bridge the gap of the literature, the goal of this paper is to provide a conceptual approach for identifying EB values and directing subsequent strategic planning process based on an integrated framework of business model, value creation and strategic planning. A value based management process will also be discussed. The rest of this paper is organized as follows. In section 2, an EB model framework is presented. In section 3, types and sources of business values are identified and a value based management process is discussed. The value-based EB strategic planning process is described in section 4 followed by a conclusion in the final section.

2   An e-Business Model Framework

The integrated framework for EB models presented by Yu [23,24] is adopted and modified to guide better value identification and assessment. Major constructs and their relationships of the EB model framework are illustrated in Figure 1. Key components and related rationales are described below.

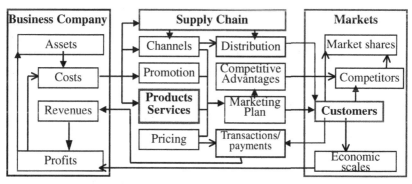

Fig. 1. An integrated framework of e-business models.

Markets: Markets are trading environments for buyers and sellers that can be classified in different ways such as by scope, targeted customers, transaction functions and processes, or by product categories. Markets can also be segmented by customer characteristics such as ages, sexes, incomes, and be clustered by customers' buying behaviors and preferences. Markets provide opportunities for making profits.

Customers: Customers are buyers of the markets and can be categorized in several different types including individuals, businesses, organizations, and communities. Major goal of the e-business is to create customer values and to gain customer shares.

Competitors: Competitors are other players of the same markets that provide alternative buying choices to customers and compete on market and customer shares.

Supply chain partners/participants: Supply chain partners are other types of market players including suppliers of product materials or providers of channel and payment services. Supply chain partners are strategic alliances that share information and values through established network relationships. They are also closely coordinated in transaction, production and distribution cycles to gain efficiency and effectiveness.

Business companies: Business companies are providers/sellers of products and services in specific markets. They conduct business by allocating assets and resources, developing products and services, setting up supply chain, launching marketing plans and handling transactions in order for creating business values and making profits.

Products: Products, physical or digital in forms, are one of the target objects of business transactions that are offered by sellers to potential buyers. Products can be positioned and differentiated by specific features that are perceived by customers as valuable and worthy to buy.

Services: Services are other targeted objects of business transactions that can be classified into a variety of categories including information, brokerage, recommendations, advertising, intermediary marketplaces, payments, trust, utilities, networking, community, affiliate, and personalized services.

Assets and resources: Assets, as financial supports for conducting businesses, are major business resources that can be measured in monetary terms. Tangible assets consist of fixed and floating capitals such as equipment, cash reserves, stocks, and money collected from venture capitals and/or initial public offering (IPO). Intangible assets and resources include trademarks, brand awareness, technology infrastructure, patents, human resources (HR), management capabilities, and domain knowledge.

Costs: Costs are necessary expenditures for starting up and sustaining business operations. Essential costs include expenses and charges on products and services development, websites and IS implementation, marketing, purchasing, inventory, distribution, transaction processing, HR, application and other intermediary services, investment and acquisition, and goodwill amortization, etc.

Prices: Prices are specified money values for customers to pay in exchange of products and services. Besides of the fixed pricing method, the frequently used dynamic pricing methods include negotiation and auction. Billing methods include charging the customers by product volume, by service time/times, by monthly fees, by project costs, by number or amount of transactions, as well as charging the advertisers.

Channels: Channels are intermediary mechanisms with interactive processes between buyers and sellers for facilitating communications, sales, and deliveries.

Promotion: Promotion is one of the marketing activities that aim at capturing customer attentions and stimulating their buying desires. Possible types of promotion include advertisement, price discount, gift, and trade show. Push marketing techniques can be used to reach better-matched customers for achieving better promotion effects.

Distribution: Distribution is an activity to deliver information, products and services through online and/or physical channels. Physical products require establishing and operating physical channels or allying with some existing distribution channels.

Transactions and payments: Transactions and payments represent activity processes for customers to get information, place orders and issue payments for acquiring products and services.

Revenues: Revenues are incoming money received from prices paid by customers who actually buy products and services. Revenue sources include products, services, and advertising sales, as well as transaction fees and trading commissions etc.

Profits: Profits, reflecting company's business performances, are net earnings that equal to the difference between total revenues and total costs. E-companies are trying hard to design and implement profitable e-business models to ensure profitability.

Market shares: Market share, representing portion of the market size owned by the company, is a percentage number obtained from dividing the company's volume of sales or size of customer body by that of the entire market.

Economic scales: Economic scale is a targeted size of customer body that indicates the company's break-even point and a starting point for gaining profits.

Competitive advantages: Competitive advantages represent strength and capabilities of the company to outperform competitors by offering better values to customers, obtaining higher market shares and business profitability.

Marketing strategies and plans: Marketing strategies and plans are strategic marketing decisions and action processes related to products, prices, promotions, and places (4P) factors, as well as their mix. The objective for implementing marketing plans is to increase competitive advantages, market shares and to make profits.

An e-company preparing to enter a new market must raise enough capitals and properly plan the usage of assets to cover all possible expenses and costs for ensuring continuous business operations. They need to identify target customers, develop products and services that match customers' needs, and set up supply chains for strengthening company capabilities and attaining better business qualities. By implementing a well-designed marketing mix plan, an e-company should be able to develop and offer products and services to customers of the targeted markets with better values in terms of product quality, channel availability, price attractiveness, as well as brand awareness and trust than their competitors and thus to gain competitive advantages. The company can then expect to attain higher growth rates on revenues, market shares, and ultimately gain profits when the economies of scales are reached. When an e-company experiencing financial losses but still expecting increasing revenues, they must make sure that current assets and future funding are capable of supporting the business operations longer enough to break even and start making profits. As for the customer site, they should be able to activate online transaction processes easily for searching and browsing desired information, placing orders, paying prices, and then receiving products and services through established sales and distribution channels. Greater customer satisfaction on the e-company's products and services as well as marketing and security mechanisms ensures higher customer loyalty, and in consequence, leads to the fulfillment of the e-company's objectives of sustaining competitive advantages and business profitability.

3 Value Identification and Management

Based on the e-business model presented in the previous section, value types and sources can be identified and value based management can be processed.

3.1 Value Identification

Based on the proposed EB model framework, levels of identified value sources comprise market environment, supply chain, business company, products and services, and customers as marked in Figure 1 by block letters. Value types identified then include market value, supply chain value, enterprise value, product and service value, and customer value. Associated value functions and measures are described below.

Market value: Market value refers to the business value perceived by the market and stakeholders. Value is created when a company allocates assets and resources to enter selected markets, conducts business operations, and makes profit. Level of market competitiveness, market revenues, market shares, and market capitalization are indicators of the market value.

Supply chain value: Strategic supply chain partners include material suppliers and channel, delivery, and financial service providers. Value is derived from sharing market and customer information, and integrating transaction, production and distribution cycles. Value indicators include cost reduction in information collection and in production and operation, time reduction in response to market demand and in transaction, production and distribution cycles, as well as revenue and profit increases for all participating parties in the entire supply chain. Also observed is the level of customer satisfaction related to time and location conveniences offered by the chain.

Enterprise value: Enterprise value refers to organization resources and capabilities to sustain business, create excellence, and capture opportunities. Values reside in asset, HR, IT/IS, innovation capability, management capability, process improvement capability, domain knowledge and expertise, brand name and publicity, as well as marketing plans. Value is created through asset acquisition, allocation, and utilization; business operation and process improvement; HR and knowledge management; IS development and application; technology, process and product innovation; and marketing plan implementation. Value indicators include return on asset (ROA), asset utilization measures, cash flow ratios, operating efficiency metrics, HR skill levels and productivity ratios, return on IT/IS investments, IT/IS usability measures, innovation effectiveness metrics, marketing effectiveness measures, and profitability ratios.

Product and service value: Product and service values refer to specific features of the products and services that are developed and offered to customers to meet their needs and preferences. Competitive features include content and functions, price and supports, quality and warranty, as well as customization and personalization. Value is created when product and service features match customers' needs and outperform that of the competitors, and consequently, activate the actual transaction and payment processes. Value indicators include function, price, quality and support levels, levels of customization and personalization, as well as level of customer satisfaction.

Customer value: Customer value is generally defined as the trade-off between benefits and sacrifices (usually costs) in a market exchange of products and services. From the business perspective, customer value refers to the benefits derived from attracting, developing, and retaining customers, as well as managing and utilizing customer relationships. Value indicators include number of registered customers, customer profitability (current profits and future profit potential), and customer shares.

Based on the identified value types and elements, suitable multi-criteria value models with proper design of weights, scaling and scoring methods can be developed and applied to measure or compare EB values of e-companies.

3.2 Value Management

The value based management process consists of value planning, value analysis, value design, value proposition, value creation, value delivery, and value control stages. In the value planning stage, value types and sources are identified and business objectives for value creation are determined. The value analysis step focuses on analyzing and estimating the possibilities of value creation, potential value and profitability levels, potential costs and benefits, as well as potential efforts and risks. In the value design stage, value objects related to products and services, supply chains, and marketing plans are designed. Also designed include the value associated development, implementation, and operation processes. The value proposition activities aim at proposing values to all parties of the markets, especially to strategic partners and customers to draw attentions and stimulate interests for conducting market exchange. In the value creation stage, value is created through the engagement of actual transactions such as purchasing products and services, and sharing information within the supply chain. The value delivery stage is a step for distributing created values to participants in the value exchange process. In the final value control stage, actual values are evaluated and compared with the estimated values, problems are diagnosed and all needed corrective actions in the previous stages are taken.

Associated management functions surrounding the VBM include market management, supply chain management, corporate management (comprising asset and financial management, human resources management, process management, marketing management, information management, and knowledge management, etc.), production and operating management, as well as customer relationship management.

4 Value Based e-Business Strategic Planning

The purpose of strategic planning in a company is to set goals and make strategic decisions to guide the development of action plans for gaining profit and leveraging capabilities. Six Internet-related principles of strategic positioning outlined by Porter [17] include sustained profitability, value proposition, distinctive value chain, trade-off, fit together, and continuity. By using the proposed e-business model framework and value settings as guidelines, a set of value-based strategies can be easily identified and the strategic planning process can be conducted and accomplished in a more systematic way. Five major value-based EB strategies to be planned include market strategy, supply chain/value chain strategy, organization strategy, product and service strategy, and customer strategy. The organization strategy can be further divided into a group of intra-organizational strategies including asset and financial management strategy, web site and IS development strategy, business operation strategy, marketing strategy, innovation and competition strategy, and profit strategy.

Market strategy: This is to clarify considerations, factors, and processes for market selection, segmentation, integration, and globalization, as well as to specify goals on market shares, economic scales, and market values. Also identified include market opportunities and risks, as well as trends of the market related industries.

Supply chain/value chain strategy: This is to indicate considerations for supply/value chain establishment, partner selection, and to outline processes for supply/value chain management and operation. Also considered include information and value sharing policies, and infrastructure and production integration processes.

Organization strategy: This is to plan the ways for better allocating asset and resources to leverage organizational capabilities, capture market opportunities, create competitive advantages, sustain business operations, and ultimately make profits. The associated intra-organizational sub-strategies are described below.

(1) **The asset and financial strategy** focuses mainly on identifying sources and methods of capital acquisition, as well as on specifying directions and processes for asset allocation, management and control.

(2) **The web site and IS development strategy** is to decide on the technology adoption policies, the budgeting, and the schedule for developing and providing functions and services on the web sites/application systems. Also to be specified is an EB infrastructure including system organization and operating environment, content and communication services, commerce and customer supports, etc.

(3) **The business operation strategy** is to specify methods and processes for EB operations. Major considerations include transaction processes, billing and payment collecting methods, sales and distribution channels, business alliances and cooperation, costs and revenues management, as well as feedback control and conflict resolution.

(4) **The marketing strategy** is to clearly direct marketing decisions and policies related to brand and reputation building, as well as products and services positioning, selling, pricing, advertising and promotion, delivering and channel integration.

Basically, a 4P mix strategy is included. Also to be specified includes an implementation plan of the marketing mix strategy.

(5) **The innovation and competition strategy** is to specify distinctive organization capabilities and competence needed to outperform the competitors, and the ways to generate competitive advantages through product, process, and technology innovations. SWOT (Strength, Weakness, Opportunity, Threat) analysis and Porter's competitive forces model can be used to help illustrating the planning considerations.

(6) **The profit strategy** is to specify cost, revenue and profit sources and structures, as well as short-term, mid-term, and long-term plans to increase market and customer shares, generate more sources and volumes of revenues, maintain competitive advantages, as well as to ensure optimal profits and sustain high profitability.

Product and service strategy: This is to identify the key characteristics and features of products and services that match the market needs while proposing better values than competitors' products and services. The strategy also specifies the processes of product and service development, and life cycle management.

Customer strategy: This is to specify approaches for customer clustering and classification, to enforce efforts on personalization, customization, and community services, as well as to capture the trend of customer relationship management.

Figure 2 shows a road map for the value based EB strategic planning in which all the above-mentioned strategies are included and arranged as a flow of considerations.

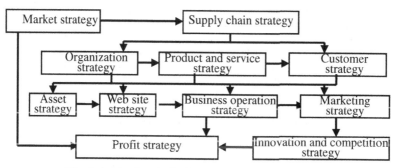

Fig. 2. A value based e-business strategic planning process.

5   Conclusion

The EB related business model, value creation, and strategic planning issues are of growing importance in recent years. Although a few research efforts have addressed these issues separately, their results show that research in this area is still in its infancy stage, and an integrated framework for efficiently and effectively guiding the EB model construction, value creation, and strategic planning is still in strong desire. In this paper, we first present a conceptual framework of e-business models, and then identify types and sources of EB values, as well as describing a subsequent value-based strategic planning process based on the integrated framework. As for business implications, the proposed integrated EB model framework provides guidelines for e-companies to better understand EB models and business values, and to efficiently and effectively plan and implement operable, measurable, and controllable value based EB strategies in hope of sustaining competitive advantages and profitability. Future research works will include: (1) developing detailed value metrics and an evaluation model to measure and compare business values of different e-companies, and (2) performing surveys, in-depth interviews, and case studies, to validate the proposed EB model framework as well as the value management and strategic planning processes.

References

1. Alstyne, M. W. V.: A Proposal for Valuing Information and Instrumental Goods. Proceedings of the 20th International Conference on Information Systems, (1999) 328-345.
2. Boehm, B.: Value-Based Software Engineering. Software Engineering Notes, 28(2) (2003) 1-12.
3. Cotter, S.: Taking the Measure of E-Marketing Success. Journal of Business Strategy, (2002) 30-37.
4. Dhillon, G. and Lee, J.: Value Assessment of IS/IT Service Provision Within Organizations. Proceedings of the 21st International Conference on Information Systems, (2000) 647-651.
5. Favaro, J.: Value Based Management and Methods. XP2003, Lecture Notes in Computer Science, Vol. 2675, (2003) 16-25.
6. Garbi, E.: Alternative Measures of Performance for E-Companies: A Comparison of Approaches. Journal of Business Strategies, 19(1) (2002) 1-17.
7. Goldszmidt, M., Palma, D., and Sabata, B.: On the Quantification of e-Business Capacity. Proceedings of the 3rd ACM Conference on Electronic Commerce, (2001) 235-244
8. Gosain, S. et al.: The Impact of Common E-Business Interfaces. Communications of the ACM, 46(12) (2003) 186-195.
9. Grey, W. et al.: An Analytic Approach for Quantifying the Value of e-Business Initiatives. IBM Systems Journal, 42(3) (2003) 484-497.
10. 10.Baida, Z., de Bruin, H., and Gordijn, J.: e-Business Cases Assessment: From Business Value to System Feasibility. International Journal of Web Engineering and Technology, 1(1) (2003) 127-144.
11. Kim, J., Suh, E., and Hwang, H.: A Model for Evaluating the Effectiveness of CRM Using the Balanced Scorecard. Journal of Interactive Marketing, 17(2) (2003) 5-19.
12. Kodama, M.: Customer Value Creation Through Community-Based Information Networks. International Journal of Information Management, 19(6) (1999) 495-508.
13. Moller, K. E. K. and Torronen, P.: Business Suppliers' Value Creation Potential: A Capability-Based Analysis. Industrial Marketing Management, 32(2) (2003) 109-118.
14. Mooney, J. G., Gurbaxani, V., and Kraemer, K. L.: A Process Oriented Framework for Assessing the Business Value of Information Technology. The DATA BASE for Advances in Information Systems. 27(2) (1996) 68-81.
15. Osterwalder, A. and Pigneur, Y.: Modeling Value Propositions in E-Business. Proceedings of the 5th International Conference on Electronic Commerce, (2003) 430-437.
16. Pather, S., Erwin, G., and Remenyi, D.: Measuring E-Commence Effectiveness: A Conceptual Model. Proceedings of the SAICSIT, (2003) 143-152.

17. Porter, M. E.: Strategy and the Internet. Harvard Business Review, 79(3) (2001) 62-78.
18. Seddon, P. B., Graeser, V., and Willcocks, L. P.: Measuring Organizational IS Effectiveness: An Overview and Update of Senior Management Perspectives. The DATA BASE for Advances in Information Systems, 33(2) (2002) 11-28.
19. Sharma, A., Krishnan, R., and Grewal, D.: Value Creation in Markets: A Critical Area of Focus for Business-to-Business Markets. Industrial Marketing Management, 30(4) (2001) 391-402.
20. Ulaga, W.: Customer Value in Business Markets: An Agenda for Inquiry. Industrial Marketing Management, 30(4) (2001) 315-319.
21. Ulaga, W.: Capturing Value Creation in Business Relationships: A Customer Perspective. Industrial Marketing Management, 32(8) (2003) 677-693.
22. Walter, A., Ritter, T., and Gemunden, H. G.: Value Creation in Buyer-Seller Relationships. Industrial Marketing Management, 30(4) (2001) 365-377.
23. Yu, C. C.: An Integrated Framework of Business Models for Guiding Electronic Commerce Applications and Case Studies. EC-Web2001, Lecture Notes in Computer Science, Vol. 2115, (2001) 111-120.
24. Yu, C. C.: A Business Model Framework for E-Business Planning. Proceedings of the 1st International E-Services Workshop, The 5th International Conference on Electronic Commerce, (2003) 38-45.
25. Zott, C., Amit, R., and Donlevy, J.: Strategies for Value Creation in E-Business: Best Practice in Europe. European Management Journal, 18(5) (2000) 463-475.

Author Index

Lecture Notes in Computer Science

For information about Vols. 1–3070

please contact your bookseller or Springer

Vol. 3124: J.N. de Souza, P. Dini, P. Lorenz (Eds.), Telecommunications and Networking - ICT 2004. XXVI, 1390 pages. 2004.

Vol. 3123: A. Belz, R. Evans, P. Piwek (Eds.), Natural Language Generation. X, 219 pages. 2004. (Subseries LNAI).

Vol. 3122: K. Jansen, S. Khanna, J.D.P. Rolim, D. Ron (Eds.), Approximation, Randomization, and Combinatorial Optimization. IX, 428 pages. 2004.

Vol. 3121: S. Nikoletseas, J.D.P. Rolim (Eds.), Algorithmic Aspects of Wireless Sensor Networks. X, 201 pages. 2004.

Vol. 3120: J. Shawe-Taylor, Y. Singer (Eds.), Learning Theory. X, 648 pages. 2004. (Subseries LNAI).

Vol. 3118: K. Miesenberger, J. Klaus, W. Zagler, D. Burger (Eds.), Computer Helping People with Special Needs. XXIII, 1191 pages. 2004.

Vol. 3116: C. Rattray, S. Maharaj, C. Shankland (Eds.), Algebraic Methodology and Software Technology. XI, 569 pages. 2004.

Vol. 3114: R. Alur, D.A. Peled (Eds.), Computer Aided Verification. XII, 536 pages. 2004.

Vol. 3113: J. Karhumäki, H. Maurer, G. Paun, G. Rozenberg (Eds.), Theory Is Forever. X, 283 pages. 2004.

Vol. 3112: H. Williams, L. MacKinnon (Eds.), Key Technologies for Data Management. XII, 265 pages. 2004.

Vol. 3111: T. Hagerup, J. Katajainen (Eds.), Algorithm Theory - SWAT 2004. XI, 506 pages. 2004.

Vol. 3110: A. Juels (Ed.), Financial Cryptography. XI, 281 pages. 2004.

Vol. 3109: S.C. Sahinalp, S. Muthukrishnan, U. Dogrusoz (Eds.), Combinatorial Pattern Matching. XII, 486 pages. 2004.

Vol. 3108: H. Wang, J. Pieprzyk, V. Varadharajan (Eds.), Information Security and Privacy. XII, 494 pages. 2004.

Vol. 3107: J. Bosch, C. Krueger (Eds.), Software Reuse: Methods, Techniques and Tools. XI, 339 pages. 2004.

Vol. 3106: K.-Y. Chwa, J.I. Munro (Eds.), Computing and Combinatorics. XIII, 474 pages. 2004.

Vol. 3105: S. Göbel, U. Spierling, A. Hoffmann, I. Iurgel, O. Schneider, J. Dechau, A. Feix (Eds.), Technologies for Interactive Digital Storytelling and Entertainment. XVI, 304 pages. 2004.

Vol. 3104: R. Kralovic, O. Sykora (Eds.), Structural Information and Communication Complexity. X, 303 pages. 2004.

Vol. 3103: K. Deb, e. al. (Eds.), Genetic and Evolutionary Computation – GECCO 2004. XLIX, 1439 pages. 2004.

Vol. 3102: K. Deb, e. al. (Eds.), Genetic and Evolutionary Computation – GECCO 2004. L, 1445 pages. 2004.

Vol. 3101: M. Masoodian, S. Jones, B. Rogers (Eds.), Computer Human Interaction. XIV, 694 pages. 2004.

Vol. 3100: J.F. Peters, A. Skowron, J.W. Grzymała-Busse, B. Kostek, R.W. Świniarski, M.S. Szczuka (Eds.), Transactions on Rough Sets I. X, 405 pages. 2004.

Vol. 3099: J. Cortadella, W. Reisig (Eds.), Applications and Theory of Petri Nets 2004. XI, 505 pages. 2004.

Vol. 3098: J. Desel, W. Reisig, G. Rozenberg (Eds.), Lectures on Concurrency and Petri Nets. VIII, 849 pages. 2004.

Vol. 3097: D. Basin, M. Rusinowitch (Eds.), Automated Reasoning. XII, 493 pages. 2004. (Subseries LNAI).

Vol. 3096: G. Melnik, H. Holz (Eds.), Advances in Learning Software Organizations. X, 173 pages. 2004.

Vol. 3095: C. Bussler, D. Fensel, M.E. Orlowska, J. Yang (Eds.), Web Services, E-Business, and the Semantic Web. X, 147 pages. 2004.

Vol. 3094: A. Nürnberger, M. Detyniecki (Eds.), Adaptive Multimedia Retrieval. VIII, 229 pages. 2004.

Vol. 3093: S. Katsikas, S. Gritzalis, J. Lopez (Eds.), Public Key Infrastructure. XIII, 380 pages. 2004.

Vol. 3092: J. Eckstein, H. Baumeister (Eds.), Extreme Programming and Agile Processes in Software Engineering. XVI, 358 pages. 2004.

Vol. 3091: V. van Oostrom (Ed.), Rewriting Techniques and Applications. X, 313 pages. 2004.

Vol. 3089: M. Jakobsson, M. Yung, J. Zhou (Eds.), Applied Cryptography and Network Security. XIV, 510 pages. 2004.

Vol. 3087: D. Maltoni, A.K. Jain (Eds.), Biometric Authentication. XIII, 343 pages. 2004.

Vol. 3086: M. Odersky (Ed.), ECOOP 2004 – Object-Oriented Programming. XIII, 611 pages. 2004.

Vol. 3085: S. Berardi, M. Coppo, F. Damiani (Eds.), Types for Proofs and Programs. X, 409 pages. 2004.

Vol. 3084: A. Persson, J. Stirna (Eds.), Advanced Information Systems Engineering. XIV, 596 pages. 2004.

Vol. 3083: W. Emmerich, A.L. Wolf (Eds.), Component Deployment. X, 249 pages. 2004.

Vol. 3080: J. Desel, B. Pernici, M. Weske (Eds.), Business Process Management. X, 307 pages. 2004.

Vol. 3079: Z. Mammeri, P. Lorenz (Eds.), High Speed Networks and Multimedia Communications. XVIII, 1103 pages. 2004.

Vol. 3078: S. Cotin, D.N. Metaxas (Eds.), Medical Simulation. XVI, 296 pages. 2004.

Vol. 3077: F. Roli, J. Kittler, T. Windeatt (Eds.), Multiple Classifier Systems. XII, 386 pages. 2004.

Vol. 3076: D. Buell (Ed.), Algorithmic Number Theory. XI, 451 pages. 2004.

Vol. 3075: W. Lenski (Ed.), Logic versus Approximation. IX, 205 pages. 2004.

Vol. 3074: B. Kuijpers, P. Revesz (Eds.), Constraint Databases and Applications. XII, 181 pages. 2004.

Vol. 3073: H. Chen, R. Moore, D.D. Zeng, J. Leavitt (Eds.), Intelligence and Security Informatics. XV, 536 pages. 2004.

Vol. 3072: D. Zhang, A.K. Jain (Eds.), Biometric Authentication. XVII, 800 pages. 2004.

Vol. 3071: A. Omicini, P. Petta, J. Pitt (Eds.), Engineering Societies in the Agents World. XIII, 409 pages. 2004. (Subseries LNAI).